THE

ORATIONS OF S. ATHANASIUS

AGAINST THE ARIANS

The Ancient and Modern Library of Theological Literature.

THE

ORATIONS OF S. ATHANASIUS

AGAINST THE ARIANS

LONDON:

GRIFFITH FARRAN & CO.

NEWBERY HOUSE, 39 CHARING CROSS ROAD

PREFACE.

S. ATHANASIUS, one of the most renowned Fathers of the Church, was born at Alexandria in A.D. 296. Of his early life we know but little. He was brought up in the Christian Faith, and received a learned education. His ability attracted the notice of Alexander, who was at that time Bishop of Alexandria. The Bishop made him his private secretary, and afterwards admitted him to ordination. In the year 325 we find him, as Archdeacon of Alexandria, accompanying his Bishop to the great Council of Nicæa. In the deliberations of this Council S. Athanasius took a prominent part, and thereby incurred the fierce displeasure of the Arian faction. The Council, composed of three hundred and eighteen Bishops, besides priests and deacons, and presided over by Hosius, Bishop of Cordova, was assembled to combat the Arian heresy, which denied the Eternal Divinity of the Second Person of the Holy Trinity. The immediate result of the session of this, the first General Council of the Church, was the putting forth of the Nicene Symbol, which is substantially the same as our present "Nicene Creed," although the articles after the clause "I believe in the Holy Ghost" were subsequently added. The Creed proper was followed by an anathema against the Arian heresy. Shortly after his return from Nicæa Alexander died, and, in accordance with his dying recommendation Athanasius was chosen by general acclamation as his successor. For forty-six years he held the see, and during that time he devoted himself with all his powers to the assertion of the orthodox doctrine on the subject of our Blessed Lord's Divinity. In the words of Robertson, "To his abilities and constancy is due, under the Divine Providence, the preservation of the Eastern Church, and perhaps even of the whole Church, from the adoption of the Arian heresy, or from a vague and creedless system, which would probably have issued in an utter abandonment of Christianity." "Athanasius the Great," says Dorner, "made it the work of his long and eventful life to defend the Creed put forth by the Nicene Council, with all the weapons of science and spiritual chivalry, against the vacillating and shortsighted on the one hand, and the apostate on the other; and to him was given the happiness of seeing that to which he had devoted his life attain ever-widening influence and recognition, and to sink into his grave crowned with honour, and laden with the fruit of his labours."

The life of S. Athanasius was one long struggle for the Faith. The Arian party, in full possession of court influence, made an unscrupulous use of it to eject such Catholic Bishops as stood in their way. They attempted especially to get rid of S. Athanasius. In the year 336 he was falsely accused before the Emperor Constantine of treason, and was banished to Treves. It was in this year that Arius suddenly died, on the eve of an attempt to compel the Patriarch of Constantinople to admit him into communion with the Church. Upon the death of Constantine in 337 S. Athanasius was recalled from exile, after an absence of about two years and a half, but a new attack upon him was commenced before long. In 341 a Council was held at Antioch, from which all the orthodox Bishops had withdrawn, and the Arian party proceeded to deprive S. Athanasius of his see, and to elect in his room Gregory, a native of Cappadocia. A second time an exile, Athanasius took refuge at Rome, where he was solemnly declared innocent, in a synod of fifty Bishops, of the charges laid against him. Strange to say, the Emperor Constantius, who favoured Arianism, after a time became eager for reconciliation with Athanasius, and invited him to resume his see. He did so, returning after an absence of nearly five years to Alexandria, where the people welcomed him most thankfully. But there was not peace for long. After Councils held at Arles and Milan, in which the Arian party was dominant, S. Athanasius was obliged to flee for his life. This was in A.D. 356. Three years later four hundred and fifty Bishops assembled at Rimini, and an Arian profession of faith was put forth. In S. Jerome's words, "The world was thunderstruck with astonishment at suddenly finding itself Arian." The position now was "Athanasius contra mundum." After an exile of six years, the tidings reached Athanasius of the death of Constantius, and setting out for Alexandria, he was received there with the greatest enthusiasm. However, the new Emperor, Julian ("the Apostate"), who knew and feared his character, ordered him once more into banishment. He remained in concealment until the death of Julian in 363. Henceforward the great ecclesiastic was allowed to pass his days in comparative tranquillity, and he remained peacefully at Alexandria till his death, at upwards of seventy-six years of age in A.D. 373.

The Four Orations of S. Athanasius are the outcome of his conflict with the Arians. They were probably written during one of his enforced periods of exile. Their value has been witnessed to by many writers both ancient and modern. Photius says, "They are written in a clear and simple style; they are full of feeling and vivacity, and contain strong and weighty arguments. This work alone would suffice to destroy utterly all the strongholds of Arianism." Montfaucon tells us that these Orations "are the sources whence arguments have been borrowed by all who have since written in behalf of the Divinity of the Word."

The opinions of Arius, which S. Athanasius so strenuously opposed, cannot better be defined than in the anathema appended to the Symbol of the Nicene Council. It runs as follows :—" The Catholic and Apostolic Church anathematizes those who say that there was a time when the Son was not ; and that He did not exist before He was born ; and that He was made of what did not exist ; or that the Son of God is of a different substance or essence from the Father, or that He was created, or is variable and changeable."

Of S. Athanasius it has been said (by S. Gregory Nazianzen), "To commend him is to commend virtue itself ; he was the pattern for Bishops, and his doctrine the rule of orthodoxy ; he was an eye and a light to the world, the pillar of the Faith, and a second John the Baptist." Most appropriately may we apply to him the words of S. Jude, for certainly he was one who " earnestly contended for the Faith once delivered to the Saints." For forty-six years he was a Bishop, and for twenty years an exile for the truth's sake. At one time he was well-nigh alone in his championship of the orthodox Faith, and at all times his efforts were unceasing in its defence. He has left his abiding mark upon the pages of Church history, and upon the Church's Creeds. His Orations are printed in this series, with the hope that many may be glad to possess the sayings of him whom Cardinal Newman so well describes, as

" Royal-hearted Athanase
With Paul's own mantle blest."

W. C. L.

CONTENTS.

Contents

THE

Orations of S. Athanasius.

THE FIRST ORATION.

1. IT is clear enough that all the heresies and false doctrines that were ever heard of have only been insane inventions, and their impiety has been long ago made manifest to everyone. What S. John has written of their authors is certainly true, that "they went out from us," for their doctrine never was, neither is, with us (1 S. John ii. 19). Therefore, as our Saviour says, "as they do not gather with us, they scatter with the devil" (S. Luke xi. 23); and, when men sleep, they watch their opportunity and shed abroad their deadly poison, and involve as many others as possible in their own destruction. The last false doctrine which has lately arisen, as a forerunner of Antichrist, is that which is called the Arian heresy, and a subtle and hateful thing this is; for, as she finds her elder sisters marked and branded, she adopts the plan of her father the devil, and by hiding her blasphemies under Scriptural phrases, she employs all her powers to force an entrance into the Paradise of the Church. By taking upon herself an outward appearance of Christianity she would deceive people into impious opinions concerning the Blessed Lord, by plausible and specious arguments. And some foolish people have been corrupted already, and, like Eve, having been first prevailed upon to listen, they have proceeded further to touch and taste, and are now so utterly incapable of discernment as to call a bitter thing sweet (Isa. v. 20), and a detestable heresy the true Faith. And so I have the duty imposed upon me, of plucking out, so to speak, the bosom of this horrible heresy, and of manifesting its abominable character to all the world, that those who so far have escaped it, may be free from its snares; and that

those who have been imposed upon may be brought to a better mind; that they may recover the sight of their understanding, and be truly convinced, that as certainly as darkness is not light, nor falsehood truth, so neither is the Arian heresy the orthodox belief. To speak plainly, they miserably go astray who call the Arians Christians; they only show how they neither know the Holy Scriptures, nor anything whatever about Christianity.

2. What resemblance, indeed, have the Arians found out between their heresy and the true Faith, that they have the absurdity to pretend that what they say is right and good? Why, this is to declare Caiaphas to be a Christian man, and to number the traitor Judas amongst the Apostles! It is to argue that those did the proper thing who sought for the release of Barrabas instead of our Saviour, and that Hymenæus and Alexander (1 Tim. i. 20) were upholders of the Faith, and that S. Paul accused them falsely! Nay, no good Christian can bear to hear such things said; he thinks instead that only a madman could assert such things to be true. They put Arius in the place of Christ, as the Manichæans did Manichæus. In the same manner they have discarded Moses and the other holy writers, and have put into their place a certain Sotades,* with his infamous poetry, and also the daughter of Herodias. For, it is according to such models that Arius has framed that effeminate poem of his which he calls "Thalia," † where he speaks in his wanton blasphemies against the Blessed Lord, and where he so excites the spirits of his companions that they become perfectly insane, and "change the glory of the uncorruptible God into an image made like to corruptible man" (Rom. i. 23), and so lose the name of Christians and take that of Arians instead, and have this name as the title of their impiety. And let no Arians imagine that they can retort in some similar fashion, and give any names that may occur to them to the true members of the Church, calling them after any of their particular superiors. Let them not do this from any vexation, but rather take shame to themselves, and hide themselves away, or else give up their wicked errors. For it is simply impossible that Christians should receive any appellation from their Bishops or rulers. We can only be known by the Name of Him, in whom we believe, and whose Faith we profess. This Faith the holy Apostles published and made known to us, and yet we are not called after their names.

* An Egyptian poet, whose songs were notorious for their indecency.
† Called *Thalia*, from the Muse of Comedy, supposed to inspire such ditties for popular entertainment at dances and banquets.

It is only Christ Himself whose we are, and after whom we are known as Christians. But since the faith of our opponents comes to them from other hands, and in another way altogether, it is fitting that they should bear the name of him who is their master.

3. Thus formerly, when we were all united Christians both in doctrine and name, Marcion became a heretic and was excommunicated, and those who sided with the Bishop that had expelled him retained the name of Christians, whilst those that continued with him were called Marcionists. So, too, Valentinus, Basilides, Manichæus, and Simon Magus, gave their names to those who became their disciples. These were named after them—Valentinians, Basilidians, Manichees, and Simonians. Likewise the Cataphrygians take their name from Phrygia, and the Novatians from Novatus. Also Meletius, after he had been excommunicated by Peter, Bishop and Martyr, no longer called his associates Christians, but Meletians. Exactly in this way, after Alexander, of blessed memory, had excommunicated Arius, those that kept with Alexander were known as Christians as before, but those that separated with Arius abandoned our Saviour's name, and from that time were denominated Arians. And since Alexander's death, those that are in communion with his successor, Athanasius, and with such other Bishops as he is in communion with, keep the same title ; and not only do they call themselves Christians, but everyone does so everywhere as a matter of course. We have, no doubt, a succession of teachers and disciples ; nevertheless, because we are taught Christ's religion and nothing besides, we are still, and always were, called Christians. But, on the contrary, let heretics have an innumerable succession of teachers, yet they will always bear the name of him who first started the heresy. So, although Arius be dead, and has left a train of successors behind him, still those who propagate his opinions are even now called after him. And an argument which carries with it considerable weight is this, that when any pagans renounce idolatry and enter the Church, they are called Christians, from Christ Himself, and they do not take any name from those who brought them within the fold. On the other hand, those that take up with our adversaries, or who leave the Church to adopt their views, lay aside the name of Christian, and are henceforth denominated Arians, as those who no longer profess the true Faith of Christ, but are given up to this insane Arianism.

4. How then can it be right to call those Christians, who are nothing of the kind, but who are really Arians ? How can those

be considered as members of the Holy Catholic Church, who
have abandoned the Apostolic Faith, and who have originated
hateful novelties ; who have thrown aside Holy Scripture, and call
the "Thalia" of Arius the newly-discovered wisdom ? And this,
indeed, they may very well call it, for it declares a new heresy.
How strange, too, it seems to be, that such doctrines as this
Thalia contains are neither to be met with in all the commen-
taries and homilies that have been written upon the Old and
New Testaments, nor are even found amongst the best heathen
writers, but are only the amusement of fools and buffoons over
their cups.   It would be a great matter for surprise that this wonderful man Arius should fall into the scurrilities of Sotades, if we
did not know already his ignorance of ordinary decent behaviour,
as well as the way in which he has appropriated to himself the
heresies of others.   When he had made up his mind to insult
and affront our Blessed Lord, how could he do it so well as by
abusing Him in these shameful and effeminate ditties ?   The
Book of Wisdom tells us, "A man shall be known by his words"
(Ecclus. iv. 24), and so we may say that the effeminacy and
viciousness of the mind of Arius is clearly enough seen in his
verses.   In fact, he could not impose upon mankind.   For, after
all his contortions and twistings he has fallen straight into the
error of the Pharisees.   Just as they pretended to search very
deeply into the law of God, and at the same time made up their
minds that they would violate its precepts ; and just as they were
determined to deny the Christ who was now present with them,
and whom they professed to be expecting; charging Him with
blasphemy for calling Himself God, saying, "Why dost Thou,
who art a man, make Thyself God?" (S. John x. 33), and why do
you say, "I and My Father are one"? (S. John x. 30); so, in
like manner, this wretched imitator of Sotades, named Arius,
pretends when he uses the words of Scripture, that he uses them
properly of God.   But this, indeed, is part of his atheism, whilst he
denies the Son of God, and accounts Him to be a mere creature.

5. The opening or preface of this impious and empty "Thalia" of
Arius is to this effect :—"These doctrines," he says, "were taught
me by good and right-thinking men, wise in all respects, being
taught of God ; and they contain the belief of the elect holy
children of God, such orthodox sons as were full of God's wisdom,
and had received His Holy Spirit.   I hold the same views as
they do.   I follow in their footsteps.   I am that remarkable
man, who has obtained true wisdom, and the knowledge of these
things from God, and who has suffered great hardships in pro-

moting the glory of God." Now these are samples of the abominable pleasantries and hateful impieties which the book contains. He remarks, "that God was not always a Father. He was God alone and solitary, before He was the Father, and afterwards He became a Father. The Son had not always a being, for, as all other creatures were made out of nothing, so likewise was the Word of God; and there was a time when He was not; nor had He any being till He was created. First of all God existed alone by Himself, and His Word and Wisdom were not with Him. Afterwards, when it was His good pleasure to create us, then He created a certain Person whom He called His Word, His Wisdom, and His Son, that He might be His agent in the work of our creation." Therefore Arius holds that God has two Wisdoms, one His proper and essential one, which was belonging to Him always; and then that by this Wisdom the Son was made, and called by the name of Wisdom and the Word. Wisdom, he remarks, came by Wisdom, by the will of the wise God. In like manner, he makes out that there is another Word in the Godhead besides the Son, by partaking of which, the Son, through grace and favour, becomes the Word of God and the Son. Besides these absurdities, there is that other curious notion, which so frequently occurs in these heretical books, the multiplication of the powers belonging unto God. They declare that one power of God is that which was from everlasting essentially in Him, but that Christ is not this power, but only one of those who are called His powers. Just as the locust and the cankerworm are styled in Scripture, not only the power, but the great power of God (Joel ii. 25). They assert, moreover, that there are several other powers of like character with the Son, especially those mentioned by the Psalmist, where he speaks of God as the Lord of Hosts or Powers (Ps. xxiv. 10). There is the same nature in the Son as there is in us. He is liable to change and variation; He may turn into evil ways, if He is so inclined; His nature, like ours, is mutable. For, they argue, God gave Him this glory or eminence, which, when He became man, He merited by His good works, upon His foreknowledge that He would be an excellent being, and that it was in consequence of this, that He made Him such as He is.

6. Further, Arius dares to say that the Word is not the true God. When He is called God, he says, it is only a figure of speech, referring to the privileges He is endowed with by God. All things connected with Him are distinct and separate from the Father. The Son has to do with created things and persons, of

whom He is one. And he proceeds to assert, with devilish arguments, that the Father is invisible to the Son, and that the Son is incapable of a true and perfect knowledge of the Father. When the Son is said to know and behold Him, it is only meant that He does so as far as He has the capacity to do so, just as we imperfectly apprehend Him. Through this deficiency the Son is not only ignorant of the nature of the Father, but of his own. The beings and nature of the Father, the Son, and the Holy Ghost are widely dissimilar. The nature and glory of the Word have no connection with those of the Father and the Holy Ghost. This impious man expressly declares that the Son is a being altogether by Himself, and has no fellowship with the nature of the Father. These affirmations are taken from that absurd and ridiculous book which Arius has written.

7. How then can anyone who hears these things and the verses of his "Thalia," think of Arius in any other way than as a buffoon, and abominate his behaviour? When he seems to name God's Holy Name it is evident that it is only for the same purpose as the serpent made use of it to the woman. Whoever reads further into his book must see his impiety as plainly as the treachery of the old serpent. Who can but be thunderstruck at these awful blasphemies? In the words of the Prophet, "The heavens are astonished at this, and the earth is horribly afraid" (Jer. ii. 12). When those indignities and sufferings were endured by the Lord of all, which He voluntarily bore for our sakes, the sun highly resented it, and could not bear the sight, but turned itself away, withdrew its rays, and turned the day into darkness. And shall not all mankind be covered with shame at the blasphemies of Arius? Shall they not shut their ears, and close their eyes, that they may neither hear nor behold either the doctrine or the teacher? Else how deservedly will the Lord apply to their impiety and ingratitude those words of Hosea the Prophet, "Woe unto them ! for they have fled from Me : destruction unto them ! because they have transgressed against Me : though I have redeemed them, yet they have spoken lies against Me" (Hos. vii. 13) ; and again, a little afterwards, " They imagined mischief against Me, they are turned into nothing " (Hos. vii. 15, Sept.). And, indeed, these heretics may be truly said to have turned or fallen aside into nothing, who have thus forsaken the true Word of God, and have substituted for it some idea of their own. For this reason a General Council excommunicated Arius, and uttered an anathema upon such wicked blasphemy. Since then his opinions have been considered to have exceeded all

former heresies, and he stands marked and distinguished by being known as the great enemy of Christ, and the forerunner of Antichrist. The authority and sentence of this Council against this vile heresy are certainly sufficient to implant a righteous indignation against it; especially in the minds of all those who profess themselves good Christians. But, nevertheless, because some who are reputed such are so foolish or so indifferent as to think it a matter of trifling importance, or because they imagine that these heretics may still be numbered amongst good Christian people, I shall proceed further to reveal this subtle iniquity. Perchance by doing this I shall convince many minds, so that they will fly from this evil, as they would from a serpent.

8. Perhaps these people approve of the blasphemies of "Thalia," because it contains some Scriptural words and phrases. Well then, if you go to the Jews, you will hear them repeating the Law and the Prophets; but they, too, deny our Blessed Lord. The Manichees are constantly reciting passages out of the Gospels. Are they then to be justified for abandoning the Old Testament? If they infer such things and lightly talk in such a strain about them, let them learn from the Bible that the devil is the originator of these heresies, and that his method of preventing them from being perceived is to veil them over with phrases of Scripture. This is the way in which he conceals his deadly poison, that he may thus instil it into the hearts of the simple. This was the way he corrupted Eve. This is his plan for introducing heresies, and after this fashion he has in-veigled Arius to do battle against other heresies, that he may the more readily establish his own. But this artifice will not do. The evil one could not altogether hide his presence. When he first arrayed himself against the Divinity of the Son of God he abandoned Christianity itself, and everyone knew that this was not the only thing in which he displayed his ignorance, but that he held false doctrine on other points as well, and was a hypocrite into the bargain. For how can he discourse about the Father who denies the Son, since it is from the Son we derive knowledge of the Father? How can he have right opinions about the Holy Spirit who thus impiously speaks against the Son, by whom the Holy Spirit is given to us? What shall we think of him who denies that Christ became for us the "First-born from the dead" (Col. i. 18), when we hear him preaching upon the subject of the resurrection? How entirely must he misunderstand the Son's Incarnation who puts aside his eternal generation? Even as the Jews, as soon as they had

denied the Christ, and exclaimed, " We have no king but Cæsar'
(S. John xix. 15), were quickly deprived of everything; their
lamps ceased to give light, the odour of their ointment failed,
they could not understand their own prophecies, truth itself
forsook them; they seemed unable to comprehend anything,
and they wandered about in darkness. For who ever heard
of such extraordinary ideas? Where did these profligate hire-
lings learn their absurdities? Did they, once upon a time,
learn these things in their Catechism? Who ever taught them,
as a part of Christian truth, that the worship of creatures having
been for some time abolished, we are to return to it again?
But if they confess that such a commandment was never heard
of before, will they not also allow that this heresy of theirs is a
modern invention, and that it has no support or favour from
antiquity or tradition? But what a wretched thing must that
be which the Fathers knew nothing of, but which has newly been
thought of. Is it not such a matter which S. Paul refers to
when he writes, " In the latter times some shall depart from the
faith, giving heed to seducing spirits, and doctrines of devils;
speaking lies in hypocrisy, having their conscience seared with a
hot iron, and turning themselves away from the truth" (1 Tim.
iv. 1, 2; Tit. i. 14).

9. We, on the other hand, very confidently prove the true
Catholic Faith out of the Holy Scriptures. We place it as a
candle on a candlestick. We assert that the Son is naturally and
essentially the Son of the Father, of the same substance with
Him, His Only-begotten Wisdom, the true and only Word of
God; that He was not made nor created, but begotten of one
substance with the Father. Therefore we say, that He is true
God, being of one substance with God the Father. Whereas the
gods mentioned by the Psalmist in the passage, " I have said, ye
are gods " (Ps. lxxxii. 6), are only entitled to that description so
far as they are partakers of Divine grace, which the Son bestows
upon them from the Father through the Holy Ghost. The Son
is the representation of the Person of the Father (Heb. i. 3). He
is Light of Light. He is the true and genuine Power and Image
of His Father's substance, according to what He says of Himself, " He that hath seen Me hath seen the Father" (S. John
xiv. 9). He always was, and is, and never was not; for the
Word and Wisdom of the Father must certainly be eternal as
well as the Father. In opposition to this, what says the hateful
" Thalia"? Let those that admire it and its author only read it
over first, to inform themselves how low they have fallen, if our

contempt may have any effect upon them, and then let them say what they think. They will find such rubbish as this. God was not always a Father, but afterwards became so. The Son did not always exist, nor had He any being until He was begotten. He does not owe His being to the Father, but He was produced out of nothing. He has not the same nature with the Father, since He was created and made. Christ is not true God, but He is so only by participation. The Son does not know the Father perfectly, nor is He the true and only Word of the Father. He is only called figuratively the Word and Wisdom, the Son and the Power of the Father. He is not unchangeable, as the Father is, but His nature is mutable, like that of other created beings, and His capacity is unfitted for a full and perfect comprehension of the Father. This is an extraordinary heresy, which contains such unreasonable ideas, and which, instead of godly discourses, amasses together such gross blasphemies. Suppose we were to ask anyone that has examined and compared our Creed and this together, which of them he thinks the more reasonable, and the more suitable to the attributes of God. Why, let any of the admirers of Arius fairly tell us, what they should inform us about the nature of God? (For, "the Word was God," S. John i. 1.) Let us compare one of these confessions with the other, to make it appear which is more sensible. Whether of the two is better, "He was," or "He was not"? "From all eternity," or "No longer ago, than when He was begotten"? "From everlasting," or "of a successive existence"? "True and genuine," or "by adoption, participation, and designation only"? Shall we say that He was "created by the Father," or that He is "in the essence of the Father"? Is He "of a different substance with the Father," or is He "of the same substance with Him"? Was He "created Himself," or were "all things created by Him"? Is He "the only Word of the Father," or besides Him is there "another Word and Wisdom, that gave Him His being; and this second and lower Word or Wisdom, is it only such by name, and as far as it is made a partaker of the higher Wisdom and Word"?

10. Of these two expositions, which is more worthy of God the Father, and of His Son our Lord Jesus Christ, let anyone judge. Is it better to believe in these ridiculous paradoxes of the Arians, or in those doctrines which we both assert and can prove out of Holy Scripture? If indeed our Saviour is neither God, nor the Word, nor the Son, then let the Arians be no longer ashamed to think and talk as pagans and Jews do. But if He

is the Word, and the proper Son of His Father; if He is God of God, and " over all, blessed for ever " (Rom. ix. 5), then shall we not utterly destroy this " Thalia," this novel doctrine and language of Arius, as if it were some horrible idol? Shall we not grind it to powder? Shall we not warn all men of this fearful abyss of error, into which even great and important personages have fallen, and which still gapes wide to receive others? Our enemies are not ignorant of this, and therefore they deceitfully put on false colours, and disguise their odious novelties with words improperly applied. For if they were to use plain language, they could not possibly escape universal condemnation. As soon as they disclose their secret opinions they are undone; they find themselves entirely overwhelmed and crushed by the authority of Scripture. No wonder then, that these children of this world, being conscious that the oil of their lamp is only that of the wild olive, which they are afraid will soon be extinguished, cover it with the bushel of hypocrisy, for Job tells us " the light of the wicked shall be put out " (Job xviii. 5); no wonder they glance off to other matters and topics, such as the power of their particular faction, and how we have come under the displeasure of the Emperor. By the use of such methods they work upon the minds of their converts, and prevent them from dwelling too much upon their abominable doctrines. It would be detestable enough if only for this, that its friends and followers are afraid to let it be seen, and keep it out of sight, as if they were hiding away a serpent. How did they learn this new language, and who taught it them? Surely they cannot tell who it was who first handed it down to them. For would anyone, Greek or Barbarian, who worshipped any god, venture to say He was one of His own creatures, and had no being till He was made? Would anyone who believes his own existence disbelieve God Himself when He asserts that such a one is His Beloved Son (S. Matt. xvii. 5), and say instead that He is not His Son, but only one of His creatures? It cannot but follow that all mankind are indignant with this ridiculous nonsense, which is so extremely unintelligible. Besides, there is no foundation for such doctrines in Holy Scripture. As has been shown before, and as shall be shown again, Holy Scripture gives them no warrant at all. The consequence is that the parent and originator of such abominations, the devil himself, has schooled them in this folly. Therefore against this arch-enemy, whose tools they are, we shall fight. We trust that God will give such strength and success to our arguments that Satan himself may be routed by them. Then, when his allies shall see their champion dead, may they be filled with shame and confusion at their being deceived by him, and come to learn at last, though late, that they cannot be Arians and Christians too.

11. You Arians say and believe, at the suggestion of Satan, that there was a time when the Son was not. This is the first of your outworks which we must assail. Tell us then, you blasphemers, what was it which had a being before the Son had any? If you say the Father had, this is a more unpardonable statement than the other. For to say of Him that He was heretofore or at some time or other is appalling insolence. For He has always been what He is now, the Father of the Son, and therefore so likewise is the Son the Son of the Father. But if you had rather say, that the Son was heretofore, when He was not, there cannot be a more foolish and absurd contradiction. Here then you are in a miserable fix, and under a necessity of confessing fairly, that there was heretofore a time when the Son was not. This is the unavoidable meaning of the expression "heretofore." It is as much as to say "at a certain time when." And to the same purpose and effect is that other proposition of yours, "the Son was not before He was begotten." The sense of both is plainly this, that there was a time when the Son did not exist. How then have you imagined such extravagant theories? Why have you thus "furiously raged with the heathen," and have "imagined vain words against the Lord, and against His Christ"? (Ps. ii. 1, 2). The Holy Scriptures have not the least hint of any such thing. On the contrary, they declare our Saviour to have existed from all eternity in union with the Father. So S. John writes, "In the beginning was the Word, and the Word was with God, and the Word was God" (S. John i. 1). And in the Book of the Revelation he says of Him, "Which is, and which was, and which is to come" (Rev. i. 4). And who is there who dares to deny that these words refer to His eternity. So, too, S. Paul, arguing with the Jews in his Epistle to the Romans, says, "Of whom as concerning the flesh Christ came, who is over all, God blessed for ever." And again, where he is seeking to convince the Gentiles, he tells them that "the invisible things of Him from the creation of the world are clearly seen, being understood by the things that are made, even His eternal power and Godhead" (Rom. i. 20). What and who this Power of God is, the same Apostle informs us in another place, where he tells us, that "Christ is the power of God, and the wisdom of God" (1 Cor. i. 24). That meaning which you are accustomed

to give of the passage is not the true one, when you say that the Father Himself is meant here, as if the Apostle had said, "The Father is His own eternal Power." This is but a wretched evasion. For it is not said here that God Himself is the Power, but that Christ is God's Power. Everyone knows the difference between being a person, and belonging to a person. Not that the latter implies always separation, but rather the contrary. So I would bid you read carefully what comes afterwards in S. Paul's Second Epistle to the Corinthians. He there says, "The Lord is that spirit" (2 Cor. iii. 17), and you, if you will turn unto the Lord, will see very plainly that the passage under dispute (Rom. i. 20) refers to God the Son.

12. Having mentioned the creation, it is by no means to be wondered at, that the Apostle should at the same time say something of the Power of the Creator. This Power is the Word of God, by whom all things were made. If, then, the works of the creation are of themselves sufficient to make God known without the Son, let us take care that we do not go on to say that those works were made without Him. For if all things were created, and continue to subsist, by the Son, then it follows that our contemplation of the creature should lead us to the contemplation of the Word that created it, and that through Him we should begin to know the Father. Now then, if according to our Blessed Saviour, "No man knoweth the Father save the Son, and he to whomsoever the Son will reveal Him" (S. Matt. xi. 27), and if in answer to that request of S. Philip, "Show us the Father," He did not refer him to the works of the creation, but said, "He that hath seen Me hath seen the Father" (S. John xiv. 9), surely S. Paul, when he was blaming the Gentiles for taking no notice of God the Word, at the same time that they were contemplating the symmetry and harmony of His works (as indeed it is certain that the creatures discover their Creator), and because they did not learn from them the knowledge of the true God, and renounce their idolatry; surely, I say, he might very well put them in remembrance of God the Son in that place where he mentions His "Eternal Power and Godhead" (Rom. i. 20). Further, when the holy writers say that the Son "existed before all things" (Col. i. 17), and that the world was made by Him (Heb. i. 2), they mean that He must be the Son of God from all eternity, and they affirm and declare Him to be properly God. In this manner Isaiah calls Him "the Everlasting God, the Lord, the Creator of the ends of the earth" (Isa. xl. 28). Susanna addresses Him "O Everlasting God" (Susan. 42).

Baruch writes, " I will cry unto the Everlasting in my days," and again a little after, " My hope is in the Everlasting that He will save you ; and joy is come unto me from the holy one" (Bar. iv. 20, 22). The writer of the Epistle to the Hebrews describes Him as " the Brightness of His Father's glory, and the express Image of His Person" (Heb. i. 3). David sings concerning Him in the eighty-ninth Psalm, that He is " the Glory of our strength" (Ps. lxxxix. 17), or "the Brightness of the Lord is upon us" (Sept.), and elsewhere he says, " In Thy Light shall we see Light" (Ps. xxxvi. 9). What madness then it is to doubt whether the Son always existed ! When did anyone ever see light without brightness? Why, then, should anyone presume to say that there was a time when the Son was not, or that He had no being before He was begotten? It is impossible to reconcile that statement of the Psalmist, " Thy dominion endureth throughout all ages" (Ps. cxlv. 13), with the supposition that there was even so much as a moment when the Word did not exist. For if every single moment is included in the ages and generations that have ever been, and if the Word is the creator and originator of all ages and generations, it is impossible that there should be a single moment of time before He existed. So it is downright madness to say that there was a time when the Son was not, and that the Son was made out of nothing. Besides, when our Blessed Lord says, " I am the Truth," he does not say, " I am made or become the Truth." He always uses this expression, " I am this or that," not " I became this or that." He says, for instance, " I am the Shepherd," " I am the Light" (S. John x. 14 ; viii. 12). Again, " Ye call Me Master and Lord : and ye say well, for so I am " (S. John xiii. 13). It cannot be imagined that the Word and Wisdom of the Father would use such descriptions as these of Himself, if they were not true of Him in the fullest and truest sense. Who then that finds Him thus speaking can avoid believing that the phrase " I am " plainly refers to His generation and existence from all eternity?

13. We have so far proved that the Holy Scriptures assert the Son to have existed from all eternity. Next we proceed to show that those affirmations of the Arians, " He was not," " Before that," and " heretofore," are in the same Scripture properly and only used concerning created beings. For so Moses in narrating the history of the Creation says :—" Every plant of the field *before* it was in the earth, and every herb of the field *before* it grew : for the Lord God had not caused it to rain upon the earth, and there was not a man to till the ground" (Gen. ii. 5).

And in Deuteronomy he writes, "*When* the Most High divided the nations" (Deut. xxxii. 8). Our Lord Himself speaks thus: —"If ye loved Me, ye would rejoice, because I said I go unto the Father: for My Father is greater than I. And now I have told you *before* it come to pass, that *when* it is come to pass, ye might believe" (S. John xiv. 28, 29). Solomon, too, speaks about the Creation as follows:—"I was set up from everlasting, from the beginning, or ever the earth was. *When* there were no depths, I was brought forth; *when* there were no fountains abounding with water. *Before* the mountains were settled, before the hills was I brought forth" (Prov. viii. 23). Again we read, "*Before* Abraham was, I am" (S. John viii. 58). Jeremiah writes, "*Before* I formed thee in the belly I knew thee" (Jer. i. 5). David sings, "Lord, Thou hast been our refuge, from one generation to another. *Before* the mountains were brought forth, or ever the earth and the world were made: Thou art God from everlasting and world without end" (Ps. xc. 1, 2). Again we read, "Then Susanna cried out with a loud voice, and said, O everlasting God, that knowest the secrets, and knowest all things before they be" (Susan. 42). Therefore it seems that these expressions, "Heretofore He did not exist," "Before He was begotten," "When as yet," and the like, are very applicable to created beings, but by no means to God the Word. If, then, these are terms which the Scripture uses of created beings, and the same Scripture uses the word "ever" in speaking of the Son, it is clear, ye enemies of God, that the Son was not made out of nothing, and that He is no creature, but His Father's eternal Image and Word, the everlasting Brightness of that everlasting Light from all eternity. How then did you come to think of a time before the Son existed? Or why should you affirm that the Word began to exist after a certain period of time, when He Himself created everything that existed in time? How do you think that there could possibly be such a thing as time, till He was in being who made everything, and "without whom nothing was made that was made"? Or why do you not speak out plainly, when you are speaking of time, and say, "There was a time when the Word was not"? No doubt the word "time" is carefully avoided, because you are afraid of alarming the minds of simple folk. But your meaning and opinion are too evident to be disguised or concealed. For *time* is really what you mean when you omit the word, and only say, "There was when," instead of "There was a *time* when He was not;" and "He was not before He was begotten," instead of "before the *time* when He was begotten."

14. But when we argue thus, our opponents have the shame-lessness to urge the following objection. If, they say, there was a time when the Son was not, but if He is from all eternity and co-existent with the Father, does it not follow that He is no longer the Son, but the brother of the Father? O foolish and perverse ones! If indeed we asserted that He only existed at once with the Father, but was not the Son, there might be some excuse for this absurd notion. But when we confess that He is from all eternity Son of the Father and begotten of the Father, how can such a thought be possible as to imagine that the Father begets Himself a brother? And where is the least hint of this brotherhood in our Confession of Faith in the Father and the Son? How can the Word be said to be brother to Him, whose Word He is? Nor do they themselves think that this objection is weighty, for they know what the truth is well enough. It is a lame argument at best, and worthy of men "who desire," as Solomon says, "to depart from the truth" (Prov. xviii. 1, Sept.). For when neither the Father nor the Son have derived their being from any principle that existed before, how can they be said to be brothers? The Father is simply the Father, the Principle of substance and being to the Son, and not the Son of any other being. The Son, like-wise, is simply His Son, and not the brother of any other being. And so we speak the language of reason when we say that the Word is the everlasting Son of the Father. For the nature of the Father was always so perfect, that there was nothing lacking to it. The generation of the Son is not like that of a man, which requires an existence after that of the Father, but the Son of God must, as such, have been begotten of the Father from all eternity. As regards man's nature it is impossible, as his nature is finite, but that his generation should be in time; but the nature of the Son of God, being infinite and eternal, His generation must, of necessity, be infinite and eternal too. Therefore, our adversaries must first prove that the Son is not the Son, but a creature made of nothing. Then, when they have done this, they may clamour as they like of His not being before He began to exist. It is, no doubt, true enough that all created beings once were not. But then if it be true, as God the Father declares of Him, and the Scriptures assert, that He is the Son; and if that which is be-gotten of the Father is His Word, and His Wisdom, and His Glory, what shall we infer from the assertion of these men, who say that the Son was not before He existed, but that it is an attempt to rob God of His Son, and openly to vilify Him,

and blasphemously declare that once upon a time He was without His Wisdom and Glory, as it were like some barren and dry fount. For as they carefully avoid using the word Time, and ready as they are to confess that the Son existed before time, or before the periods or events in which they say He existed, because they are afraid of bringing disgrace upon themselves, that must still be considered as a makeshift as long as they allow that there were certain periods in which God the Father had no Word or Reason.

15. But if they agree to adopt the title of Son, lest everyone should condemn their opinions, whilst at the same time they deny that He is the true and genuine substance of the Father, as if that must imply division and parts in the Godhead, they as really deny Him to be the Son of God as if they expressly rejected the Name with the thing itself. Besides, do they not grievously err, who make no difference in their arguments between beings corporeal and incorporeal, and who deny that the nature of God is capable of what even their own frail nature is incapable of? These foolish people, who thus judge of the Son of the Father from what they see among men, are led to deny the being of God, even the Father, since they cannot possibly reconcile these ideas together. And as reasoning and arguing in this manner concerning the Son's Godhead is pitiable in the extreme, they must let me proceed to put a few more questions to them, and see if perchance I can do anything to recall their common sense. Now, if you say the Son is of nothing, and had no being before He was begotten, does it not follow that the Son is by participation God and the Wisdom of the Father, even as all other beings that are sanctified and glorified? But whose being does the Son partake of, will you inform us? All other creatures partake of the Spirit. Does the Son then partake of the Spirit? Now the Son Himself tells us that "the Spirit receives" or "partakes of the Son" (S. John xvi. 14), which plainly shows that the Son sanctifies the Spirit, and not the Spirit the Son. Whom or what then is it possible for the Son to be partaker of, but the Father? And how otherwise is He partaker of Him than of His very substance and nature? For if He is only partaker of something external to that brought thus into being, then He does not partake of the Father, but of that foreign created being. And He cannot, therefore, be second in place and order after the Father, because that foreign being would come before Him. Nor can He any longer be said to be the Son of the Father, but only the Son of that same being, by participation of whose nature He is called

the Son of God. But what a ridiculous and wicked thing this is to say when the Father declares, "This is My Beloved Son" (S. Matt. xvii. 5), and when the Son says that "His Father is God" (S. John viii. 54). Therefore it follows that the Son is not a partaker of any such foreign being, but that He partakes of the substance of the Father. But if it be said that that which partakes is any other besides the substance of the Son, the same absurdity still exists if there is an intermediate being between the nature of the Father and the nature of the Son.

16. And thus, from these ridiculous opinions, which seem to contradict one another, we are compelled to arrive at the truth, which is, that the Son is properly and entirely of the substance of the Father. For when it is said that the Son participates, that is the same as saying that He is begotten, and this implies that He is God's Son. Well then, all creatures are partakers of the Son, according to that grace of the Spirit, which He is pleased to communicate to them. From that it is clear that He Himself partakes of nothing but the substance of the Father, and in consequence of this participation, He is the proper Son of the Father. But we, since we are made partakers of the Son through grace, are said to be partakers of God. Thus S. Peter says, "That ye might be partakers of the Divine nature" (2 S. Peter i. 4). S. Paul says, "Know ye not that ye are the temple of God?" (1 Cor. iii. 16), and "Ye are the temple of the living God" (2 Cor. vi. 16). Our Lord declares, "He that hath seen Me hath seen the Father" (S. John xiv. 9), meaning that all our knowledge and comprehension of the Father are derived from the Son, because He is of the substance of the Father. And as to the objection that participation argues a passive condition and a division in the Divine nature—for that such a participation there is in God, and that it is the same with the eternal generation we have already shown and proved—we remark that in affirming the Son to be begotten of the Father, we do not regard this nature as passive, or that there is any division of the Godhead. It is surely not impossible to believe that God has a Son, begotten of His own nature. And when we call this person His Son, and His Offspring, we do not intend to imply that there is a passiveness or division in the Godhead; but this we believe, that the Son is the true and Only-begotten Son of God. After we have made it thus clearly manifest, that what is begotten of the nature of the Father is the Son of the Father, there remains no manner of doubt but that this Son is that Wisdom and Word of the Father, in and by which He creates and makes all things. This is He,

I say, whose Brightness illuminates all things, and who reveals Himself to whomsoever He will. This is that express Image of His Person, in which He is discerned and contemplated, and in regard of which both the Son and the Father are one. In a word, this is that Christ, by whom we all have been redeemed, and who has made us " a new creation" (2 Cor. v. 17). And since the Son is certainly this being, it is utterly unsuitable as well as most dangerous doctrine, to assert that He was made out of nothing, or that He was not before He was begotten. For whosoever says such things as these of Him, who is of the very substance of the Father, is guilty of blasphemy against the Eternal Father Himself, and plainly shows that He believes no better things concerning Him than He does about His Son.

17. This, then, is really enough to overturn the whole Arian heresy. However, let us proceed from this to another argument, which may further show its folly. If God is the Maker and Creator of all things; if He creates all things by His Son, and nothing is or has been made, which was not made by the Son; is it not, then, the height of impiety to assert that this Word and Wisdom, which was the Maker of all things and the Worker together with God, at one time did not exist? Is not this as much as to deny that God is the Creator of everything? Since, if this be true, the Word, which created all things, was not His own Reason or Word, working by His authority, but some foreign and alien being, and not of His Father's substance. Another difficulty which they have to solve before they can justify their doctrine of the Son's non-eternity either to us or themselves, is this—that if the Word did not exist from all eternity with the Father, then there was not a Trinity from all eternity. Only a Unity existed first, and afterwards it became and grew to be a Trinity. This is the kind of theological doctrine these men teach. Moreover, if the Son is not properly and essentially the Son of the Father, but was made out of nothing, it follows that the Trinity also rose out of nothing, and that there was a time when there was no Trinity, but a Unity only. And so the Trinity must have been at one time imperfect, at another time entire. It was imperfect until the Son came to be created, and then entire afterwards. Then this created Son began to be numbered in the Trinity, and He, who at one time did not exist, was considered as equal with Him who had existed from all eternity. The Son, in fact, then became God, and as such became worthy of Divine honour and worship. Moreover, this follows, which is worse than all, the Holy Trinity must thus be dissimilar and inconsistent with itself,

made up of different kinds of natures and substances, the real meaning of which is to call the Trinity something made or created. What sort of religion or theology is this, the foundation of which is so uncertain and changeable, and which at one time stands in one way, and at another time in another way? If it is like this, it may go on adding more and more Persons to the Trinity, and this indefinitely; and then, doubtless, such a Trinity as this is capable of decrease too. For, whatever admits of increase is certainly liable to diminution.

18. But God forbid that these inventions should be considered as true doctrine. The Holy Trinity is no created being. The Divinity of it, the Glory of it, is eternal, equal, and undivided. How then do you Arians presume to distribute it into a diversity of natures? Why, since you allow that the Father is eternal, do you assert of the Son, who is enthroned with Him, that there was a time when He was not? In doing this you drag the Son down from the Father's side. The Holy Trinity is the Maker and Cause of all things. Yet, you are not afraid to number the Blessed Persons amongst created things; you do not hesitate to place the three infinite Persons on the same level as their own servants, and to number the Lord of Sabaoth amongst His own subjects. Leave off, then, from confounding and blending these natures into one, which never can be one. Do not unite into being those things which are not with those that are. These notions, so far from conducing to God's honour and glory, are in every way injurious and hurtful to it. For whosoever dishonours the Son dishonours the Father. If the doctrine of the Trinity be that which we hold now to be the true one, and if the Trinity be now the true and only object of religious worship, it must have been always so. Unless, indeed, you will be so foolish as to say that that which is right and true can have additions made to it, and that the first elements of theology need continual accretions, so that either the Trinity was properly so from all eternity, or if it was not, it is not so now. Now this is such fearful blasphemy, and such hateful heresy, that no Christian can possibly stand it. This doctrine is only fit for pagans, to say that the Trinity was created and made. The gods of pagans may be imperfect, and may increase or decrease. But Christianity only knows of a Holy Trinity which is perfect, uniform, and invariable. We believe that the Blessed Trinity was always the same, not consisting of fewer persons at one time, and of more at another. For nothing more wicked can be supposed. Wherefore, we are careful to keep the Holy Trinity free from any

notion of being mixed up with created beings, and we assert and adore the individuality and unity of the Godhead. We detest and abominate the wild blasphemies of the Arians, and we know and confess that the Son existed from everlasting. For He is co-eternal with the Father, whose Word He is. This will further appear from what follows.

19. God is declared in Scripture to be the Fountain of Wisdom and Life. So Jeremiah says, "They have forsaken Me, the Fountain of living waters" (Jer. ii. 13); and again, "A glorious high throne from the beginning is the place of our sanctuary. O Lord, the Hope of Israel, all that forsake Thee shall be ashamed, and they that depart from me shall be written in the earth, because they have forsaken the Lord, the Fountain of living waters" (Jer. xvii. 12, 13). So likewise it is written in Baruch, "Thou hast forsaken the Fountain of Wisdom" (Bar. iii. 12). And it is evident that the nature of this Life and Wisdom does not belong to any foreign substance, but is exactly the same with that of the Fountain of it. It is not a being by itself; and it does not exist in time, but from everlasting. Now the Son declares Himself to be this Life and this Wisdom. He says, "I am the Life" (S. John xiv. 6), and "I Wisdom dwell with prudence" (Prov. viii. 12). What an impious wretch, then, must he be who says, "There was a time when the Son was not!" What is this but plainly asserting, that there was a time when the infinite Fountain of Life and Wisdom was perfectly dry and unproductive. If it was this, it could not be a fountain; for that cannot be a fountain which produces nothing. And this is the height of absurdity! For God has promised to those who will perform His will, that they shall be like a fountain whose waters fail not. For so He speaks by the prophet Isaiah, "And the Lord shall guide thee continually, and satisfy thy soul in drought, and make fat thy bones: and thou shalt be like a watered garden, and like a spring of waters, whose waters fail not" (Isa. lviii. 11). And yet these men are so hardened as to affirm of that God, who is, as He is called, the Fountain of Wisdom, that there was a time when He brought forth no Wisdom, but was altogether bare and destitute of it. But these things which they assert are falsehoods and lies. Reason and truth, and Scripture as well, bear witness that God is the eternal Fountain of His own Wisdom. If the Fountain be eternal, the Wisdom must certainly be so too. And indeed it is that Wisdom by which all things were made, and of which the Psalmist declares, "In Wisdom hast thou made them all"

(Ps. civ. 24); and of which also Solomon says, "The Lord by Wisdom hath founded the earth; by understanding hath He established the heavens" (Prov. iii. 19). This is that Wisdom which S. John tells us is the Word, "by whom all things were made, and without whom nothing was made" (S. John i. 3). In short, this Wisdom is Christ Himself. "For to us there is but one God the Father, of whom are all things, and we in Him; and one Lord Jesus Christ, by whom are all things, and we in Him" (1 Cor. viii. 6). If all things are by Him, then He is not to be numbered amongst all things. For it will be as reasonable to assert that God the Father, "of whom are all things," is amongst the number of "all things," as to say that our Lord, "by whom are all things," is amongst them. So that whosoever would look upon it as the greatest absurdity possible, that God the Father should not be separated from all created things, must also allow that His Only-begotten Son, who is of the very substance of the Father, must be separated too. And if He is not so separated, then it is a wicked lie to say of Him that "there was a time when He was not," and "He was not before He was made." These imperfections are only to be found in created beings; but not in the Son, who is of the same nature with the Father, His co-essential Offspring, Word and Wisdom. In this is the true relationship of the Son towards the Father, and likewise of the Father towards the Son, so that it cannot be said that there ever was a time when God the Father was without His Word or Wisdom, or that there ever was a time when the Son did not exist. Why, indeed, should He be called the Son, if He was not of the substance of the Father? or, why should He be called the Word and Wisdom of the Father, if He was not so always and essentially.

20. When, I ask, was God without anything which essentially and properly belonged to Him? or, how can it be conceived that whatever is His essentially should be deemed of some foreign and diverse nature? Created things have no affinity with their Creator. They cannot be compared. They are outside Him altogether. They have received their being from the Word, and by His pleasure and appointment; and, if it pleased their Creator, could at any moment cease to be, since that is the nature of created things. It must, therefore, be the height of folly and wickedness, to suppose that a being which is of the nature and essence of the Father (and this we have now proved the Son to be), came originally from nothing, was begotten or made in time; that He is adventitious, and could at some time or other cease to exist. As soon as anyone imagines such folly, let him

ask himself, whether the perfection and infinity of the Father's nature is capable of being withdrawn. And then that he may more perfectly understand this ridiculous Arian heresy, let him reflect, that the Son is the Image, the Brightness, the Character, the Truth, and Reality of the Father. For if Light no sooner shines forth, but the Brightness, which is the Image of it, does so too; if when the Substance exists, its Form and Figure does so likewise; if, in short, when the Father exists, His Truth and Reality exists at the same time; then let our opponents begin to consider into what awful blasphemy they have fallen, by making no more than a created being of the Image and Character of the Deity. For if the Son had no being before He was begotten or made, and it is asserted that this Reality or Truth was not always in God, that is the vilest heresy that can be uttered. As certainly, therefore, as the Father always existed, so certainly the Truth, which is the Son, who declares of Himself, "I am the Truth" (S. John xiv. 6), always existed in Him. It is quite necessary that the express Character and Image of the Divine Substance should exist along with that Substance from eternity. For this Image is no external representation of God, but is Himself begotten of God, such as delights Him with a just and true idea of Himself, as the Son says, "I was daily His delight, rejoicing always before Him" (Prov. viii. 30). When, then, was there a time that the Father did not contemplate Himself in His own Image? When was there a period in which He did not rejoice in beholding it? Who will dare to say that His Image was produced out of nothing, and so that the Father could not rejoice in it until it was born or made? And besides, who can possibly conceive that the Maker and Creator of all things could contemplate Himself in a created being? Therefore it follows that the express Image of the Father must be exactly of such a nature as the Father is Himself.

21. But now come and let us inform ourselves distinctly in what manner the Son is the true and proper Image of the Father. The attributes of the Father are these: He is eternal, immortal, omnipotent; He is the Light, the King, the universal Governor, the great God, the Lord, the Creator and Maker of all. And if the Son were not truly and properly all these, it could not be true that he who sees the Son sees the Father. Unless He were these things, He would be, as the Arians imagine, a creature, and not the eternal Son, nor the true and proper Image of the Father. Unless, indeed, laying aside all candour, they would say that the Son is only called the Image of His Father, but that

this does not imply a sameness of substance, for it is only an appellation. Tell me then, ye enemies of the Lord, is a name of a thing an image and a representation of it? Is there any likeness between creatures and their Creator? Are being and not being so very like one another that you make no difference between them, although you would have us believe that the last was heretofore the case of the Son? In such a fashion do you Arians argue, to surround us, as you imagine, on all sides with difficulties. If the Son, you say, is in all respects the express Image of the Father; if there is no difference between them; then the Son ought to beget another Son; as the Father begets Him. He ought to be a Father too, as well as His Father; and for the same reason the Son's Son ought to beget another Son, and so on without limit. If otherwise, there will be one respect at least in which the Son is not like the Father. How shamelessly do these inventors of blasphemies, these enemies of God, weave together their horrid schemes, rather than allow that the Son is the genuine Image of His Father. They ascribe corporeal and earthly properties to the Father. They subject Him to the possibility of separation and division of substance. If, indeed, they conceive the nature of God and man to be similar, then they may very well suppose that the Divine generation is much the same as the human, and that sons ought to be begotten one from another in an unlimited fashion. But God is not a man, that we should suffer ourselves to form any notions of Him, as if He were so. The brute creation and mankind, by virtue of the law of their being, which was implanted in their natures at the first, from time to time propagate their species, ever since which the relations of the father and son have alternately descended; he that was only a son in his order and time, becoming a father, by the transmission of the same law, which he himself derived from his father. And therefore there is no such thing, properly speaking, as father and son in the animal world; or, at least, theirs is but a very slender and variable sort of paternity and sonship. Among them the same person is frequently both a father and a son at the same time. But anything of this nature is incompatible with the Deity. There is no such thing here as a Father of a Father. There is no procreation of a Son that is afterwards to be a Father. Nor is the Son begotten of a Father who received His being before from another Father. Nor is He in any sense so begotten of the Father, as that He can, in like manner, beget another Son. From all which it is evident, that the truest and most essential paternity and sonship are only to be found in the Deity. The relationships of Father and Son are always and for ever exactly the same; the Father is always the Father, and the Son is always the Son.

22. Whoever, therefore, makes the enquiry, why cannot the Son beget another Son? may just as well ask, why the Father had not a Father? Either of the questions is as impious and absurd as the other. For as the Father was always a Father, and can never be a Son; so the Son was always a Son, and can never be a Father. And indeed there is nothing in which the Son is more expressly and evidently the Character and Image of the Father, than in that absolute and invariable state of being, which He derives from the Father. If, therefore, the Father was mutable, or capable of any alteration, then He that is the express Image of Him must be so likewise. Else there would be something wherein the Son would by no means resemble the Father. But if the Father is incapable of any kind of change; if He is always, and in all respects, one and the same; then must He that is His express Image be always so too. Nor can it be imagined, that the nature of the Son should vary in the least from the nature of the Father, unless it could be proved that He is not of the substance of the Father. In vain, therefore, do these foolish people harbour such ridiculous nonsense, seeking to separate God's Image from Himself, in order that they may make His Son on a level with His own creatures. This shows how the Arians, conforming to the doctrine of Eusebius,* make a creature of the Son, and represent Him with all those imperfect properties which belong to His creatures. Thus have they widely erred from the truth. And think how, publishing abroad their iniquitous doctrines ever since they have devised this heresy, they have gone about everywhere; even some of them, as they do at this day, encountering the children in the streets and asking them such questions as these, proceeding not out of Holy Scripture, but " out of the abundance of their heart" (S. Luke vi. 45). " Did He," they say, " create Him out of nothing that yet was not, or did He create Him that was already in being? Did He produce Him that was, or Him that was not produced before? Is there one, or are there two self-existent beings? If the Son has not in Himself a power of acting and willing independently of the Father, is not His nature as insensible as a stone? Or if He has His freewill, may He not vary His own measures in the exercise of it, whereas all God's decrees and purposes are ever-

* Eusebius, Bishop of Nicomedia, was condemned at the Nicene Council, and, refusing to conform to its decrees, was exiled.

lasting and unchangeable?" Then they also accost women and ask them indecent questions after this sort: "Did you ever have a son before you brought him forth? If you have not, then just so the Son of God did not exist before He was begotten." Such bandying of jokes these low people delight in, placing God's nature upon an equality with their own. And these are they who have the face to call themselves Christians, at the same time that they are acting the part of heathens, in endeavouring to "change the glory of the uncorruptible God into an image made like to corruptible man" (Rom. i. 23).

23. These objections are so senseless and dull that they do not even deserve an answer. Still, lest their heresy should have any foundation at all, it may here be worth while to expose its emptiness; the more so on account of the women, who are easily deceived by them. I should therefore like to know why, when they thus speak, they never think of asking an architect, "Can you build a house without materials? If you cannot, whether it does not follow that God could not make the universe without materials?" They ought to demand of every man they meet, "whether he can exist without place? and if he cannot, whether it follows that God is in His place?" So they would bring contempt upon themselves from those who heard them. Why is it that, on hearing that God has a Son, do they deny Him by the standard of their own conceptions? Whereas, if they are told that He creates and makes, they no longer object their human ideas. They ought in creation to act in the same manner, and to supply God with materials, and so deny Him to be the Creator, till they join themselves to the Manichees. But if the sublimity and dignity which our thoughts entertain concerning God supersede such low ideas as these; if everyone at once is sure that God does not exist as we do; that He does not make or create as we make, but in a manner peculiar to His own infinite nature; then we cannot but be convinced at the same time that the Divine generation is as absolutely different from, and as little to be compared with, the human. For God does not imitate man; but rather men are called fathers of their own children on account of God, who is alone truly and properly Father of His Son. For "of Him the whole family" (or "every fatherhood") "in heaven and earth is named" (Ephes. iii. 15). The assertions of these men seem plausible enough at first sight, but if anyone will take the trouble to enquire into them closely, they will soon find they are only fit to be ridiculed and despised.

24. The first of their queries is very dark and unintelligible. They put an indefinite question without saying what it is they would enquire about, as if they did not wish to receive an answer. They talk in general terms of " He who is," and of " Him who is not." But who is " He who is," and what " are not," ye Arians? Or who " is," and who " is not"? What are said " to be," and what " not to be"? It is in the power of Him that is, to make those things which are not, and those things which are, and those things which were before. If he has but proper materials provided for him, any mechanic, goldsmith, or potter, each according to his own calling, can make those vessels he pleases; and even thus the great Creator of the world Himself was pleased to make man out of that dust of the earth which He had already created, but which was not in existence till He had so created it by His own Word. So then, if this is the meaning of their question, the creature, on the one hand, plainly was not before its generation; and men, on the other, must have materials before they can make anything out of them; and, therefore, their reasoning is at fault, because there is nothing more considered than the making of those things which already are, and the making of those things which were not. But if they speak concerning God and His Word, let them complete their question, and ask, " Was there ever a time when He who is God was without His Word?" " Was He who is Light at any time without Brightness?" " Did the Father of the Word always exist?" Or suppose they put it thus :—" Has the Father who exists made the Word, who did not exist before?" Or, " Has He ever with Him His Word, as the proper Offspring of His substance?" By thus clearing up the question, it appears immediately how these men do but presume and profanely dispute about God and the Son of God. Who, indeed, can bear to hear them say that God was ever without His Reason or Word? For this is the difficulty they strike upon at last, although they endeavour to keep clear of it and to hide it with their sophisms. But it is all in vain. They can never pretend to prove that there was a time when the Word was not, without asserting and proving that God was not always a Father, but came in time to be so. Who will not stop his ears to keep such blasphemy out of them? Who, I say, that has ever thought of any of these arguments we have already laid down, or has read S. John's saying, " In the beginning was the Word " (S. John i. 1), or S. Paul's texts, " Who is the Brightness of His glory " (Heb. i. 3), and " Who is over all, God blessed for ever. Amen" (Rom. ix. 5).

25. They had much better have been silent ; but since they will not take this advice, the best way to meet their shameless questions is to put some bold ones to them. Perhaps if we do, they may be disposed to lay down their arms and submit to the truth, when they themselves are beset and entangled in the way they would inconvenience us. After many prayers, then, that God would prosper our cause, we might ask them in turn, " Did He who is God come afterwards to be made, since He did not exist before, or was He in being before He was made ? " " Did He create Himself after He had previously existed, or when as yet He had never been ? " " Did He arise out of nothing, and suddenly start into being ? " Such questions as these are, doubtless, very wild and absurd ; they are unsuitable, moreover, to God's honour and dignity. But then they are exactly of a piece with those of our adversaries. If it is very blasphemous and wicked to propose such questions with regard to God the Father, it will be just as bad to ask them concerning His Word. But if there is yet occasion for a direct and serious answer to those senseless and foolish queries, there is this clear and easy answer, Since God is, He was eternally ; and that as the Father is, so the Brightness of the Father's glory, which is His Word, must be so too. Again, God who is has from Himself His Word who also is ; nor was the Word born afterwards, whereas He was not before ; because the Father never was without the Word. In fact, He that affirms that the Son is only a being remote from the Divine nature, and created to serve the wise purposes and counsels of the Father, insults the Father no less than the Son. Upon the whole, then, this question of theirs deserves to be slighted and neglected. Since they deny the Word or Reason, they in consequence ask irrational and absurd questions. Would any reasonable person when he is looking at the sun, ask concerning its radiance, " Were the rays of the sun made by it when as yet they were, or when as yet they were not ? " I think that man would be held to reason foolishly in the extreme, because he supposed that what is from the light was external to it, and because he was asking questions when, and where, and whether it were made. In like manner thus to speculate concerning the Son and the Father, and to entertain such notions is far greater madness, for it is to imagine that the Word of the Father is external to Him, and to confound generation with creation. But in order that they shall not complain that we have answered their questions only in the negative, we will grant that in one sense the Father did create or make the Son, for " the Word was made

flesh" (S. John i. 14), and the eternal Son hath now in the end of the world condescended to make Himself the Son of Man. This they will not deny, I suppose, unless with Paul of Samosata,* they say that He had no being before He became man.   Thus much may suffice in reply to the first of their questions.

26. And now, on your part, O Arians, remembering your own words, answer for us the following questions.   " Did He that is stand in need of Him who was not, or of Him that already was, in order that He might create and make all things ? "   For you said that the Father created the Son out of nothing, to be such an instrument as it was necessary for Him to make use of in the creation of the universe.   Which, then, is the superior being, He who needs, or He who is wanted?   Or, does not each supply the other's deficiency ?   The notion that you have formed of the Son's mere subserviency reflects in a shameful manner upon the weakness of the Maker, as if He could do nothing for Himself, but is like some mechanic or shipwright, who can do nothing until he is provided with axe and saw.   Can anything be more shocking than this ?   But why do we dwell so long upon its grossness, when enough has been said already to show quite clearly that their doctrines are mere fanciful inventions.   And as for that other very foolish enquiry, which they put to women, no other answer is needful than that which has been already given, namely, that the manner in which the eternal Son is begotten of the Father ought not to be compared with human generation.   But to leave them in this particular without excuse, it will not be foreign to our purpose to make them sensible that their own parallel is directly against them.   Since they enquire of parents about their children, let them consider whether every child is not of the substance of its parents.   It is true that no one can be said to be a father before he has a son; but after he has one, the original nature of that son is not something foreign and external, but derived out of his own being, a part of his own nature, and so perfectly his own image and likeness, that the father may be said to be seen in the son, and the son in the father.   So that if our opponents will make the Divine generation parallel to the human as regards time, it is but reasonable that they should allow them to answer one another in that identity and propriety of substance which exists between parents and children.   But

* Paul, a native of Samosata, in Syria, was Bishop of Antioch.   Dionysius of Alexandria says, "he had a low and abject opinion of Christ, contrary to the doctrine of the Church, as if He had been no more than a man."   Paul was excommunicated by the Council of Antioch, A.D. 269.

they only want to make use of whatever seems to suit their purpose, just as serpents only suck those juices out of the earth, which will turn to poison. Those who make enquiry of parents, and ask of a mother whether she ever had a son before he was begotten, ought to add another question, and that is, " Whether her son was something quite foreign to herself; whether she purchased him as she would a house or anything else ? " Her answer, I need not tell you, would be this, " I did not buy my son, but bear him. He is not a part of my goods and chattels, which can pass on from one person to another ; but he derives his very nature and being from mine, and they are substantially the same as mine. He was not a being conveyed to me, but he received his being from mine, so that I can say that my whole nature is truly in him, although I am personally distinct from him." And, indeed, it is impossible but that a father and mother amongst men should commence and continue so, according to the succession of time, because every father and mother commenced themselves as a son and a daughter, the finite character and successive donation of human nature not admitting of the son's existing as soon as the father exists. And yet the Apostle gives us to understand that Levi was in the loins of Abraham, his great grandfather, before even Isaac, his grandfather, was born. Till a certain age human nature is incapable of propagation ; and so many years at least must the son be younger than the father.

27. Therefore, if when our adversaries ask parents about their children, they are told that every child is of the substance and nature of his parents, let them acknowledge also that the Word of God is altogether of the Father's substance and nature. And if they make any objection as to the time, let them say what is to hinder God Almighty ? It seems indeed necessary to prove their impiety from those very things they seem to ridicule. Well then, I say, let them tell us what is there to hinder God from being always the Father of the Son ; for it is granted us that whatever is begotten must be from its father. And as for these people who have such unworthy opinions respecting the Deity, let us turn the tables on them. Let them stand self-condemned, and when they question women on the subject of time, let them enquire of the sun concerning its brightness, and the fountain concerning the streams which flow from it. These instances will show them that the cause sometimes no sooner exists than the effect exists too. Besides, if that which is born of human nature came from that nature, and yet when the being

exists separately is nevertheless truly a part of that nature, why do they not speak out plainly, and openly declare to the world that they have meaner notions of the power and perfections of God, than of those of His creatures. But if they do not dare to say this openly, and if at the same time it must be granted, as we have shown it must be, that the Son of God was not in the nature of an addition, but begotten out of the nature and substance of the Father; and that there is nothing which is a hindrance to God, for God is not as man, and His glory is far greater than even that of the sun, of which He is the ruling power; it is evident that the Son, by whom the Father gave all things their being, is of the same nature with the Father, and has existed with Him from eternity. Therefore it is certain, even from the nature of the case, that the Son does not come of nothing, but is eternal and from the Father; and the question of these heretics, which they are fond of putting to parents, exposes their malice. For, as soon as they are compelled to own that the Son is of the same nature as the Father, they find out that they are only covered with shame, and are defeated on those arguments which they raise as to the particular of time.

28. As we have already stated, so we now repeat, that the Divine generation must not be compared with the nature of men, nor the Son considered to be part of God, nor generation to imply anything of passion. God is not as man. That passion, which exists in man, whose body consists of divisible parts, and which grows up by degrees to a capacity of procreation, does not exist in God, and ought not to be ascribed to Him. He is an uncompounded indivisible being, without parts or passions. And Holy Scripture remarkably defends this doctrine, and guards against any gross error which might arise upon it. For the Word of God is God's Son, and the Son is the Word and Wisdom of the Father. Now, as the Word and Wisdom of God cannot be a created being, so neither can they be a part or portion of the substance of Him whose Word and Wisdom they are. Nor do they imply any kind of passion. To express the reality and propriety of His Sonship, that He is of the same nature and substance with the Father, Holy Scripture declares Him to be the Son of God. And again, to keep us from imagining that He is such, and by the same means, a Son as are the sons of men, it also affirms Him to be of and in the Divine nature, calling Him God's Word, Wisdom, and Brightness. From this we understand that the Divine generation has nothing whatever in it of passion, but that it is from eternity,

and such as is altogether suitable to the greatness of Almighty God. Here is another question which these madmen may well ask themselves. " What part of the Father, or what passion in Him, do they take His Word, His Wisdom, and His Brightness to be?" Why should not they question men about their words or speech, as well as women about their children? Why do they not want to know, whether words which men put forth are a part of their being, or of their passions? If then, parts or passions cannot be implied in the words or speech of men, although human bodies consist of divisible parts and are subject to passions; why should these men ascribe passions and parts to the Divine nature, which is incorporeal and indivisible, and why should they deny that the Son is the true and natural Son of God, begotten of His Father? We have now much more than sufficiently proved that what God begets He begets without any sort of passion. Now we will particularly show the same as to His Wisdom. God is not like man; and we must not in this instance think of Him as if He were so. Now, men are capable of receiving wisdom, but God cannot derive or acquire it. He is the Father of His own Wisdom, of which those who are partakers may lay claim to be called wise. And this Wisdom of the Father is no part of Him, nor passion in Him, but His genuine Offspring. Therefore, He was always the Father; and as His nature is unchangeable, so His Father-hood must have been eternal. For if it is a good thing that He be Father, yet if He has not always been the Father, then His nature has not been ever perfect.

29. But then our adversaries say, God was always a Creator, and that the power of creating did not come to Him at any time subsequently. Will you say, then, because He is the Author of all things, that His creatures also are eternal, and we ought not to affirm of them that they were not before they were made? How extremely foolish are these Arians. For is there such a similarity between what God begets and what He creates, that what may, and indeed must, be said of Him as a Father may as truly be said of Him as a Creator? After that abundant proof which we have produced of the infinite difference there is between the Son and the creatures of God, can they think there is anything material in this reply? Let me, therefore, say once more, that a work is external to the nature, but a Son is the proper offspring of the substance. There is, therefore, no necessity that the works of God must have had an eternal existence, for it depended entirely upon His own pleasure and choice how soon

or how late He would give them their being.   But this could not be the case when He would beget a Son, because the substance of the Son must be from Himself, and His generation of Him not an arbitrary but an essential act.   Besides, a man may be properly called a maker before he has done his work, but a man cannot be called a father before he has a son.   And if they will yet be so perverse as to ask why God was not always as willing as He was able to create, this is indeed the presumption of madmen, for " who hath known the mind of the Lord, or who hath been His counsellor ? " (Rom. xi. 34), or " how shall the thing formed say to Him that formed it, why hast Thou made me thus ?" (Rom. ix. 20).   However, not to leave even a weak argument unanswered, they must be told that although God had always the power to create, yet created beings as such are absolutely incapable of existing from eternity.   For they came into being out of nothing, and were not before they were made ; and how could that which had a beginning of existence always co-exist with the eternal God ?   Wherefore God, considering what was most fitting and suitable for them, did not give His creatures their being until they might exist to most advantage, and best be preserved.   For, as He did not think well to send His Word into the world in the beginning of it, in the days of Adam, Noah, or Moses, but postponed His appearing till later times, because He saw that this would be far the better plan for the whole creation ; so did He make, in the same manner, things generated, when He would, and when He saw it was most for their benefit.   But the matter with regard to the Son stands otherwise, for as He is of the Father's own nature and substance, He has always existed. Inasmuch as the Father always has existed, so what belongs to His substance cannot but have existed with Him, and in Him from eternity ; and this is His Word and His Wisdom.   That creatures should have this necessary incapacity so to have existed, does not at all disparage the power of the Creator ; for He was able to have created them before had He so pleased.   But to suppose that His own Offspring did not always co-exist with Him, this would indeed be a disparagement of the perfection of His substance.   His works were called into being when He would, through His Word ; but the Son is ever the proper Offspring of His Father's substance.

30.   These reasons then, whilst they are perfectly satisfactory to the faithful, distress and trouble these heretics, for they see their false doctrines utterly crushed by them.   And how little sincerity is in their views, how deceitful and crafty they are, ap-

pears plainly from that other question, "whether there is one, or are there two unmade beings?" They propose this difficulty, not with any serious intention of honouring God the Father, but only out of a malicious desire to dishonour the Son. So that if anyone, unaware of their subtlety, replies, "There can be but one unmade being," immediately they dart out such poison as this, and say, "That, then, the Son must be one of those beings which God made, and that they have well said that He was not before He was made by God." They are quite willing to disturb and confuse everything if only they can but separate the Son from the Father, and bring the great Creator to the same level with His creatures. How clamorously they have accused the Nicene Bishops for assuming unscriptural terms, although these are very innocent and inoffensive ones, but suitable enough for subverting their heresy, and yet they themselves have done the very same thing, and have invented unscriptural terms on purpose to dishonour our Blessed Lord, "understanding neither what they say nor whereof they affirm " (1 Tim. i. 7). Their expressions cannot be found in Scripture; they have invented them themselves; perhaps they have borrowed them from some of the Gentiles. If so, they had better enquire of these Gentiles about their meanings and significations. And here, I fancy, they will soon perceive that they have been talking without understanding what they mean. For instance, let us take for example that word " unmade." Sometimes it signifies a thing that may be, but is not yet made; as wood which is not yet made into a boat, although it is fit and ready to be made so. Again, " unmade " may also mean that which is never made nor can be made; as a triangle cannot be made a square, nor an equal number an unequal one. Again, " unmade " may signify a being which may be said to exist, but which has never been generated at all. Indeed, Asterius, that unprincipled philosopher, who is such a champion of this heresy, tells us in one of his essays that " unmade " means that which is not made, but that which always exists. So that our adversaries ought to determine in what sense they understand this word, before they can expect that anyone should answer their question.

31. But if they still insist upon asking, " Is there one unmade being, or are there two?" we must deal with them as ignorant people, and tell them that as there are many unmade beings in one sense, so there are none at all in another. There are many that may be made, but none that cannot be made. But if they think, with Asterius, that the " unmade " is that which was not made, but which always is, let them know that the Son of God

is such a being, and may be truly called so. For, as we have shown already, He is no part of the creation, and He is no work of the Father, but He always has existed with the Father, whatever these blasphemers may wish to say to the contrary, when they remark that He "arose out of nothing," and "He was not before He was born." But if, failing at every turn, they say they had rather understand by the expression alluded to "that which already exists, but has no external origin and is unbegotten," our answer is, that God the Father is in this sense the unmade being, and the only one. So will they gain nothing on hearing this. For they will never be able to prove, that because the Father is the only unmade being in this sense, therefore the Son is a made or created being; until they can disprove these arguments, which we have brought forward before, that the Word is of the same nature with Him that begat Him. Therefore, although the Father is an unmade being, it does not therefore follow that the express Image of His Person, His Word and Wisdom, must be made. On the contrary, it shows that He is truly begotten of Him. For a thing created cannot be the express Image of a being that existed of Himself from eternity. I am sorry to repeat these arguments so often, but I am obliged to do so to prove my point. What similarity is there, I ask, between the creature and the Creator? Can he who beholds the former, behold it in the nature of the latter? If they say they are alike, they will next affirm that the Creator is the express image of His creatures. The end of all this is to turn everything into confusion; to exalt the creature into an equality with the Creator; and to bring down the unmade being to the same level with the things which He has made; and the object and aim of all is, that they may consider God the Son a mere creature.

32. However, I imagine, that they will hardly venture to such lengths as the philosopher Asterius. For he, although he zealously advocates this Arian heresy, and maintains that the unmade is one, nevertheless he goes against them in saying that the Wisdom of God is unmade and without beginning, as appears from the following passage out of his writings :—"S. Paul," he says, "did not say that he preached Christ the Power of God *or* the Wisdom of God, but without the word *or*, the Power of God *and* the Wisdom of God (1 Cor. i. 24); thus implying a real and personal distinction between God and that power which is innate in Him, uncreate, and existing with Him from eternity." And soon after he writes : "Although His eternal Power and

Wisdom, which must evidently be without beginning and unmade, cannot but be always one and the same." For though, misunderstanding the words of the Apostle, he considers that there are two Wisdoms, yet he expressly allows and asserts that the Wisdom which co-exists with God is uncreated. And this is the same as saying, that there is more than one uncreated being, or that one uncreated being co-exists with another. For what is co-existent, co-exists not with itself, but with another. If, then, they agree with Asterius, let them never ask again, " Whether the unmade consists of one or two beings," or they will have to contest the point with him; if, on the other hand, they differ from him, let them lay aside his book too, and no longer make advantage of it. For, " if they bite and devour one another, they are in danger of being consumed one of another" (Gal. v. 15). So much then may suffice concerning their ignorance; but who can express himself sufficiently strongly about their hypocrisy and wickedness? What resentment does their odious madness raise in the minds of all people! When they are shown it is impossible to say that the Son of God " arose out of nothing," and that " He was not before His generation," then they say He was " unmade." For they know that if they can persuade ordinary folk to believe that the Son is a creature, then it must follow that He arose out of nothing, and there was a time in which He did not exist. Such characteristics of a made or created being must, of course, be implied.

33. Had these men really confidence in themselves, they would keep to their first assertions, and not change about so variously. But this they will not do, because they think they will easily attain success if they do but shelter their heresy behind the word " unmade." But now it is plain enough, that, in spite of their clamour, the contrast between made and unmade does not lie between the Father and the Son, but between the Creator and the creatures. The like consideration will hold good with regard to the terms " Almighty " and " Lord of the Powers." For as truly as the Father governs and directs all creation, and exercises this jurisdiction by and in the Word ; and as truly as the Son possesses this power, and overrules all things as God's Word and Image ; it is quite clear that nothing can be more absurd than to place the Son amongst created beings, and to say that God is called Almighty with reference to Him, and not with reference to those things which He created by the power of His Son, and still governs by His direction and superintendence. This alone is enough to show that the word " unmade " does not

properly distinguish the Son from the Father, but only has to do with created beings. And it very well serves this purpose, since God is not like created things, but is the Creator and Maker of them through the Son. And as the word "unmade" is no more than the opposite of "made," so the word "Father" has only relation to the "Son;" so that when we speak of God as the creator of things, and consequently as "unmade" and "uncreated," this has reference to, and is understood of, things created and made. But when we consider Him as a Father, then at once we consider and think of Him with reference to His Son. And here, again, our adversaries betray their obstinacy and folly. Although the word "unmade" admits of a very good sense and application, and may be religiously used, yet these men are fond of it, only so far as it is capable of being misapplied for the dishonour of the Son. I suppose they have forgotten what the Scripture says, "That all men should honour the Son, even as they honour the Father," and "He that honoureth not the Son, honoureth not the Father which hath sent Him" (S. John v. 23). Had they really consulted the honour and glory of the Father, they ought not to have gone out of the way to acknowledge God to be the Father, if at the same time they deny Him to be so. As often as they speak of God as "unmade" or "uncreated," they call Him so, as I said before, from His works, and as Maker and Creator only, because they think they can argue from this, according to their fancy, that the Word is only a created being. Whereas when we call God a Father, we celebrate a much higher principle in His nature, and acknowledge His proper relation to that Son by whom He created whatever was created. The very Gentiles know and confess that God is "unmade," being convinced of it by the things that are made. They only deny him to be Father; and so far heathens and Arians are agreed. But he who calls God Father names Him from the Word, and he believes this Divine Word to be, not one of the creatures, but the Creator and Maker of all things.

34. Therefore it seems more in accordance with religious feeling and truth to call God the Father from His relationship to the Son, than to name Him only from His works, and to call Him the "Unmade." He that says God is an uncreated being, declares no more than that He caused so many beings to exist, which before did not. But he that declares Him to be the Father, magnifies Him in a much higher sense, even with reference to the eternal generation of the Son, who caused the existence of all created things, according to the Father's will. And

that the consideration of God's being a Father is of more importance than even of His being a Creator, even as much more as
the doctrine of the Godhead of the Son is more agreeable than
that He should be deemed a creature, may be seen also from
this, that Holy Scripture does not call God " unmade " or " uncreated," but avoids it, as not being as accurate as it should be,
and in many ways liable to puzzle our minds. But the word
Father is very simple and Scriptural; it explains itself at once,
and informs us that God the Father has a Son. The Gentiles,
who were altogether strangers to the Son, were the authors of
the word " unmade ; " whereas our Lord Himself commonly
spoke of God as His Father, and has taught us in like manner
to use and apply the name. He certainly knew whose Son He
was when He said, " I am in the Father, and the Father in Me,"
and, " He that hath seen Me, hath seen the Father," and, " I
and My Father are one " (S. John xiv. 10, 9 ; x. 30). Nowhere in Holy Scripture does the Son call the Father the " unmade." And when He teaches us to pray, He does not say,
" When ye pray, say, O God unmade," but rather, " When ye
pray, say, Our Father, which art in heaven " (S. Luke xi. 2).
And in the same way the form of baptism, which contains the
summary of our Faith, does not refer to the name of the unmade
and made, or of the creator and created, but we are to be
baptised " into the name of the Father, and of the Son, and of
the Holy Ghost " (S. Matt. xxviii. 19); which initiation, whilst it
makes us, although we are but creatures, adopted sons, also
shows us that God the Son is in the essence of the Father. This
argument, then, about the term " unmade " is a vain thing, and
we have clearly proved that it is nothing but an absurd fantasy.

35. It is quite superfluous to enter into dispute with these
men upon the doctrine of the Son's mutability. It is enough
simply to write down what they say, and so show their glaring
impiety. These are the kind of trifling questions they ask :—
" Is He a free agent or not ? Is He morally good in consequence of a right use of His own freewill ? Or, being capable of
changing and varying His resolutions and actions, can He abuse
or misapply that freedom if He pleases ? Or, has He no such
faculty, and is He destitute of any sort of voluntary determination,
as a stock or a stone ? " It is but of a piece with their heresy
so to speak and think ; for, when once they have formed the
notion of a God who arose out of nothing, and a Son who has
been created, they also adopt such terms as are suitable to a
creature. However, when these men are engaged in controversy

with true Catholics, and when they hear them discoursing of the
genuine and only Word of the Father, yet they venture thus to
speak of Him ; is not, then, their doctrine of the most infamous
character ? Is not this belief so blasphemous that whoever first
hears it is so startled that he is obliged to stop his ears, although
he may be unable to frame a direct reply to it ? For if the Word
is a variable and unsettled being, in what degree is He so ?
Where are we to make a stand ? and when will it be certain that
He has reached the most perfect state of His nature ? Again,
how can a fickle and mutable being be the express Image of
an Immutable one ? How should He that has only seen a
mutable being be considered to have seen the Immutable ? In
which of His states shall we be able to behold in Him the
Father ? For it is plain that the Father cannot be always
constantly seen in the Son, if the Son's nature is always changing, and subject to all kinds of fluctuation. The Father's nature
is invariable and immutable, absolutely and entirely the same
from everlasting to everlasting. If, then, the Son's nature be
variable and of a shifting character, how can the Son be the express Image of His Father, " with whom is no variableness neither
shadow of turning " ? (S. James i. 17). How can He be said to
be in the Father, the disposition of whose will may be contrary
at one time to what it is at another, and very likely because He
is advancing daily towards perfection, is not yet perfect ? But
now let this madness of the Arians disappear, and let the light of
truth arise and shine forth, and overwhelm these infatuated
people with evidence and conviction. For can they conceive
that there should be any disparity whatever in Him who is equal
with God ? Can His nature be mutable who is one with the
Father, the genuine Offspring of His nature ? As therefore there is
no change or variation in the nature of the Father, so neither is
there in Him, who is truly begotten of that nature. And if they
slanderously impute alteration to the Word, let them seriously
consider the awful sin and danger of such treatment of the Son of
God. " The tree is known by its fruit " (S. Matt. xii. 33). Hence
it is that he that has seen the Son has seen the Father, and whoever has knowledge of the Son has knowledge of the Father also.

36. It appears, then, that the Image of the immutable God
cannot be mutable ; for " Jesus Christ is the same yesterday,
and to-day, and for ever " (Heb. xiii. 8). The Psalmist asserts
the same, " Thou, Lord, in the beginning hast laid the foundation of the earth, and the heavens are the work of Thy hands.
They shall perish, but Thou shalt endure, they all shall wax old

as doth a garment. And as a vesture shalt Thou fold them up and they shall be changed, but Thou art the same and Thy years shall not fail" (Ps. cii. 25-27). And the Lord says of Himself through the Prophet, "See now that I even I am He" (Deut. xxxii. 39), and "I change not" (Mal. iii. 6). It is true that it may be said that these references have to do with God the Father. Still, they are equally true of the Son, and they are more directly applicable to Him because He was made man; notwithstanding which He declares Himself to be always and immutably the same, and so obviates any objections which those might make, who might argue His mutability from His Incarnation; and I hope that these holy men, or at least God Himself, is to be believed before the perverse statements of the impious. For Holy Scripture in that Psalm we have already cited, where all created beings, implied in the words "the heavens and the earth," are declared to be changeable in their nature, and the Son is as plainly declared not to be one of those beings, puts it beyond dispute, that, as the Son is no created being, so He is the Author of all the changes that follow the nature of created beings, without any variableness or change in His own nature. " Thou art the same," we read, "and Thy years shall not fail." And this is truly so. For that created beings arise out of nothing shows their existence to be, as it were, a state of change; but the Son, who is of the very substance of the Father, can no more be changeable than the Father Himself. For it would be a most sinful thing to say that from that nature which is unalterable was produced an alterable Word and a changing "Wisdom." How can He be any longer the Word if He be alterable? Can that be eternal Wisdom which is changeable? Unless perhaps they will say, that the Son or Wisdom is nothing else but an indwelling grace or habit of virtue and excellency, which may be imagined to dwell in the Divine nature, as an accident does in its subject, and is consequently capable of being added to it and taken from it. This is an evasion which our adversaries often seek to make. But this is not the orthodox Faith of Christian people. For they would have it that as often as God speaks of His Word, and His Son, and His Wisdom, we must think He does not refer to His true Word, and Son, and Wisdom, but some other. But how can that which alters and changes, and does not continue in one settled condition, be true and real, whereas our Lord says of Himself, "I am the Truth" (S. John xiv. 6). Where then, I should like to know, did these profane and impious creatures obtain their absurd and peculiar notions, in contradiction to the words of our Lord, and the constant tradition and testimony of holy men, and indeed to the first principles and conceptions we have concerning the Deity? Where did they get them, I ask once more, but out of the wickedness and corruption of their own hearts?

37. And since we find them so clever in misinterpreting Scripture and explaining it away to suit themselves, we must defend it and show the true meaning, and expose their errors. From those words of the Apostle, "Wherefore God also hath highly exalted Him, and given Him a Name which is above every name: that at the name of Jesus every knee should bow, of things in heaven, and things in earth, and things under the earth" (Philip. ii. 9, 10), and from those of the Psalmist, "Therefore God, even Thy God, hath anointed Thee with the oil of gladness above Thy fellows" (Ps. xlv. 7), they argue in the following manner, as they pretend very closely. If Christ was exalted and received grace, and was anointed, is not this a reward of His using His will aright? But if He must needs make use of His freewill, then He must have a nature liable to change. This is what Eusebius and Arius have not only dared to say but to write, and their disciples and friends are always conversing about it in the streets, without even reflecting upon the insanity of the doctrine they are asserting. For if it was the consideration of mere reward that prevailed with our Saviour to act as He did— and He could not obtain it until He had finished His work, and unless He needed it, although His great piety and His obedience might in one sense have entitled Him to be called Son and God— yet this would not make Him a true and genuine God or Son. That He cannot be, unless He is of the substance of His Father; as Isaac and Joseph were the true sons of Abraham and Jacob, and as the brightness of the sun really arises out of it. Those who are called sons by favour and courtesy are only such in dependence upon that, and they are not so by nature. That which makes them so is no physical principle or part of their being. This is only such a sonship as results from being made partakers of the blessed Spirit; the same as is to be understood in those words of the prophet, "I have nourished and brought up children, and they have rebelled against Me" (Isa. i. 2), and these truly since they were not sons by nature, were capable of becoming degenerate and disobedient, and when they became so, the Spirit was taken away and they were disinherited. And again, on the other hand, when they repented, through God's goodness and mercy they were in a position to receive again their privileges and glorious light, and to be called His children once more.

38. But if our adversaries speak in this manner of the Saviour, it follows that He is neither true God or a true Son, nor like the Father, nor in any way has God for His Father according to substance; but the Father only imparts to Him a special grace, and is in no other sense the Author of His being than He is of any part of the creation. Had He been this kind of Son, He could not be said to have been always a Son. If that title was the reward given to Him for His good work and merit, it could in no way belong to Him, until such a time as He assumed human nature and the form of a servant. It was not till then that He became obedient even unto death, and for that obedience was exalted and received "a Name which is above every name, that at the name of Jesus every knee should bow" (Philip. ii. 10). Well then, if He was not exalted until after His Incarnation; if Divine honours were not paid Him, nor Sonship ascribed to Him until then, what was He before that time? For if Christ was promoted to His Sonship upon His Incarnation, He was so far from dignifying and exalting human nature, that His own nature gained an advantage by assuming ours. Let us then ask again the question, a question we are obliged to ask that it may reveal the hideousness of their tenets, "What was the Son of God before He became incarnate?" For if He is God, and the Son, and the Word, and if He was none of these before He was made man, the consequence will be, either that He was something else distinct from these powers conferred on Him as a reward of His merit and services; or else it must follow that these men must be forced to condemn themselves, and own that He had no being at all before His Incarnation, and that He is nothing else but a mere man. But this is not the Faith of the Church, but the doctrine of Paul of Samosata, and of the Jews at this day. Why, then, if they think as Jews, do they not submit to be circumcised, and no longer profess the Christian Faith, whilst they act as its foes. For if Christ did not exist before His Incarnation, or if He had only a defective and incomplete being, how could He be that one by whom all things were created? If His nature was imperfect, until in process of time its condition was made better, how could the Father delight in Him? Or again, how did He before rejoice in the presence of the Father? If Divine adoration was neither due to Him, nor paid Him, until after His death, how is it that Abraham worshipped Him in His tent (Gen. xviii.), Moses in the bush (Exod. iii.), and Daniel saw thousands upon thousands of angels administering unto Him?

(Dan. vii. 10). If He had no glory until recently, how comes He Himself to mention so plainly that Divine glory which He had before the foundation of the world, when He said, " And now, O Father, glorify Thou Me with Thine own self, with the glory which I had with Thee before the world was"? (S. John xvii. 5). If, as they tell us, His condition was once so lowly, how could it be true of Him that before His exaltation " He bowed the heavens and came down," and that being "the highest" He "gave His thunder"? (Ps. xviii. 9, 13). Therefore, if even before the world was made, the Son had that splendour, and was Lord of Glory, and the Most High ; if He descended from heaven, and is ever to be worshipped ; it follows that He did not come to this world in order to advance Himself to a state of glory and perfection, but to supply the defects and improve the circumstances of other beings which needed His assistance. He did not receive the titles of Son and of God as the reward of His good offices in our behalf ; but He condescended to humble Himself so low that He might raise us to the position of His brethren. He vouchsafed to be made man, in order to make men like gods.

39. He was not, therefore, first man and then God ; but first God and then man, in order that He might make us as gods. For if, when He became man, only then He was styled Son and God ; and if before He became man God called the Israelites His sons, and made Moses a god to Pharaoh (Exod. vii. 1) ; and if the Scripture makes mention of several gods when it says, " God standeth in the congregation of gods" (Ps. lxxxii. 1, Sept.), then it is plain that He had neither Sonship nor God-head later than these had. How, then, can it be true that " all things were created by Him" (S. John i. 3), and that " He is before all"? (Col. i. 17). Or, how is He " the First-born of the whole creation" (Col. i. 15), if others, declared to be both sons and gods, existed long before Him ? And how is it that those first partakers of God's adoption are not also partakers of His Word? This opinion is utterly false ; those who uphold it are neither more nor less than Judaizers. According to this belief, what becomes of the Fatherhood of God? There cannot be adoption apart from the real Son, who speaks thus, " No man knoweth the Father save the Son, and he to whomsoever the Son will reveal Him" (S. Matt. xi. 27). How could anyone be made a god without and before the existence of the Word, according to those words with which our Lord argued with the Jews, the brethren of those gods, " If," He says, " He called

them gods, unto whom the word of God came?" (S. John x. 35). If none of all these sons and gods, whether in heaven or earth, were made so but by the Word, and if the Son of God is that Word, then it must follow that they entirely owe those two relations to Him ; that He was in being before them all, that He was only in a proper and true sense His Son, very God of very God ; that He did not receive these titles as a reward of His virtue, as being something distinct from Himself, but He was these by the fact of His nature and being. In a word, that He is the Son of His Father's substance, and consequently cannot but possess a nature as immutable as the Father's.

40. Hitherto our work has been, with God's assistance, to expose the wretched folly and absurdities of the Arians from the generally received notion of what is implied in the term " Son." In the next place, we must go on to prove the immutability of the Son's nature more directly from the Holy Scriptures, and to show that as His nature is the same as His Father's, so it is as unalterable. Consequently, we see how abominable their belief is who deny this doctrine. In S. Paul's Epistle to the Philippians we read the following :—" Let this mind be in you, which was also in Christ Jesus : who, being in the form of God, thought it not robbery to be equal with God ; but made Himself of no reputation, and took upon Him the form of a servant, and was made in the likeness of men : and being found in fashion as a man, He humbled Himself and became obedient unto death, even the death of the Cross. Wherefore God also hath highly exalted Him, and given Him a Name which is above every name ; that at the Name of Jesus every knee should bow, of things in heaven and things in earth, and things under the earth ; and that every tongue should confess that Jesus Christ is Lord, to the glory of God the Father" (Philip. ii. 5-11). Can anything be plainer and more express than this? He was not advanced from an inferior position to a higher one ; but rather, existing as God, He took the form of a servant, and in taking it He did not exalt Himself, but humbled Himself. Where, then, is there here any reward of virtue, or what promotion or improvement of His nature? If, being God, He became man, and when He descended from the height of glory, He is said to be exalted ; where, I should like to ask, can He be exalted to, since He is Almighty God? As certainly, therefore, as God the Father is Most High, so, too, is God the Word and Son Most High. Where and to what place could He be exalted higher, who was from eternity in the Father, and in all respects is like unto the Father? It is plain that the

opinions of the Arians are utterly false upon this point, as God the Son is beyond the need of any more exalted place. For though the Word did descend in order to be exalted, for so the Scripture informs us ; yet why should He humble Himself, as if He needed to seek that which He possessed already? What grace did He want who is the great Distributor of grace to all? or how did He receive a name or title which should render Him an object of Divine worship, when He was always worshipped from all eternity by His own Divine Name? Before He was made man He was invoked by the Saints of old. "Save me, O Lord, for Thy Name's sake," says the Psalmist" (Ps. liv. 1) ; and again, "Some put their trust in chariots and some in horses, but we will remember the Name of the Lord our God" (Ps. xx. 7). The Patriarchs worshipped Him, and so did the holy Angels, concerning whom it is written, "Let all the Angels of God worship Him" (Heb. i. 6).

41. But if, as David sings in one of the Psalms, "His Name remaineth before the sun, and before the moon from one generation to another" (Ps. lxxii. 17-5, Sept.), why did He descend from heaven to be put in possession of that which was His own from all eternity, and which He had before He came down from heaven? How can He be exalted higher, who was the Most High before His exaltation? How, again, did He receive the privilege of becoming an object of worship, who long before, even from everlasting, had been worshipped by right? "In the beginning was the Word," says S. John, "and the Word was with God, and the Word was God." This is no riddle or paradox, but a heavenly mystery. This Word, which was God, was afterwards made flesh for our sakes. That expression, therefore, of the Apostle's, "God hath highly exalted Him," cannot mean an exaltation of His Divine nature, for in that He was from eternity equal with God, but of His manhood only. And we nowhere find any such expressions applied to Him as that "He humbled Himself," and that "God exalted Him," before He was made flesh. This plainly shows that only His human nature is concerned in them. For nothing but that which is first in an inferior state can be raised to a higher state. That His humiliation consisted in His taking our nature upon Him, is not denied. And ought not His exaltation, then, to be understood of the same nature, whose weakness and imperfection, especially its mortality, very well qualified it for marks of honour? He that was the very Image of His Father, and God the Word from everlasting, took upon Him the form of a servant, and in human

shape submitted even to death for our sakes, and as a sacrifice of propitiation to His Father for us. And, likewise, it was for our sakes and for our advantage that the same Person was exalted and glorified ; that as our human nature died in His, so it may be raised, exalted, and glorified in His, at that day when our bodies shall arise from their graves and ascend up into heaven, "whither the forerunner is for us entered, even Jesus" (Heb. vi. 20). "For Christ is not entered into the holy places with hands which are the figures of the true, but into heaven itself, now to appear in the presence of God for us" (Heb. ix. 24). Christ was that Lord who created heaven and the heaven of heavens ; and therefore when He entered into heaven for us, this was His exaltation for us. Again, when He who sanctifies all things is said to sanctify Himself for us to the Father, it cannot be supposed that that sanctification has any effect upon the eternal Word and Son of God, but only that He sanctifies our human nature in His own. And, in like manner, we ought not to put such an interpretation upon God's exalting Christ, as if the Most High, and consequently Christ who is so, was capable of receiving additional exaltation ; but we must give that expression this meaning, that, having satisfied God's justice for us, and made atonement for our sins, He exalted us in Himself, and so we may enter now the gates of heaven, which He has also opened for us, those who heralded us thither exclaiming, "Lift up your heads, O ye gates, and be ye lift up ye everlasting doors ; and the King of Glory shall come in" (Ps. xxiv. 7). That the gates of heaven should be shut against the great Creator and Lord of all things is not possible. But for our sakes, and in reference to us, is this written, against whom the gates of Paradise are closed ; and, therefore, the lifting up of the gates and the entrance of Christ must be understood of His human nature, as the expressions "the Word was God," "the Lord," and "the King of Glory," can only belong to His Divinity. This exaltation of our nature in the person of Christ is what the Holy Ghost foretold by the Psalmist in these words, "And in Thy righteousness shall they be exalted, for Thou art the Glory of their strength" (Ps. lxxxix. 16, 17). The Son being that Righteousness, neither wants to be nor can be exalted. But it is we who are exalted in that Righteousness, which is our Blessed Lord Himself.

42. Again, when it is said that God "hath given Him a Name which is above every name," this does not refer to the Son's Divinity, for before He became man He was worshipped by the Angels and the whole creation with as much propriety as was God

the Father. But this, too, is written for our sakes, and only concerns our interest in Him. It was His human nature that died and was exalted. As God He was never without those graces which He received as man, and by that means communicated to our nature; His union with which will by no means affect His Divinity, so as to give it any occasion of soliciting such graces. On the contrary, it highly glorified the nature it assumed, and very richly benefitted the race of man. As the Word of God, and as being in the form of God, His creatures always adored Him; and, although He has become man, even the man Christ Jesus, He still exercises an absolute dominion over the whole creation. All bend their knees at this Holy Name, and acknowledge that the Incarnation and cruel death of the Son of God, instead of derogating from, do rather conduce to, the glory of God the Father. For it is indeed to the glory of the Father, that man, created and afterwards lost, should be found again; and should be snatched from death and given life once more, and should become the very temple of God. How highly is our nature dignified, since the Son of the Most High God is adored Incarnate! Angels and Archangels and all the heavenly host now sing those praises to the Blessed Jesus, which before they had always sung to God the Word. And so after this, it will not be a matter of such great surprise to the heavenly host to see such bodies as ours, of the same nature and form as our Lord's, admitted and welcomed into those glorious mansions; as otherwise we may suppose it must have been. For this would not have happened unless He, who is in the form of God, had taken upon Himself the form of a servant, and had been pleased to humble Himself to suffer the cruel death of the Cross.

43. Behold, then, what men considered unworthy of the Wisdom of God, namely, the infamy of the death of the Cross, has become of all things the most glorious! For the certainty of our resurrection entirely hinges upon this; and hence it is, according to the prediction of the Prophet, not Israel only, but the whole Gentile world renounce their idols, and acknowledge the true God, the Father of Christ Jesus. The impostures of evil spirits are all defeated, and the true God alone is worshipped in the Name of our Lord Jesus Christ. For since, when our Lord is believed on as the Son of God in the nature of man, and by the name of Jesus, and the knowledge of the Father is conveyed to us through Him, it is plain, as has been shown, that not the Word, as such, but our nature receives additional graces and privileges. For it follows from His having a body of the same nature

as ours, that we are become the temples and the sons of God, so that even in us the Lord is now worshipped, and they who behold us may cry out in the words of the Apostle, that "God is in us of a truth" (1 Cor. xiv. 25). As S. John also says in his Gospel, "As many as received Him, to them gave He power to become the sons of God" (S. John i. 12) ; and again, in his Epistle, "Hereby we know that He abideth in us by His Spirit which He hath given us" (1 S. John iii. 24). And this is an instance of His great goodness towards us that He has thus exalted our human nature by personally uniting it with His Divine nature. This He condescended to do for our sakes, that Almighty God, from whom all our good things do come, should surpass all other manifestations of His favour in enlarging the object of them by the addition of a part for the redemption of the whole. Our Saviour humbled Himself exceedingly when He took upon Him our frail unworthy nature. He assumed the form of a servant in making that flesh, which was enslaved to sin, a part of Himself. He received no advantage from doing this. It was impossible for the Word of God to do so, whose being is incapable of any improvement. Our nature gained all the benefit, for "He is the Light which lighteth every man that cometh into the world" (S. John i. 9). And, therefore, the Arians argue to little purpose when they lay stress on the word "wherefore" in those words of S. Paul, "Wherefore God also hath highly exalted Him." For this exaltation does not imply any reward of virtue or any advancement of any kind, but only the exaltation of our nature in Him. And what is this but that He who existed in the form of God, the Son of an infinite Father, humbled Himself and became a servant in our behalf and for our sakes. For our redemption from sin and from death must have been impossible had not God Himself vouchsafed to be made man. We should have remained for ever in the region of the dead; we never could have ascended into heaven ; we should have lain in Hades. Therefore in those expressions, "God hath highly exalted Him," and "He hath given Him a Name," the Apostle chiefly considered what was done for our sakes and on our account.

44. This, then, I take to be the interpretation of the passage, and one which is in accord with the judgment of the Church. However, there is another explanation possible, and that which agrees very well with the other, namely, that God the Word, as such, did not rise from a lowly to a higher condition (for, as we said before, He is Most High and equal to His Father), but that, as man, He was exalted by His resurrection from the grave. For

after saying, "he humbled Himself even unto death," He immediately adds, "Wherefore God hath highly exalted Him;" as if the Apostle had said that although as man He died, yet as the Principle of Life to us He was exalted by rising again; for "He that descended is the same also that ascended" (Ephes. iv. 10). He descended in body, but He rose again, because He was God Himself united to that body. And this may very well be the reason of the word "wherefore," to signify not any reward of virtue or accession of dignity, but the natural efficient cause of His rising again. The reason why other sons of Adam have died and never revived has nothing to do with Him, whose body, alone of all men, rose entire, as it was buried, from the grave. The cause is this, which the Apostle had mentioned before, namely, that He was God as well as man. Those other sons of Adam died, since they were only men, and death had dominion over them. This "second man" is "from heaven" (1 Cor. xv. 47); for "the Word was made flesh" (S. John i. 14). And this man is said to be "from heaven" and "heavenly," because the Word came down from heaven, and therefore He could not be the prisoner of death. For although He humbled Himself so far as to submit His body to undergo death, because it was capable of death, yet it was highly exalted from the grave, because the Son of God was united to that body. Accordingly what is said here "Wherefore God also hath highly exalted Him," is of the same meaning as S. Peter's words in the Acts of the Apostles, "Whom God hath raised up, having loosed the pains of death, because it was not possible that He should be holden of it" (Acts ii. 24). For as S. Paul says, that "He, being in the form of God, was made man, and humbled Himself even unto death, therefore God hath highly exalted Him;" so S. Peter argues that "because He was God made man, and manifested Himself to be so by the signs and wonders which He wrought, therefore it was impossible that He should be held captive by death." It was not possible for man to conquer here, for death is man's common end; so on that account the Word, being God, became flesh, that, being put to death in the flesh, He might raise us all to life by His Almighty Power.

45. But since He is said Himself to be "exalted," and because it is written, "God gave Him," &c., and so these heretics say that these expressions are derogatory to the Divinity of the Word, it becomes necessary to explain the meaning of them. As our Saviour's death is here spoken of, so He is said to be raised and exalted from the lower parts of the earth. The death

and resurrection are both His, for it was His body, and no one else's, that was raised from the dead, and received up into heaven. The body, therefore, being His, and the Divinity being united to that body, it follows that, upon the resurrection and exaltation of that body, He must be said to be raised and exalted as man, and because of that body. So that if He was not man these things could not be said of Him. But if the Word was made flesh, then the resurrection and exaltation in these places of Scripture must be understood of His manhood, in order that His death should be the propitiation of our sins and the abolition of death; and that the resurrection and exaltation should, for His sake, afford us the security of ours. It is said of Him that "God hath highly exalted Him," and that "God hath given unto Him," to let us also understand that the Father Himself was not made flesh, but that His Word or Son was made man; and that in His human nature He received from, and was exalted by, the Father, as we observed before. Now, it is granted on all sides that whatsoever the Father gives He gives by the Son. And this is indeed astonishing and marvellous, that the grace which the Son gives from the Father, that the Son Himself is said to receive; and that exaltation, of which the Son is the author by the Father's power, is the exaltation of Himself as man. The Son of God being become the Son of man, as the Son of God, distributes the graces of His Father; for whatever the Father does or gives, He effects by the agency and administration of the Son. The same person, as the Son of man, receives in His human nature what He bestows or imparts in His Divine; because His humanity, which is capable of additions of happiness and glory, is, since His Incarnation, within His very Person. Thus the Son of man became God, and that indeed was the glorious exaltation of the human nature. But such a change of state and condition the Word was absolutely incapable of, since He always partook of His Father's Godhead and perfection.

46. This is the true explanation of the Apostle's words, and it clearly confutes the Arian doctrine. And what the Psalmist says gives also the same meaning, which they misinterpret, but without success. He says, "Thy Throne, O God, is for ever and ever; the sceptre of Thy Kingdom is a right sceptre. Thou hast loved righteousness and hated iniquity; wherefore God, even Thy God, hath anointed Thee with the oil of gladness above Thy fellows" (Ps. xlv. 7, 8). These very words are enough to convince any Arian who will duly consider their true sense. The Psalmist calls us all the "fellows" or "companions" of the

Lord. Had the Son of God, therefore, been a created being, we should not have found Him here excepted out of that number. Those words "Thy Throne, O God, is for ever and ever," are only applicable to the eternal God, who is plainly distinguished from the creatures who are His "fellows." So it is evident that He is not one of the creatures, but that He is the genuine and substantial Word of His Father, the Brightness of His Glory, and the Fulness of His Wisdom, of which He is pleased to make us partakers, giving us the sanctification of the Holy Spirit. This "unction" here alluded to was not to make Him a God, since He was God before. It was not to make Him a King, for from eternity He reigned with His Father, as being His express Image, as the Scripture testifies. This, then, as before, is written for our sakes. The kings of Israel were anointed when they were made kings. They were not kings before, as David, Hezekiah, Josiah, &c. Our Blessed Saviour, on the contrary, although He had been God from everlasting; although the sceptre of His Father's Kingdom was His sceptre; although He always conveyed and distributed the unction of the Blessed Spirit; yet He, as man, was anointed with the Holy Ghost, that He might make us a habitation of the Spirit, as well as partakers of His resurrection and exaltation. This indeed is the very thing He has Himself told us in the Gospel according to S. John, "I have sent them into the world, and for their sakes I sanctify Myself, that they also might be sanctified through the truth" (S. John xvii. 18, 19). In saying this, He has shown that He is not the sanctified but the Sanctifier. He sanctifies Himself that we might be sanctified in His truth. He who sanctifies Himself is the Lord, the Principle of sanctification. His meaning, therefore, must be this, "I, who am the eternal Word of My Father, communicate the grace of the Holy Spirit to My human nature; in order that, being myself thus sanctified as man, I, who am the Truth" (for "Thy Word is truth"), "may sanctify all those who are in Me."

47. If, therefore, He sanctified Himself for our sakes when He became man, then it is very clear that when the Holy Spirit descended upon Him at His baptism, it descended upon us, whose nature was then united to His Divinity. And this descent did not convey any sort of advantage to Christ, but it was again for our sanctification, that we might be partakers of His unction, and that it might be said of us, "Know ye not that ye are the temple of God, and that the Spirit of God dwelleth in you" (1 Cor. iii. 16). When our Lord, as man, was baptised in Jordan,

we were cleansed in Him and by Him; and His receiving the Spirit gave us the right and title to receive it. The oil with which He was anointed was not like that which was poured on Aaron, or David, or others, but of a far superior kind, such as had not been vouchsafed to any of His fellows. It was " the oil of gladness," which, as we learn from the Prophet, was the Holy Spirit of God, " The Spirit of the Lord God is upon Me, because the Lord hath anointed Me" (Isa. lxi. 1). The Apostle S. Peter also says that " God anointed Jesus of Nazareth with the Holy Ghost " (Acts x. 38). When, then, was He thus anointed, but in His human nature at His baptism in the river Jordan by the descent of the Holy Spirit upon Him? Our Blessed Lord, speaking of the Holy Ghost, says, " He shall receive of Mine," and "I will send Him" (S. John xvi. 14, 7), and to His disciples, "Receive ye the Holy Ghost" (S. John xx. 22). And nevertheless, He who, as God the Word, and the Brightness of His Father's Glory, bestows the Holy Spirit on others, now is said to be sanctified, because now He has become man, and the body which is sanctified is His. In consequence of which, we, the members of His body, are anointed and sealed, as S. John has told us, " Ye have an unction from the Holy One " (1 S. John ii. 20), and S. Paul also informs us, " Ye are sealed with that Holy Spirit of promise " (Ephes. i. 13). Therefore, as I have remarked before, these assertions are all written on our account, and in our behalf. Where, then, is there any foundation for those inventions of the Son's being advanced to some higher position, or that He was to receive some additional reward or some special grace ? If He had not been God at first, and was afterwards made one ; or if He had not been a King, and was afterwards made one ; then there would have been some ground for their remarks. But if He is truly God, whose Throne has been from everlasting, in what way could God advance? or how could there be anything wanting to His happiness, who was sitting on His Father's Throne ? And if, as our Lord declares, the Holy Spirit is His, if it receives of Him and is sent by Him, it cannot be conceived that the Word and Wisdom of God, as such, should receive an unction from that Spirit which He Himself bestows. It was His human nature which was thus anointed, and He Himself thus anointed it, and for this purpose, that the sanctification, which, by this unction He conveyed to Himself as man, might come to all men by Him. " The Spirit," He tells us, " does not speak of itself" (S. John xvi. 13) ; it is the Word who gives it to those who are worthy of it. For this is like the passage considered above ; for, as the Apostle has written, "Who, being in the form of God, thought it not robbery to be equal with God, but made Himself of no reputation, and took upon Him the form of a servant" (Philip. ii. 6, 7) ; so David celebrates the Lord as the eternal Lord and King, but sent down to us and made man. For this is what he means in the Psalm where he says, "All Thy garments smell of myrrh, aloes, and cassia" (Ps. xlv. 9). This became literally true of Him, when Nicodemus "brought a mixture of myrrh an aloes about an hundred pounds weight" (S. John xix. 39), and when Mary and her companions "brought the spices which they had prepared" for the burial of the Lord's body (S. Luke xxiv. 1).

48. What advantage, then, could it be to Immortality to assume mortality, or what benefit is it to the Eternal to put on that which is temporal? What reward can be gratifying to the great and everlasting God and King, who was always in the bosom of His Father? Is it to be denied, that this dispensation was entirely for our benefit, and that whatever is said of it must be understood to this effect, that God became man in order that He might make us immortal, and incorporate us into His Everlasting Kingdom. What shameless wretches, then, are these who seek to fasten such false interpretations on Holy Scripture. For when our Lord Jesus Christ came into the world, He made a glorious change in our condition, for He ransomed us from the power of sin, but there was not the least change in His own. He was still the same (I am obliged to repeat it) after He was made man, as He was before ; for the prophet says, "The Word of God abideth for ever" (Isa. xl. 8). And by the same Spirit, which, before He became man He communicated to His saints, He since sanctifies all them that come unto Him. He says to His disciples, "Receive ye the Holy Ghost" (S. John xx. 22). This is He who gave of the same Spirit to Moses and the seventy elders. Through Him also David prayed to the Father, saying, "Take not Thy Holy Spirit from me" (Ps. li. 11). Indeed, when He was made man, He said that He would send unto His disciples "the Comforter, even the Spirit of Truth" (S. John xv. 26); and He sent Him, as He could not fail to do, as He Himself is the God of Truth. Therefore "Jesus Christ is the same yesterday, and to-day, and for ever" (Heb. xiii. 8). He remains unalterable, and He both gives and receives. He administers as God what He receives as man. His condition as God admits of no improvement, for He was from eternity per-

fection and happiness itself. The profit and advantage of His receiving as man are ours. His unction and baptism are ours, as He gives us very clearly and definitely to understand in those words which He addresses to His Father, "And the glory which Thou gavest Me I have given them ; that they may be one, even as We are one" (S. John xvii. 22). He sought or desired no glory, but what should be for our advantage. The receiving, the giving, the exalting, had no other tendency, but that we might receive, that He might give to us, and that we might be exalted in Him; even as He sanctifies Himself for our sakes, that we might be sanctified in Him.

49. But if our adversaries still strive to twist for their own purposes the word "wherefore" in that passage of the Psalmist, "Wherefore God, even Thy God, hath anointed Thee," and if they seek to drag it, if possible, into the service of their cause, then let these inventors of blasphemy and these unlearned barbarians know, that, as before, it cannot imply what they would make of it. It cannot have reference to the words receiving a reward for His virtue or conduct, but it only relates to His coming upon earth and receiving in His human nature the unction of the Holy One, in order that we also might receive it. There is not the least intimation that the object of this anointing was to make Him a God, a King, the Son, or the Word. He could not be made any of these, for, as we have shown already, He was all these from everlasting, and, indeed, His being so was the very reason of His unction :—"Since, O Lord, Thou art God and King, therefore Thou was anointed, for no other but Thou, who art the express Image of Thy Father, and in whose image and likeness we were created, could possibly effect so close a union between the Spirit of God and the nature of man ; for that Holy Spirit is Thine." The noblest parts of the creation were unworthy and unqualified to undertake this work. Angels had fallen, and men had sinned, and it was only and entirely in the power of the Word of God, as being Himself very God, to redeem us from the sentence and curse of the law. Christ, as such, could not possibly have a beginning of existence, for then He must have been a creature, and a sharer in those imperfections, which rendered every created being incapable of redeeming us. But being God, the Son of God, the eternal Majesty, Brightness, and Image of His Father, He was perfectly qualified for the office and work of the expected Messiah, whom the Father had announced to mankind by the mouth of His holy prophets. So He, who had given us our being, was ordained to recover and save us from de-

struction, and to reign over us as the subjects of His Kingdom for ever and ever. And this is the cause of His Incarnation and unction, foreseen by the Psalmist, who, speaking of the Godhead and dominion of Christ, proclaims them in these words, "Thy Throne, O God, is for ever and ever ; a sceptre of righteousness is the sceptre of Thy Kingdom." And in the next verse, speaking of Him as man, He adds, "Therefore God, even Thy God, hath anointed Thee with the oil of gladness above Thy fellows" (Ps. xlv. 6, 7).

50. What, then, is there to marvel at or to disbelieve in our Lord's being said to be anointed with the Spirit, although He is Himself the bestower of it ; since, when the occasion demanded it, He plainly and readily declared His inferiority, as man, to the Holy Spirit? When the Jews said that He cast out devils through the power of Beelzebub, He confuted their blasphemous notions by saying, "I cast out devils by the Spirit of God" (S. Matt. xii. 28). He that dispenses the Spirit here declares that He casts out devils by the power of the Spirit, meaning that as man He is assisted by the Spirit. For since man's nature is not equal of itself to cast out devils, but only so far as it is aided by the Spirit, therefore, as man, He said, "I cast out devils by the Spirit of God." And so He tells the Jews that the blasphemy against the Holy Ghost is of a far more serious nature than that against Himself as Son of man. "Whosoever," He says, "speaketh a word against the Son of man, it shall be forgiven him" (S. Matt. xii. 32), such as were those who said, "Is not this the carpenter's son?" (S. Matt. xiii. 55). But those who blaspheme against the Holy Ghost, and ascribe the deeds of God's Word to the devil, shall receive inevitable punishment. To the Jews, in whose eyes our Lord was no more than a man, He here speaks as a man, but when He addresses His disciples He uses quite different expressions. And so when He speaks to those who knew Him to be God, He gives them to understand that He is not in any way inferior to the Holy Spirit, but in all respects equal to it. In this sense He gave the Holy Spirit to His apostles, saying, "Receive ye the Holy Ghost" (S. John xx. 22). And He tells them before that it is "He that sends the Spirit," and that "the Spirit shall glorify Him," and that "the Spirit shall speak whatsoever He shall hear" (S. John xvi. 7, 14, 13). That God, who alone is the Giver of the Spirit, affirms, nevertheless, that it is by the power and help of the Spirit that He is able, as man, to cast out devils. The same Giver of the Spirit very expressly declares of Himself, "The

Spirit of the Lord is upon Me, because He hath anointed Me" (Isa. lxi. 1), that is to say, "after He was made flesh," as S. John says (S. John i. 14). And it is plainly implied in both these declarations of our Saviour, that we can no more be sanctified without the grace of the Spirit, than that we can cast out devils without the Spirit's power. And from whom should this grace proceed, or who should bestow it, but God the Son, whose this Spirit is? And when was it possible for us to be made partakers of it, unless it was when the Son assumed our nature? As, therefore, it is evident from the passage already referred to in S. Paul's Epistle to the Philippians, that if He, who was in the form of God, had not taken on Him the form of a servant, we could not have been redeemed here nor glorified hereafter; so we learn from the words of the Psalmist, that unless God the Word had received, in our nature and for our sakes, the unction of the Holy Ghost (although He Himself gives the Spirit), we could not have been partakers of the Spirit, nor have obtained its sanctification. And, therefore, we have securely received it, since Christ can be said to have been anointed in the flesh. His human nature was first sanctified by receiving the Spirit; and He, being said to have received it as man, in regard of His humanity, "of His fulness have we all received" (S. John i. 16), even the grace and influence of the same Holy Spirit.

51. Those words of the Psalm, "Thou hast loved righteousness and hated iniquity" (Ps. xlv. 7), our adversaries would also try to prove have reference to the mutability of the Word; whereas, rightly understood, they tend to show that He is unchangeable. For since the nature of created beings is liable to change; and since, as we have before observed, some of these have transgressed the Law, and others have not obeyed it; and it often happens that He who is at one time good and true at another time is wicked and unrighteous; it was necessary that He, who was to be unto us and for us an example and instance of perfect and entire obedience and goodness, should be unalterably just and good. And the reasonableness of this argument commends itself to all sensible people. For since the first man Adam changed for the worse, and through his sin death entered the world, therefore it was needful that the second Adam should be incapable of any alteration; that the serpent's insinuations and temptations, if the serpent should assail Him too, might be defeated; so that we might lay hold of the immutability of our Lord, as a security and help to defend us against the efforts of that formidable enemy. For, as by the sin of Adam, sin entered in

C

and overran all mankind; so since our Lord, made man, has conquered the serpent, He has made us sharers in the advantages of that victory, and has enabled our nature to pursue it, so that everyone of us may say, "We are not ignorant of His devices" (2 Cor. ii. 11). Who, then, but He, who cannot but always love justice and hate iniquity, because of the immutability of His nature, which was the same from eternity, was so well qualified to be anointed and sent? that by the stability and constancy of that perfect obedience, which He was to perform in our changeable frail nature, He might "condemn sin" in that nature, and in His person enable us "to fulfil the righteousness of the Law;" upon which account we may now say, "We are not in the flesh, but in the Spirit, if so be that the Spirit of God dwelleth in us" (Rom. viii. 9).

52. In vain, then, once more, ye Arians, have you imagined these things; in vain have you sought to pervert the words of Holy Writ. The Word of God is unchangeable, but is the same from everlasting to everlasting. He is in unity with the Father, and exactly as the Father is. For how otherwise could He be said to be like Him, unless He was so? Or, how could He say that all things that the Father has are His, if He had not this attribute of immutability? His continual love of good and hatred of evil are not from any obligation and fear of laws, nor are they attended with any possibility of any alteration. There is nothing of passion or infirmity to be apprehended, no motive of interest to be considered. The strictness of His justice, His affection for virtue, and His power of conferring these perfections, are the result and property of His nature, as being God, the eternal Son and Word of the Father. His "loving righteousness and hating iniquity" must be understood in a natural sense, that the one is essentially agreeable, and the other essentially repugnant to his attributes; as much as to say, that He loves and patronises holy and good men, but rejects and dislikes the wicked and disobedient. And the same thing is affirmed of the Father too in Holy Scripture, "The righteous Lord loveth righteousness" (Ps. xi. 8); and, "Thou hatest all them that work iniquity" (Ps. v. 5); and, "The Lord loveth the gates of Sion, more than all the dwellings of Jacob" (Ps. lxxxvii. 1); and, "Jacob have I loved, but Esau have I hated" (Mal. i. 2, 3); and by the prophet Isaiah God declares of Himself, "I the Lord love judgment, and I hate robbery of unrighteousness" (Isa. lxi. 8.) Let, then, our adversaries explain the former and the latter passages too, for the former also are written of the Image of God;

otherwise, if they misinterpret the latter as they do the former, they will ascribe mutability to the Father as well. But if they were to dare to utter such an awful blasphemy as this, whoever believes in the existence of a God would be shocked to hear such a thing. For all religion teaches this, that God's love of righteousness and hatred of iniquity is not the consequence of any previous compassion or deliberation in Him, or of anything which could imply any possibility of making an erroneous choice between the one and the other. This sort of thing can only belong to created and finite beings. It is from His essential justice that God loves and patronises that which is good, and is averse to everything that is evil. And so must He, who is the true and genuine Representation of His Father, be conceived to love and hate in the same sense and manner as His Father. He that is truly such must be perfectly of the same nature as His Father, although the Arians are so blind and senseless that they can neither find out this, nor indeed the truth and meaning of anything else in Holy Scripture. For when they are bewildered, and their imaginations are disordered with their foolish and absurd fancies, they fly to Scripture, and hope to find some countenance from it for their folly. But here, too, from want of understanding, as usual, they are as much in the dark as before; for laying down their own opinions as a rule of interpretation, they wrest the whole of the Divine Oracles in accordance with them. And, therefore, as often as they appeal to them or quote from them, that rebuke of our Saviour ought to be applied to them, " Ye do err, not knowing the Scriptures, nor the power of God" (S. Matt. xxii. 29). Or, if they are fortified against this reproof, they must be put to silence by the words, " Render unto man the things that are man's, and to God the things that are God's" (S. Matt. xxii. 21).

53. But our opponents say it is written in the Book of Proverbs, " The Lord created Me, the beginning of His ways, for His works" (Prov. viii. 22); and in the Epistle to the Hebrews the Apostle says, " Being made so much better than the Angels, as He hath by inheritance obtained a more excellent Name than they" (Heb. i. 4). And a little after he writes, "Wherefore, holy brethren, partakers of the heavenly calling, consider the Apostle and High Priest of our profession, Christ Jesus, who was faithful to Him that appointed Him" (Heb. iii. 1, 2). In the Acts we find S. Peter saying, "Therefore let all the house of Israel know assuredly, that God hath made that same Jesus, whom ye have crucified, both Lord and Christ" (Acts ii. 36).

These passages, the meaning of which they entirely fail to grasp, they try and pervert to their own ideas, misapplying them so as to make them teach that the Word of God is a mere created being; and thus they deceive the thoughtless, by rejecting the true meaning of the text, and by the sound only of the words insinuating the poison of their heresy. Did they rightly understand the passages, it is to be hoped they would not thus attack the Lord of Glory, nor thus have perverted the wholesome words of Scripture. Or, if they are resolved to follow the example of Caiaphas and to become like the Jews, and will not understand what the Scriptures foretold, that "God should dwell upon the earth" (*cf.* Zech. ii. 10), let them forbear from making any use of the Apostolic writings, whose authority Jews have no right to make use of; or, if they wish to rank themselves with the godless Manichees, and will deny that the Word was made flesh and dwelt among us in our nature; then they must confess that the text alluded to from the Proverbs is entirely against them, for it utterly confutes the Manichees. But if, either from fear of losing preferment, or from the shame of incurring disgrace and infamy, they are restrained from denying the Incarnation of the Word, which Scripture asserts so plainly, let them rightly explain these passages to refer to the nature and advent of the Messiah, or else they will have to deny also that our Lord was made man. For it is an unseemly thing to confess that "the Word became flesh," and yet to be confounded at those things which are written of Him, and so, on account of this, to pervert and distort the sense of Scripture.

54. Let us first examine the text which says, "Being made so much better than the Angels." And here the same rule of interpretation ought to take place, by which we should govern ourselves in finding out and determining the sense of all other passages of Scripture. That is to say, we are carefully to observe upon what occasion the Apostle speaks, who is the person he speaks of, and for what purpose he speaks; because a mistake, wilful or otherwise, in any or all of these particulars, may be far from the true meaning. It was a wise and judicious question of the eunuch to S. Philip, "I pray thee, of whom speaketh the Prophet this? of himself or of some other man?" (Acts viii. 34). He was afraid of mistaking the person meant in that place of Scripture, and so of misunderstanding it. Again, when the Apostles were curious to know when those things which our Lord foretold them of were to come to pass, they enquired, "When shall these things be? and what shall be the sign of Thy coming?"

(S. Matt. xxiv. 3). And again, when they heard their Master discoursing about the end of the world, they were curious about the time of it, for fear they should fall into error about the matter, and afterwards draw others into the same mistake. And so, when they were answered by our Blessed Lord, they knew how to set the Thessalonians right who were going wrong (2 Thess. ii. 2). When anyone knows these points properly himself, then his faith rests upon a sure and right foundation; but if he makes a mistake on these things, he most likely at once falls into heresy. Thus Hymenæus and Alexander, when they said that the resurrection was past already, went unhappily astray (1 Tim. i. 20; 2 Tim. ii. 18); and the Galatians also erred from the faith. The former ante-dated the resurrection, and the latter insisted on circumcision, when it had been done away with. And so are the Jews in grievous error about the person of the Messiah. They think that one of themselves is alluded to in the words, "Behold a Virgin shall conceive and bear a son, and shall call His name Immanuel; which, being interpreted, is, God with us" (Isa. vii. 14; S. Matt. i. 23). They also imagine that the words, "The Lord thy God will raise up unto thee a Prophet" (Deut. xviii. 15), is spoken of one of their own Prophets. And because they will not admit that S. Philip was right in his explanation of the words, "He was led as a sheep to the slaughter" (Isa. liii. 7), they allege that they must be spoken of Isaiah himself or some other of the Prophets.

55. This, then, has been the state of things under which these haters of our Blessed Lord have plunged themselves into this damnable heresy. For had they considered the person, the thing, and the time of which the Apostle is speaking, they had not thus so madly thrown themselves into this gulf of impiety, by applying to our Lord's humanity what belongs to His Divinity. And this anyone will readily perceive, if he rightly understands the beginning of the passage. The Apostle's words are these: "God, who at sundry times and in divers manners spake in time past unto the fathers by the prophets, hath in these last days spoken unto us by His Son." And shortly after he says, "When He had by Himself purged our sins, He sat down on the right hand of the Majesty on high; being made so much better than the Angels, as He hath by inheritance obtained a more excellent Name than they" (Heb. i. 1, 3, 4). It is plain here that the Apostle is speaking of that time when God spoke to us by His Son, and when a purging of sins took place. Now, when was it that God thus spoke to us? When was it that this purging of sins took place? When was

it that God was made man, unless it was after the times of the Prophets, in the latter days? Moreover, it must be considered, that as this late dispensation of the Gospel is the subject of the Apostle's discourse, it was natural for him to begin by telling us that God had also communicated His will to the world in the earlier ages by the mouth of the Prophets. Therefore it seems that, first of all, there is the ministration of the Prophets; and secondly, the promulgation of the Law by Angels; and lastly, the Incarnation of the Son. And because the Son came in order to minister, it was necessary to add, "Being made so much better than the Angels." For we cannot but see that his meaning is this, that the ministry of the Son is so much more excellent than the ministry of God's ordinary servants, as the nature of the Son is better than their nature. Contrasting, then, the old dispensation and the new, the Apostle demonstrates to the Jews how much the former is inferior to the latter, which those words imply, "Being made so much better than the Angels." He does not say, He was made greater or more honourable, for that might have given us occasion to think that He was of the same nature with them. But He uses the word "*better*," a word which admirably expresses the infinite distance of His nature from that of all created beings. The same word is used in this manner in other places of Scripture. David says in the Psalm, "One day in Thy courts is *better* than a thousand" (Ps. lxxxiv. 10). Solomon has these words, "Receive my instruction and not silver, and knowledge rather than choice gold. For wisdom is *better* than rubies; and all the things that may be desired are not to be compared to it" (Prov. viii. 10, 11). Will anyone confound the nature and substance of wisdom with the nature and substance of stones? Is there any affinity between celestial courts and earthly habitations? Are spiritual and eternal things in any way allied to things temporal and mortal? Isaiah was sensible of the difference, for he says, "Thus saith the Lord unto the eunuchs that keep My Sabbaths, and choose the things that please Me, and take hold of My covenant; even unto them will I give in Mine house, and within My walls a place and a name *better* than of sons and of daughters: I will give them an everlasting name, that shall not be cut off" (Isa. lvi. 4, 5). In like manner, no comparison can be instituted between the Son and the Angels; and so the Apostle does not use the word "better" in the sense of comparison, but in that of distinction, as showing the immense disparity between the nature of the Son and the nature of Angels. And the Apostle himself gives us this very explanation of the word "better," when he calls the one the Son, and the other the servants of God. The Son, as such, sat down on the right hand of the Father; but the Angels only stand round His Throne, to receive and execute His orders and commands.

56. Thus, ye Arians, you may see that Scripture is so far from favouring your opinion, that the Son is a creature; that it plainly distinguishes Him from every order of created beings, even the highest; it declares Him to be of one substance with the Father, and places Him in His bosom. The word "made" does by no means imply that the nature of the Son was made or created, as you fancy. Had no other word been joined with it, it might possibly have been said to bear an Arian construction; but the Son had been mentioned before, and such things were said of Him which plainly distinguish His nature from that of the creatures. And, further, the word "made" is not absolute, nor does it stand by itself, but is joined, both in place and construction, with the word "better," and can indeed signify nothing if it is separated from it. After the Apostle had declared this person to be the true and genuine Son of God, he might, without any fear of mistake, very well say that He was "made better," that is to say, that He was and is so. For in speaking of things begotten, it does not much matter if we say they were "made," or they "became" what they are. But, on the other hand, of things made, which are only the handiwork of him that makes them, it cannot be said rightly that they are begotten. It is true, allegorically and improperly, we may be said ourselves to be begotten of the truly begotten Son of God; not that we derive our nature and being from His, but only as we are made spiritual partakers of His grace. Instances of this distinction occur frequently in Holy Scripture. The word "made" is applied to things created or formed, whether by God or man. Thus, "All things were made by Him; and without Him was not anything made that was made" (S. John i. 3); and, "In wisdom hast Thou made them all" (Ps. civ. 24). Concerning persons begotten we read, "There were born" (or "made") "to Job seven sons and three daughters" (Job i. 2); and, "Abraham was an hundred years old when his son Isaac was born" (or "made") "unto him" (Gen. xxi. 5); and Moses said, "If any man has sons born" (or "made") "unto him." Therefore, as certainly as the Son is to be distinguished from the creatures, and is alone the proper Off-spring of the Father's substance, so certainly our adversaries have failed to prove anything by arguing about the word

" made." If the shame of this defeat should drive them to another subterfuge, and put them to the necessity of asserting that there is no more than a comparison of dignity referred to, and that it is of the nature of comparison, that the things compared should agree in kind or species, this will oblige them to ascribe the nature of Angels to the Son. And then the question arises, whether or not they will be ashamed to own the faith and agree with the doctrines of Valentinus, Carpocrates, and heretics of this description? For it is notorious that Valentinus affirmed that Christ and the Angels were of one and the same nature, and Carpocrates asserted that the world was made by the Angels. Very probably they have taken a liking to such teachers as these, and will have the hardihood to speak out as plainly as they do, that the Son of God is no better than an Angel.

57. Surely, if they do imagine such vain things, they will be somewhat moved when they think of the sayings of the Psalmist, " Who is he among the gods that shall be like unto the Lord ? " (Ps. lxxxix. 7) ; and, " Among the gods there is none like unto Thee, O Lord" (Ps. lxxxvi. 8). Nevertheless they must be answered, in order that they may learn the truth if they have any mind to do so, that comparisons only lie between things of the same kind, and not between things of a different nature. So, for example, no one would compare God with man, men with beasts, wood with stone, because their natures are dissimilar. God cannot be compared with anything else ; man may be compared with man, wood with wood, and stone with stone. Now, in such cases, we should not use such a word as " better," but such words as " rather" or " more." Thus, Joseph was comely rather than his brethren, and Rachel than Leah. We should not say one star is " better" than another star, but is " more excellent " in glory. The excellency of nature implied in the word " better," is only such as supports a comparison between things of a different nature ; such as, wisdom is said in this sense to be " better" than a stone, that is to say, of a higher order of things. Had the Apostle said, " The Son does by so much take precedence of the Angels," or " The office of the Son is so much higher than that of the Angels ; " such a comparison as this of the Son with the Angels might have given our adversaries some pretence for the meaning they would assign here. But when He says that He is " better," and that He is no more an Angel than a servant is a son, is not this a clear and essential distinction between the nature of the Son and that of Angels? Again, when He affirms that the Son " laid the foundation of

all things" (Heb. i. 10), He assures us that the Son is a distinct being from whatever was created. And, if this is so, who will dare to make a comparison, or to seek a resemblance between, an uncreated being and any created one whatever? But if they have any such thoughts, let S. Paul himself convince them, who speaks to the very point at issue, " For unto which of the Angels said He at any time, Thou art My Son, this day have I begotten thee? And of the Angels He saith, Who maketh His Angels spirits, and His ministers a flame of fire" (Heb. i. 5, 7).

58. Thus we see that created things only are properly said to be "made," and are the production of Divine power. But when the Apostle comes to speak of the Son of God, he does not speak of His being "made," nor of His "becoming" anything. On the contrary, He exclaims in the following terms concerning His eternity, His kingly power, and His being Creator and Framer of all, "Thy Throne, O God, is for ever and ever," and "Thou, Lord, in the beginning hast laid the foundation of the earth, and the heavens are the works of Thine hands; they shall perish, but Thou remainest" (Heb. i. 8, 10, 11). Those men must be strangely blind that cannot observe here the Creator distinguished from His works; that He who created all things is God, and that these things were of His making and forming, and called by Him into being out of nothing. That expression, "They shall perish," is not here to be literally understood, as if all created beings were actually to perish and vanish away. But the purpose of it is to signify the dependency of their nature, that their existence is precarious, and only perpetuated for the sake of those ends which the Creator has ordained they should serve for. Whatever is capable of perishing, although its existence be perpetuated as long as its maker pleases, yet is still no more than a thing made out of nothing, and witnesses of itself that it was not always in being. Thus it is with all created beings, and in these respects the Son is here distinguished from them. His eternity stands opposed to their capacity for perishing in those emphatic words, " But Thou remainest." It was impossible that He should perish or cease to be, because He never was made or began to be, but He has the power of eternal duration. Having that principle in His nature, He cannot with any propriety be said or supposed to have been out of being ; until such time as He was begotten, He must have existed with the Father from all eternity. And even if the Apostle had not thus written in the Epistle to the Hebrews, still his other Epistles, and indeed the whole tenor of the Scriptures,

could never be reconciled with such strange notions as these concerning the Word of God. But, in the place above, the Apostle has very clearly explained himself, and we have shown from that and other passages of Scripture, that the Son is begotten of the very nature and substance of the Father; that He was the great Creator and Maker, and that all other things were His work; that He is the Brightness of His Father's glory, His Word, and Image, and Wisdom; and that all created beings were in subjection to the will of the Blessed Trinity, existing at its pleasure, and serving its purposes. Therefore it follows that the nature of the Son is infinitely superior to that of the creatures, and it is indeed the same as that of the Father. And hence is that when our Lord declares that " His Father is greater than He " (S. John xiv. 28), He does not use the word " better," from which it might have been concluded that His nature was distinct and separate from that of the Father. The word " greater " expresses a priority, not in any order of time, and a pre-eminence, not as to plenitude of essence, but in consequence of the Son's eternal generation from the Father. And that very word " greater " implies, indeed, that He is of the same nature with Him who is greater than the Son in that essence.

59. These words " Being made so much better than the Angels," cannot carry in them a comparison of natures between the uncreated Word and His created works, for they admit of no comparison with one another. But that which the Apostle referred to was the Incarnation of the Word, and the new dispensation which was then introduced. The comparison He was making lay between the instruments and ministers of the first Covenant, and the great Administrator of the second. He observes that the excellency and grace of the latter was, in proportion, as much greater and more abundant than that of the former, as the Son of God is of a higher and more superior character than that of the Angels. The servants of the householder could do no more than demand the fruits of the vineyard, but the Son and the Lord had it in His power to loose men's debts and transfer the vineyard to others. To this purpose the Apostle proceeds to show the excellence of the Son over all created things. He says, " Therefore, we ought to give the more earnest heed to the things which we have heard, lest at any time we should let them slip. For if the Word spoken by Angels was stedfast, and every transgression and disobedience received a just recompence of reward; how shall we escape if we neglect so great salvation, which at the first began to be

spoken by the Lord, and was confirmed unto us by them that heard Him?" (Heb. ii. 1-3). Had the Son been only one of God's creatures, His nature must have been perfectly on an equality with theirs. And, if so, how could rejection of His revelations, and disobedience to His commands, deserve a severer punishment than the obstinacy of men against the declarations of God's ambassadors in the times before Him? We do not find any distinction made between the revelations made by different Angels or by different Prophets, either as to excellency of nature, or as to degrees of penalty. In the old Law there was one fount of authority, and the punishment inflicted was of one kind. But our Blessed Lord, being not a creature, but the Word and Son of His Father, the punishment of rebellion against His administration ought to be so much severer than that of opposition to the authority of God's inferior ministers, as His nature, acts, and operations are more excellent than theirs. Our adversaries, therefore, would do well to consider the grace which results from the dispensation of the Son, and the knowledge and consideration of this should be enough to convince them that the Son cannot be a creature, but is essentially and substantially in the Father and the Father in Him. Let them remember what the Apostle has told them, that the Law spoken by Angels made nothing perfect; that this was not to be done but by the visitation of the Word, but the Incarnation of the Word has perfected and completed the work of the Father. Death reigned from the time of Adam's transgression to that of Moses, but the presence of the Word abolished death. In consequence of which we now no longer die in Adam, but obtain eternal life in Christ. Again, the Law was only proclaimed from Dan to Beersheba, "In Jewry was God known" (Ps. lxxvi. 1); but now the sound of the Gospel is gone forth into all lands, and the whole earth is filled with the knowledge of God. All the world has received the glad tidings from Apostles and Disciples, and we now see fulfilled Isaiah's prophecy, "They shall be all taught of God" (Isa. liv. 13). That which was revealed of old was but declared in type and symbol, but now the truth itself has been manifested. And this, too, the Apostle afterwards observes more clearly, saying, "By so much was Jesus made a surety of a better testament" (Heb. vii. 22); and again, "But now hath He obtained a more excellent ministry, by how much also He is the mediator of a better covenant, which was established upon better promises" (Heb. viii. 6); and, "For the law made nothing perfect, but the bringing in of a better hope did" (Heb. vii. 19); and again, "It was therefore necessary that the patterns of things in the heavens should be purified with these, but the heavenly things themselves with better sacrifices than these" (Heb. ix. 23). In all which places, and indeed throughout the Epistle, does he ascribe the word "better" to the Lord, who is thus distinguished from, and considered far superior to, mere created beings. Thus His sacrifice of Himself, and the blessed hope which stands firm upon that foundation, and the promises also which are made to us through Him, are all "better," not only in degree, but quite of another kind from, and much nobler than, any other sacrifices, or the benefits and good fruits of them, which they could not be unless He, who thus procured for us all these privileges, was of a nature infinitely superior to that of created beings.

60. Moreover, the words "He was made surety," point directly to His suretiship for us. Now, as it is plain that He became our Surety by virtue of His human nature, and accordingly we ascribe His being so to Him as man, that is to say, as so far a created being, so the word "made" must here be understood in this sense, that He was made man, and as man He became our Surety. And this alone may suffice to let these obstinate and perverse corrupters of the Faith understand that they fail in this their wicked purpose. S. Paul, who very well knew, and as expressly declares, our Blessed Lord to be the Son, and the Wisdom, and the Brightness, and Image of the Father, cannot be supposed, in those other passages where He uses the word "made," to mean that His nature or essence was made or created. But he refers to the ministry of that covenant in which death, which once had the dominion, is overthrown and destroyed. It was this great victory which rendered His ministration so much more glorious than those that preceded it, because "What the Law could not do, in that it was weak through the flesh, God sending His own Son, in the likeness of sinful flesh, and for sin, condemned sin in the flesh" (Rom. viii. 3), thus delivering our nature from the captivity of guilt, in which state the Divine grace could not enter into our hearts. And, having qualified our flesh to receive His Divinity and grace, He made us walk no longer "according to the flesh but according to the Spirit," so that we may repeat over and over again, "But we are not in the flesh but in the Spirit" (Rom. viii. 9). "For God sent not His Son into the world to condemn the world, but that the world through Him might be saved" (S. John iii. 17). All mankind had formerly incurred the sentence of the

Law, and were guilty criminals; but the Word of God took upon Himself the punishment to be inflicted, and thus justice was satisfied; and, by undergoing punishment in our nature, He applied to our persons the redemption wrought by it. And this was what S. John meant when he exclaimed, "The Law was given by Moses, but grace and truth came by Jesus Christ" (S. John i. 17). How much more excellent is grace than the Law, and how far superior is truth to a shadow of it.

61. And, indeed, it was impossible that this state of things should have been brought about in this excellent manner by any one but the Son of God Himself, who sits at the right hand of the Father. And what does His session there denote but that He is the genuine Offspring of the Father, and that His Divinity is the same as His Father's? If He sits on the Throne of His Father, it must be confessed that He is also invested with the same dominion as His Father; and since the Son is contemplated in the Father's Godhead, therefore the Word of God is truly God, and he that sees the Son sees the Father, and thus there is one God. Nor does it follow from His session of the right hand of His Father, that His Father has His place at the left hand of Him. Whatever is right and belonging to eminence in the Father, that also belongs to the Son, according to our Lord's declaration, "All things that the Father hath are Mine" (S. John xvi. 15). Thus it is that the Son, though sitting on the right hand, also sees the Father on the right hand, although He says of Himself, with regard to His human nature, "I have set God always before Me, for He is on My right hand, therefore I shall not fall" (Ps. xvi. 9). This shows, moreover, that the Son is in the Father, and the Father in the Son. The same place of pre-eminence is common to them both, for even while the Son sits at the Father's right hand, the nature of the Father is in the Son. The business and employment of Angels is ascending and descending; but concerning the Son God says, "And let all the Angels of God worship Him" (Heb. i. 6). And when Angels minister they say, "I am sent unto thee," and, "The Lord has commanded;" whereas the Son, although as man, He says He is sent, and come down to do the work and accomplish His Father's will, yet as the Word and the Image of God, He says, "I am in the Father and the Father in Me," and "He that hath seen Me hath seen the Father," and "The Father that dwelleth in Me, He doeth the works" (S. John xiv. 10, 9). For those miraculous works, which Christ performed whilst on earth, were the operations of the Father's omnipotence. And these argu-

ments ought to be sufficient to silence our adversaries, and make them hide their faces. But if still they maintain that the expression "being made better" bears their false interpretation, and they will not understand it in the sense of "becoming," or "coming to be;" and if they will not be brought to confess the truth of our construction, that the term "better" bears no relation to the nature of the person, but only to the nature of the dispensation; if still they will affirm from this expression that the Word was made and created, let them listen to our arguments again in a concise form, since they have forgotten what has already been stated.

62. If the Son is only one of the Angels, then let Him be said to be "made" in the same sense as the Angels; let Him not differ at all from them in nature. If the Son is only an Angel, let all the Angels be sons too. Let all sit together enthroned at the right hand of the Father, or else let the Son, as a ministering Spirit stand and bow before the Throne of God in company with His brethren, and let Him be a messenger, as they are. But then what becomes of all those distinctions which S. Paul has assigned to separate Him from whatever is created? Could He imagine the Son to be Angel when He was asking that question, "Unto which of the Angels said He at any time, Thou art My Son"? (Heb. i. 5). Besides, if, as we are told, the Son created heaven and earth, and the Angels themselves were the work of His hands, if the Son sits upon the Throne with the Father, and the Angels stand by ministering, will anyone be so foolish as to interpret the "being made better" of the substance or person of the Word, and not of the ministry, which He took upon Him as man? For the Second Person of the Trinity assumed our nature, and in that nature, by virtue of that union, He became as much more a glorious Administrator of His Father's will than any of the Angels, and accomplished a purpose of God as much more stupendous than that which any Angel could have done; as the condition of a Son is superior to that of a servant, and the nature of a Creator to that of a creature. Let them cease, therefore, from interpreting this word "made" of the nature of the Son, for He is not one of created things; but let them admit that it simply has reference to His ministry and the new dispensation of things which He introduced. And if anyone desires to know how there could be any addition to that person, in respect of His office, to whom there could be none, in respect of His Divine nature, we have enlarged more than enough in answer to that question, and those who propose it, ought in modesty to withdraw it. But

if there is no other way of bringing these men to reason, it may be proper to try yet another method to confound them, and that shall be to observe to them that such expressions as these, which they object against the Divinity of the Son, are used in Scripture of the Father Himself. This may seem to prevail with them to refrain their tongue from evil, or may bring them to some sense to acknowledge the depth of their folly. It is written in the Psalm, " Become my strong rock and house of defence that Thou mayest save me " (Ps. xxxi. 3); and again, " The Lord became a defence for the oppressed " (Ps. ix. 9). There are, besides, many other parallel places. Will our adversaries tell us that these passages are to be understood of the Son ? If they will, I will so far grant that they may be right. But let them then acknowledge that the person here called upon for assistance and as a refuge was not a created person ; and, therefore, that the words " made " or " become " ought to be understood of His incarnate presence. For then did He become a " strong rock " and " house of defence," when He bare our sins in His own body upon the tree, and when He said, " Come unto Me, all ye that labour and are heavy laden, and I will give you rest " (S. Matt. xi. 28).

63. But if they refer these passages to the Father, will they, when it is here also written " made " or " became," argue from these words that God the Father too is a made or created being? Yes, they will dare, as they argue thus concerning His Word, for the same expressions which they allege for the Son's being a creature in one part of Scripture, will oblige them in another part to deny the Divinity of the Father. Almighty God forbid that such monstrous notions should ever enter the hearts of His servants ! For neither is the Son in the number of created things, nor do the words of Scripture alluded to, " made " or " became," have any reference to the beginning of being, but only to some part or act of the interposition of the Divine goodness. God is the same, in the same manner affected from eternity, in all respects. Men were once nothing, and afterwards they received their being from the Word at what time the Father willed it. The Divine nature is invisible and inaccessible to all created beings, and especially to men upon earth. And, therefore, when men in their infirmity call upon God for succour, when we cannot relieve ourselves under oppressions and persecutions of any kind, then He, who is invisible, discovers Himself at hand to support and help us in effects and manifestations of His beneficence ; which aid He affords us in the person and ministration of His essential

Word. And forthwith the Divine favour is proffered to everyone according to his need, and He becomes thus strength to the weak, to the persecuted " a strong rock and house of defence ; " and with these cheering words He speaks to the injured and oppressed, " Thou shalt cry and the Lord shall say, here I am" (Isa. lviii. 9). Therefore, whatever help or succour comes to anyone through the Son, each one says that God has benefitted him in this respect, since it is through the agency of His Blessed Son that God sends this assistance. And this is as common an expression as is the same kind of thing among men. Often succour comes to man from man. One man becomes the avenger of an injury done to another, as Abraham avenged the quarrel of Lot (Gen. xiv. 16). Another has made his house a refuge for the persecuted, as Obadiah sheltered and provided for the sons of the prophets (1 Kings xviii. 4). Another has entertained a stranger, as Lot hospitably received the Angels (Gen. xix. 3). Another has relieved the wants of his poorer brethren, as Job was charitable to those who asked aid of him (Job xxix. 12). We see, then, there is no absurdity in using this expression of our friends, saying, " Such a one became my benefactor," or " Such a one became my protector," or " Such a one assisted me ; " and yet here the making or the made has nothing to do with the nature or essence, or the beginning and birth of the person spoken of, but it concerns them only as it has reference to their good offices. And in like manner when the sacred writers say concerning God "He was made," or " He became," this has nothing whatever to do with any original becoming ; for God never had any beginning, nor was He ever made ; but all that is implied in such expressions is God's relation to us as the Saviour of all men.

64. No more, then, need be said to guard and determine the senses of such expressions as these when applied to the Son, " He was made," and " Be Thou made," or " Do Thou become," and " Being made so much better than the Angels," to satisfy any sensible person. It cannot be inferred from them that the Word of God was begotten in time, and is only a creature, and that those expressions, particularly in the Epistle to the Hebrews, relate only and entirely to what He was pleased to make Himself for our sakes, when He became incarnate. For when " the Word was made flesh and dwelt among us " (S. John i. 14), when He came to minister and to grant salvation to all, then He was made our Saviour, He was made our Life, He was made our Propitiation. Then the old administration or dispensation of things which He undertook for us was introduced, and it became much

better than that of the Angels. He became our Way to heaven, and our Resurrection from the grave. And so, in conclusion, His being said to be "made so much better than the Angels," and "He became," and "By so much is Jesus become a better surety," are no more proofs or arguments that His nature had a beginning or was created, than that prayer of the Psalmist, "Become my strong rock," is a demonstration that the nature of God the Father was created. It refers, of course, to His loving-kindness, as has been clearly shown before. These passages do not signify, God forbid that they should, that the substance of God the Son was ever created, but they only have reference to those great privileges and benefits whereof we are partakers through His Holy Incarnation. And this is the absolute truth, although these heretics are unthankful and ungrateful for these mercies, and although they are resolved to persist in their own detestable opinions.

THE SECOND ORATION.

1. I HAD, indeed, hoped that the arguments I had brought forward against the blasphemies of the Arians, and against the absurdities and errors of their doctrines, would have been sufficient to entirely confute these heretics, and to reduce them to silence; and to make them sensible of, and sorry for, the impieties they have invented and uttered against the Blessed Lord. But alas! it is no easy matter to make them acknowledge their errors. Just as swine and dogs wallow in their own vomit and mire, even so do they revel in their irreligion, and invent further fallacies. Thus they will misinterpret the verse in the Proverbs, "The Lord created Me, the beginning of His ways, for His works" (Prov. viii. 22), and also the words of the Apostle, "Who was faithful to Him that made Him" (Heb. iii. 2), and would make them assert that the Word of God is a creature. Had not their understanding been entirely withdrawn from them, what has been urged before upon the plain authority of Holy Scripture, must have effectually convinced them that the Son of God is not a being made out of nothing, and that there is not the least affinity between Him and any created being whatsoever. Since He is God He cannot possibly be a creature, and it is the height of blasphemy to say that He is one. It is only of beings who are made and created that we can say rightly they were made out of nothing, and they did not exist before they were born. But because they will not give up their false position, they continue their misconstructions of the aforesaid and other passages of Holy Scripture, which are themselves full of sacred truths, but which are violently arrested by these men, to be brought, if possible, into conformity with their own notions. Let us, then, proceed to examine and determine the true sense of these passages, not only to confirm the minds of the faithful, but in order to show that our adversaries are extremely ignorant of the first

principles of Christianity. If this was not the case, they would not have shut themselves up in the unbelief of the Jews of the present time, but they would have made enquiry, and have learned that, " In the beginning was the Word, and the Word was with God, and the Word was God" (S. John i. 1). And because this is so, it follows that the Word, according to the good pleasure of the Father, "was made flesh" (S. John i. 14), and then it might be truly said in the words of S. Peter, " He hath made Him both Lord and Christ" (Acts ii. 36). Of the same person, as Solomon says, it is certainly true, that "The Lord created Him, the beginning of His ways, for His works" (Prov. viii. 22); and that, as the Apostle says, He was "made so much better than the Angels" (Heb. i. 4); and again, that He "made Himself of no reputation, and took upon Him the form of a servant" (Philip. ii. 7); and again, it is said, "Wherefore, holy brethren, partakers of the heavenly calling, consider the Apostle and High Priest of our profession, Christ Jesus, who was faithful to Him that made Him" (Heb. iii. 1, 2). These, and several other similar passages of Holy Scripture, have all the same sense and meaning, which is agreeable to our holy religion, expressive of the Divinity of the Word, at the same time that they are worded in ordinary language, and are only applicable to our Blessed Lord in regard to His Incarnation and humanity. And although this consideration ought to be a full and sufficient reply to our adversaries, still, because they will continue to misinterpret the Apostle's words (to begin with them), " Who was faithful to Him that made Him," and because this text is so foolishly urged by them to prove the Word of God to be a creature, I have thought it needful to silence this further statement of theirs, by making use of the same method of argument as before.

2. Suppose, then, that the Word is not the genuine Son of God, what must He be called? The answer is plain : He must be a creature. And whatever we find affirmed of creatures in Holy Scripture, must be affirmed of Him, and so we must no longer call Him God's Son, or Word, or Wisdom. And so, too, God Himself must no longer be a Father, but only a Creator and Framer of things which He causes to exist. And so a creature must represent the Image and Expression of His operating will, and the fecundity of His nature must cease ; and there can be neither Word, nor Wisdom, nor Image, of the Father's substance. If He is not the Son, He cannot possibly be the Image of the Father. And, if He is not God's Son, how then can we say that God is the Creator, since all things, whatever were or are

made, the Father communicated their being to by the operation of His Word and Wisdom, and without that was nothing made that was made? On the contrary, you say the Father is destitute of that in which and by which He assures us He made all things. For if the Divine substance be without its glorious attributes of fruitfulness, as they imagine; if they represent the Majesty of Heaven as a barren thing, a light without rays, and a dry fountain, will not this content them, without denying His power of creation too? What shame and confusion ought to cover those men, who endeavour to deprive the great God of so glorious a perfection of His Divine nature, and make the mere operations of His will, not only equal, but superior and antecedent to the eternal properties and essentials of His being? As if it were not most certain, that He must be a Father, before He could be a Creator. He was not a Creator until He gave being to those things which had no existence before, and afterwards had only such a one as was foreign and external to His that made them. But He must have been a Father before, even from everlasting; because His Son could not be properly and truly His Son, unless He were of His very substance, which substance is from everlasting. For, if they attribute to God the willing about things which are not, why is it that they do not recognise that to exist in God which is far superior to the will? But it is something that surpasses will, that God should be by nature the Father of His own proper and essential Word. If, then, that which comes first, which is according to nature, does not exist, as these foolish people would have it, how can that which is inferior come to be, which is a mere act of His will? For it is certain that the Word or Son of God existed before anything else was created. This will be true, whatever these blasphemers assert to the contrary; because all things that were created were made by the Son, and by the Son, not as something external to the Creator. For, if He had been external to the nature of the Creator, He must Himself have been a created thing, but He made all things as the genuine and proper Son of the Father. And this I am obliged to repeat over and over again. The Divine nature has its power of will, and the energy of this power is productive of the essences of all created beings; and the Word or Son produces and creates these essences. Can anything, then, be more evident, than that He is the living will and energy of His Father? that He is of the same substance with Him? and that He is that genuine Word and Person, by whom all things consist and are directed and supported? I suppose it will not be questioned, but that the artificer must be antecedent to, or elder, than His own work. And, after what has been now said, it is as clear that God's Fatherhood must have preceded His Creatorship from eternity. The Son's existence flows immediately and essentially, and therefore from everlasting, from the substance of the Father; but the creature's existence is altogether external to the substance of the Divine nature, and was imparted only by an act of God's will, which He exerted by and in the genuine and eternal Offspring of, His own nature.

3. Hence, therefore, it appears that those who say that our Lord is not the Son of God, but only an ordinary creature, are guilty of the greatest folly. They ought to acknowledge that there is a necessity laid upon all to confess our Lord to be the true and genuine Son of His Father. And if He be the Son, as indeed He is, and there is no such thing as a son who is not of the substance of his father, then, as I said before, what occasion is there to quarrel about mere expressions? If the sacred writers have used the words "He who made Him," instead of saying "He who begat Him," in speaking of Him, who is so expressly and plainly declared to be the Son and Word of God, what advantage will this afford our adversaries? When there is an agreement as to what His nature is, what expressions are used are by no means material. Words will never alter or destroy the nature of things; on the contrary, they ought to be shaped and adjusted to it. For nature was before language, and not language before nature. Thus, when we are speaking of a nature that was made or created out of nothing, then those expressions which are properly applicable in any instance of mere workmanship, as "He made it," or "It was made," and "He created it," are to be understood in that proper sense. But when we are speaking of a nature or thing which was not made, and which is also plainly and expressly styled a Son and an Offspring, then, if we find those expressions applied to it, "He made Him," or "He was made," or even "He created Him," we must understand them, not properly, as implying that the thing was the workmanship of Him that made and created, but improperly. And thus to be "made" may be sometimes very well used of the same person that was "begotten." It is not at all unusual for fathers to call the children born of them their servants; and they do this without in any way hinting that they are, therefore, not their children. On the other hand, it frequently happens that masters, in kindness and consideration for good services, call their servants children, and this without intimating that they

were originally anything more than a part of their property. In the first appellation the fathers express their natural authority over their children ; and in the second, the masters declare their affection towards their servants. Thus Sarah called Abraham lord, although she was not his servant, but his wife (Gen. xviii. 12). The Apostle speaks of Onesimus the servant, as brother to Philemon the master (Philem. 16). Bathsheba, although mother, calls Solomon her son, David's servant, in speaking to David ; she says, "thy servant Solomon," and Nathan the Prophet does the same afterwards (1 Kings i. 19, 26). Nor were they sensible of any impropriety in calling the son a servant. There was no fear of a mistake, either in the persons who spoke, or as regards the persons spoken to, about Solomon being the son of his father. They all knew he was so. And, accordingly, the petition then presented was, that David would be pleased to declare him, whom they mentioned to him under the name of servant, his heir, as having been naturally begotten of him.

4. And why must the construction and the application differ so widely, where the cases answer and are parallel ? If we can hear Solomon called the servant of David, when he was his father's natural and genuine son, why cannot we read those places of Scripture where the words "made" and "created" and "servant" (as, "I am Thy servant and the son of Thy hand-maid," Ps. cxvi. 16), and all expressions of the same kind, are applied to our Lord, without inferring that He is not the genuine Son of the Father, and when the Scripture fully and plainly asserts Him to be so ? If it is reasonable in the case of David and Solomon, why is it not right also in the case of the Father and the Son ? For if our opponents do not entertain the least doubt of Solomon's being the son of David, when they find him expressly called his servant, are they not guilty of most unpardonable impiety, whilst they deny our Lord the justice of such an interpretation ? As often as they find Him plainly declared to be the Son, and Word, and Wisdom of His Father, they avoid and reject the plain sense of these words, and immediately seek to invent false notions to deny the Son's natural and genuine generation from the Father ; and as often as any word or phrase, which is only applicable to something created or made, comes in their way, it is at once used in argument to imply that the Son is only a creature, although these expressions are easily capable of reference only to our Lord's humanity. Are not these men proved to be "an abomination unto the Lord," as having "divers weights" with them (Prov. xx. 23), because,

on the one side, they measure and estimate those other instances, and on the other, they place blasphemies against the Lord? Now, perhaps, they grant that the word "servant" is used of Solomon under a certain misunderstanding, but they lay particular emphasis on the text, "Who was faithful to Him that made Him," as the very corner-stone of their heresy. However, this is but a poor refuge, a reed shaken with the wind, too weak to keep their cause from sinking. For their own conscience must tell them this, if they are at all familiar with the style and manner of expression used in Holy Scripture. For as Solomon, although a son, is called David's servant, to repeat what I have already said, so children may be very intelligibly said to be made, formed, or created by the parents, and yet at the same time they do not deny their nature in any way. So Hezekiah, in the Book of Isaiah, said in his prayer, "From this day will I make children, who shall make known Thy truth, O God of my salvation" (Isa. xxxviii. 19, Sept.). He then said, "I will make," but the prophet in the same book, as also in the Book of Kings, thus speaks, "The sons who shall come from Thee" (Isa. xxxix. 7; 2 Kings xx. 18). He uses "made" for "begotten," and the children are said in effect to be the creatures of their parents; and yet these expressions never occasioned any suspicion that the children here spoken of were not the natural offspring of those parents. Again, Eve, on bearing Cain, said, "I have gotten a man from the Lord" (Gen. iv. 1); thus she, too, used "gotten" for "brought forth." For first she saw the child, yet next she said, "I have gotten." Will anyone, from Eve's saying, "I have gotten," consider that Cain was not born of her, but only bought with her money? Again, the patriarch Jacob said to Joseph, "Thy two sons, Ephraim and Manasseh, which became thine in Egypt, before I came unto thee into Egypt, are mine" (Gen. xlviii. 5). And it is said of the seven sons and three daughters of Job, that "they were made" unto him (Job i. 2). And Moses, too, in the Book of the Law, uses these modes of expression, saying, "If sons shall be made to anyone," and "If anyone shall make a son."

5. Thus we see that the sacred writers put the words "made" and "become" very often in the place of the word "begotten." For they knew that whilst sons were acknowledged to be such, it was quite indifferent whether they were spoken of under this or that particular term. For nature and truth direct the meaning in such questions. For, if it be asked, whether Christ is a creature? we are first to enquire whether He is the Son, and

Word, and Wisdom of God. For, if this is shown, the matter will no longer bear disputing about, because a created being cannot be the eternal Son and Word of God, nor could the eternal Son be a created being. The force of this reasoning, candidly and fairly considered, shows how little service that expression of the Apostle, "Who was faithful to Him that made Him," can be expected or pretended to serve the cause of our adversaries, or rather, how strongly it condemns it. We have shown that it is no unusual thing in Holy Scripture for such a word as "making" to be applied to the birth of natural children; so that if we learn beforehand from Scripture that our Lord is the proper and genuine Son, and Word, and Wisdom of the Father, we ought not to infer from such expressions elsewhere, as "God made Him," or "He was made," that He is, therefore, no more than a creature. For we might just as reasonably conclude that Cain, and Solomon, and the children of Hezekiah, were not properly begotten, but made or purchased by them. Therefore let these enemies of Almighty God, notwithstanding their repeated misconstructions, which they persist in bringing forward in support of their heretical opinions; let them, I say, submit and resign themselves, before it be too late, to the strength and evidence of those arguments we have laid before them. Let them renounce their errors, and confess that the Saviour of the world is not a part of the creation, but by nature the eternal Son, the Word and Wisdom of the Father. If He were only a created being, I would ask, by what Word and Wisdom of God He was created? God made all things by the operation of His Word and Wisdom, as it is written, "In wisdom hast Thou made them all" (Ps. civ. 24); and, "And all things were made by Him, and without Him was not anything made that was made" (S. John i. 3). But if it be He who is the Word and Wisdom by which all things were made, how then could He Himself be in the number of those things that were made? The Son, therefore, could not be a created Son; and if He could not be a created one, He must be an uncreated one, eternal and infinite, and consequently of the very substance of His Father.

6. For, just consider, in the next place, what a very serious error it is to call the Son of God one of His works. Solomon has declared in a certain passage in Ecclesiastes, that "God shall bring every work into judgment, with every secret thing, whether it be good, or whether it be evil" (Eccles. xii. 14). If, then, the Word of God is indeed one of His works, this plain text of Scripture forces our adversaries to confess that He is to

be brought amongst the rest into judgment. And where, then, will be the judgment when the Judge is brought to trial? From whose mouth are the good and faithful servants to receive their blessing, and from whom will the wicked receive their punishment, if the Messiah Himself is to stand a trial as well as His fellow-creatures? And by what law is the Law-giver to be judged? It is a certain characteristic of every created being, that he shall in due season be brought before the Judge at last, to be either blessed or punished. Therefore let Solomon instruct you to fear this Judge, and give good heed to what the wise man says. Can anything be clearer than this? Whatever has been made shall be brought into judgment. The Son is so far from being one of those things which shall be judged, that He is to sit as Judge over every single creature. Therefore the Son is not a work or a creature, but the Word of the Father, the Creator and Judge of whatever is made. But, perhaps, they may yet extract another objection out of the words "Who was faithful," and confound the faithfulness here ascribed to Him with that which is common to all believers, as if it were only such a grace or moral perfection as made Him capable and worthy of a reward. If this must be the sense of *faithful* where it is ascribed to a person who is God, how will they be able to justify or excuse either Moses or S. Paul, the former of whom calls God "faithful and true" (Deut. xxxii. 4, Sept.), and the latter assures us that "God is faithful, who will not suffer us to be tempted above that we are able" (1 Cor. x. 13). We must not imagine that when the sacred writers spoke thus they meant us to understand these and the like expressions, when they used them of God, in a sense that belongs to them when used of men. They acknowledged two senses of the word "faithful" in Scripture, very different from one another. Sometimes it signifies him that believes or trusts, and sometimes the person that deserves to be believed or trusted. In the former sense it is applied to men, and in the latter to God. Thus Abraham is said to be faithful because he believed God's word, and God is called faithful because, as the Psalmist says, "The Lord is faithful in all His words" (Ps. cxlv. 14, Sept.), that is to say, He is trustworthy and cannot lie. The same word signifies the person believing, in the verse, "If any faithful woman have widows" (1 Tim. v. 16); and again, we read, "It is a faithful saying" (Tit. iii. 8); and here the word denotes that which ought to be believed, because it is true and cannot be otherwise. Accordingly, our Lord's words, "Who is faithful to Him that made Him," must be distinguished from the expressions used of His disciples and servants. They are said to be faithful simply on account of their belief and sincerity, but He is so because He is the Son of the True God, and ought to believed in all He says and does. He remains the Truth immutably, and has lost nothing of His eternal and infinite veracity by his Incarnation and His office as the Son of man.

7. We have said enough, in spite of the shameless obstinacy of our adversaries, to confute their detestable doctrines from the single expression " He made," which they pretend is so much in their favour. We have hitherto only argued for our meaning of the passage, and determined the time and occasion to which the words relate. We shall now confirm our own interpretation, and show the folly and nonsense of our opponents to be more blameworthy than ever from the context, where we find the fact and state of things of which the Apostle was discoursing, and where He made use of the words in question. Now we are not here concerned with things which took place antecedently to the creation, but only with what related to, and was consequent on, the Son's Incarnation. For thus it is written : " Wherefore, holy brethren, partakers of the heavenly calling, consider the Apostle and High Priest of our profession, Christ Jesus, who was faithful to Him that made Him." Now, when was it that our Lord became " Apostle," but when He put on our flesh ? And when did He become the " High Priest of our profession," but when He raised from the dead that body which He had offered a sacrifice for us on the Cross ? And does He not still bear that character and exercise that office, by bringing near and recommending those that believe on Him to the Father, and by making the ransom He has paid, and the satisfaction He has wrought for them, effectual to their salvation ? How ridiculous it is, then, to apply those words, " Who was faithful to Him that made Him," to the nature or generation of the Word (who was so far from being made, that He is declared to be the Maker of all things), when the words so clearly and undeniably relate wholly to His Incarnation and High Priesthood. And this may be further illustrated from the account given of the Law and of Aaron. Aaron did not come into the world as a high priest, but only as a man, and afterwards, when God willed it, he was ordained high priest, and the solemnity or form of his being made so was a thing of much importance. He did not merely wear the ordinary vestments of the priests. There were the ephod, the breastplate, and the robe, to distinguish him in a special manner. The

vestments were the work of the women, according to God's special direction. Attired in these garments, he entered into the sanctuary to offer sacrifice for the people, and he there placed himself as the medium between the presence of God and the worship of men. In like manner, when our Lord, who from eternity was the Word, the Word with God, and God the Word, was, according to His Father's will, to enter upon the great work of our redemption, and to make us worthy recipients of God's grace, He took upon Him our flesh, as Aaron did his robe, and assumed a body like ours, having Mary for the Mother of His Body, as it were of virgin earth, that as our High Priest, having somewhat to offer, He might offer Himself as a sacrifice to the Father, and might by shedding His blood cleanse us from all our sins, and release our bodies from the dominion of death.

8. Whatever happened under the old dispensation was but a shadow of the new. And so the priesthood of Aaron under the Law prefigured that of the Messiah. Now then, as Aaron was a man before he was a priest, and his priestly vestments did not change his nature, but only his outward appearance, so that had anyone seen him executing his office and had said, " Behold this day Aaron has been made high priest," no one would have thought that the word "made" so used implied that Aaron was not a man before he was high priest, or that the person speaking meant any more than this, that he perceived Aaron had become high priest, since he saw him wearing those vestures which had been appointed for the holder of that dignity. In the same way, when we hear of our Lord's becoming or being made this or that, there is no reason to suspect that any alteration befell His eternal nature when He assumed ours ; but what we are to understand by those expressions, is only that He united our nature personally to His. It is impossible to fancy that the eternal Word of God, as such, should in process of time "become" or "be made" anything whatsoever which He was not before. But that, as being the Creator of all things, He should make or create Himself a body, when the fulness of time was come ; that He should make Himself our High Priest ; that He should join this body to His Divinity, and then offer it up to atone for our sins ; this is intelligible enough. I do not see which way the Arians will solve this difficulty, unless they will make up their minds to assert with us, that our Lord was not made man. For if He was made man, in what other terms would they have had the Apostle speak of Him as such, than in those they argue from "Who was

faithful to Him that made Him." It was certainly as proper to say of Him in regard of His manhood, that He "became" or was "made," as to say of Him considered as God, "In the beginning was the Word, and the Word was with God, and the Word was God." How natural it would have been for any of us, if we had seen the Lord walking and acting as another man, but still declaring Himself to be God, and proving it by His miracles, to ask, who was it that had made Him man? And would not anyone, who had been asked this question, have answered, that His Father had made Him so, and ordained Him to be our High Priest. And, indeed, if we will but carefully notice the Apostle's reasoning, introductory to this place, we shall find, not only that this was the general sense, but the particular meaning too, as to the time and person. For his discourse is here linked together in one chain, and relates to one and the same person. He writes, then, in the Epistle to the Hebrews, as follows :—" Forasmuch then as the children are partakers of flesh and blood, He also Himself likewise took part of the same ; that through death He might destroy him that had the power of death, that is the devil ; and deliver them who through fear of death were all their lifetime subject to bondage. For verily He took not on Him the nature of Angels ; but He took on Him the seed of Abraham. Wherefore in all things it behoved Him to be made like unto His brethren, that He might be a merciful and faithful High Priest in things pertaining to God, to make reconciliation for the sins of the people. For in that He Himself hath suffered, being tempted, He is able to succour them that are tempted. Wherefore, holy brethren, partakers of the heavenly calling, consider the Apostle and High Priest of our profession, Christ Jesus, who was faithful to Him that made Him " (Heb. ii. 14-18; iii. 1, 2).

9. Who can read this whole passage, without condemning Arius, and admiring the holy Apostle, who has spoken so excellently? For when could our Lord be "made" or "become" Apostle, unless at the time when He took part in flesh and blood? And when did He become a merciful and faithful High Priest, except when in all things He was made like unto His brethren? And then was He "made like" when He became man, having put on Him our flesh. And, therefore, it is true that S. Paul was speaking only of our Lord's human nature, and of His human dispensation, when he said, "Who was faithful to Him that made Him." And thus, again, the enemies of truth may be convinced, that the Word of God is not a creature, but

the Only-begotten Son of the Father's substance; and this should bring them to right reason and a sober mind. Our, Lord, then had brethren, when He took upon Him our flesh, that He might offer Himself as a sacrifice for us. By this act He became our High Priest, and is said to be our merciful and faithful High Priest; merciful, in respect of the great mercy He showed in offering Himself for us; and faithful, not in the same sense as His believing people are said to be so, not as deriving from God the gift of faith or trust in Him, but because He deserves our entire belief and trust in whatever He says or does; and, moreover, as having offered upon the Cross a faithful sacrifice, one which is abiding and perpetual, and not merely transient and passing away. There was a necessity for a daily repetition of the sacrifices of the Law; a succession of sins was to be followed by a succession of atonements. But Christ's sacrifice of Himself, being made once for all, made all things perfect, and is become faithful, since it remains for ever. And, once more, Aaron had successors, and the high priests had to follow one after another, as fast as death made a vacancy. But our Lord's High Priesthood never changes or alters. He never dies and leaves it to a successor. He abides a High Priest for ever, and, therefore, He has become a faithful High Priest. He is also faithful in regard of His promise. He never fails to attend to the prayers, nor does He ever deceive those who make application to Him. We may learn this from those words of S. Peter, "Wherefore let them that suffer according to the will of God commit the keeping of their souls to Him, as unto a faithful Creator" (1 S. Peter iv. 19). For He is faithful, since He does not depart from, but because He performs, what He has promised.

10. The deities of the heathens are faithful in neither of these respects, neither in their nature, nor in their promises. The same gods do not exist everywhere, and it is only a matter of time before they exterminate themselves, and cut off their own memorial in the very places where they were honoured. And this is the character which the Son of God gives of them, that "faith is not strong in them" (Jer. ix. 3), but they are "waters that fail" (Jer. xv. 18), and that "there is no faith in them" (Deut. xxxii. 20). Whereas the true and only God is faithful and always the same, and says, "See now that I, even I, am He" (Deut. xxxii. 39), and "I change not" (Mal. iii. 6). And, therefore, His Son is faithful, immutably the same, incapable of failing either in His nature or His promises. So the Apostle says of Him, "Faithful is He that calleth you, who also will do it"

(1 Thess. v. 24). He performs as certainly as He promises. And he thus writes in another place as to the meaning of the word "unchangeable," "If we believe not, yet He abideth faithful; He cannot deny Himself" (2 Tim. ii. 13). So that the Apostle, discoursing concerning the Incarnate Word of God, might very well style Him "an Apostle, and faithful to Him that made Him," showing us that, even when made man, "Jesus Christ is the same yesterday, and to-day, and for ever" (Heb. xiii. 8). He was and is immutably the same. And again, as the Apostle, contemplating His Priesthood, speaks of our Lord's human nature, so, at a little distance from this place, he makes mention of His Divinity, as if on purpose to prevent any misconception of any part of his discourse which concerned our Lord, considered in His state of humiliation. In very expressive terms He asserts and magnifies His equality with the Father. For instance, he says, "Moses as a servant, but Christ as a Son"; "Moses was faithful in all his house, but Christ is over His own house," as having Himself built it, and being its Lord and builder, and as God sanctifying it (Heb. iii. 5, 6). Moses, a man, showed himself to be faithful, in believing what God revealed to him by His Word. But the Word was not a mere man. He was not one created being united to another, a finite spirit enclosed in a human body. He was God Himself Incarnate, the great Author and Creator of human nature united personally to the work of His own hands. The bodies of men are one half of their being; they must have them in order to exist; but this necessity was not the cause of the Son's Incarnation. He did not take our flesh to perfect His own nature, but to sanctify ours. It was only for this purpose that the Lord of all took upon Him the form of a servant, for all created things are subject to the Word, and by Him everything was made and caused to exist. And so it further appears, that the Apostle's expression "He made," does not prove that the Word is made, but no more is implied in it than that He assumed a body of like nature with ours; that He was made man, and in consequence of His humanity, became one of our brethren.

11. But since it has been shown before that the sacred writers used the word "made" instead of the word "begotten," and since it has been so clearly proved that the Son is not a creature, but the Son of His Father's substance, although as His agent and administrator He was for our sakes made man, when so it seemed good to the Father, and in that respect He is said to be "made" by the Apostle when he tells us, "He was faithful to

Him that made Him," and in the Proverbs He is even said to be created (Prov. viii. 22), I cannot conceive what further perverse expedient our adversaries will have recourse to next. For if they will not deny that, as being Incarnate, He was made man, those terms and expressions, as I observed before, with which they would attack His Divine nature with will not help their cause at all, such as, for example, "became," "made," "created," "formed," "servant," "son of the handmaid," "son of man," "constituted," "took his journey," bridegroom," "kinsman," "brother." For as man such expressions might be, and were, very applicable to Him; they prove Him indeed to be a man, but they have no effect upon the doctrine of His Divinity. The same is the meaning of the passage in the Acts of the Apostles, where S. Peter says that "God hath made that same Jesus whom ye have crucified both Lord and Christ" (Acts ii. 36), which the Arians are so foolish as to produce against us. And this also requires the same interpretation as the former. Is it said here that God made this Jesus His Son or His Word? The thing in question, if our adversaries will be pleased to remember it, is not the office of Christ, but His Sonship. Now then, let them find a place of Scripture, if they can, where God declares He has made Himself a Son, or has created Himself a Word, and that the Word, in plain terms, is a creature, a mere dependent being. Let them direct us where to find any such assertions as these in all the Bible. And, if they cannot, even this ought to convince them of the falsity and rashness of their doctrine. But, if instead of answering this challenge, they will still insist upon their old argument of expression, "God made Him," and "He has been made," it is to be feared lest, when they came to read the first chapter of Genesis, "In the beginning God made the heaven and the earth," and "He made the sun and the moon," and "He made the sea," they should come in time to call the Word the heaven, and the Light which was made the first day; that He is the earth, and, in a word, the whole creation; so as to come to imitate the Stoics, as they are called, who make their god a mere composition of the several constituent parts of the universe. For in this manner the Arians deal with God the Son when they assert Him to be a created being, and, at the same time, say He is the instrument of creation and continuance to all other created beings.

12. But here they must have the same answer as before, and first be told that the Word is truly God's own Son, and no created being; and that the phrases and passages of Scripture,

which they allege to the contrary, if the occasion and analogy of them be duly enquired into, ought not to raise the least doubt of the Divinity of His nature, because they plainly concern and relate to His Incarnation and humanity. For S. Peter, after saying, "God hath made Him both Lord and Christ," immediately added, "this Jesus, whom ye have crucified" (Acts ii. 36). And this makes it plain even to the most obstinate among them, if they will but compare the facts of this discourse plainly together, that the meaning of those words is only that our Lord was "made" in respect of His human nature. For what was crucified but His body? And how could any more appropriate word be used in speaking of His human nature than the word "made." And yet that very word here admits of, and seems to call for, another construction as little favourable to the Arians. S. Peter does not say, " God made Him His Son or His Word," but he says, " He made Him Lord," nor that in general terms, but "among us," and "in the midst of us." So that "made" is here the same as "manifested," as appears very plainly from the following words, " Ye men of Israel, hear these words ; Jesus of Nazareth, a man approved of God among you by miracles and wonders and signs, which God did by Him in the midst of you, as ye yourselves also know" (Acts ii. 22). The expression "made," which he used in the verse before referred to, is best explained by the word " approved " in this verse here before us. The signs and miracles which He wrought were a clear evidence and proper testimony of our Lord's Divinity. They proclaimed Him to be much more than man, even God Incarnate, the Lord of the universe, and the Anointed of the Father. And this further appears from that passage in the Gospel according to S. John, "Therefore the Jews sought the more to kill Him, because He had not only broken the Sabbath, but said also that God was His Father, making Himself equal with God" (S. John v. 18). For the Lord did not then fashion Himself to be God, for it is impossible that the Divine nature should at any time be made such ; but by His miraculous powers He gave a convincing proof that He was indeed the God and Author of nature. As He says of Himself, " Though ye believe not Me, believe the works ; that ye may know and believe that the Father is in Me, and I in Him " (S. John x. 38). And thus has God made Him Lord and King in the midst of us, and proved Him to be so to us who were once disobedient. Therefore it is certain that His dominion and kingship did not commence at the time the Evangelist here is speaking of, but about this time He began to show His Lordship and to manifest it to the world, even to those, too, who were ignorant of His sovereignty over them.

13. If, then, our adversaries suppose that our Saviour was not Lord and King until He was made man and suffered on the Cross, and that then and not till then He began to be both, they had better candidly confess themselves adherents of the doctrine of Paul of Samosata. At the same time, let them inform themselves how clearly we have proved that He is the eternal King and Lord from the plain and undeniable statements of Abraham, Moses, and David. The first of these worshipped Him as God; the second says of Him, "Then the Lord rained upon Sodom and upon Gomorrah brimstone and fire from the Lord out of heaven" (Gen. xix. 24); and the last says in the Psalms, "The Lord said unto my Lord, sit Thou on My right hand" (Ps. cx. 1); and again, "Thy Throne, O God, is for ever and ever; the sceptre of Thy Kingdom is a right sceptre" (Ps. xlv. 7); and, "Thy Kingdom is an everlasting Kingdom" (Ps. cxlv. 13). And so it is quite evident that He was Lord and King before He was made man, even co-eternally with His Father, as being His Word and Image. And the Word, being the eternal Word and King, it is very plain, again, that S. Peter did not say that the substance of the Son was made, but he only meant that He became our Lord and Master when He was made man, and when He bought us on the Cross with the price of His own Blood. So that if our adversaries will still insist upon the expression "God made Him," and if either their ignorance or their obstinacy will not suffer them to put the construction of "showed" or "approved" upon it, let them listen to another reasonable explanation of S. Peter's words. He who becomes the Lord and Master of others comes into the possession of beings already in existence. But if our Lord is the Maker of all things, and the eternal King, yet in another respect He was made in time, and then became our Master, when He took on Him our human nature. And so, again, no conclusion can be drawn from the words of S. Peter against our Lord's Divinity, for they will refer to His being invested by His Father with the dominion of all things, and to His being appointed Ruler over all things as their Saviour. And this is just the same as we have said before, for as we then quoted the words, "Do Thou become my strong rock and house of defence" (Ps. xxxi. 3), and "The Lord was made" (or became) "a refuge for the oppressed" (Ps. ix. 9); and we showed that these expressions did not at all concern the nature of God, but they referred to His acts and appointments, so the same sense must be taken here.

14. The Son of God, who is the Word, is indeed Lord of all. But as for us, we were subject from the first to the slavery of corruption and the curse of the Law, and then by degrees we took to making for ourselves gods to worship; we served, to use the Apostle's expression, "them which by nature are no gods" (Gal. iv. 8); we forgot and forsook the great Cause of all, and substituted mere shadows and phantoms for the Truth itself. In process of time, just as the ancient people, when they were oppressed in Egypt, groaned, so the force and light of the Law of nature had so good an effect upon us, that with those groanings of the Spirit which cannot be uttered (Rom. viii. 26), we began to make our intercession, "O Lord our God, take Thou possession of us" (Isa. xxvi. 13, Sept.).   And now it was, that He, who makes or renders Himself a house of refuge, and a God to defend the oppressed, was pleased to make or render Himself our Lord and Master by our redemption. Not that His Person then had first a beginning, but we then began to have Him for our Lord. For the gracious and merciful God, the Father of our Lord, moved with pity for our state, and earnestly desiring to recover us to the knowledge we had lost of the Deity, condescended to clothe His everlasting Son with human nature, to make Him perfect man, and to call Him Jesus, that He might, by the sacrifice of Himself in that nature which He had given Him, offer Himself for all, and free us from all sin and error, and make Himself our Lord and King. And this is the proper meaning of S. Peter's assertion, that God made Him our Lord and sent Him as Christ. It is as much as to say that He made Him man (and man He could not be until God was pleased to make Him so), and that having made Him man, He made Him our Lord and Master too, and the bestower of that unction by which He sanctifies us to Himself.   Nor did this union of the human nature with the Divine at all take from the Perfection and Majesty of the latter. The Form of God received no diminution from taking the form of a servant.   The Word, assuming our human nature, became he means and occasion of enhancing the glory of the Person in whom these two natures were united.   For the Divine nature exalted the human; and so that very Word, who was by nature Lord and was then made man, has, by means of a servant's form, been made the Lord of all and the Messiah, and has caused Him to be the means of our sanctification by the unction of the Holy Spirit.   And as God, when He becomes a refuge and protector to His people, and tells Him "He will be to them a God," He must not be conceived to mean such an absurd thing as that He

will give a beginning to His own existence, but only that He will exert those attributes of benevolence in their favour which were essential in Him from eternity ; so, when our Blessed Saviour is said to be made our Lord and King, that expression must not be understood as if His dominion only began at His mission, and that He was not our Lord and King from everlasting in right of His Divine nature. But the sense of the text is plainly this, that He, who was our Lord from everlasting as God, became, in the fulness of time, our Lord as man ; and that, having redeemed us all by His Blood, He became in this sense also the Lord both of the living and the dead. For all things from henceforth serve Him ; and this is what David means in the Psalm, where He says, "The Lord said unto my Lord, sit Thou on My right hand, until I make Thine enemies Thy footstool" (Ps. cx. 1). And, indeed, it was fitting that only He, who was our Lord by nature, should be so also by redemption. Otherwise, we should have been in this condition : we should have been created by the Son, but should name some other one Lord and Master ; and thus we should fall into that insane imagination in which the Arians and the heathen are agreed, namely, to serve the creature instead of the God who is the Creator and Maker of all things.

15. And this, in my poor judgment, is the true meaning of S. Peter's words. And we shall think it to be so the more if we consider that his discourse was directed to the Jews. For they, in the blindness of their hearts, live in expectation of another Messiah, one that shall not suffer and die ; speaking about what they do not understand, and saying, "We have heard out of the Law that Christ abideth for ever ; and how sayest Thou, the Son of Man must be lifted up?" (S. John xii. 34). The King they expect to deliver them and reign over them is not God Incarnate, but an ordinary mortal, such as any of their former monarchs were. And even Cleophas and his fellow-disciple made this mistake, until our Lord informed them that "Christ must first suffer" (S. Luke xxiv. 26). And elsewhere He confutes the Jews, by showing them that God Himself was to come among them to be their Ruler, saying, "If He called them gods, to whom the Word of God came, and the Scripture cannot be broken ; say ye of Him, whom the Father hath sanctified and sent into the world, Thou blasphemest, because I said, I am the Son of God?" (S. John x. 35, 36).

16. Thus S. Peter had been instructed by His great Master, and thus he argues with the Jews upon their own principles. He says, "O Jews, the Holy Scriptures announce that a Messiah was

to be sent to you, and you consider that this person is to be no more than an ordinary man, one of the posterity of David. But the same Holy Writings show very plainly that in saying this you make a very grave mistake, and assure you, that this Messiah is God Himself, the great Author of life and immortality. For Moses thus speaks, 'You shall see your Life hanging before your eyes' (Deut. xxviii. 66, Sept.); and David says, 'The Lord said unto my Lord, sit Thou on My right hand, until I make Thine enemies Thy footstool' (Ps. cx. 1); and again, 'Thou shalt not leave My soul in hell; neither shalt Thou suffer Thy Holy One to see corruption' (Ps. xvi. 11). That David himself is not the subject here of his own prophecy, is evident from his giving the title of Lord to the person he speaks of. Besides, you yourselves know that the Psalmist is dead, and his bones are buried in your land. You will not, then, deny that Christ is such as the Scriptures proclaim Him to be. These writings are the infallible oracles of God Himself, and it is impossible that they should contain anything false or untrue. If, then, you can prove that a person, answering to the description here given, has been sent to you at any time before, and who has manifested His Divinity by miracles, it must be confessed that you have gained a considerable advantage over us. But if you cannot prove this; if you are still expecting the coming of the Messiah, consult the Prophet Daniel as to the time when He was to manifest Himself, and you will find that his words exactly refer to the time when He did appear. If, then, the present season be that which was declared beforehand, and if you have been spectators of the mighty miracles which have accompanied His advent, be quite sure, that this same Jesus, whom you have crucified, is the promised and expected Messiah. As for David and all the Prophets, they are dead, and their sepulchres remain with you to this day. Whereas the Scriptures inform you very clearly, that, as the Messiah was to die, so He was very soon afterwards to rise again. This Jesus undoubtedly did, and He has, therefore, this remarkable testimony of the Scriptures, among many others, of His being the Messiah. The Crucifixion was foretold by those words quoted just now, 'Ye shall see your Life hanging.' And the spear which pierced His side fulfilled that prophecy of Isaiah, 'He is brought as a lamb to the slaughter' (Isa. liii. 7). This Jesus rose from the dead. And not only did He rise Himself, but He restored to life, and released from their graves, several other persons that had been long dead, and many of you have been eyewitnesses of this. Here is the completion of those other prophecies, 'Thou shalt not leave my soul in hell' (Ps. xvi. 11); and, 'He will swallow up death in victory,' and 'God will wipe away all tears' (Isa. xxv. 8). For the miracles which He actually wrought sufficiently prove that He was God Incarnate, and the Fountain of Life, and the Lord of death. For it was impossible that that Christ, who was to communicate Life to us, should Himself be held a prisoner by death; and yet it must have been so, had He been, according to your notion of Him, only an ordinary man. But He is not so; He is the Son of God, and not one of those poor mortals who are under the dominion of death. No longer, therefore, let any man have a doubt about it; but let all the house of Israel know assuredly, that the same Jesus, whom you beheld with your eyes truly man, and working such wonders as never any man did, is indeed the very Christ, and the great Lord of all. He was made man, and His name was called Jesus, as we said before. But, so far was His assumption of human nature from lessening His Divine Majesty, that, contrariwise, in taking upon Him our flesh He is thereby manifested as the Lord of quick and dead. For since, as the Apostle says, 'After that in the wisdom of God the world by wisdom knew not God, it pleased God by the foolishness of preaching to save them that believe' (1 Cor. i. 21). And so, since mankind would not acknowledge God, who had been revealed to them through His Word, nor serve the Word of God, whose subjects and property they were, it pleased God to manifest and exercise this sovereignty of His in the person of a man, and by this method to draw all men unto Him. But then it would have been most unseemly that this person should only be a man, lest, having a man for our Lord and Master, we should become worshippers of a mere mortal. Therefore the Word and Son of God was made flesh, and the Father called His name Jesus, and so made Him both Lord and Christ. And so exalted was that dominion He gave Him, that as every knee must bow at the name of Jesus, whom you have crucified, so it is the duty of all to recognise and worship God the Son as our Heavenly Lord and King, and to worship and serve the Father by and through Him."

17. This discourse of S. Peter, we find, made such an impression on many of the Jews, that it cleared up their understandings, and opened their hearts for a ready reception of the Christian Faith. But because the Arians, on the contrary, choose to remain Jews, and oppose S. Peter's teaching, let us in the next place look out for some other parallel instances of the same kind

of speaking in the Scriptures. Who knows but when they plainly perceive that the Scriptural usage is directly contrary to them, they may recollect and submit themseves. Those arguments and authorities we have urged already, put it beyond dispute that Christ is our eternal Lord and King. As the Son of God, He must be the express Image of His Father, and this He could not be if He were inferior to His Father in might and dominion. And, therefore, He might well say, "He that hath seen Me hath seen the Father" (S. John xiv. 9). But to proceed. The benediction of Isaac (although the instances be widely different, and the illustration somewhat of a faint character) affords another proof that S. Peter's words, "He hath made Him both Lord and Christ," are not to be taken in that sense which our adversaries would attach to them. Isaac there says to Jacob, "Do thou become lord over thy brother," and afterwards he says to Esau, "Behold, I have made him thy lord" (Gen. xxvii. 29, 37). Here the making of Jacob lord most certainly does not refer to the production of his being or his birth. Why, then, must the same expression, when it is applied to the Son and Word of God, be supposed to refer to the origin of His nature? Even if the expression might be taken with a reference to Jacob's birth, it would not be right so to apply them to our Lord, for the Son of God is no creature, as Jacob was. If they would only enquire the meaning from some indifferent person, they could not go so sadly astray. If, then, they do not understand the words of our Lord's substance, nor of His coming into being, although Jacob was both created and made, is not their madness simply diabolical? If it is the fact, as it seems to be, that what they dare not ascribe in consequence of a like phrase even to created things, that they attach to the Son of God, to force a proof that the Son of God is a creature, is not this fiendish wickedness? The thing is plain. There is nothing more intimated in those words of Isaac, "Do thou become," and "I have made thee lord," than the superiority and mastery which Jacob was to have, and afterwards had, over his brother Esau. No one can suppose, that the being of his person, or the beginning of his life, was at all concerned in them ; for the words were spoken more than thirty years after Jacob was born.

18. Much more, then, did S. Peter speak the words we have referred to without in the least meaning that the Word of God was a created being; especially since the Scriptures inform us, that he not only knew Him to be the Son of God, but openly confessed Him as such, saying, "Thou art the Christ, the Son of

the living God" (S. Matt. xvi. 16). He meant that by grace Christ was made not long before our King and Lord. And while saying this, he asserted Him to be truly and properly God, the eternal Son of the Father, for he had already ascribed the communication of the Holy Spirit to our Lord. Now, to dispense and convey the Holy Spirit at pleasure, is a thing peculiar to the Divine Power, and it is an impossible thing for any made or created being to do so. The Holy Spirit is emphatically the gift of God. Again, all creatures are capable of being sanctified by the Holy Spirit. But the Son is so far from deriving any sanctification of His nature from that Spirit, that He Himself is the Giver and Distributor of the Spirit's gifts and graces. This He could not be, if He were only in an improper sense the Son of His Father, and not of the Father's very substance. And yet this Dispenser of the Spirit is also said to be "made." And so He was "made" first truly and properly man, and then in that nature, too, our Lord and Master. But He is unmade and without beginning, because He is God's Word and Son, and, therefore, qualified to give us the Holy Spirit. As such, He was and is from everlasting the Blessed Son of God, the Lord and Sovereign of all creation, being similar in all His attributes to the Father, and as He Himself has said, "All things that the Father hath are Mine" (S. John xvi. 15). And now, in the next place, let us examine that passage in the Proverbs, "The Lord created Me, the beginning of His ways, for His works" (Prov. viii. 22); although this, after all, is unnecessary, since in showing that the Word was not made, it has also been proved that He was not created. Made and created are only two words for the same thing, and, therefore, these arguments which demonstrate He was not made, as clearly prove that He was not created. And so we are greatly amazed again at these men, thus planning excuses for their impiety, and nothing daunted at the refutations with which they are met at every fresh turn they take. For first they begin by deceiving simple-minded people by questions of this kind, "Did He, who existed, make Him who did not exist, or Him who did exist, out of nothing?" and, "Did you ever have a son before you begat one?" And then, when this has been proved untenable, they next invented the question, "Are there two unmade or uncreated beings, or is there only one?" And when this is answered, they immediately want to know this, "Has the Son freewill or not, and is His nature variable?" And when again you have parried this query, they strive to hide themselves under that expression

of the Apostle's, " Being made so much better than the Angels."
And when the truth has exposed this delusion, then once more
collecting all their impieties together, they think to recommend
their heresy with repetitions of the words "made" and
"created." For they mean the same old things over and over
again, they still keep to their worn-out blasphemies, and they
turn and twist them about in various ways, so that, if it were
possible, they may deceive some unstable ones by dint of this
variety. Although, then, I seem to be giving myself needless
trouble, after having abundantly proved the weakness of their
cause, yet seeing they make that text in the Proverbs one of their
strongholds, and are continually repeating and boasting of it, and
are attacking the simplicity and ignorance of untried Christians
with it, it will be necessary to examine that saying, " He created,"
as well as " Who was faithful to Him that made Him ; " that here,
as in other places of Scripture as well, we may convict our adversaries of novelty and invention in their explanation of the text.

19. And the first thing we have to do, is to consider the
original phraseology of this heresy, in which it addressed and
delivered itself, at its first appearance, to my predecessor Alexander, of blessed memory. He wrote as follows : " He is a
creature, but still is not as one of the creatures ; He was made,
but still is not as one of those things that were made ; He is
begotten, but still is not as one of those things that were and are
begotten." Let everyone consider the guile and subtlety of this
heresy, for knowing how hateful and vile a thing it is, there was
a necessity to throw a covering of nonsensical and unintelligible
distinctions over it. The doctrine was to be published, that the
Son of God is a creature. But then they think they will be able
to tone down such a harsh statement as this, and so they add,
" But He is not as one of the creatures." And will this carry
weight ? Instead of mending the matter, it rather makes it
worse. For if He was created or made at all, why is it necessary
to add the pretence, " But He is not as one of the creatures "?
What sort of a limitation or exception is meant ? And if He is
indeed begotten, but not as one of the things which were and
are begotten, we again see the poisonous character of the heresy
manifested. For is not this introducing a large family of sons ?
our Lord, indeed, as the Elder Brother, but, if this be true, not the
Only-begotten one. What use, then, is this pretence of saying
that He is a creature, but still not as one of the creatures ? I
will prove this sophism of yours to be a wretched and paltry one.
For you still assert Him to be one of the creatures ; and what-

ever a man might say concerning other created beings, such you declare to be the case also concerning the Son. Surely you are both fools and blind to say that such absurdities can be true. Now, is any single one of the creatures just what another is? And if not, what reason had you to think that the Son would be exactly like some other of His fellow-creatures? God created the whole visible world in six days. In the first, He made the light which He called day ; in the second, the firmament ; in the third, He gathered together the waters into one place, formed the dry land, and covered it with trees, fruits, and herbs ; in the fourth, He made the sun, the moon, and all the number of the stars ; in the fifth, He created all the fish in the sea, and the birds in the air ; in the sixth, He formed all the beasts of the earth, and last of all, He made man. " And the invisible things of Him from the creation of the world are clearly seen, being understood by the things that are made" (Rom i. 20) ; and the light is not like darkness ; nor is the sun like the moon ; nor the irrational beasts like rational man ; nor is one order of Angels like another. And yet these beings were all created, but everyone is confined to his own nature and species ; and what they were made such they remain in their own substance and nature.

20. Either, then, let the Word of God be no more degraded into the condition of a creature, but let Him, as Creator of all, be restored to His Father's side, and let Him be confessed to be by nature the true Son of Almighty God. Or, if He simply be a creature, do not take so much pains to make Him seem more than He really is. Do not make a mere contradiction of His nature for fear of not exalting it high enough. Call every creature plainly a creature, and no more. Let the terms " begotten " and " made " (which, indeed, are in your construction the very same, as appears from your own words) indiscriminately belong to whatever is so. Do not talk any more of this creature as one of the creatures, and of that creature not as one of the creatures. For the Son of God, in your account of Him, is but a creature still. Let Him be considered as far superior in the excellence of His nature to all His fellow-creatures ; yet there are distinctions of this kind to be found between the several sorts and ranks of them too. " One star differeth from another star in glory" (1 Cor. xv. 41) ; and so, too, all the works of God have their respective degrees and shares of usefulness and beauty, and stand at wide distances from one another. And yet one is not the object of the other's worship, and the other is not the subject of another's power. This one does not give being

to this, and that one does not hold its being from that. They are equally created, equally dependent, and alike in subjection. And they celebrate together with one voice the attributes of their Creator, as the Psalmist says, "The heavens declare the glory of God; and the firmament showeth His handiwork" (Ps. xix. 1); and as Zorobabel the wise says, "All the earth calleth upon the Truth, and the heaven blesseth it; all works shake and tremble at it" (1 Esdr. iv. 36). Here is the whole earth adoring, blessing, trembling before its Creator, even before that Truth, which can be no other than the Son and Word of God, who declares of Himself that "He is the Truth" (S. John xiv. 6); that is to say, He is the very Principle and Origin of all reality and existence. And, therefore, He cannot be, in any sense, a creature. He must be co-essential with His Father, and as in unity of nature with Him, He created and disposed, and still governs the whole frame and course of nature, so, in the same unity, He receives from His own works all those praises and adorations which are the just tribute of every creature to its Creator. And this is the very thing He tells us of Himself, "I was by Him disposing all things" (Prov. viii. 30, Sept.); and again, "My Father worketh hitherto and I work" (S. John v. 17). And the word "hitherto" expresses and proves beyond all dispute the Son's eternal existence in nature of the Father. For as He works and creates in Him and with Him, in one common act, so it is certain His nature is not distinct from, and foreign to, that of the Father.

21. If, then, the effects of the Father's Power are as properly the effects of the Son's, and if all that is of the Son's creation is of the Father's too, then, if the Son is one of His Father's creatures, He must either create Himself, and will give Himself His own being, as being one of those works or effects which are to be ascribed in common to the Son and the Father (and this is absurd and impossible); or, it must be confessed, that as He made and created whatever the Father made and created by Him, He Himself cannot be a creature, unless you will say, that the efficient Cause of all things is one of His own effects. In which case, indeed, He could not be that efficient Cause. For if He had a beginning of existence, and was made out of nothing, how should such a dependent being be capable of creating all other things out of nothing? or why must He be the only creature that can produce another creature? Why should it not be as much in the power of all other creatures to create? And if these have the power of creation too, one would think that the more perfect and excellent kinds of them might be employed in the

case of the Son, to give being to the less perfect ones. Or, at any rate, one might think that everything that is brought into being could have heard in the beginning the words of God the Father, "Become" and "Be made," and so would have come into existence. But this is plainly contradicted both by reason and Scripture. No creature whatsoever can produce another creature. And all things were altogether the production of the Power of the Word; and yet all could not be so, if that Word had Himself been one of them. The highest orders of Angels are but creatures, and, therefore, they cannot be capable of creating; although Valentinus, and Marcion, and Basilides (those whom our adversaries are trying to rival), foolishly supposed them able to do so. The sun could never, since it is a creature, make what is not into what is, nor could one man ever create another, nor could one stone produce another, nor could one piece of wood cause another piece to exist. It is God alone who fashions man in the womb, and who has arranged the mountains, and has planted the trees. It is true, that man is able by his intelligence to compound or unite, to proportion and work upon the parts of that matter, which God has created. God finds materials, and man can use his skill, but even that only by the help of God. For a very short experience convinces us, that all our dependence is upon His Power and Providence, and teaches us whenever we feel our need of anything, to ask for aid from God.

22. Suppose that extraordinary idea of the Gentiles were admitted, that God made the world out of various materials, and that He never was a Creator but only an artificer; yet, even in that case, it might be imagined very well that the Son should work the materials at the direction and according to the good pleasure of His Father. But if the Father created things which before had no existence by the operation of His Son and Word, then that Word could not be in the number and a part of those created things then called into being. He could not be so, unless there was, indeed, another Son and Word of God which created Him. For the Word and the Son of God was the sole Creator of whatever was created. And all created substance whatsoever cannot be of His creating, if He Himself is a created substance. He must, therefore, be the uncreated Word and Son of God; and, indeed, He manifests His infinite attributes in all those productions and works which He created and made, in conformity to the will and appointment of the Father. He is " in the Father and the Father in Him," and " he that hath seen Him hath seen the Father" (S. John xiv. 11, 9), because of the

consubstantiality of His nature with that of the Father, and because He is in all points like Him. He must needs be His Father's Word and Wisdom, because the Father creates all things by Him, and He cannot Himself be made or created out of nothing, but must be the Son of His Father's substance, because He is that very Word and Wisdom. Again, if the Son is only one of created beings, if His existence is as successive and dependent as theirs, how does it come to pass that He alone reveals the Father, and He alone perfectly knows the Father? Why should He not at least partake of these privileges in common with His fellow-creatures, if the Father's perfections are not absolutely incomprehensible to any one of the creatures? Why should not the faculties of every intelligent creature besides be proportionately capable of grasping more or less of the knowledge of the Infinite? All of them are works, as He is. But that no made or created being whatsoever is capable of a direct sight and intimate knowledge of the Father's Divine nature; that the powers of all finite souls are too narrow to receive, and too weak to sustain, that tremendous idea, both God the Father and God the Son assure us. "No man," says the Father, "shall see My face and live" (Exod. xxxiii. 20); and "No man," says the Son, "knoweth the Father, save the Son" (S. Matt. xi. 27). Our adversaries must, therefore, deny that the Son only comprehends the nature of the Father, and declare that they will not believe Him when He tells them, that "Not that any man hath seen the Father, save He which is of God" (S. John vi. 46); and that "No man knoweth the Father save the Son," or else they must confess that the Son cannot be a creature. Were He not in a literal and proper sense the only-begotten Son of God, why should it be absolutely impossible for other intelligent beings to reach a just and adequate knowledge of the Father? And how can He be literally and properly a Son, unless He is indeed of the very substance of the Father? I trust that my frequency of repetition will be pardoned, when the vast importance of the occasion is considered. To assign the Son of God a place amongst His own works and creatures is monstrous blasphemy. It is irreligious and foolish to call Him "a creature, but not as one of the creatures," and to say that "He was made, but is not as one of those things that were made; and that He is begotten, but yet He is not as one of those things that are begotten." And how, indeed, is He not as one of those, if, as they say, He was not before He was begotten? All God's creatures came alike out of nothing, and one as much as another had no being until it was made, however different they may be from one another in those qualities that distinguish them into kinds and species ; and this variety and disparity runs through all parts of creation. It is common to the intellectual and invisible, with the visible and material world, although it is discerned by us only in the latter.

23. If it were possible for the Son of God to be that strange thing which these heretics represent Him to be, a mere created being, although not as one of the creatures, because of His excelling them in glory, we should certainly have had some information of it from the Holy Scriptures. There we should have found such a comparison between the Son of God and God's other creatures in point of circumstances or qualities as implied in their being alike created. We should have been told that He is far greater than the Archangels and more honourable than the Thrones, that He is brighter than the sun and moon, and that He is greater than the heavens. But this is by no means the way in which He is represented to us in Holy Scripture. The Father speaks of Him in quite another style, and He calls Him His Son, His own Son, His Only-begotten Son. He says, " Thou art My Son" (Ps. ii. 7), and " This is My Beloved Son, in whom I am well pleased" (S. Matt. iii. 17). The Angels ministered unto Him, as if to one who was their Lord and Master " (S. Matt. iv. 11), and they worship Him, not as being only greater in glory, but as being someone far superior to all creatures, and superior to themselves, even as being God's Only-begotten Son, and the Son of His Father's nature and substance. For if He was worshipped by them because He was simply a more glorious creature than they are, then every superior order of beings in the rest of creation would have a right also to the worship of what was inferior and subordinate. And yet it is certain that no creature whatsoever ought to be the object of another's worship. This homage is due, and must only be paid, to the great Lord and God of heaven and earth. Thus, when Cornelius fell down at S. Peter's feet and worshipped him, the Apostle immediately hindered him from so doing, saying, " I myself also am a man " (Acts x. 26). And when S. John fell down to worship an Angel, as related in the Book of Revelation, he was at once forbidden, the Angel saying, " See thou do it not ; for I am thy fellow-servant, and of thy brethren the Prophets, and of them which keep the sayings of this book : worship God" (Rev. xxii. 9). The holy Angels are not ignorant that they are the noblest part of the creation. But then they know also that still they are no more

than creatures, and that they cannot claim any right to be worshipped, but that even they must only worship the Lord God. Thus that Angel that was sent to Manoah, the father of Samson, would not suffer him to offer a sacrifice to him, but said, "If thou wilt offer a burnt offering, thou must offer it unto the Lord" (Judges xiii. 16). On the other hand, the Lord is worshipped even by the Angels, for it is expressly written, "Let all the Angels of God worship Him" (Heb. i. 6). And thus, as the Prophet Isaiah tells us, all the nations of the earth adore Him, "The labour of Egypt, and merchandise of Ethiopia and of the Sabeans, men of stature, shall come over unto Thee, and they shall be Thine; and they shall fall down unto Thee, and shall make supplication unto Thee, saying, Surely God is in Thee; and there is none else, there is no God" (Isa. xlv. 14). And our Lord accepts His disciples' worship, and commends them for it, and requires them to continue it, saying, "Ye call Me Master and Lord, and ye say well, for so I am" (S. John xiii. 13). And when S. Thomas said to Him, "My Lord and my God" (S. John xx. 28), He permits the use of such language, and does not correct or reprove him, but rather approves his words. He is the same whom the Psalmist and the rest of the Prophets often mention under the title of "The Lord of Hosts" (Ps. xlviii. 7), and the "Lord of Sabaoth," which is interpreted "The Lord of Armies" (Ps. xxiv. 10). And He is the great God of all, the true and the omnipotent One, although this news may cause the Arians to become quite frantic with rage.

24. If our Lord were no more than a creature, He had never thus been distinguished by characteristics and titles so peculiar to the Divine nature, neither would He have admitted of such modes of address or acts of worship. But being the very Son of His Father's substance, and as truly God as the Father, He is, in as full and proper a sense, the object of our adoration, and of our faith and obedience, and is as much the Lord of Hosts, the great Almighty Sovereign of the universe, as the Father Himself. He has said Himself, "All things that the Father hath are Mine" (S. John xvi. 15). This can only be true of a Son that is of the very substance of His Father, for no other is capable of representing the whole nature of His Father. It was impossible that any other should be the agent of His Father's will in the mighty work of creation, and in the preservation of all things. And here we have a few questions for our opponents to answer, the very proposing of which discovers the frightful character of their doctrine. Let them tell us if the Son of God

is really a creature, and had a beginning of existence, as all other creatures have? what could be the reason why God created and "made all things by Him"? and why "without Him was not anything made that was made"? (S. John i. 3). Again, why is it when "all things" are spoken of, that no one thinks the Son is signified in that number, but only those things that were created by Him? And why, when Scripture speaks of the Word, does it not understand Him to be in the number of all created things, but it always places Him on an equality with the Father? Why should Scripture always take it for granted that this Son is employed by and acts for His Father in supporting the existence, and conducting the affairs of, the whole creation, although the same command that created the Son could have as easily created all things without Him? Do they think the work of creating would have been a fatigue and weariness to Almighty God? Or, was He under any necessity of creating such a Son to be His Instrument for the production of all other beings, because of any defect of power, which made Him incapable of creating them without Him? Is there any occasion for an Infinite Being to take time, or pursue a certain method, in the work of creation? Does not one single act of His will immediately cause all things He wishes to exist, and "no one hath resisted His will" (Rom. ix. 19). Why, then, were not all things brought into being by God alone at that same command and act of His power, which He exerted at the creation of His Son? And why must all other creatures receive and hold their existence from the Son, who is Himself but a creature? These questions our adversaries find very difficult to answer, and they have nothing to urge in reply except that which is absurd and ridiculous. However, when they have nothing better to say, they speak in such terms as these, "The strength of God would have been too violent, and His hand too heavy, to be applied immediately in the production of His creatures. They could not sustain the force and vehemence of so powerful an impression, and, therefore, God found it convenient to create first of all a certain one whom He calls His Son and His Word, that through Him, as a kind of medium, all things might very advantageously receive their being." And this very solution of the difficulty, Eusebius, Arius, and the sacrificer Asterius, have dared to make use of, not only in conversation, but in their writings as well.

25. Is not this an overwhelming proof of that irreligion with which they have filled themselves? No Bacchanalian, inflamed

with wine and madness, could blaspheme with more delight or vehemence. For if they will be so impudent as to allege this reason for God's creating Himself a Son, that He did it because He would not take the trouble to make all other creatures Himself, the whole creation will cry out against them, as offering an insult to the Divine Majesty; and Isaiah, too, testifies against them when he says, "Hast thou not known? hast thou not heard that the everlasting God, the Lord, the Creator of the ends of the earth, fainteth not, neither is weary? there is no searching of His understanding" (Isa. xl. 28). And if they suppose that God created the Son to save His own honour, because He thought it beneath His dignity to make the rest, but committed them to the Son as a mere assistant, such a thought reflects quite as impiously upon God's goodness, for God has no pride in Him. And the Arians will be forced to own this, unless they will say that our Lord was mistaken when He said, "Are not two sparrows sold for a farthing? and one of them shall not fall on the ground without your Father, who is in heaven" (S. Matt. x. 29). And again, "Take no thought for your life, what ye shall eat, or what ye shall drink; nor yet for your body, what ye shall put on. Is not the life more than meat, and the body than raiment? Behold the fowls of the air: for they sow not, neither do they reap nor gather into barns; yet your heavenly Father feedeth them. Are ye not much better than they? Which of you by taking thought can add one cubit unto his stature? And why take ye thought for raiment? Consider the lilies of the field, how they grow; they toil not, neither do they spin: and yet, I say unto you, that even Solomon in all his glory was not arrayed like one of these. Wherefore, if God so clothe the grass of the field, which to-day is, and to-morrow is cast into the oven, shall He not much more clothe you, O ye of little faith?" (S. Matt. vi. 25-30). It seems, then, that God does not look upon it as at all beneath His dignity to extend His Providence and care to things of such little account as the sparrows, the grass of the field, and even the hairs of our head. And, therefore, much less could He think it to be undignified to give them their being. As He is pleased to take them under His special protection, so it is not to be doubted but that He created them, too, by the power and agency of His Word. And then there is a worse difficulty still to be solved by the men who hold these opinions. For if there is anything in this distinction, that creation is the work of the Father, but the creatures the work of the Son, it unavoidably follows, either that the Father created all other things as well as the Son; or, if all created things were created by the Son, that the Son Himself is not a creature.

26. But we have now another objection to bring forward. If creatures, as such, are too feeble to endure the force of the Father's immediate creating power, and if the Word Himself is but a creature, how could this Word, being a creature, alone be able to endure this force of the Father's power, as our adversaries say He did? If it was not too violent for one creature, why should it be so for any of the rest? And if it was, then the Word Himself could not be created by it, and for this very reason, because He was a creature. Must a mediator be introduced, because an immediate application of Omnipotence is inconsistent with the weakness of a created being? Why, then, when this Word of God was created, there must have been the operation of some other medium, in order that He might be created; the weakness of His nature, as being a created one, absolutely requiring such an agent, as the weakness of all other created beings as such required it. Here, then, our adversaries will have occasion for another medium between God and His Word. And, again, that medium will signify nothing without another, and so they will go on multiplying mediators without end. The consequence of which will be that there neither is, nor can be, any such thing as a created being. For there can be no such thing without a medium, and there can be no medium without another one; because all the mediators must be creatures too, and every creature, as such, is incapable of enduring the force and power of God's action. What extraordinary nonsense all this is, which obliges these foolish ones to confess that all created beings which now exist could not possibly have been created! Or to extricate themselves out of this endless seeking of mediators, perhaps they will, instead, deny the existence of all created beings. They have no other choice but either to embrace this height of absurdity, or to renounce their error, which is not only senseless but the doctrine of madmen.

27. But again, they urge a reply. Did not God, they say, conduct the children of Israel out of Egypt, and give them the Law by the ministry of Moses, although he was no more than a man? It seems, then, that like can bring like things into being. They should cover their faces when they make such a parallel, for fear they should incur more contempt and derision than they can bear. Did Almighty God commission or employ Moses to create things for Him, "to call those things which be not, as though they were" (Rom. iv. 17); to fashion his fellow-mortals like himself? It was

only to transact and manage affairs between the Israelites and King Pharaoh. And this is not to be compared with the other function; for God's creatures are qualified to execute His commands as servants, but they can by no means make things out of nothing. This power pertains only to God Himself, and to His essential Word and Wisdom. Accordingly this power is only ascribed to the Son of God, for "All things were made in Wisdom" (Ps. civ. 24), and "Without the Word was not anything made that was made" (S. John i. 3). But as regards ministrations, these are not limited to any of God's creatures, but are distributed among many of them, according as it seems good to God to employ them. There are innumerable multitudes of Archangels, Thrones, Powers, and Dominions, "thousand thousands, and ten thousand times ten thousand minister unto Him and stand before Him" (Dan. vii. 10), ready to receive and execute His orders. And thus Prophets and Apostles, and S. Paul, and Moses, and Aaron, and the seventy Elders upon whom the Holy Spirit rested, and Joshua, the son of Nun, and after him a series of Judges, and a succession of Kings, were all instruments to perform His will. And why, then, if the Son be no more than a creature, should it not be supposed that God has many such Sons? Why may there not have been a multitude of Sons? that God might have many such ministers, just as well as a numerous retinue of other attendants. And yet it is certain that there is but one Word of God, although the creatures that serve Him consist of a great variety of species, and those of numberless individuals. And this one consideration may satisfy our adversaries that the nature of the Son has nothing in it in common with that of the creatures; and that as there is but one Son and one Word of God, so that one Son is properly and substantially the Son of God, and that one Word His express Image or Character. But they proceed yet further, and say, " Behold there is but one sun and one earth." And why do they not in the same absurd manner ask us, too, whether there is one element of water, or one element of fire in the world? as if this or that individual or species were singly sufficient for that service which it has to perform, for this reason, because it is an individual or a species. Is this the meaning of what God said at the creation? " Let there be light in the firmament of the heaven, to give light upon the earth, and to divide the day from the night; and let them be for signs, and for seasons, and for days, and years. And God made two great lights; the greater light to rule the day, and the lesser light to rule the night: He made the stars also. And God set them in the firmament of the heaven, to give light upon the earth, and to rule over the day and over the night" (Gen. i. 14-18).

28. Behold! there are many lights, and not the sun only, nor the moon only, but every one of them is single in the individuality of its nature; and yet the service of all is one and common, and what each lacks is supplied by the other, and the office of lighting is performed by all. Thus the sun performs the part of shining throughout the day only, and the moon throughout the night only, and the stars together with them cause the seasons and the years to fall in their proper order, and become for signs to us, indicating to us the several stages of life. Thus again, the earth does not serve for all uses and conveniences. Its function is to provide fruits and various kinds of food, for supporting the life of those creatures that dwell upon it. And the firmament serves another purpose; dividing between the waters and the waters, and to be a place wherein the stars are placed. Fire, water, and the other elementary bodies, are provided as the general ingredients of nature. No one single thing stands by itself. The whole is compounded together, so to speak; and is made up of an infinite number of correspondent parts and members. And all men should join in stoning such blasphemous wretches, as make the Word of God to be no more than one of these parts, subservient equally, and in concert with, the rest of God's creatures carrying on the various appointments with which they have been entrusted. And if our adversaries can have no other notion of the Son of God but this absurd and impious one, let them acknowledge instead that He is the Son of His Father's substance, and not one of God's creatures, but the Creator and Maker of them all. But, once more, they say, " Although He is a creature, and one of those things which were made, yet He might learn the art of creation. God may have taught Him, as a master teaches a scholar, and when He saw that He understood the art thoroughly, then He let Him work at it." And truly such an abominable statement is not very surprising in the writings of a man that had learnt how to deny Christianity altogether, as we know the sophist Asterius has done. But then one would think that anyone might have seen to what a frightful absurdity this would lead. For there can be no such thing as teaching anyone to create. If making things out of nothing is a trade, did God the Father learn it, and did anyone show Him how it should be done? And if He got this knowledge by industry, perhaps He might come in time to forget and lose the power. And how

could it be the Wisdom of God that created all things, if the way of doing it was to be first learned or acquired? It would be rather God's skill than His Wisdom; for it seems His Wisdom was insufficient for these things, until it had been put into a method. And thus His Wisdom could not be of His true substance, but was only a kind of accomplishment which He took some pains to attain, and which He must be at some trouble to retain. For he that has made himself master of any part of knowledge by diligently learning it, may by neglect and disuse come to be in time as ignorant of it as if he had never known it. Now such conceptions and representations of the Divine nature as these might be imagined by some heathen; but to anyone that has the least knowledge of Christianity, what can be more absurd or execrable?

29. Does not such a strange notion as this imply either jealousy or else weakness in Almighty God? It implies jealousy, because it seems that He only allowed one of His creatures to learn how to create, instead of teaching many how to do so, such as the Angels and Archangels. And it implies weakness, because it makes it necessary for Him to provide Himself an assistant before the work of creation could begin. And yet it must begin at God, and can only be by the effort of His Omnipotence (as has been proved already), because if the Son were a creature, God only could create Him. And may God forbid that we should think so meanly of Him as to think He stands in need of anything whatsoever, for He hath said Himself, "I am full" (Isa. i. 11). Nor did the Word become the Creator of all things by learning the art of creation, but because He is the Image and Wisdom of the Father, therefore He does the Father's work. And the Father did not create the Son simply for the use to be made of Him in creating things; for the Father Himself still creates and operates, even after the supposed creation of the Son, as our Lord Himself says, "My Father worketh hitherto, and I work" (S. John v. 17). If, however, as you suppose, the Son was created for the purpose of working God's works and making His creatures, and yet the Father goes on working Himself after this Son is in existence, what occasion was there for the production of the Son? Besides, the Scripture is very clear in this matter, and assures us that by a single act of will God can make or do whatsoever He pleases. "He hath done," says the Psalmist, "whatsoever pleased Him" (Ps. cv. 3); and the Apostle asks, "Who hath resisted His will?" (Rom. ix. 19). If, then, God's will by itself is sufficient for the creation of all things,

the office of a mediator is altogether superfluous. As for those other ministrations you have brought forward concerning Moses and the rest, and the sun and moon, what has been already said quite proves that those arguments will not bear weight. But we have something else quite as impious and incongruous as what we have alleged against them already, to lay to the charge of the Arians, upon the supposition that the purpose of God's creating the Son was His desire to create the world.

30. For, in the first place, if God had not created Him but for the sake of our creation, it plainly follows, that it was not for the Son's sake that we were created, but that the Son was created for ours. Therefore the Son ought to be thankful to us for His being, rather than that we should be thankful to Him for ours. And the case would be much the same between us and Him, as that between the man and the woman, " For the man," says the Scripture, "was not created for the woman, but the woman for the man." Therefore, "as the man is the image and glory of God, but the woman is the glory of the man " (1 Cor. xi. 9, 7), so we are made in God's image and for His glory; but the Son is our image, and exists for our glory. God's chief purpose, it seems, was our existence, and He had not concerned Himself about creating His Word, but simply to make use of Him instrumentally, when we were to be created. And, therefore, it must be said that He created Him, not in favour to Him, but in kindness to us. Now those that can conceive such monstrous thoughts are worse than madmen. For the Word cannot take precedence of us with God, if it was only for our sakes that God created Him. He was not in or with God, until after our creation was determined upon. And when our creation was resolved upon, then, according to these men, God began to think of creating His Word for this end and object. If this be the true state of the case, it may well be supposed, that the Father deliberated with Himself whether He should create the Son at all. For the existence of the Son, as such or in itself, was not the thing which the Father proposed, but our existence, and His only in subserviency to ours. The Son, indeed, if there were any truth in this detestable opinion, is now altogether superfluous, if He was the last and lowest in God's design. He is like an instrument, after the work is finished for which it was made to be used; since now those things are completed, which He was formed to produce. And another difficulty arises. If the Father made the Son, because no one else could make Him; and if the Son made us, because it was impossible we should receive our being

immediately from the Father, how came we to be first and the Son last in God's counsel and purpose of creation? Again, how comes He, whose excellency of nature was such that only the Father could create Him, to be in any way subordinate to those beings whose natures were so feeble, as to be incapable of enduring creation from the hand of the Father? And why did not the Son, who was created first, also hold the first place in the counsels of God? Or why, if God first deliberated about us, did He not create us first, since one act of His will would have been sufficient to create all things? But you say that God's chief design was to create us, and yet He created Him before us; and that being whose existence He least valued, He created before those beings whose existence he principally intended. And, what is still more strange, He calls us only His creatures, but He calls Him, who He only forms so as to make use of Him in the work of creating us, His Son and the Heir of all things. But surely we, for whose sake He made Him, ought much rather to be called sons; or certainly He, who is His Son, may reasonably be supposed to have been the highest concern and the principal purpose of God's creation; and it may be thought, too, that we were given our being only for the sake and honour of the Son. These are the nauseous productions of these heretics, of which we have now had a surfeit.

31. We must proceed forthwith to declare the truth of the subject, and to carefully enlarge upon it. Well then, it is evident that the Word of God was not created simply on our account, but rather He was the cause of our creation, for "by and in Him were all things created" (Col. i. 16). And it was not, God forbid, that the Father made the Son, because He only could make Him, and that He made Him to serve as a mere instrument in the work of our creation; because such weak creatures as we are, were incapable of being created by the immediate force of Almighty God. This is utterly absurd. For although the Father had never been disposed to create the world or any part of it, yet still the Son would have been with the Father, and the Father in the Son. And at the same time, it is true, that if there had been no Word of God, the world could not have existed; and, therefore, it is not surprising that the Scripture tells us that "all things were made by Him." It is impossible they should have been made without Him, because He is united in essence with His Father; He is of the Father's substance and in Him. Just as the light enlightens all things by its brightness, and without that brightness there would be nothing but darkness;

so also the Father operates by His Word and Son, as by an arm of strength, and without Him He makes or creates nothing. Therefore God said, as Moses tells us, "Let there be light," and "Let the waters be gathered together," and "Let the dry land appear," and "Let us make man" (Gen. i.), and, as David says in the Psalm, "He spake and it was done; He commanded and it stood fast" (Ps. xxxiii. 9). He did not deliver His Father's commission at second hand, as our servants do, who must wait upon their masters to receive their commands, and have to enquire upon what work they are to be employed, before they can set about it. This is proper enough to creatures, but to entertain such an idea of the Son is most profane and unseemly. For the Word is the Performer of God's decrees; He executes them all, and that with the Father's full approbation. The Scripture nowhere tells us, that the Son or Word of God attended on His Father to receive His instructions; that He asked Him what He was to do, and in what manner He would be pleased to have it done, and then made answer accordingly. God only said, "Let it be made," and it is added, "And it was so." What the Father wished to be created, immediately was made and completed by the Word. But this is very different from what passed at any time between God and His Angels, or when He conversed with Moses, or made promises to Abraham. The Patriarch was obliged to ask the question, "Whereby shall I know?" (Gen. xv. 8). Moses said, "Choose some other person" (Exod. iv. 13); and again, "If they ask me what is His Name, what shall I say unto them?" (Exod. iii. 13). The Angel said to Zacharias, "Thus saith the Lord;" and he asked the Lord, "O Lord of Hosts, how long wilt Thou not have mercy on Jerusalem?" (Zech. i. 17, 12), and He waits for an answer of good and comfortable words. To these and all such inferior ministers of His will, God revealed Himself by His Word and Wisdom as a Mediator, by whom He made known His will. But when that Word Himself works and creates, there passes no such thing as enquiries and replies. Whenever any Divine decree is to be put into execution, the Father is in Him and He in the Father, and so one effort of will suffices, and whatever it is their pleasure to effect is forthwith done. The verse expresses this act by the words, "He said," as being most suitable for our comprehension. And then follow the words, "And it was so," denoting the action of God's Word and Wisdom which performs the work, that action also including the will of the Father. "God said" is explained in "the Word," that is, God is conceived to say in and by His Word. And so Scripture says, "In Wisdom hast Thou made all things" (Ps. civ. 24); and, "By the Word of the Lord were the heavens made" (Ps. xxxiii. 6); and, "There is but one Lord Jesus Christ, by whom are all things, and we by Him" (1 Cor. viii. 6).

32. It is plain, then, from all this, that the Arians are not really fighting with us about their heresy. Whilst they pretend they are waging warfare with us, they are in actual fact directing all their powers against God Himself. For if that were our voice which said, "This is My Son" (S. Matt. xvii. 5), we should not think so very much of their accusations. But when the Father Himself declares our Saviour to be His beloved Son, and when this declaration has been both attested by those disciples who heard it uttered, and confirmed by our Lord Himself, who says that "Before the mountains and hills was He brought forth" (Prov. viii. 25), are not they fighting against God, like the giants in the fables? and is not their tongue, in the Psalmist's words, "a sharp sword," since they make use of it for the utterance of such blasphemy"? (Ps. lvii. 5). And we cannot wonder that if they will not listen to the Father and the Son, neither will they be persuaded or convinced by the testimony of holy men; one of whom tells them that the Word is "the Brightness of His Father's glory, and the express Image of His Person" (Heb. i. 3); and that "Christ is the Power of God and the Wisdom of God" (1 Cor. i. 24). Another says in the Psalm, "With Thee is the well of life, and in Thy Light shall we see light" (Ps. xxxvi. 9); and again, "In Wisdom hast Thou made them all" (Ps. civ. 24). And the Prophets say, "The Word of the Lord came to me" (Jer. ii. 1). S. John says, "In the beginning was the Word" (S. John i. 1). S. Luke says, "Even as they delivered them unto us, which from the beginning were eye-witnesses and ministers of the Word" (S. Luke i. 2). And David again says, "He sent His Word and healed them" (Ps. cvii. 20). All these passages utterly confound in every possible manner the Arian heresy, and they establish the doctrine of the Son's co-eternity with the Father, and that He is consubstantial with Him. Did ever anyone see a light without brightness? or a just image and representation of anyone that was unlike the original? Can anyone, then, be so insane as to fancy that there was a time when God's Word, His Reason, and His Wisdom, were not in His essence? These are resemblances and allegories, which God has thought it convenient to make use of in revealing this great mystery. And indeed they are well

adapted for suggesting as just and answerable a notion as our human understanding can possibly receive, although even that must be a very defective and obscure one of the incomprehensible nature of Almighty God. As, then, the universe is a demonstration of the Being and Providence of God, " for by the greatness and beauty of the creatures proportionally the Maker of them is seen " (Wisd. xiii. 5) ; and as the plain and express declarations of God in Holy Scripture supersede all questions and debates upon this head ; and as both these proofs united convince us with double force that there is an Infinite Being, who created and formed all things out of nothing, and who governs and directs the whole course and order of nature with His marvellous Providence ; so those proofs and arguments we have now brought from Scripture and reason so clearly and fully prove the proper Divinity of God the Son, that hereafter it will not only be superfluous, but the height of folly and of madness, to dispute about it any more, or to enquire in an heretical fashion such impertinent questions as, " How can the Son be co-eternal with Him whom He proceeds from ? " and " How can He be of His Father's substance without being a part of His Father ? " and " If He be a part of His Father, how can the Father's essence be entire and indivisible ? "

33. These are all disgraceful sophistries of vile heretics, and indeed, although we have already shown their worthlessness, a fair explanation of terms, and a right apprehension of the things alluded to, will be more than enough to show the hollowness of their opinions. Are not the principles of reason co-existent with the mind, and do they not flow from its nature ? Are they not both conceived to be in being at the same moment with one another ? Do we not see that brightness comes from the sun, and belongs to its essence and substance ? And yet that substance is not divided or impaired, and the brightness is not prejudicial either to the sun that furnishes the light, or to the light itself that flows from the sun. We understand, in a similar fashion, that the Son of God is of one substance with His Father, and yet that Father's substance remains entire and undiminished ; that the Father's express Image or Character has co-existed from everlasting with His Person, and loses nothing of that exactness of similitude, in consequence of which he that has seen the one may be truly and properly said to have seen the other. And, indeed, the attributes of the Divine substance can be seen in those miraculous operations of the great Image and Character. And this is what we are taught by our Lord Himself, when He says, " The

Father that dwelleth in Me, He doeth the works that I do," and
" I and the Father are one," and " I am in the Father, and the
Father in Me" (S. John xiv. 10; x. 30).   Therefore let the upholders of this absurd and abominable heresy first attempt to
disjoin those things which nature has made inseparable by the
instances before us.   Let them tell us, at what time did the sun
exist without brightness?   Or, will they dispute whether brightness, after all, has the nature of light in it? and whether it could
not shine by itself without any union with that luminous body
which sheds it forth?   Let them undertake not only to abstract
in imagination, but to extract in reality, form or figure, brightness,
motion, or strength from the substances in which they adhere.
But if this is too hard a task for them, and if this is such an attempt
which they are forced to shrink from, can anything equal their
insolence and rashness in thus pretending to fathom and comprehend the nature of a being immensely and infinitely superior
to their own, and to the essence of all other creatures whatsoever?
Does their boasted philosophy consist at last in reconciling contradictions, and practising impossibilities?

34. If created and material beings result from one another
without any diminution of those essences whence they derive
theirs ; if offsprings are found which are not parts of the substances from which they are produced ; then our opponents must
be mad in seeking to ascribe this to the incorporeal essence of
God Himself, making out that He has parts and passions, and
trying to reconcile divisible with immutable and impassible.
This is all in order to perplex the understandings, and to shipwreck the faith of their illiterate and simple hearers.   Whereas,
who hears of a son, but immediately thinks of that which is
proper to the father's substance?   Is it not reasonable to suppose
that even Catechumens are no sooner told that God has a Son,
and that He made all things by His proper Word, that they
understand the same things that we mean by those expressions?
When first this noxious heresy of Arianism manifested itself,
were not all men thunderstruck at it, as some frightful novelty?
Did not everyone consider it to be a new gospel and seed which
had never been sown before in the field of God's Church?   For
it had always been taught till then, that God has truly and
properly a Son and a Word, who is His Wisdom and Power, the
Brightness of His Glory, and the express Image of His Person,
and, in consequence, that the Son is from everlasting of the
substance of His Father, like and equal unto Him, and absolutely unmade and uncreated.   It was an enemy that took his

opportunity of sowing this fatal Arian seed while the husband-men slept. The soil was only of late sown with such tares of doctrine as the Son of God's existing in time, and the impossibility of the contrary. And as soon as these wicked men had spread abroad these corruptions, how diligent and active did they become, like so many thieves and robbers, in stealing away the good and wholesome doctrines which before prevailed? How shamelessly and openly did they show forth their hateful opinions, and venture to say such things as these, "How can it be that the Son should have existed as long as the Father? It would be a great marvel amongst men if a father should have a son as old as himself, for there is always a long space of time between their births. The father is often thirty years old before he has a son, and it is certain every man must be begotten before he has his being." And, again, they are fond of whispering, "How can God's Word be His Son, or the express Image or Representation of His Person? for the words of men are composed of so many sounds or syllables, and they only last for a moment, being altered at the will of the speaker, and then they vanish away and cease to be."

35. Thus, forgetting all the difficulties with which they were beset before, they are constrained once more to bind themselves round with the cords of impiety. But the truth entirely confounds them. Let them think and speak what they please about the sons and words of men; but when the topic is the great Creator of all, let them no longer entertain mere human ideas, but rather those which are far above human nature. The nature of the offspring cannot but be the same as that of the parent. Now, just as a father among men was himself begotten in time, and has a temporary duration, so he begets a son in time, whose existence is as successive as his father's. And as the word or speech of a man is unsubstantial, so it is transitory and dies away. But "God is not as man" (Judith viii. 16), as the Scripture testifies; "He is what He is" (Exod. iii. 14), that is to say, He is the ever-existing One; and, therefore, equally so, His Word is so too, and was from everlasting in the essence of His Father, as brightness is incorporate in light. And man's word is composed of syllables, and there is no principle in it of life and action. It only just interprets the thoughts of the speaker, and then immediately disappears, and it is as though it had never been uttered. The fruit of a man's lips is not as the fruit of his body. It has no living principle in it, nor any organic faculty. It resembles the nature of him that utters it in

nothing so much as in its fleeting character and end. But the Word of God is not merely an echo, so to speak. It is not an empty resonance, or a pronounciation of sounds or syllables. It is not an audible promulgation of God's decrees. It is, on the contrary, the substantial Offspring and Fruit of His very Being, and results from that as perfect and complete a subsistence, as light is produced from a luminous body. And thus it is that the Person of God the Son exhibits and represents the Person of the Father in all the embodiments of infinite perfection. Thus, also, it is that "the Word was God" (S. John i. 1), not accidentally, or as an effect or external cause, but His Word substantially and essentially. And man's words are of no avail for operation; and so our hands, not our words, perform the work of life, for they are effectual for this, whilst our words are not. But, again, the Apostle informs us that "the Word of God is quick and powerful, and sharper than any two-edged sword, piercing even to the dividing asunder of soul and spirit, and of the joints and marrow, and is a discerner of the thoughts and intents of the heart. Neither is there any creature that is not manifest in His sight; but all things are naked and opened unto the eyes of Him with whom we have to do" (Heb. iv. 12, 13). He is, then, the Creator and Maker of all, even that Almighty Being without whom nothing ever was or can be made.

36. And now, if anyone should be tempted to enquire, why it is, or how it can be, that God's Word bears no manner of resemblance in its nature to ours? what we have observed before is a full and effectual reply, namely, that there is no affinity between the Divine nature and ours. And if we should be called upon to determine the method by which this substantial Word, this eternal Son, this Infinite Brightness of His Father's glory, has His Personality communicated to Him from the essence of the Father, my answer is, that he who demands replies to such questions must be treated as out of his mind. A man must be mad to desire an explanation of such a deep mystery as this, if he will not be satisfied until we teach him to comprehend what is peculiar to the Divine nature, and what only is and can be known to the Father and the Son. Such an enquirer might just as well want to know, where God is? and how God exists? and what the Father's nature is like? There is as much gross infidelity and barbarism in proposing such rash and profane questions about the Eternal Generation and nature of His Son, as to seek to find out the attributes and perfections of the Father. It is as much the height of folly and as full of contempt of God, to make an

estimate of His Son's nature, as of His own, from ours. When our minds are wearied with such problems as these, we must at last come to Holy Scripture. Here we must rest, and believe things exactly according to the obvious sense revealed there. If any doubts or difficulty arise, the safe course to take, is not to question or reject the general truth of the doctrine according to what seems the exact meaning of the words before us, although we may suspend our judgment as to any particular perplexities. This is far better than at once to throw aside, and to stand out against, revelation, because it has happened that some of our conceptions of it have not been altogether clear. A suspense or hesitation is pardonable enough, because we may be so far inquisitive, consistently with a resignation of understanding and the obedience of faith. But when anyone is led by his difficulties to form for himself doctrines which God disapproves of, and when He makes the most of them in defiance of Him, and when He misrepresents the Deity out of His own oracles, this is an unpardonable abuse of God's loving-kindness. For the Scriptures can often solve our difficulties and thereby afford us comfort, when we understand rightly what is written, and can make a good and satisfactory use of the sense and application of the figurative language of "the Son," "the Word," and the like. For instance, the term "Word" so far represents something to us in God, that we conceive it to result from the essential properties of His nature, just as speech is derived from ours. We do not think God's Word is any more an external thing in Him, than that our words are so many mechanical productions in us. Although, at the same time, we know this cannot resemble the speech of a man, for this were to suppose that the Divine nature was just the same as ours. Moreover, men's words and discourses are continually being uttered, and are always rapidly passing away. They quickly follow one another, and swiftly disappear altogether. This is so, because their authors are human beings, and as one generation succeeds another, so their devices and thoughts are born and die. As fast as the mind alters its ideas, the organs of speech keep pace with it in an orderly circulation of words, which our tongues are perpetually giving utterance to. But the speech of man is interrupted at any moment, and is cut short when he perishes. But there is nothing of all this in the Word of the Father. This Word is perfect and entire in the Unity, Immutability, and Permanency of its nature, for "The Word of the Lord endureth for ever in heaven" (Ps. cxix. 89). There is no former nor latter, no before or after, in this Word, but He existed the same always. For as there can be only one God, so there cannot be more than one express Image, one Word, or one Wisdom.

37. Is it not, then, a matter of great astonishment, that they who profess to believe in only one God, should so wickedly invent such novelties, and say that there are so many express Images, Words, and Wisdoms of this one God? They say that there is a Word existing in the Father's nature by which He created another who is His Son, called also His Word, but this only metaphorically, as He is called the Vine, the Way, the Door, and the Tree of Life. They say that He is called Wisdom also only in name and title, affirming that the Father has another unbegotten Wisdom, inherent in His nature, which always existed with Him, and by which, as He made His Son, so He was pleased to call that other Son His Wisdom too, as partaking of a share of His nature. This our adversaries have not only asserted with their lips, but Arius has said in his " Thalia," and the sophist Asterius has written what we have stated above, as follows :—" It is observable," he says, " that when the Apostle calls Christ ' God's Power and Wisdom' (1 Cor. i. 24) he omits the article, which is as much as to say, that He is not the true Power of God nor the true Wisdom of God. God, moreover, has His physical and inherent Power besides, an Only-begotten one, which always co-existed with Him ; that productive one by which He created Christ, and all the other parts of the universe. And this is the Wisdom meant by S. Paul in that passage of his Epistle to the Romans, ' For the invisible things of Him from the creation of the world are clearly seen, being understood by the things that are made, even His eternal Power and Godhead' (Rom. i. 20). For as everyone will readily grant, that the Divinity there mentioned is properly that of the Father ; so by the ' Eternal Power and Godhead' must be understood the Father Himself, and not His Only-begotten Son. That was another Power, another Wisdom of God, which manifested itself in the person and actions of Christ." And a little after, the same Asterius says, " That eternal Power and Wisdom of God, which truth assures us must have been without beginning and unbegotten, the same must surely be one. But then besides this, there is a numerous collection of Wisdoms, individually distinct from one another, and created by this ungenerated Wisdom. Of these the chief and Only-begotten is Christ, who in company with the rest equally depend upon the arbitrary pleasure of God. But He and they are very appropriately named the

" Powers " of God, as being created by Him, serving His purposes and ministering to Him. Thus the locust, appointed and sent by God to execute His vengeance upon His rebellious people, is called by the Prophet, not only " the Power," but " the great Power" of God (Joel ii. 25). And the Psalmist calls upon God's " Powers " as well as His Angels to praise and worship Him."

38. Now, are not the Arians to be rightly detested by all men for reciting these horrible blasphemies? If, as they hold, the Son be not begotten of the Father, and of the same nature with Him, but is only his nominal Word or Reason, as being an instance or effect of God's essential Word or Reason; if He is only a nominal Wisdom, as being an instance and instrument of that other inherent Wisdom ; if He is only a Power, as being a production of, and subservient to, God's natural Power ; if He is only a Son, as being one of those works which God has called Sons ; who knows whether He is any other than a mere intellectual operation of God in the production and preservation of God's creatures? What, then, will they make of Him at last ? What, indeed, if there can be nothing but a mere empty name and abstraction in all these characters? What if all His offices and titles, and, indeed, His very being were given to Him upon our account, and that is all? Is not this truly some awful imagination of the devil, or, worse still, if these men are not unwilling that they should exist in fact and reality themselves, but think that the Son of God exists in name only? Is it not a terrible thing to say, that, notwithstanding God's Wisdom existed with Him from eternity, yet Christ is not His Wisdom, much less His only-begotten Wisdom ; but only one amongst many Powers and Wisdoms, all created and made, although, indeed, the foremost of them ; and that the locust and the cankerworm are, in as true and proper a sense, the Power of God as our Lord Himself? As often as they hear us asserting that the Father and the Son co-exist from everlasting, they tax us with imposing upon their understanding, and ask us, whether there can be two self-existent and unmade principles? And yet they can perceive no absurdity when they themselves affirm that God has an unmade Wisdom which co-existed with Him from eternity. Moreover, what folly is there in that other idea of theirs, that this unmade Wisdom is indeed the Father Himself, and yet co-existent with the Father ; whereas no one can possibly understand how the same thing can be said to co-exist with itself. We read in the Gospel that our Saviour was with His disciples. Now it would be a curious

comment if we should say, that when He was with His disciples the meaning was, He was all alone. One thing cannot exist along with another, unless there are two things. Or, are our adversaries disposed to make a compound being of the Divine nature, and to annex this perfection of Wisdom to it, as a sort of appendage, but yet created, unmade, and that which formed the universe? It is not unlikely that they will do this rather than that the Son shall have the honour of being supposed to create it; for they had rather do anything than justice to the Creator and Saviour of the world.

39. What Scripture or tradition ever told them that God has another Word and Wisdom besides His Eternal Son, that they should manufacture such a doctrine? Indeed it is written, "Is not My Word like as a fire? saith the Lord; and like a hammer that breaketh the rock in pieces"? (Jer. xxiii. 29). And in the Proverbs we read, "I will make known My words unto you" (Prov. i. 23). But these words are God's precepts and commandments, delivered to His saints through His essential and only-begotten Word. Of these the Psalmist says, "I have refrained my feet from every evil way, that I may keep Thy word" (Ps. cxix. 101). That such words as these are not our Lord Himself, appears not only from what He says of them, but because He says in His own person, "The words that I speak unto you" (S. John vi. 63). These words are not so many Sons of God, not so many creating Words, nor express Images of the Father, nor made men for our sakes; nor will all of them together constitute such a Word as that substantial and Only-begotten One, whom S. John tells us was "made flesh," and "all things were made by Him" (S. John i. 14, 3). Therefore of our Lord Jesus Christ, whose unity with the Father in substance and nature the Holy Scripture so plainly declares and asserts, the Father Himself has expressly informed us that He is the only-begotten Son and Word; and as holy men have learned this from Him, so they have taught it to us. And, indeed, the works of creation, which God wrought by the Son, is of itself a clear proof of this. For all things, visible and invisible, were created by the Son, and "without Him was not anything made that was made" (S. John i. 3). But concerning anyone else these writers have not a thought; there is no mention of any other Words, or Wisdoms, nor of anything created or done by any other Sons. These were all invented and imagined in the wicked and base hearts of these enemies of Christ. And they, too, would not have thus twisted the common meaning of words and the sense of things; they would have contented

themselves with an individual Word and an Unity of Wisdom in God, but that they were resolved to deny this one Word and Wisdom, and not be out-done in apostacy by the Manichæans. For they, too, turn the works of creation and the methods of Divine Providence into an argument against the attributes of the Creator, and have substituted to themselves another god in His place, about whom, or any work or operation of his, Holy Scripture is silent.

40. Well then, if Holy Scripture gives not the least intimation of any other Wisdom besides the Son, and if nothing of the kind has ever been the doctrine of the Church ; and if the Fathers of the Church have, all of them, confessed by word of mouth, and written down as well, that the Wisdom of the Father is an uncreated Being, consubstantial and co-existent with Him and the Creator of the world ; then it follows that this Wisdom must be the very Son of God, who, even by the concession of our adversaries, co-existed with Him from everlasting. For that this Wisdom of God is the Creator of the world is asserted plainly in those words of the Psalmist, " In Wisdom hast Thou made them all " (Ps. civ. 24). And, indeed, Asterius himself, as if forgetting what he wrote before, in his subsequent writings, where his dispute is with the Gentiles, is carried away, insensibly as it were, like Caiaphas, by some over-ruling impulse, into an acknowledgment of the truth, that God has not many Wisdoms, as he told us before, but that He has only one Wisdom, without a word of the caterpillar. He says, " There is but one Word of God, although there are many creatures endowed with intellectual faculties. And although there is a wisdom and a goodness which many of God's creatures share in common, yet the Wisdom of God Himself is but one in substance and nature. And soon afterwards he says again, " Who are these that seem worthy in the eyes of the Gentiles to be called the sons of God ? For no one will presume to say that these sons can be so many Words of God. No one will be so foolish as to suppose that God has several Wisdoms. For nothing can be more absurd than to distribute the nature of the Word amongst a multitude of sons, or to call them so many Divine Wisdoms ; because, as we have shown, no more than one Word and one Wisdom can belong to the nature of God." Such plain and express contradictions as these are as to the opinions of Asterius quoted before, make it no longer surprising that the Arians should battle with the truth. We may well expect no favour from them when they fall out in this manner amongst themselves, and disagree with each other.

At one time they say God has many Wisdoms; at another they maintain but one. At one time they place on the same level God's Wisdom and the caterpillar; at another they say the Father's Wisdom is of His essence and nature, and always existed with Him. Sometimes they say it is impossible that there should be any more than one unbegotten being, even God the Father; at other times His Wisdom and Power are confessed to be unbegotten too. And as for us, we must not be allowed to affirm constantly that the Word of God is from everlasting. But they seem to imagine that they may enjoy the privilege of contradicting themselves, and may say, if they like, that God's Wisdom is an uncreated being, and that it existed with Him from eternity. Such a curious giddiness has seized their understandings, that they deny the true Wisdom of God, and have invented another one, first found out by themselves; even as the Manichæans did, who make to themselves another Divinity, after denying the existence of the true and only God.

41. But in opposition to the Manichæans and all other heretics, we affirm and teach that our Lord has but one Father, who creates and governs all things by the agency of His substantial Word. Against these Arians especially we assert the Unity of the Word of God, and His consubstantiality with the Father. This is the doctrine we must abide by, seeing that we are taught it by our Lord Himself. If the Son were not what we affirm Him to be, how is He thus God's agent in creation? and why does the Father reveal Himself to whom He will in the person of the Son? and how does the Son come to be capable of illuminating and sanctifying? Why, once more, is the Son joined with the Father in the form of Baptism? Surely they will not say that the Father alone was unqualified for these things, for this would be altogether too shocking. And yet, if no more than the Father was necessary, why was the Son given an equal share with the Father in the work of creation? How comes He to act together with Him in the work of our regeneration? And what communion or fellowship can a mere creature have with its Creator? We are initiated into the Church in the name and act of God. How then comes this form of initiation to be in the name of a creature too? or, at least, why is it in the name of one Creator, and of one creature, as the Arians say? If a creature may be the object of our faith and worship, why may not more creatures than one be so? If the purpose of this institution be a close fellowship with the Divine nature, how comes a finite creature to be concerned in that? or is He framed in the form in order that

we should be united to Him, and incorporated into a mystical fellowship with Him, although He is a creature? If this is so, then there was no occasion for God's creating Him, because He could have made us His sons, and as much His sons as the Word Himself, without Him. And, therefore, the name of the Son might just as well be left out of the form of Baptism, if He is only such a Son as our adversaries would make of Him. The general properties of all rational creatures are the same. And if the Son be no more than one of these, He must be so far from enjoying that prerogative of shedding abroad Divine influence and grace on others, because He, being a creature, will need grace as well as they. We have said enough before about the Son's Creatorship. And now as the current of our discourse has brought us to the topic of Holy Baptism, it would not be right if I did not set this matter in a true light, and allege the reason which I firmly believe to be the true one, why the Son is joined with the Father in that sacramental form. It is not because the Father Himself is not all-sufficient, nor is it mentioned just casually and, as it were, accidentally, but because the Word of God is His essential and inherent Wisdom, and that eternal Brightness which belongs to His nature, and was of His very substance from eternity. Therefore it is impossible if the Father bestows grace, that He should not give it in and through the Son ; for the Son is in the Father, just as the brightness is in the light. Nor was it out of necessity, but simply from the principle of Fatherhood in His nature, that " God by Wisdom founded the earth " (Prov. iii. 19), that He made all things by that Word, and sanctifies the laver of regeneration in the name of that Son, which is of His very substance. For where the Father is, there is also the Son ; as there cannot but be brightness where there is light. We learn from our Saviour that whatever the Father does, He does by the Son. He says, " The Son can do nothing of Himself, but what He seeth the Father do ; for what things soever He doeth, these also doeth the Son likewise " (S. John v. 19). It follows from this, when anyone is baptised, that whom the Father baptises, the same also the Son baptises ; and whom the Son baptises, he is sanctified by the Holy Spirit. And, again, just as when the sun shines we can truly say that its brightness illuminates the things it rests upon, for the light is one and indivisible, and it cannot be separated into parts ; so, likewise, the presence or act of the Father implies and includes the presence and co-operation of the Son. And, therefore, it is clear that the form of Baptism must contain the name of the Son as well as that of the Father, for where one is named the other must be named too.

42. Accordingly, when He made His promise to the sacred writers, He joins Himself with the Father, " I and My Father will come unto him, and make our abode with him " (S. John xiv. 23) ; and again, " That they all may be one ; as Thou, Father, art in Me, and I in Thee, that they also may be one in us " (S. John xvii. 21). And as S. Paul writes in every Epistle, the grace imparted is as much ascribed to the Son as to the Father, and is pronounced of both alike, " Grace to you, and peace from God our Father, and the Lord Jesus Christ " (Rom. i. 7 ; 1 Cor. i. 3). Light and brightness are never to be disunited, and the brightness must be looked upon together with its own light. And thus the Jews and Arians by denying the Son forsake and oppose the Father. When the Jews abandoned the " Fountain of Wisdom " (Bar. iii. 12), as Baruch reproaches them, they shunned and fled from the true Wisdom which flows from that Fountain, even our Lord Jesus Christ, and would have Cæsar to be their king (S. John xix. 15) instead of that Christ, who is " the Power of God and the Wisdom of God " (1 Cor. i. 24). And what was the punishment which God inflicted upon them for their infidelity and rebellion? Their city as well as their reasoning came to nought. Besides, it is much to be doubted, whether the Baptism administered by our adversaries is valid. There are, indeed, the names of the Father and the Son in it; but this is such a Father, as according to them is really no Father, as having no Son of His substance who is equal to Him in nature ; and the Son they mean is really no Son, but only a mere creature made out of nothing. Can it be supposed that the Blessed Trinity should ratify such a Baptism as this, in which the Holy Name is not invoked, but mocked? Can God's blessing follow a Baptism of this kind ? For let the Arians say the words as they please, they do not baptise in the Name of the Father and of the Son, but in the name of the Creator and one of His creatures. And, therefore, although they retain the words of the Scripture form, yet their Baptism has, in truth, no more of Christ's ordinance and institution in it, than there is of the nature of a creature in the Divinity of God the Son. Not every one that says " Lord, Lord," administers an effectual Baptism. The words will not do, where there is a professed denial of the faith. On this account, therefore, our Saviour did not simply issue a command to baptise, but first says " Teach," and then " Baptise into the Name of the Father, and of the Son, and of the Holy Ghost " (S. Matt.

xxviii. 19). The world was to be duly instructed about the object of their faith, and then they were to be baptised in the Name of the Holy Trinity, in whom they steadfastly believed.

43. And this is the case with regard to many other heresies too, which use the words of the form only, quite contrary to the proper sense of them. Such baptisms as these, wanting that which is essential, the substance of that faith or belief, which the form itself requires, are unprofitable and useless ; and instead of benefitting those who use them, they rather render them more than they were before, children of wrath. So the heathen also, although they often mention the name of God, still are very far from rendering worship and service to the Almighty, because they deny the real and true God, even the Father of our Lord Jesus Christ. So the Manichæans, the Phrygians, and the disciples of Paul of Samosata, are destitute of the true faith, although they keep to the right forms of it. The Arians, likewise, follow in their footsteps, and, although they pronounce the words of Scripture, and use the right forms, yet those poor creatures who are baptised by them are shamefully deceived. For no other heretics have so egregiously misapplied those words in a sense so derogatory to the honour of God ; and they seek, moreover, to excuse themselves by entire recklessness of speech. For other heretics have indeed mutilated the sense of Holy Scripture in various ways, either erring concerning the Body of the Lord, denying that He assumed our flesh of the substance of the Blessed Virgin ; or, as if He was really and substantially a man, affirming Him to be no more than a phantom, and saying that He showed Himself to His disciples only as the image of one friend presents itself to the imagination of another in a dream. But the Arians seem openly to defy the Majesty of God Himself, for hearing in Holy Scripture that God has declared His Son to be Brightness of His Glory, and the express Image of His Person, they dare to utter the blasphemy, that this Son is only a creature. As soon as you come into contact with the Arians, you are told " The Son was not before He was created," and they carry about with them base expressions of this kind, and are always ready to scatter them about like deadly poison wherever they go. Then, whereas their doctrine is hateful to all men, forthwith they are obliged to support and maintain their heresy with human authority, lest it should give way altogether ; in order that simple people, who do not understand their wretched arguments, may be overcome by this parade, and may be frightened into believing it. How deplorable and how piti-

able is the case of those miserable beings who are cheated by them! It is enough to make one weep, to think that they have made so foolish an exchange, as to purchase the satisfaction of this life at no less a price than the comfort of a clear conscience now, and the hope of future glory.   For what can be the benefit of such a pretended baptism, administered in the name of a person who does not exist?   And if He does exist, what advantage do they expect to gain from one who is, after all, a mere creature like themselves?   It is necessary for the efficacy of the Sacrament, that we believe the Son to be what He really is, the proper Son of the substance of His Father, in the essence of His Father, as the Father is also in Him.   But these wretched dupes believe in no such person, but in a phantom of their own inventing, in a being unallied to the Father in essence, and unlike Him in properties and perfections.   And thus their wicked guides basely lead them astray, and circumvent them in this all-important matter, and leave them in the same unregenerate state in which they found them.   And how completely ruined will these men perceive themselves when death has finally cut them off from their enjoyment of the pleasures of this life!   What will they do when they see the Lord, whom they have denied, sitting enthroned at the Right Hand of His Father, and judging the quick and dead?   Will they call for aid and protection to those by whom they were so vilely betrayed?   They will see the authors of their woes also at the judgment-seat, and too late bewailing their deeds of iniquity and impiety.

44. We have said so much by way of preface to our explanation of the passage in the Book of Proverbs—and this seemed very necessary in order to remove the absurd notions which our adversaries had invented—that we might give proof and evidence of our Lord's Divinity as might anticipate the false construction they put upon the text in question; which admits, moreover, of very good sense and meaning.   Now, it is written, "The Lord created Me, the beginning of His ways, for His works" (Prov. viii. 22).   Since, however, these words are found in the Book of Proverbs, we must consider them as proverbial sayings, that is to say, we must not take them in a strict and literal sense; nor can we safely determine the meaning of them before we have enquired and considered who is the person said to be created in them.   Our Lord Himself remarks that proverbs are full of inner meanings, and must not be understood in the most obvious sense, saying in the Gospel according to S. John, "These things have I spoken unto you in proverbs; but the time cometh, when I shall

no more speak unto you in proverbs, but I shall show you plainly"
(S. John xvi. 25). Therefore if we would not run the risk of
mistaking and perverting a part of God's revelations, we must not
take that sense of the words which appears at the first glance
—that construction which lies upon the surface—but we must
proceed with deliberation and examine a little deeper. If, then,
the words "created me" are here affirmed of any Angel, or any
other of God's created works, there is no reason why they should
not be taken in their literal sense. But if they refer to the
Wisdom of God, by whom God gave all His creatures their
being; if this Wisdom is here speaking of Himself; then nothing can be more absurd than to suppose He used the word
"created" in its proper sense, which would have made it a contradiction to His eternal generation. No one will dare to say
that He had forgotten He was the Creator and Maker of all
things, or that He was so ignorant of the difference between the
Creator and the creatures that He confounded one with the
other, and reckoned Himself a part of what His own power had
formed. Consequently, the meaning of the passage must lie
deeper, and we ought to interpret it according to that method
which is usual in proverbial and prophetical writings. At a
little distance from this passage there is another figurative expression which explains and illustrates the truth of this. "Wisdom,"
we read, "hath builded her house" (Prov. ix. 1). And what is
Wisdom's House but that human Body, which our Saviour
assumed at His Incarnation? What is this but that flesh of
which S. John rightly says the "Word was made"? This Wisdom of God did not dictate to Solomon any such expression as
this, "I am a creature." There is, on the contrary, a particular
caution observable in the text. For it is written, "The Lord
hath created Me, the beginning of His ways, for His works," not
simply, "created Him that He might have existence," nor
"because He had a creature's beginning and generation."

45. That which is here said to be created is only our Lord's
humanity, and the functions and offices peculiar to it, and not
His Divine nature. He does not say of Himself, "I, the Person
now speaking by Solomon, am a creature, or was made out of
nothing; but My Father created Me, who am His proper Son
and His fellow-worker." For the creatures, having a created
substance, are being made by God, and this is what creation
means. But, then, the mere term "He created" does not
necessarily apply to the nature or existence of a thing, but only
to its condition or circumstances. And thus an uncreated nature

may be created something else; as by the accession of a character or office which it had not before, or by its personal union with a created nature. This distinction Holy Scripture fully recognises, saying concerning the creatures, "The earth is full of Thy creation" (Ps. civ. 24, Sept.), and "The whole creation groaneth and travaileth in pain together" (Rom. viii. 22). Again, in the Book of Revelation, we read, "And the third part of the creatures which were in the sea, and had life, died" (Rev. viii. 9). Again, S. Paul says, "Every creature of God is good, and nothing to be refused, if it be received with thanksgiving" (1 Tim. iv. 4); and in the Book of Wisdom it is written, "Thou hast ordained man through Thy Wisdom, that he should have dominion over the creatures which Thou hast made" (Wisd. ix. 2). Of these creatures also our Lord is speaking, where He says, "From the beginning of the creation God made them male and female" (S. Mark x. 6). Moses, too, speaks in a similar fashion in his song, where he says, "Ask now of the days that are past, which were before thee, since the day that God created man upon the earth, and ask from the one side of the heaven unto the other" (Deut. iv. 32). And S. Paul, in his Epistle to the Colossians, says, "Who is the Image of the invisible God, the First-born of every creature : for by Him were all things created, that are in heaven, and that are in earth, visible and invisible, whether they be Thrones, or Dominions, or Principalities, or Powers ; all things were created by Him and for Him ; and He is before all things" (Col. i. 15, 16).

46. Many more expressions of this kind might be produced from Holy Scripture, but these passages may suffice to remind us that creation, in the proper sense of the word, is applied by Scripture only to created substance. But then it is as plain that elsewhere it does not signify the production of a substance out of nothing. For instance, David says in the Psalm, "This shall be written for the generation to come ; and the people which shall be created shall praise the Lord" (Ps. cii. 18); and again, "Create in me a clean heart, O God" (Ps. li. 10). Likewise, S. Paul, in the Epistle to the Ephesians, writes, "Having abolished the law of commandments contained in ordinances, for to create in Himself of twain one new man" (Eph. ii. 15) ; and again, "That ye put on the new man, which after God is created in righteousness and true holiness" (Eph. iv. 24). The people of whom the Psalmist spoke were not a race of men created out of nothing, and the heart which he prays God to create in him was not another besides that which he possessed at the

time. What was meant in these places is a spiritual regeneration, and a renewal of the state of grace. And when S. Paul speaks of a new man being created, and of one new man being created of two, this creation here is not of any new substance; it is not of the person made by God out of nothing, but the new man is only the new life, or that state which is suitable to a regenerate person. The two men, likewise, out of whom one new one is created, are the people of the Jews and the people of the Gentiles, who are renewed in Christ. And thus, in that passage in the Book of Jeremiah, "The Lord hath created a new salvation for a plantation, in which salvation men shall walk hither and thither" (Jer. xxxi. 22, Sept.) ; the creation is not of any new substance of a creature, but it is a prophecy of the renewal of salvation among men, which we obtain in Christ Jesus. And thus it evidently appears that it is one thing for a substance to be said to be created out of nothing, and another for a person, already created as regards his substance, to be said to be created or made something as regards his condition or circumstances. If our adversaries know of any text of Scripture where our Lord is directly called a creature, let them produce it and resolutely insist upon it. But if they can find out no such text; if only what He says about Himself in the Book of Proverbs, "The Lord hath created Me; " let them admit, to their confusion, the force of our distinction between created substance and created condition ; and also let them consider our observation, that proverbial sayings must be interpreted according to the method of proverbs. Let them blush and confess that the creation here is not to be understood of our Lord's eternal nature, but only of His human nature, whose substance only could be created. Indeed, is it not evidently most inconsistent in you, when both David and S. Paul say "He created," not to understand any creation or production of a new substance, but only a renewal ? yet when the Lord says "He created," to say that He uses the word in an entirely different sense, and that He means His whole substance was made out of nothing, as well as that of all other creatures. Again, when Scripture says, "Wisdom hath builded her house, she hath hewn out her seven pillars" (Prov. ix. 1), they own that "house" must be understood allegorically ; but they take the words "He created" as it stands, and say it must be literally understood, and so they draw it into an argument for their doctrine of the Son being a created being. It seems, then, that neither His being the Creator and Framer of all has any weight with you, nor have you feared His being the proper and the Only-begotten Son of God ; but you have set yourselves in array against Him, and struggle hard to establish in the world as mean and as unworthy notions of Him as you can, and use Him more despitefully than you would treat even an ordinary man.

47. The true interpretation of the passage proves clearly enough that it is a gross misapplication of it to call the Lord a creature. Our Lord knew Himself to be what He calls Himself frequently, the Wisdom of God, His Father's Only-begotten and uncreated Son, and different from all created beings; and so He says in kindness to man, "The Lord hath created Me, the beginning of His ways," as much as to say that His Father had prepared for Him a body, and had made Him a man, in order that He might be the author of our salvation. We might as well imagine that S. John, when he tells us "the Word was made flesh," means a conversion of the Godhead into flesh, and that He did not assume our nature at His conception, but was always man and nothing else from everlasting. We might as well suppose that S. Paul's words, where he tells us that " Christ is made a curse for us" (Gal. iii. 13), and where he says, " He hath made Him to be sin for us, who knew no sin" (2 Cor. v. 21), mean that Christ's very nature and person has become cursed and sinful, instead of signifying that He has taken upon Himself the malediction due to us, as the Apostle has said, " He has redeemed us from the curse of the Law" (Gal. iii. 13); or in Isaiah's words, " He has borne our griefs and carried our sorrows" (Isa. liii. 4); or as S. Peter has written, " He bare our sins in His own body on the tree" (1 S. Peter ii. 24). So, if it is said in the Book of Proverbs, " He created," this does not imply that the whole nature and substance of Christ is created, but that God created Christ's human nature and made Him man, that He might re-establish us in the favour of God and in the privileges of His grace, and make us co-heirs with Himself. What, then, has deceived you, madmen that you are, first to make a creature of your Creator, and then so stubbornly to persist in, and so proudly to boast of, the absurdity of your imagination? The word "created" is in the Book of Proverbs, but what then? Does Solomon tell you that the Son is a creature? Does he not, in fact, call Him the contrary? For, according to that distinction we have noted to be observed in Scripture between "He created" and " creature," does he not confess and declare Him to be the Only-begotten Wisdom of the Father and the Creator of the world, and consequently the Son of His Father's nature and substance? Therefore, the Father's creating Him has no relation to His Divine substance, but only refers to His being made

the beginning or principle of God's manifold ways with His creatures; and His creation, as such, is opposed to His generation, as He is God's eternal Son. As the first, He is the beginning of God's ways; as the latter, He is the Only-begotten Son of the infinite God.

48. Now, if the Word is begotten at all, how, then, can He be a creature? It is unusual for fathers to call their children creatures, or to say they have created a son when they have begotten one. And again, if He is Only-begotten, how does He become the beginning of His ways; for of necessity if He was created a beginning of all things, He is no longer alone, because there were many other creatures made after Him. Reuben was the beginning or the first begotten of the sons of Jacob, but he was not his only-begotten son. He was, indeed, older than his brethren, but they were as properly men and sons as he was. And thus, if the Word be nothing else but such a beginning of God's ways, the first-made of His creatures, then He and His fellow-creatures are of one nature, although of different ages. The first stone that is laid in the foundation of a city is of the same character as the other parts of the city are, and all the stones being joined together make the city complete and perfect. It is just as all the members of the body are joined one to the other. The foundation comes as much under the direction of the builder, and is as much a part of his workmanship as the whole superstructure. The materials which are first made use of have no advantage on that account, and are of no more importance than those which are used last. Both are equally passive under the hand of the workman. And thus our Lord, if He is the beginning of God's ways and works, only as He is the first formed of them, cannot be God's only-begotten work, but makes only one portion of all His works. His being first-made does not make Him the only-made. Such a primogeniture would not make Him the Lord and Governor of all the other parts of the creation; but, as being a creature, He would be equally subject with His fellow-creatures to Him that created Him. Again, how is it that He should be created singly by Himself, and before all other creatures whatsoever? Why should there not be intervals also between the creations of the several kinds of the other parts of the creation; which, however much some might excel others in glory, were all created without any interval? For individual stars and the great lights were not called into being one after another, but they were all created on one day, and they all started into existence at one command.

And all the individuals of the same kind or species, beasts, birds, fishes, and plants had, as it were, but one birth. And even the whole human race may be said to have been created along with Adam, for in him were the means of the succession of the rest of mankind.

49. Moveover, from the visible creation, we clearly see that His invisible things also, "being understood by the things that are made" (Rom. i. 20), are not independent of each other; for they were not created one after the other, but they all began to exist at once. And, therefore, the Apostle, when speaking of the celestial beings, does not word himself in the singular number, saying, "Whether Angel, or Throne, or Dominion, or Principality," but he says in the plural, "Whether Angels, or Archangels, or Principalities" (*cf.* Col. i. 16). It seems that this was God's particular method which He adhered to in the creation of all the several parts of the universe. And so, if His Word had been created too, however much He might excel in glory all other creatures, still it is reasonable to conclude that He would have received His being in company with all the other Powers, and not have come before them as an exception to a general rule. For we find it to be the case with regard to these blessed ones, that they at once, all together, with no intervals of time between their creation, began to exist. They differ from each other in glory; some have their station on the right hand of the Throne, and some on the left, and some encompass it, but they one and all praise the Lord, and with one accord they render to Him their service and ministry. Therefore, if the Word be a creature, He would not be the first or the beginning of the others. But if He be indeed, as He certainly is, before them and all other creatures, if He is God's first and Only-begotten Son, then it follows that He is not the beginning of God's ways as to His substance, for what is the beginning of all is in the number of all. And if He is not such a beginning, then He is not a creature at all, and if not a creature, then His substance and nature is absolutely distinct from, and infinitely superior to, that of any created being conceivable. It must be the only and adequate Representation and Image of the only true God. And thus in Holy Scripture we never find Him ranked among the creatures; and those who dare even to think of Him as such incur David's rebuke, when he says, "Among the gods there is none like unto Thee, O Lord" (Ps. lxxxvi. 8), and "Who among the sons of God can be likened unto the Lord?" (*cf.* Ps. lxxxix. 6.) And Baruch says, "This is our God, and there shall

none other be accounted of in comparison of Him" (Bar. iii. 35). For He is the Creator, the rest are His creatures. He is God's Word and Wisdom, of His very essence and substance, and they are the things which this Word and Wisdom has made out of nothing.

50. Your assertion, therefore, that the Son is a creature is false; its only foundation is in your disordered imagination, and Solomon reproves and condemns you for having so often misinterpreted his words. He affirms that the Son is not one of God's creatures, but is His essential Offspring and Wisdom, saying, "The Lord by Wisdom hath founded the earth" (Prov. iii. 19), and "Wisdom hath builded her house" (Prov. ix. 1). And the very passage in question proves your irreligious spirit, for it is written, "The Lord created Me the beginning of His ways, for His works." If the person here said to be created existed before all things; and if He was created, not in order that He should create all other things, but "for the works," that is for the benefit and advantage of the works already existing; then one of these two things will follow, either that He succeeded Himself in being, or that His existence commenced later than those works, since at His creation He found them already in being, and this notwithstanding it was for their creation that He was created. But if this is so, how could He be said to exist before them? How were all things made by Him, and how did they consist by His power? It is plain the Arian heresy must suppose the existence of the works antecedent to that of the Son; for which works, you say, He is created and sent. But this is all falsehood and delusion. The Word of God is not a creature, but the Creator; and He says, according to the manner of proverbs, "He created Me," when He assumed our human nature. And something besides may be understood from the passage. For here He, who is the genuine and substantial Son of God, calls His Father His Lord, in regard of that dependent nature, that form of a servant, which He assumed by His Incarnation. As He is truly of the substance and essence of God, He calls God His Father, as children call their parents by this title. And, as He took upon Him the form of a servant, and by that wrought the work of our redemption, He styles His Father His Lord, which was the name due to Him from His created nature. We find in the Gospel that our Saviour Himself taught His disciples this distinction, where He says, "I thank Thee, O Father," and then, "Lord of Heaven and earth" (S. Matt. xi. 25). For He calls God His Father, but He describes Him as Lord of all

created beings ; as showing clearly from these words, that then it was He called the Father Lord, when He assumed our created nature. And the Holy Ghost has intimated the same distinction in that prayer of the Psalmist, "Give Thy strength unto Thy Child, and help the Son of Thine handmaid" (Ps. lxxxvi. 16). Here the proper and essential Son is distinguished from the improper and adopted. The one has the strength of His Father, His dominion and power ; the other, the children of the handmaid, the works of creation, stand in need of His succour and salvation.

51. If our adversaries will find fault upon the word "child," which signifies a servant, as well as a son, let them remember that Isaac is called the child of Abraham (Gen. xxi. 8), and the son of the Shunamite her child (2 Kings iv. 18). It would be surprising if our Saviour, as man, did not call His Father Lord, as we do. And this He did from love to man, that by the communication of His Divine Spirit and grace to the human nature, He was pleased to qualify us to call Him our Father who is by nature our Lord. But as we, in calling the Lord Father, do not deny our natural servitude ; for we are His works, and "it is He that hath made us and not we ourselves" (Ps. c. 2), so when the Son, on taking the servant's form, says, "The Lord hath created Me the beginning of His ways, let them not deny the eternity of His Godhead," and that "in the beginning was the Word," and "all things were made by Him," and "in Him all things were created." For the passage in the Proverbs, as I have before mentioned, does not speak of any other creation than that of His human nature, because the creation here mentioned was "for the works," that is, not a creation of His substance, but a creation of office or employment, of which God's works already in being were the object. And this creation pre-supposes the actual existence of the person in this sense created. There are two ends proposed by God in the work of creation. The one is that certain beings should exist ; and the other, that when they do exist, they should answer the end of their creation, in the discharge of those duties, which the Wisdom of God has thought fit to prescribe. And thus it is with all created beings. For Adam was created, not that he might perform certain works, but that first of all man might simply be brought into existence. The duty and obedience which God required of him was subsequent to this. And God created Noah, not because of the ark, but that first he might exist and be a man ; and after this he received the com-

mand to make the ark. The same observation holds good in all other instances of this nature. Thus the great Prophet Moses was first made a man, and some years passed before he was caused to be the governor and leader of God's people. Therefore we must understand exactly the same thing concerning our Blessed Lord. The Son is not created in order to exist, for "in the beginning was the Word." But this Eternal Word and Son was afterwards created "for the works," that is, He was created God's agent to accomplish His dispensations. For before any creature began to be, God's Eternal Son is in existence, and there was not yet any need that He should be created. But when the works were created, and when they had fallen from their original state of happiness, in which they could not be reinstated, unless the Son of God interposed on their behalf; then it was that, in His goodness and mercy He stooped to that humble condition in which He assumed our nature; and all this is very truly implied in the word "created." There is a passage in the Prophet Isaiah which signifies the same thing:—"And now, saith the Lord that formed Me from the womb to be His servant, to bring Jacob again to Him, that Israel may be gathered to Him, and I may be glorious in the eyes of the Lord, and My God shall be My strength" (Isa. xlix. 5).

52. And notice that His "being formed" in this verse does not mean His entrance into being, but it has reference to the gathering together of the tribes, which existed before He was thus formed and sent. The word "formed" here exactly answers to the word "created" in the text of the Proverbs, and the "bringing again" is parallel to the import of the words, "for God's works." Therefore it is not to be doubted, but, as the "forming" in the one place supposes the previous existence of the person formed, so the "creating" in the other alludes to the previous existence of the person created. And as the tribes of Israel, whose bringing back He was formed to accomplish, were in being before His birth or formation; so those works of God, for whose benefit He was created, were in being long before He was so created. As He was the Word and Son of God, He was "in the beginning," prior to the existence of all created beings. As He was Man, He was created many ages after the world began to be; and not till that time came, which the Wisdom of God chose as the most fitting period for the doing of that work for which our Lord assumed our nature to perform. It is just as if some son, when his father's servants had been made prisoners in consequence of the incursion of enemies,

and through their own negligence and carelessness; if, suppose, the son was sent by his father, on account of the extreme urgency of the case, to recover them out of the enemies' hands; and if the son should disguise and dress himself like one of the servants and take upon him their name as well, for fear the spoilers, when they knew who was pursuing them, should betake themselves to flight, and leave the prisoners hidden in some cave underground; if, I say, the son were then asked what was the meaning of it all, he should say that his father had thus constituted and instructed him for this work. Would any one infer from this reply that he was his father's servant, or one of his works, or that he was not his father's son, or that his words meant any more than a discovery or declaration of his affair and commission? Would it, then, have been a very extraordinary thing if any one should have asked the Son of God, clothed with human nature, and " found in fashion as a man " (Philip. ii. 8), what was the purpose of this wonderful and amazing combination; and He had answered, " The Lord has created Me the beginning of His ways, for His works," and " He has formed Me to gather together Israel?" This is the very thing of which the Holy Spirit prophesied in the Psalms, " Thou makest Him to have dominion over the works of Thy hands " (Ps. viii. 6). And thus has our Lord spoken of Himself in the words, " I am set as King by Him upon God's holy hill of Sion " (Ps. ii. 6, Sept.) And yet, when He shone in the body upon Mount Sion, His reign or His being did not then commence; but since He was God's Word and everlasting King, He condescended to come down from the throne of His glory and to pitch His tent on the holy mountain, that He might deliver both His own peculiar people and us Gentiles from the state of captivity in which we were detained by sin, and that He might bring us triumphantly home to His Father's House. And in this sense He was created and constituted " for the works," not for things which did not yet exist, but for the creatures already in being, who were in need and distress for want of His assistance and succour.

53. Those expressions, therefore, "He created," " He formed," and " He appointed," are to be understood in one and the same sense. They do not denote the beginning of His being, or that He is a creature. They have reference to that great and gracious work of our regeneration and redemption which He effected for us. Accordingly, although He thus speaks, yet He taught also that He existed before this, when He said, " Before Abraham was, I am " (S. John viii. 58), and " When He prepared the

heavens, I was there ;" and, "I was by Him, disposing and adjusting His works" (Prov. viii. 27, 30, Sept.). And just as He was in being before Abraham, and the people of Israel came after Abraham, so it is plain that our Lord existed before He was created or formed. Consequently, when He is said to be so, the existence of His nature cannot be meant, but His assumption of ours ; by His union with which He qualified Himself to bring Jacob again. His Divinity, therefore, co-existed with the Father from everlasting, and in concert with the Father He gave all creatures their being. So it is evident that whatever was created had no being till after Him, and His being said to be created implies no beginning of existence in Him, but only His undertaking that work or office, which He accomplished in our nature. It was necessary that our regeneration should be the work of an uncreated being—that is to say, of their Creator, that in His person He, being made man for our sakes, might repair our fallen nature and make us a new creature. For when He said, " He created," it is to be observed that the reason immediately follows, naming " the works," that His creation for the works might signify His becoming man in order to restore them to their original state of perfection. And, indeed, it is usual in Holy Scripture when it speaks of the Word's Incarnation, to mention the cause or occasion of it. Whereas, when either our Lord Himself or His servants are discoursing of His Divinity, their expressions are positive, and free from all manner of restriction or limitation, and without any reason being added. There is no hint of any design or purpose, for which He existed as the Brightness of His Father's glory, any more than why or to what end and purpose the Father Himself exists. Thus it is written, " In the beginning was the Word, and the Word was with God, and the Word was God" (S. John i. 1) ; but there is no reason assigned for it. But we are no sooner told that " the Word was made flesh," but the reason and purpose of this is declared in the next words, " And dwelt among us " (S. John i. 14). And again, when the Apostle says, " Who being in the form of God," he does not state the reason. But when He mentions the fact that " He took on Him the form of a Servant," He tells us for what end He did so, for " He humbled Himself, and became obedient unto death, even the death of the Cross " (Philip. ii. 6-8). It was for this purpose that the Word both became flesh and took upon Him the form of a servant.

54. Our Lord very commonly taught and discoursed in parables, and yet we never find Him doing so, when His own

Divine nature is the subject He speaks upon. Then His words are always clear and express. He says, "I am in the Father, and the Father in Me" (S. John xiv. 10); and, "I and My Father are one" (S. John x. 30); and, "He that hath seen Me hath seen the Father" (S. John xiv. 9); and, "I am the Light of the world" (S. John viii. 12); and, "I am the Truth" (S. John xiv. 6). In all these passages there is no reason assigned for His existence, and this is certainly withheld lest He should seem second to those things for which He was made. As man, the necessity is plain that those things or persons should exist before Him, because it was upon their account that He was pleased to become so. S. Paul, for instance, "separated an Apostle for the Gospel, which the Lord had promised afore by the prophets" (Rom. i. 1, 2), did not become a minister of the Gospel, until that Gospel itself was in being; and Christ as God was before S. John, who was the messenger sent before His face as man to prepare the way before Him. But there being no purpose for which our Saviour was to be the Word, save only that He is the Father's Offspring and only begotten Wisdom, no cause for His existence could be suggested, till He signified that He was about to become man. Then He plainly declares the reason why He was about to assume our nature. Human nature and mankind must have been older than He was as man; because they were the cause or occasion of His taking our nature upon Him. Thus our Lord Himself has acquainted us with the necessity and reason for His Incarnation in the following words, "I came down from Heaven, not to do mine own will, but the will of Him that sent Me. And this is the Father's will which hath sent Me, that of all which He hath given Me I should lose nothing, but should raise it up again at the last day. And this is the will of Him which sent Me, that every one which seeth the Son and believeth on Him may have everlasting life, and I will raise him up at the last day" (S. John vi. 38-40). And again, "I am come a light into the world, that whosoever believeth on Me should not abide in darkness" (S. John xii. 46). And again, "To this end was I born, and for this cause came I into the world, that I should bear witness unto the truth" (S. John xviii. 37). And S. John has written, "For this purpose the Son of God was manifested, that He might destroy the works of the devil" (1 S. John iii. 8).

55. This, then, was the reason why the Saviour came among men, to bear witness to the truth of God, to die upon the Cross for our redemption, to raise us up from the dead, and to defeat

all the machinations of the devil. Had it not been for these ends, He had never assumed our flesh; had not the resurrection of His Body been necessary for ours He had not died; and He could not have died unless He had taken upon Himself a mortal body. This is what He taught S. Paul, and what that Apostle teaches us, "Forasmuch then as the children are partakers of flesh and blood, He also Himself likewise took part of the same; that through death He might destroy Him that had the power of death, that is the devil; and deliver them who, through fear of death, were all their lifetime subject to bondage" (Heb. ii. 14, 15). And, "For since by man came death, by man came also the resurrection of the dead" (1 Cor. xv. 21). And again, "For what the Law could not do, in that it was weak through the flesh, God sending His own Son in the likeness of sinful flesh and for sin, condemned sin in the flesh; that the righteousness of the Law might be fulfilled in us, who walk not after the flesh but after the Spirit" (Rom. viii. 3, 4). And S. John says, "For God sent not His Son into the world to condemn the world, but that the world through Him might be saved" (S. John iii. 17). Our Blessed Saviour again says of Himself, "For judgment am I come into this world, that they which see not might see, and that they which see might be made blind" (S. John ix. 39). It was, then, entirely for our sake and advantage, and not at all for His own, that He came down from heaven. The purpose that brought Him here was that of destroying death, condemning sin, giving sight to the blind, and life to the dead. And if it was our interest and not His that was the occasion of His advent, then His creation, too, was for our advantage and not for His. And if the end and object of this creation is not for His interest, but wholly for ours, then it cannot mean a creation of His nature, for that would be principally for His own advantage. It must certainly, therefore, signify that creation of His office and manhood, which was entirely for ours. And this interpretation of the text is exactly the meaning of what we may learn from S. Paul's Epistle to the Ephesians, where we read these words, "Christ hath broken down the middle wall of partition between us, having abolished in His flesh the enmity, even the law of commandments contained in ordinances, for to make in Himself of twain one new man, so making peace" (Eph. ii. 14, 15). Here we find two created in His body, or human nature. If, then, He bears those two in Himself, He may be very truly said to be created. As they were united in Him, so was He in like manner in them. And, therefore, in consequence of their creation in His nature, it might very truly be said of Him that "The Lord had created Him." In consequence of our infirmities which He took upon Him, He is said to be weak and infirm ; which yet He could not be, as being himself the Power of God. And because He bare our sins and underwent the curse which was pronounced against them, He that never did sin is said to be a sin and a curse for us. Why, then, although uncreated, might He not say, "God created Me for His works," from His creating us in Himself?

56. For if, as our adversaries imagine, it is here affirmed that the substance of the Word was created, then it is plain that He was thus created for His own benefit, and not for ours. And if He was not created for our sake, the consequence will be that we are not created in Him. And if we are not created in Him, then He is not in us, but wholly without us; that is to say, He leaves our nature as He found it, and has concerned Himself no more about us than as a teacher with his scholars. And if this is all He has done for us, then the dominion of sin is still in our flesh, and was never purged out of it. And this does not at all agree with S. Paul's assertion a little before, where he says, "We are his workmanship, created in Christ Jesus" (Ephes. ii. 10). It must, therefore, be granted that we are created in Christ; and if so, it is very clear that the creation in the text must be interpreted, not of His being a creature, but of our being created in Him. The Creator here represents Himself a creature, with reference to our spiritual creation in His person. The verse does not signify that the Word in whom we are created was Himself created. It only asserts that we, who are His workmanship, are created in Him. And as, since the Father is from everlasting, so also is His Word, as He Himself assures us, saying, "I was daily His delight, rejoicing always before Him" (Prov. viii. 30) ; and, "I am in the Father, and the Father in Me" (S. John xiv. 10). In like manner, when He has occasion to mention His being made man, He speaks as one of us who are created in Him would have done, "The Lord created Me." This means that by His Incarnation sin might be destroyed in our flesh, and the whole of our nature might be illuminated and exalted. For what ought He, according to the Arians, to say, when He was made man? Should He say, "In the beginning I was man"? This expression would not have answered His meaning, neither would it have been true. And as it was not at all fitting that He should say this, so it is natural and proper in the

case of man to say " He created," and " He made Him." It is for this reason that the words " He created " are added ; it was for the benefit of His works. If we attend to that, then the whole passage can very easily be explained. Thus here, when He says. " He created," He informs us what sort of creation is meant. On the other hand, there is no cause or reason assigned when His Eternal Generation is the subject of His discourse a little before. Then what He tells us is that " Before the hills He was brought forth" (Prov. viii. 25), as it is said elsewhere, " In the beginning was the Word" (S. John i. 1). It is not said that His Father begat Him before the creation " for the works," or that the Word was in the beginning God " for the works." For, if they had never been created, He had still been the Word of God, and the Word had still been God. Nor had this Word of God been made man, if man could have been saved without it. Therefore it is quite certain that the Son of God is not a creature. Had He been a creature, He had not said, " He begets Me," for whatever is made or created has nothing in it of the nature and substance of the maker. It is only an external being formed by His power and wrought with His hands. But things begotten are derived from the very nature and substance of their fathers. And, therefore, whatever is or can be created is one thing ; but the Word of God, His Only-begotten Son, is another.

57. In the history of the creation Moses said, " In the beginning God created the heaven and the earth" (Gen. i. 1) ; not that, in the beginning He begat them, nor that in the beginning they existed. And thus David says in the Psalm, " Thy hands have made me, and fashioned me" (Ps. cxix. 73) ; but nowhere " Thy hands have begotten me." And he constantly uses the words " made" or " created," whenever he speaks of the creatures ; but when he speaks of the Son of God he uses no such terms, but only such expressions as denote a proper generation, such as " This day have I begotten Thee" (Ps. ii. 7) ; and " Out of My heart has proceeded a good Word" (Ps. xlv. 1). Therefore it is said concerning the creation of the world, " In the beginning God made" ; but concerning the Son we read, " In the beginning was the Word " (S. John i. 1). Whatever was created, besides, must have had a beginning, and that first moment of existence must be continued in a succession of duration. So when Moses tells us God made His creatures in the beginning, it is the same thing as if he had said He made them from a certain beginning. And our Blessed Lord, who certainly knew

what was best to be said of the things He Himself had made, made use of this expression in one of His disputes with the Pharisees, for He said, " He, which made them from the beginning made them male and female" (S. Matt. xix. 4). No created substance can acquire existence, but from the act of a principle, which existed without beginning before itself. And the Holy Ghost has signified this very thing in the Book of Psalms, saying, " Thou, Lord, in the beginning hast laid the foundation of the earth" (Ps. cii. 25); and again, " O think upon Thy congregation, whom Thou hast purchased from the beginning" (Ps. lxxiv. 2, Sept.). Now the being of that which holds its existence according to a beginning, must be traced back to a certain first moment or instant. And, no doubt, there was a certain point of time when God first purchased His congregation. " In the beginning God created," we find to be the same as God " began to create," which is the expression of Moses at the close of his history of the creation, " And God blessed the seventh day, and sanctified it, because that in it He had rested from all His work which God began to make" (Gen. ii. 3, Sept.). Thus the duration of all created beings must be successive; but the Word of God is without beginning. He does not reckon His existence by length of days, and therefore He could not begin to be made. All the works of God must have a beginning of existence, because they were made; and they must have received it from some antecedent principle. But the Word of God is not one of God's works; but, on the contrary, the cause and principle which gave being to all those works. The nature and essence of whatever is made must be finite and limited, as well as to the term of its existence as the extent of its essence. And, accordingly, God began to produce and form His creatures at a certain instant of time; and this shows us that they neither were nor could be before they were made. Now, whereas the Word of God is in the very nature and essence of His Father as He is in the principle of His subsistence; and since the Father, as even our adversaries themselves confess, exists without beginning and from eternity; consequently it follows that the Son, whom He did not make but beget, being in His nature, must in like manner exist with Him from everlasting.

58. This distinction, then, Holy Scripture very plainly makes between begotten and made or created. It declares the Son of God to be the former, and that He has no beginning of existence, but is eternal. And, on the other hand, it asserts the creature to have had such a beginning, and that the being and

substance of creatures are wholly external and foreign to the Divine nature. S. John very well understood this distinction, and how widely the words that express it differ in sense from one another. Accordingly, when he would assert the Son's proper generation and eternal existence, and obviate all difficulties that might arise from the use of improper terms, said, "In the beginning was the Word;" and not, "In the beginning became," or "was made." This expression also would do away with all notions of a successive duration in Him. How entirely, then, have our adversaries misunderstood those passages in the Book of Deuteronomy, from which they so boldly and blasphemously pretend to prove that the Son of God is a creature. Have the expressions "begotten" and "made" precisely the same meaning? Let the very texts the Arians allege make them sensible of their stupidity and impiety. The first passage brought forward is this, "Is not He Thy Father that hath bought thee? Hath not He made thee and created thee?" And shortly after, in the same Song, it is said, "Of the Rock that begat thee thou art unmindful, and hast forgotten God that formed thee" (Deut. xxxii. 6, 18). Now, the meaning of these words deserves our particular attention and regard. The word "begat" comes after the word "made," as if to prevent the words being considered synonymous, and to exclude any such erroneous conclusions from them as our enemies advance. The same Moses that informs us that God said in the beginning, "Let us make man" (Gen. i. 26), has here expressed Himself otherwise, "Of the Rock that begat thee thou art unmindful;" for he knew that "begat" and "made" were equivalent, when applied to this subject. But after the words "bought" and "made," he has added last of all "begat" to discriminate the one from the other. The word "made" implies the proper or literal creation of human nature and of human kind; the word "begat" which comes after must be understood of God's goodness and favour shown to men after He had given them their being. It is their ungrateful returns, concerning which Moses expostulates with them, as we find in the words immediately preceding, saying, "Do ye thus requite the Lord, O foolish people and unwise?" And then He adds, "Is not He thy Father that hath bought thee? Hath not He made thee and created thee?" And, afterwards, He proceeds, "They sacrificed unto devils, not to God; to gods whom they knew not, to new gods that came newly up, whom your fathers feared not; of the Rock that begat thee thou art unmindful" (Deut. xxxii. 6, 17).

59. It has pleased God not only to create us but to make us His sons, just as if He had begotten us.   For the term "begat" is a word whence sonship is properly inferred, as in that saying of the Prophet, "I have begotten and brought up children" (Isa. i. 2, Sept.).   And thus Holy Scripture generally speaks of the Son as being begotten, and not as created.   To illustrate this, let us consider these words of S. John, "As many as received Him, to them gave He power to become the sons of God, even to them that believe on His Name; which were born, not of blood, nor of the will of the flesh, nor of the will of man, but of God" (S. John i. 12).   We are to take notice here of the word "become," which stands to distinguish adoption from natural sonship, and which is followed by the word "born" or "begotten," to remind us that adopted sons are also truly sons. The Prophet tells us that the people had "rebelled against" the goodness of God (Isa. i. 2) ; which goodness manifests itself to all mankind, first, in giving us our being, and then in making us His children by giving us His grace ; and He does this when, as the Apostle says, "He sends forth the Spirit of His Son into our hearts, crying, Abba, Father" (Galat. iv. 6).   And thus it is that He gives us power to become the sons of God, by sending to us the Spirit of His Word ; for created beings are quite incapable of becoming His Sons in any other manner.   The Holy Spirit of Him, who is essentially God's Son, can only make us such by dwelling in our hearts.   And for this end "the Word became flesh," that He might qualify man for communion with the Divine nature.   This is what we find revealed long since by those two questions of the Prophet Malachi, "Hath not one God created us ?   Have we not all one Father ? " (Mal. ii. 10).   Here "created" comes first, and "Father" follows, and this shows that our nature is a created one, and that God created it by His Word ; but afterwards He adopted us as His children, and from that time our Creator becomes our Father as well.   The Father of our Lord is only a Father essentially to Him, and the Son is uncreate, and essentially the Son of God the Father ; and, there-fore, it is not anything in our nature that constitutes us sons of God, but the Son who dwells in us.   Our nature is quite of a different character from that of God, and, therefore, He makes Himself our Father simply by the indwelling of the Spirit of His Son, in whom, and because of whom, we cry, "Abba, Father." Where the Father finds anyone that has received this Holy Spirit, He acknowledges that person to be His son, and He says, "I have begotten Him," not "I have made him," for He made

Him at His creation. We were created first when it was said, "Let us make man" (Gen. i. 26) ; but we were begotten and born the sons of God afterwards, when He was pleased to impart to us the grace of His Holy Spirit. How wisely, then, has the great Prophet Moses, in his Song, said first "He bought," and afterwards "He begat," as if on purpose to remind us of the entire dependence of our nature and successiveness of our existence ; that although by grace we are sons, yet we must not forget that we are originally, and naturally, no more than mortal men.

60. And that "created" and "begotten" are not the same, but differ from each other both in nature and in the meaning of the words, our Saviour informs us even in this very passage of the Proverbs. For having said, "The Lord hath created Me, the beginning of His ways," He has added, "But before all the hills He begat Me." Had the sense of the former passage been that the nature and substance of the Divine Word was created ; and had there been no difference in meaning between "begotten" and "created," how does Solomon come to add that assertion of His being begotten ? Did not the word "created" imply it sufficiently, if "begotten" signifies here no more than "created"? Again, the conjunction "but" in the text, "But before all the hills He begat Me," seems to suggest an opposition between the "begetting" here and the "creation" before, and fixes the sense we are to put upon that "creation." For the "begetting" here, as it stands annexed to the being "created," shows the meaning of both. It shows that it is only meant in a metaphorical sense, because of the object that is mentioned with it. Whereas the words that accompany the word "begetting," show that it must be understood properly, and that it signifies a generation antecedent to that creation. Had the words run thus, "The Lord begat Me, but He created Me before the hills," then the creation must have been understood to precede the begetting. It is, therefore, as reasonable, on the other hand, that when the creation is first mentioned, and afterwards the explanation follows, "But He begat Me before the hills," the generation should be understood to precede the creation. For in saying, "Before all things He begat Me," He declares that He is different from all other created beings, which, as we showed before, were not created one after another, at distant intervals of time, but all created things began to exist at once together upon one and the same command. Therefore, neither do the words which follow "created" also follow "begat Me." "He created Me," we read, "the begin-

ning of His ways ;" He does not say, "He begat Me, the beginning of His ways." He says, "Before all things He begat Me ;" and it is certain that He who existed before all things cannot be the beginning of all these things, but must be absolutely distinct and infinitely distant in substance and nature from them. And if He is so, even distinct and separate from the first or oldest of those things, it follows clearly that He cannot be a creature. Wherefore, since it appears that the Word is not in the number of all created beings, but that He was in being before the first made of them, we can at once understand the true meaning of His being created "the beginning of God's ways for His works," namely, that it relates to His Incarnation ; and that as the Apostle has said, "He is the Beginning, the First-born from the dead, that in all things He might have the pre-eminence" (Col. i. 18).

61. Wherefore those expressions "created," "begat," "beginning of ways," and "before all," being thus compared, the doctrine intended to be conveyed in them is as follows :—God, who created all mankind, becomes also our Father by the indwelling of the Spirit of His Word in us. On the other hand, as regards His Word and Son, He is His Father by nature, and He became afterwards His Maker and Creator, when that Word assumed a created body, and was made man. The Son of the Divine substance makes the sons of men the adopted sons of God, by sending the grace of His Holy Spirit into their hearts ; whereas the Word of God is said to be made and created when He became the Son of man. If, then, we are by nature the sons of God, then it must be confessed that it will be true also, that the Word and Son of God is also a creature. But if we are sons by adoption and grace, then it is manifest that no more is implied in the words "The Lord hath created Me," than that the Word was made man, that so He might confer this grace upon our nature. And next, because by taking upon Him our nature, He became like us in body, He is, therefore, very properly called both our Brother and First-born. For although it was after us that He was made man for our sakes, and is properly called our Brother, on account of similitude in body ; still He is declared to be, and is, the First-born of us in this respect, because all men being lost by the sin of Adam, the human nature of Christ was first regenerated, redeemed, and sanctified, and so became the means of our regeneration, redemption, and sanctification, in consequence of the union between our nature and His. Our Lord united a human body to His infinite nature ; that in it He might conduct us to the Kingdom of Heaven and the presence

of His Father, saying, "I am the Way," and "the Door," and " By Me if any man enter in He shall be saved " (S. John xiv. 6 ; x. 9). He is not called "the First-born from the dead," as being the first of us that died, for we were all in a state of death before Him. But that title belongs to Him, because He freely laid down His life for our sakes, abolished the kingdom and power of death, and arose from the dead on our behalf, and it is a guarantee of our resurrection. It was necessary that He should first rise, because He was to raise us from the dead, and His Resurrection was to be the means and pledge of ours.

62. But if the Word of God is also called "the First-born of all creation," this does not signify either an equality of nature with any other of the creatures, or that He is first of them as regards time; for then He could not be the "Only-begotten" also. But it refers altogether to His amazing love towards us His creatures, in consequence of which He became one among many brethren. "Only-begotten" implies no brethren, whereas the term "First-begotten" does imply them ; and we nowhere find Him in Holy Scripture styled either "the First-begotten of God," or ."a creature of God." He is commonly called "the Only-begotten," the "Son," the "Word," and "the Wisdom" of God ; expressions which, in the common acceptation of them, relate to His being of the same substance with the Father. So we read, "we beheld His glory, the glory as of the Only-begotten of the Father" (S. John i. 14) ; and, "God sent His Only-begotten Son into the world" (1 S. John iv. 9) ; and, "O Lord, Thy word endureth for ever" (Ps. cxix. 89) ; and, "In the beginning was the Word, and the Word was with God" (S. John i. 1) ; and, "Christ the Power of God and the Wisdom of God" (1 Cor. i. 24) ; and, "This is My beloved Son" (S. Matt. iii. 17); and, "Thou art the Christ, the Son of the Living God" (S. Matt. xvi. 16). At the same time He is called "the First-born," because of His singular affection for, and wonderful redemption of, our created nature, of which He is the "First-born" in the work of our regeneration. He was created man for the sake of God's works, that is to say, in order to regenerate and sanctify His creatures. We must, therefore, consider how He can be Only-begotten and First-born too. As being First-born He cannot be said to be Only-begotten, for it is impossible that the same person should be both Only-begotten and First-born in the same respect. And so it appears, that when He is said to Only-begotten, nothing but His eternal generation can be meant ; but when He is called the First-born, we are to understand

nothing more by it than His great kindness and love which He manifested to the creation, and the brotherhood which He has made with many. Seeing, then, that those two terms understood in the same respect are irreconcilable, is it not most reasonable to suppose, that the term " Only-begotten " should belong to our Lord as the Word or Son of God ? For God most certainly has but One Word, One Wisdom, One proper or essential Son. Moreover, as was said before, there is nothing hinted of a final cause, a purpose or end of this Unity of Sonship, but it is said absolutely, " The Only-begotten Son, which is in the bosom of the Father " (S. John i. 18). Whereas, the term " First-born " has the reason assigned with it, namely our creation. As when S. Paul calls our Lord " the First-born," he immediately adds, " For by Him were all things created " (Col. i. 16). And if all things were created by Him, then must He necessarily be a distinct being from all created beings, an uncreated nature, and the Creator of all creatures.

63. And, therefore, he is not the First-born, because He is the begotten of the Father, but because all created things had their being in Him. He was the Son of God before the existence of those things which were made by Him. He did not begin to be the Word that was with God, and the Word that was God, at the time when He commenced to be the First-born of the whole creation. But since these impious men did not in the least understand this, they go about saying, " If He is the First-born of the whole creation, then He certainly must be one of the creatures." This shows how very foolish they are, for the reverse of this is the fact, because He could not be the First-born of all created beings, unless He were a distinct being from them. Had it been said indeed that He was born or begotten before the rest of the creatures, it might have been thought that He Himself is one of the creatures. But this does by no means follow from His being called the " First-born of the whole creation," because the meaning of that expression may be, and is really this, that He was born or begotten before all creatures. Reuben, for example, is not said to be the first-born of all the children of Jacob, but he is said to be the first-born of Jacob his father, and of his brethren ; lest he should be thought to be some other than one of the children of Jacob (Gen. xxxv. 23). Moreover, concerning the Lord Himself, the Apostle does not say " that He might be the First-born of all," lest He should be thought to have a different body from ours ; but his words are " among many brethren " (Rom. viii. 29), which refer to that

human nature, which is common to us all. And we cannot doubt, but that if the Word had been a creature, Scripture would have told us in plain and proper terms that He was the First-born of other creatures. And, therefore, seeing the sacred writers have so expressed themselves, saying that He is the " First-born of the whole creation," they meant us to believe that the Son of God is different from all other created things, and not a creature at all. For if He is a creature, He will be the First-born of Himself. How can this possibly take place, O Arians, unless you can make it appear, that the same person may actually exist before and after himself? Again, if He is a creature, and yet the whole creation was brought into being and exists by Him, then one of the creatures must have created all the creatures, and He must exist dependently among them at the same time that they all exist by and in Him. Now, such notions are so full of absurdities and impossibilities that they at once confute our adversaries, and establish the opposite truth, namely, that He is called the " First-born among many brethren," in regard of that nature which is common to us all ; that He is called the " First-born from the dead," because the resurrection of the dead began in Him, and will follow His ; that He is called the " First-born of the whole creation," because of the loving-kindness of the Father which was displayed towards mankind, by which it came to pass that in His Word not only " all things consist " (Col. i. 17), but the creation itself, which, as the Apostle tells us, " waiteth for the manifestation of the sons of God, because the creation itself also shall be delivered from the bondage of corruption into the glorious liberty of the children of God " (Rom. viii. 19, 21). Our Lord will manifest Himself, in this sense, as the First-born of the creation thus delivered, and of all persons that shall become the children of God. He is the first thus delivered, and their glorious liberty is the consequence of His assuming our human nature, just as an effect depends upon the cause which produces it.

64. And I imagine that our adversaries will be glad, out of very shame, to abandon their line of argument, when we show them another fearful consequence to which their exposition unavoidably impels them. If He is, as they say, the First-born of the whole creation, He must be the brother of all creatures too, and His nature the same as theirs. He must be the brother and fellow of the things without reason and life ; for, according to their theory, He is the First-born of these as well as of other creatures ; and there must be a common nature and a relation of

brotherhood between Him and them, as well as between Him and us. All the difference in the one case as well as the other, will be that He was the first made of the kind. But how can they utter such terrible things as these, without surpassing all kinds of blasphemy? Who can bear to hear them giving utterance to such impious doctrines? Who can even put up with their imagining such things? And especially is it dreadful, when we attend to the clear evidence of the contrary doctrine, that He is not the First-born of the whole creation, either with respect to His nature simply considered as created, or because He has a nature in common with the rest of the creatures; but because the Word, when He framed the creatures at the beginning, condescended to created things, that it might be possible for them to come into existence. For they could not have borne those attributes in all their splendour, which render Him the Brightness of His Father's Glory and the express Image of His Person, if He had not accommodated His Father's and His own infinite power and goodness in such a manner as was suitable for them. And by a further condescension of this Eternal Word, He has exalted us His creatures to the dignity of the children of God, that so, as has been said, He might in all respects become the First-born of them, not only by the way in which He acted at the creation, but also when He was brought into the world for the further good of His creatures. For so it is written, " When He bringeth in the First-begotten into the world, He saith, and let all the Angels of God worship Him " (Heb. i. 6). His descent upon earth is here very plainly made the foundation of that primogeniture; and, therefore, our adversaries when they hear this text ought to beat their breasts in despair. Therefore our Lord is the Only-begotten Son, as He is alone from the Father; and He is the First-born of creation, as our adoption owes itself entirely to His. Thus He is the " First-born among many brethren," as He is likewise the " First-fruits of them that slept " by His resurrection (1 Cor. xv. 20). And because it became Him " in all things to have the pre-eminence" (Col. i. 18), God also has created Him "a beginning of ways," that we, walking along it and entering through Him who says " I am the Way and the Door," and partaking of a true knowledge of the Father, may also hear the words, " Blessed are those that are undefiled in the way" (Ps. cxix. 1), and " Blessed are the pure in heart, for they shall see God" (S. Matt. v. 8).

65. Having thus clearly proved that the Divine Word cannot be a created substance; in the next place, let us more distinctly

show what is the meaning of His being called " the beginning of ways." Now, there have been two ways marked out by God for men to walk in, and the first way, which was through Adam, was lost, and instead of treading the path leading to Paradise, we turned aside to the regions of death, and we heard the words, " Dust thou art, and unto dust shalt thou return" (Gen. iii. 19). Therefore the Word of God out of His great love for man, at the will of the Father, invests Himself with our mortal flesh, that by the shedding of His precious Blood, He might purchase forgiveness and life for His assumed nature, upon which the sin of the first man had entailed mortality and death. In the words of the Apostle, He has opened for us " a new and living way, through the vail, that is to say, His flesh " (Heb. x. 20). And, therefore, as the same Apostle teaches us elsewhere, " If any man be in Christ, He is a new creature, old things are passed away, behold, all things are become new" (2 Cor. v. 17). But if a new creation has come to pass, some one must be first of this new creation. But this was a dignity, such as a poor frail creature possessing an earthly nature, and, moreover, which had trangressed God's law, could not possibly attain to. For in the first creation men had forfeited their faith, and through guilt that first creation perished and was lost. And, therefore, there was a necessity that some one else should come to bring the first creation again into being, and to preserve it, when it was renewed. Now, this " Beginning" of the new creation, this "Way," is our merciful Lord Himself, and could be no other. And so has He expressed this loving work of His very clearly and properly in those words, " The Lord created Me, a beginning of ways, for His works," that man might no longer have his mode or manner of life according to that first creation, but as having a beginning of a new creation, and in it Christ a " beginning of ways," we might find it our duty and interest to follow Him, who says to us, " I am the Way." The holy Apostle asserts the same great truth in those words of His in his Epistle to the Colossians, " He is the Head of the Body, the Church ; who is the Beginning, the First-born from the dead, that in all things He might have the pre-eminence" (Col. i. 18).

66. For if, as has already been stated, our Blessed Lord became the " Beginning" because of His resurrection from the dead, and if this resurrection did not take place until after He had assumed our nature and sacrificed Himself for us, it is evi-dent that His words, " He created Me, the beginning of His ways," do not refer to His eternal nature, but only to His Incar-

nation. His humanity only was capable of death; and so to His creation and advent in His mortal nature only are those words applicable, "The Lord created Me, the beginning of His ways." For that the Saviour was thus created in mortal flesh is meant; that He thus became the Beginning of God's ways in the regeneration or new creation of His creatures; and that this assumed nature of His is the first-fruits of ours thus renewed, appears from what we read of in the Psalms concerning the people to come, David saying, "This shall be written for the generation to come; and the people which shall be created shall praise the Lord" (Ps. cii. 18). And again, "They shall come, and the heavens shall declare His righteousness; unto a people that shall be born whom the Lord hath made" (Ps. xxii. 32). For we shall no longer hear, "In the day that thou eatest thereof thou shalt surely die" (Gen. ii. 17), but, "Where I am, there ye shall be also" (S. John xiv. 3); so that we can now say, "We are His workmanship, created unto good works" (Eph. ii. 10). And, besides, God created that work of His, namely man, perfect. But this state of perfection has been forfeited by sin, and transgression brought death along with it. And because it was most unfitting that the work of God should remain imperfect; such petitions arising from all good people concerning this, such as we find in the Psalm where we read, "The Lord shall make good His loving-kindness toward Me; despise not Thou the work of Thine own hands" (Ps. cxxxviii. 8); therefore, that perfect being, the Son of God, takes upon Himself our imperfect nature, and is said to be created for the works of God's hands. He does this, that by discharging the debt in our behalf, He might by Himself make perfect that which was wanting to man; that He might recover for him that immortality, and the way to Paradise, of which he had incurred the loss. And this is what our Saviour means by the words, "I have glorified Thee on the earth; I have finished the work which Thou gavest Me to do" (S. John xvii. 4); and again, "The works which the Father hath given Me to finish, the same works that I do, bear witness of Me, that the Father hath sent Me" (S. John v. 36). These works which He here says the Father hath given Him to do are the same for which He tells us He is created, saying, in the Proverbs, "The Lord created Me, a beginning of His ways, for His works." The expressions are perfectly equivalent, "The Father hath given Me the works," and "The Lord hath created Me for the works."

67. And if these enemies of God will but recollect at what

time His Son entered upon the doing of the works, they cannot mistake the meaning here of the word "created." Will they say that the "works" in this place mean the creation of those works out of nothing? This cannot be; for these works are spoken of as already in being, and the works of the creation were not so before He had actually created them. Nor can any works which the Word may be supposed to perform before His Incarnation be meant here; because then his Incarnation would be rendered unnecessary, if they had been performed before. So that He could receive these works to do only at the time of His Incarnation; and having received them, He actually performed them, by healing our wounds, and obtaining for us the resurrection from the dead. As, therefore, the works, for which the Word was made man, were given Him to do at the time of His Incarnation, so, it is evident, that He was created then, and not before, in order to perform those works. And, consequently, till then, as has been often urged already, He must have been an uncreated person. Our iniquity had ruined us, and had destroyed all that was excellent in us. Therefore, the Word was to be made man, that is, to be created as to His human nature, to re-establish us in a sound and perfect state, that He might present unto His Father "a glorious Church, not having spot or wrinkle, or any such thing, but that it should be holy, and without blemish" (Ephes. v. 27). Mankind, then, is made perfect in Him, and restored even as it was made at the beginning; or rather, it is advanced to a higher state of grace than before. For, at the resurrection, we shall no longer have any fear of death, but we shall for ever reign with our Blessed Lord in the heavens above. To procure these privileges for us, He, the very Word and Son of God, begotten of His Father's essence, made Himself man. Had He been only one sort of creature at first, and was afterwards made another, our case had been hopeless; and we must have remained as much excluded, and at as great a distance, from the mercy of God as ever. One created being could not presume to exalt another into a state of union with God. All created beings are equally dependent and helpless, and no one is more capable of diverting the purposes of the Creator than another, and, therefore, the best of them cannot be serviceable to any other of them in this respect. It had not been possible for the Word or Son of God, had He been only a creature, to reverse the sentence of God, and to forgive sin. For this, as the Prophet has told us, is the special prerogative of God Himself, for, "who is a God like unto Thee, that pardoneth

F

iniquity, and passeth by transgression?" (Micah vii. 18). And whereas God had said, "Dust thou art, and unto dust shalt thou return" (Gen. iii. 19), so it was that men became mortal. What creature, then, could dare to pardon those upon whom God Himself has passed judgment? Our Blessed Lord, therefore, cannot be a creature, as appears more fully from His own assertion, that we cannot be free, "unless the Son shall make us free" (S. John viii. 36). This evidently proves Him to be the essential Word and Image of the Father's substance. For, otherwise, He could not forgive us that debt which was due to His Father, and Him only; nor could He free us from that punishment to which His Father had consigned us. The Father had pronounced this sentence upon us, "Dust thou art, and unto dust thou shalt return," by His Word. And, therefore, it was fitting that this sentence should be repealed by the very Word and Son of God.

68. But here we shall be told, that whether our Saviour had been created or not, God, if He had pleased, might have pardoned us, as He inflicted our punishment, by only pronouncing the words. And to this I make reply, that although it were granted that God could do this without sending down His Son nither; yet we are not here considering what belongs to the power of God, but what is most suitable for mankind. No doubt it was in His power to have destroyed the sinful world by a deluge before Noah had built the ark, and yet He did not think fit to do so until afterwards. Without the ministry of Moses, by speaking only the word, He could have delivered the children of Israel from Egypt; and yet He was pleased to save them by the hand of Moses. God saw that it would be for the advantage of His people to be governed for a time by Judges, although He could have watched over them and protected them by His own immediate presence. Our Saviour, too, might have come in the beginning of the world, and need not have been delivered up, after He had come to Pilate; but yet He came "in the fulness of time" (Gal. iv. 4), and when He was sought for He said at once, "I am He" (S. John xviii. 5). We must judge of the expediency of the Divine methods, not by our own opinion of them, but by God's choice. He always chooses the best way, and we know He has approved this, when He prosecutes any particular plan. Accordingly "the Son of Man came not to be ministered unto but to minister, and to give His life a ransom for many" (S. Matt. xx. 18). He might, if He had pleased, have spoken the Law from heaven, but He deemed it would be more advantageous for men if He were to deliver it from Mount Sinai. He

did that, in order that it might be possible for Moses to go up, and that the majesty of the Lawgiver, as well as the Law itself, should be exhibited to the senses of those that were to obey it. Suppose, then, that God could by His own immediate voice have uttered the declaration of pardon to mankind, even as He uttered the curse ; yet it is certain that it was much more agreeable to His infinite purpose, that He should transact this affair by His Son. Had His Omnipotence spoken the word, and so the curse had been undone ; this, no doubt, would have manifested His power, and had rendered our nature the same as it was before the fall ; that is to say, we should have received grace from without, as Adam then did, but we should not have had it as we have now, within our hearts. This was Adam's condition when God first placed him in Paradise ; and it made the consequence of his sin much worse than those of our transgressions. For if this had been made his condition again after his first fall, and he had sinned again, there would have been a further necessity that God Himself should immediately repeat the act of remission ; and this necessity would have returned as often as there was sin, and we could not have helped sinning, for want of that grace within, which subdues the power of sin. Thus we should have been enslaved to sin, and although every act were from time to time forgiven, yet we could not have been in that state of freedom, wherein we now are, through God's grace dwelling in us; because we should have been altogether carnal, and under the yoke of the Law, through the infirmity of the flesh.

69. Had the Son been a creature, He could not have effected our union with God, and consequently man would have had to remain mortal. A creature does not possess the power to join itself or other creatures to God ; and no created being can save itself, much less can it be the author of another creature's salvation. And therefore to provide for this also God sent His Son, who, taking our nature upon Him, became the Son of Man, that He, who was not one of us sinners, might lay down His life as a ransom for us all who were guilty and under the sentence of death ; that so the justice of God might be satisfied by our undergoing that sentence in Him (for all died in Christ), and thus we might all be freed from sin, and from the curse which it brought with it ; and that even our bodies, being released from death might put on immortality and incorruption, and in union with our souls, live for ever in perfect bliss. For the Son of God having assumed our flesh, as has oftentimes been said, bruised the serpent's head, and healed the venom of his bite ; He cured our

mortified nature ; He suppressed our evil passions and desires ; and utterly destroyed both sin and death together, as the Lord Himself says, " The prince of this world cometh, and hath nothing in Me " (S. John xiv. 30) ; and, " For this purpose the Son of God was manifested, that He might destroy the works of the devil " (1 S. John iii. 8). And, as He obtained this victory in our nature, so we, being partakers of that nature, enjoy the benefits of it in our persons, and are in actual and immediate union with the Word. And, being joined to God, we are no longer bound down to this earth, which our bodies return to, but as He Himself has said, " Where He is there shall we be also " (S. John xiv. 3) ; and henceforth we shall no longer fear the serpent, for he was vanquished when he was assailed by our Saviour in His mortal flesh, when He bade him " Get thee behind Me, Satan " (S. Matt. xvi. 23), and thus He is cast out of Paradise into the eternal fire. Nor shall we have to watch any more against the allurements of our carnal nature, for " in the resurrection they neither marry nor are given in marriage, but are as the Angels " (S. Matt. xxii. 30) ; and, " In Christ Jesus " there will be " a new creation " (Gal. vi. 15), there will be " neither male nor female " (Gal. iii. 28), but Christ will be all and in all. Now in the presence of Christ no fear and no danger can prevail.

70. But all this would not have happened, if the Word had been a creature. For the devil, being himself a creature, would have ever maintained a struggle with one that was a creature like himself ; and man meanwhile must have stood, as it were, between the two, unable to help himself, as a captive given over to death ; and as being utterly destitute of any virtue capable of exalting his nature into union with God, without which he could not possibly attain to a state of happiness and security. So that the truth shows us clearly that the Word of God cannot be a creature, and that He cannot but be our Creator. For, as He had at first created and formed this body of ours, so now He assumed it to make it, as it were, over again, to communicate a Divine nature to it by making it a part of Himself, and thus that He might introduce us all into the kingdom of heaven after His likeness. Our nature could not have been thus joined to the Divine by virtue of any conjunction with a creature, or unless the Son were very God ; nor could man have been introduced into the Father's presence, unless He had been His natural and true Word, who had assumed our nature. As, on the one hand, we could not have been redeemed from sin and the curse, unless the flesh and nature, which the Word took upon Him had been

truly ours (for we should have had no interest by his assumption of any foreign nature); so also man could not have been united to the Divine nature, unless that Word, which was made flesh, had not been, in essence and nature, the Word and Son of God. For that was the very purpose and end of our Lord's Incarnation, that He should join what is man by nature to Him who is by nature God, that so man might enjoy His salvation and His union with God without any fear of its failing or decrease. And, therefore, those that deny that the Son of God is properly so, of His Father's nature and substance, have as much reason to deny that· He was conceived truly and properly man, of the substance of Mary ever Virgin. For He had been quite as unqualified for that work of grace, which was the occasion of His coming among us, if He had not been of the very nature of His Father, as if He had not assumed a true and proper body. And, therefore, all the raving of Valentinus will never make us believe that the Word of God is not really and truly a man; as the Arians, on the other hand, madden themselves to no purpose to make it believed that He is not properly and truly God. Having made Himself man for us, He became the beginning of a new creation, a new way to bring us to happiness by what He did and suffered for us in the flesh.

71. The Word of God, then, is neither one of His creatures nor one of His works. "Created," "made," and "work" are all one and the same thing, and, therefore, if He had been created and made, He must have been one of God's works, and then He would have expressed Himself thus, "The Lord created Me," not "for His works," but "one of His works," or thus, "The Lord made Me," not "in order to His works," but "among His works." But we find no such declarations as these to check our belief in what is His true nature and substance. He does not so much as say, "The Lord created Me for the making of His works," as if on purpose to avoid giving any cause for any such impious opinion as that of our adversaries, that He was only God's instrument, created for His use in the work of our creation. Nor does He say, "The Lord created Me before His works," for if He had been said to be created before His works as well as begotten before them, it might have given us occasion to conclude that His "being begotten" was but another way of expressing His "being created." But He has said with exact discrimination "for His works." It signifies exactly this, "The Father has caused Me to be made man for the good of mankind, His creatures." So that this passage duly explained shows us that the

Word is not a work, but begotten of God's substance. A man's going into a house does not make him a part of a house; for he is the same, and as much a man, as he was outside it. So He who is created for the works must be considered by His nature to be altogether different from those works. But if otherwise, as you think, O Arians, if the Word of God be a work, what Hand and what Wisdom was it that made Him? For we know that whatever was created received its being from the Hand and Wisdom of God. He tells us this Himself, saying, "All those things hath Mine Hand made" (Isa. lxvi. 2). And David says in the Psalm, "Thou, Lord, in the beginning hast laid the foundation of the earth, and the heavens are the work of Thine hands" (Ps. cii. 25); and again, "I do remember the time past, I muse upon all Thy works: yea, I exercise myself in the works of Thy hands" (Ps. cxliii. 5). Thus it is plain that all the creatures were given their being by the Word of God, and it is written that "all things were made by the Word, and without Him was not anything made that was made" (S. John i. 3); and again, "To us there is but one Lord Jesus Christ, by whom are all things" (1 Cor. viii. 6); and again, "By Him all things consist" (Col. i. 17). It is very plain, then, that the Son cannot be one of God's works, but that He is the Hand and the Wisdom of God. This was the faith of the Martyrs in Babylon, Ananias, Azarias, and Misael, and their confession entirely confutes Arianism. For when they say, "O all ye works of the Lord, bless ye the Lord," they recount things in heaven, things on earth, and the whole creation, as works; but they do not name the Son. They do not say to Him, "O Word of God, bless Thou the Lord," and "O Wisdom of God, bless Thou the Lord," which they certainly would have done, if the Word had been in the number of God's works which they called upon to praise Him, because they are so very particular in the recital of those works. And, therefore, they must have known that He was the Creator of those works, the Word and Wisdom of the Father, and not one who was bound to pay Divine worship, but one who was equally with the Father the object of it. And what is this, but what the Holy Spirit has most distinctly declared in the Psalms? saying, "The Word of the Lord is true, and all His works are faithful" (Ps. xxxiii. 4), and "O Lord, how manifold are Thy works, in Wisdom hast Thou made them all" (Ps. civ. 24).

72. If the Word is only a work of God, He must have been made as well as the rest by God's Wisdom. But the Scripture would not have so clearly distinguished Him from all the rest of

God's works; it had not named them works whilst it spoke of Him by the title of God's Word and Wisdom. Now, since it does this, it puts it beyond dispute, that this Word and Wisdom is not one of God's works, but the Creator of them all. This distinction is conspicuous in that passage of the Epistle to the Hebrews, "For the Word of God is quick and powerful, and sharper than any two-edged sword, piercing even to the dividing asunder of soul and spirit, and of the joints and marrow, and is a discerner of the thoughts and intents of the heart. Neither is there any creature that is not manifest in His sight; but all things are naked and opened unto the eyes of Him with whom we have to do" (Heb. iv. 12, 13). Here the creature stands expressly distinguished from the Son, whom He mentions under the title of the Word of God; and he opposes Him to all creatures, in consideration of His nature and being. And again, when He says that "All things are naked and opened unto the eyes of Him with whom we have to do," this signifies that He Himself could not be one of those things, since He could not be the Judge of all God's works and creatures, if He, as one of them, had to be judged along with the rest. And so also in that passage, where the Apostle observes that the whole creation is groaning together with us, that it might be delivered from the bondage of corruption (Rom. viii. 21, 22); the Son is thereby proved not to be any part of the creation. If He were so, He would be one of those who groan along with the rest, and would need some one who should bring adoption and deliverance to Him as well as the others. And, therefore, as certainly as the whole creation groaneth and travaileth in pain together, that it may be freed from the bondage of corruption; and as certainly as the Son is distinguished from whatever needs liberty; so certainly it is the Son Himself that makes us all sons, and sets us all free. This is what He told the Jews of old time, "The servant abideth not in the house for ever; but the Son abideth ever. If the Son, therefore, shall make you free, ye shall be free indeed" (S. John viii. 35, 36). And thus it is clearer than the light from these considerations, that the Word of God is uncreated, and that He is the proper and co-essential Son of the Father. Concerning the passage, " The Lord hath created Me, the Beginning of His ways," this is sufficient, as I imagine, although I might have argued the matter at much greater length, to prove my position. And I trust that what has been said will induce men of learning to frame still more complete refutations of the Arian heresy. But since the heretics, reading the next verse, seek to fix upon it the same false meaning; because it says, " I was set up " (or, " He founded Me ") from everlasting, from the beginning, or ever the earth was; because they say that these words refer to the Divinity of Christ, and not to His Incarnation, I must proceed now to make it appear that they are altogether in the wrong with regard to their explanation.

73. It is written, " The Lord by Wisdom hath founded the earth " (Prov. iii. 19). And if it was His Wisdom that founded the creation, how could the Founder Himself be founded? Here, then, we must have recourse to that proverbial method of interpretation, which leads us directly to this interpretation of the texts, namely, that the Father produced the earth out of nothing, and established it firm and stedfast by His Wisdom; and then that this His Wisdom was founded or created for us, as a proper and necessary instrument and principle of our renovation and new creation. He does not say, " God founded or made Me His Word or His Son from the beginning," lest that might have been taken as a proof that He had a beginning of existence, and was a creature. And that is the first thing to be enquired into, whether He that is said to be created or founded, was not antecedently, however, the Son of God? and whether the Holy Scriptures do not expressly declare Him to be so? What was S. Peter's answer, when our Saviour asked His Apostles, whom they thought Him to be? He answered and said, " Thou art the Christ, the Son of the living God " (S. Matt. xvi. 16). The first thing which the father of the Arian heresy wanted to know, was, whether Christ was the Son of God? "If," he says, "Thou be the Son of God " (S. Matt. iv. 3). He very well knew that this was the fundamental point, and the principal basis of the Christian Faith. If He was the Son of God, then the mastery of the devil would soon come to nought; but if He was only a creature, a sinful descendant of Adam, then there was an end of his anxiety. He had formerly deceived the first of our race, and he doubted not but that he could more easily overcome this descendant of his, if He were possessed of a weak and fallen nature. Again, why were the Jews so enraged, because our Lord called Himself the Son of God, and declared God to be His proper Father? Had He called Himself one of the creatures, or had He told them that He was only a work, this news would not have so disquieted them, nor could they have charged Him with blasphemy. They were well acquainted with sacred history, and knew that Angels had often been sent down from heaven to their fathers. But they could not bear that our Lord should call Himself the Son of God. For

that was a title which they were sure that no creature would assume, and, therefore, it was an open declaration that He was truly God, and of the very substance of His Father.

74. The Arians, then, ought, one would imagine, to imitate their father the devil, and make this their chief enquiry. If they found that Christ had declared of Himself, " the Father hath founded or made Me His Word or His Son," then they might reasonably maintain their present opinion. But if He has not said anything of the kind, then it is not right that they should invent what never was said. The words are these, " He founded Me," and not what they would make of them, " Before the world He founded Me as His Word or Son." The expression is proverbial ; and the founding, as was said before, has no relation to His essence and nature, but only to ours, which He assumed as a foundation for us to be built upon. S. Paul has expressed the same truth in the same language, " Other foundation can no man lay than that is laid, which is Jesus Christ. But let every man take heed how he buildeth thereupon" (1 Cor. iii. 10, 11). The materials of the foundation ought to be of the same kind as those of the superstructure, in order that they may admit of being well compacted together. Now the Word of God, as such, can have no sort or species of beings of the same nature as Himself. As He is such, He is God's Only-begotten Son, but by His Incarnation, He became, as we are, truly and properly man. And being so, He is our foundation, and we are built upon Him, as so many precious stones, into a living temple of His Holy Spirit who dwelleth in us. And as He is the foundation and we the superstructure, so He is the Vine and we are the branches, not of His Divine nature, for that is impossible ; but of His human nature, for the branches must be like the vine, since we are like Him according to the flesh. And because our adversaries have such human notions, we are ready to encounter them with their own weapons, and argue with them on their own ground with resemblances taken from human things. The expression here is not " The Lord created or made Me a foundation," which might have afforded a pretext to these people who shamelessly pervert everything, and try to make everything show that the Word is a creature, and had a beginning of existence. The words are " He hath founded Me." Now, what is founded is founded for the sake of the superstructure. A foundation is not a work of nature, but of art. The stones must be digged out of the mountain side and placed in the depth of the earth. The stone in its natural situation is not a foundation for anything ; but when the need

arises, and it is transferred from its original position, and laid in the depth of the earth, then if the stone could speak it might very properly say, "Now he has laid me for a foundation, who has brought me hither from my place in the mountain." And when our Lord assumed our body and nature, when He was separated from the substance of the Virgin Mary, then He might truly say, as He did, "The Lord hath now laid Me as a foundation;" as much as to say, "He has covered Me, being the Word, with an earthly body." And so it was, He was to be our foundation, which He could not be but in our nature. He was to be exactly such a composition of soul and body as any one of us, in order that we, as so many members, being joined to Him as the Head, and, as it were, growing into Him, might all come unto a "perfect man," and abide immortal and incorruptible.

75. And there is nothing in those expressions, "Before the world," and "before He made the earth," and "before the mountains were settled," which need raise any doubt in our minds, if it be remembered what other expressions they are connected with, namely, "He founded Me," and "He created Me." For here again allusion is made to the dispensation according to the flesh. And thus the Apostle says, "For the grace of God which bringeth salvation hath appeared to all men" (Tit. ii. 11), and this is conveyed to us in the person of our Lord. His advent has at length brought to light the reason of this, the purpose and appointment of God, which was decreed long before we ourselves or even the world was in being; and this is in exact agreement with His wisdom and goodness. For we must not think so unworthily of God, as if He made us first, and then, and not till then, took care to provide for our safety and happiness. God's foreknowledge forbids us to entertain such an idea. Wherefore, when our Almighty Father determined to create us by the power of His Word, and knowing what should befall us better than we, and foreseeing that, after He had made us good and perfect in our nature, we should transgress His commandment, and thereby incur the sentence of expulsion from Paradise; so He proceeded with such a care for the interest of His creatures, that in the same act He prepared beforehand in His proper Word, by whom also He created us, a provision for our salvation. He did this, so that even if the tempter should lead man to his destruction, as He foresaw, yet His creatures' case should not be desperate; His Only-begotten Son Himself would redeem and save us, and would become the means and instrument of our resurrection and immortality, created for our sakes "the Begin-

ning of God's ways," "the First-born of creation," "the First-begotten among many brethren," and "the First-fruits from the dead." And the following passages of S. Paul in his Epistles very well interpret the words of the Proverbs, "Before the world," and "before the earth was." For he thus speaks to Timothy, "Be thou partaker of the afflictions of the Gospel according to the power of God; who hath saved us and called us with an holy calling, not according to our works, but according to His own purpose and grace, which was given us in Christ Jesus before the world began, but is now made manifest by the appearing of our Saviour Jesus Christ, who hath abolished death, and brought life and immortality to life through the Gospel" (2 Tim. i. 8-10). And to the Ephesians he writes, "Blessed be the God and Father of our Lord Jesus Christ, who hath blessed us with all spiritual blessings in heavenly places in Christ, according as He hath chosen us in Him, before the foundation of the world, that we should be holy and without blame before Him in love ; having predestinated us unto the adoption of children by Jesus Christ to Himself" (Ephes. i. 3-5).

76. How, then, has He chosen us before we came into existence, but that this was according to the Divine resolution and decree of our redemption and salvation in Christ? And how was it possible that this decree was in the Divine will from everlasting, if the Son had not from everlasting been the determined and sure foundation of it, the means by which only it could be executed? How could we, as the Apostle goes on to say, have "an inheritance being predestinated" (Ephes. i. 11), had not this foundation been eternally laid? had it not been the firm and unalterable purpose of our Lord, to take our nature into His own person, and with it that sentence of death which it had incurred, and by this method to make us sons of God in Himself, and co-heirs with Himself? We could not have been objects of Divine love and mercy, even eternally, before we were anything at all, if these attributes had not then belonged to our Lord, as to Him, by whom they were afterwards to reach to mankind. Wherefore, also at the Judgment Day, when everyone shall receive his reward according to his deeds, He says to His faithful ones, "Come ye blessed of My Father, inherit the kingdom prepared for you from the foundation of the world" (S. Matt. xxv. 34). How, then, or in whom, could this kingdom be prepared for us before our existence, unless it was in our Saviour, whom God made the foundation of it "before the world"? that we, as built upon Him, might be partakers of the life and grace which comes

from Him, even like stones cemented together in due form and order. And all this happened, as we may think in all piety, that, as has been said before, we may rise once more after our death to an eternal life, of which we were totally incapable before; since even for us men, formed of earth, there was prepared for us " before the world " in Christ Jesus the hope of life and salvation. Therefore we can see the meaning of the Word taking upon Himself our mortal flesh, and being created as " a Beginning of God's ways for His works," that He might thus be laid as our foundation by the decree of His Father's, and in Him, of His own eternal will, before the world, and before the earth was, and before the mountains were settled, and before the fountains burst forth. Had it not been for this, we might have shared the same fate with this earth and these mountains, and all the parts of the material world. We must have decayed and wasted away, and have come to nought. But, on the contrary, God has been pleased to make human nature the survivor of all. Before we were created we had been elected, in the predestinated Incarnation of the Son, to spiritual and everlasting life and happiness. Our life was founded, it was established and hidden in Christ, before anything whatever had received its being. And in Christ it is safely deposited, so that we shall ever live in Him and He in us.

77. And upon what foundation could we so securely stand, as upon the Lord who is before all time, and through whom everything received its being? Thus all our happiness being connected with Him, we become sharers with Him in the everlasting joys of heaven. For God is good, and being good always, He willed this, since He knew that our weak nature needed the succour and salvation which He alone could bestow. And just as some wise architect, resolving to build a house, should think it convenient beforehand to take proper measures for its repair, in case at any time it should fall into decay; so it would be natural for him to lay in a stock of materials for that purpose, and give them into the care of the workmen, that thus all means of repair would be provided even before the actual building of the house. In like manner, even before man came to be created, did God provide in Christ Jesus, who alone could give unto us the means of our new creation, the way whereby our salvation might be re-established. And, therefore, this work and office of His was appointed and determined on before the creation of the world, and afterwards put into execution by Christ, who came into the world just when His presence was

most needed. The effect of this will be, that as from all eternity the Lord provided for our being first, and our redemption afterwards, so He will receive us into closest communion with Himself in heaven, when He receives us into happiness for all eternity. This, then, ought to be sufficient to prove that the Word of God is not a creature, and to make clear what is the true doctrine of Holy Scripture. But because there are more ways than one of disclosing this true belief, it may be best not to confine ourselves with one interpretation; but rather to overwhelm our adversaries, and frighten them into some sense of shame by a great show of the forces at our disposal. Now here I must refer to what has been said before, for what I have to say relates to the same proverb and the same Wisdom. The Word has not told us that His nature was a created one neither here nor elsewhere, but He has said, speaking proverbially and allegorically, "The Lord created Me;" and therefore it is certain that the literal sense in this passage is not the true one, and that we must draw aside the metaphor before we shall discover the true meaning. When that Wisdom which created all things informs us, that "the Lord created Me, the Beginning of His ways," who rests satisfied with the literal meaning of such a proposition, which directly contradicts another assertion of the same Wisdom? Who, on hearing the Only-begotten Son of God assure us that He was created "the Beginning of His Father's ways," does not at once seek to find out the meaning of the expression, wondering how it can be that the Only-begotten Son of God can possibly become the First-begotten of many brethren? Doubtless it is somewhat unintelligible at first sight, but yet we are told that "a man of understanding shall understand a proverb and the interpretation; the words of the wise and their dark sayings" (Prov. i. 6).

78. The Creator and Author of all things is the Only-begotten and essential Wisdom of God. "In Wisdom," says the Psalmist, "hast Thou made them all," and "The earth is full of Thy creation" (Ps. civ. 24). God, if He had pleased, might have made things less perfect. He might have made them without any particular beauty; but it was His good pleasure that all things should be made perfect of their kind. And to make them so, His eternal Wisdom so adapted itself to the nature of the creatures He made, as to stamp some tokens and marks of itself, not only on the universe, taken as a whole, but upon all the several parts of it too. And thus the works of God were not only made, but were made worthy of their Creator, and

were marked, as it were, with the seal of His own Wisdom. Our speech carries with it some kind of resemblance of the Son of God considered as the Word ; and our wisdom, or those intellectual faculties which God has made a part of our nature, represent the Son considered as the Wisdom of God. Our wisdom qualifies us for the reception of the creating Wisdom, and by the influence of that we attain to the knowledge of the Father ; for "He that hath the Son," says S. John, "hath the Father also" (1 S. John ii. 23) ; and, "He that receiveth Me," says our Lord, "receiveth Him that sent Me" (S. Matt. x. 40). And it is from this impression of the Divine Wisdom, that may be seen not only in us but in all God's works, that the original creating Wisdom does with reason speak of that which belongs to its own impress, and say, "The Lord created Me for His works." No more may be implied here than the created or human wisdom, mentioned as if it were the Divine, because of the affinity it bears to it. There is, then, no occasion to say that there is here such a great contradiction, as if the creating Wisdom called Himself a creature. He may be only speaking of the created likeness of Himself ; as if a man were to speak of his own picture, as if he meant himself. And as our Lord Himself has said, "He that receiveth you, receiveth Me, because we are impressed with His character and image ; so though He is not Himself a creature, yet because His image and impress is created in the works, He says, as if in His own person, "The Lord hath created Me, the Beginning of His ways, for His works." And for this reason has the Son of God impressed this mark of His Wisdom upon His creatures, that the creature might discover by it from what hand He received His being ; that he might recognise the Wisdom and Word of God as the immediate cause of it, and through the knowledge of the Son advance to the knowledge of the Father. And this is what S. Paul said, "Because that which may be known of God is manifest in them, for God hath showed it unto them. For the invisible things of Him from the creation of the world are clearly seen, being understood by the things that are made" (Rom. i. 19, 20). So, then, the wisdom in this passage of the Proverbs may be said to imply no more than that representative wisdom which the Son has engrafted in our nature, and does not in the least prove that the Divine Word is a created substance.

79. If our adversaries are resolved to reject this exposition, let them inform us, whether they think there is any wisdom to be found in God's creatures or not? If there is not, what is the meaning of that complaint of the Apostle, "For after that in the

Wisdom of God the world by wisdom knew not God"? (1 Cor. i. 21). And how is it if there is no wisdom, that we so often read of wise men in the Scripture? It is said, for example, "A wise man feareth and departeth from evil" (Prov. xiv. 16); and, "Through wisdom is an house builded" (Prov. xxiv. 3); and the Preacher says, "A man's wisdom maketh his face to shine" (Eccles. viii. 1); and the same Preacher thus reproves those who are headstrong, "Say not thou, what is the cause that the former days were better than these? for thou dost not enquire wisely concerning this" (Eccles. vii. 10). And this is the wisdom which the Son of Sirach speaks of, "He poured her out upon all His works. She is with all flesh according to His gift, and He hath given her to them that love Him" (Ecclus. i. 9, 10). The wisdom said here to be poured out cannot be the eternal and Only-begotten Wisdom of God, but signifies no more than that which is impressed upon the creatures. And thus by comparing things, we still find it less improbable, that the wisdom said to be created, may signify properly that created wisdom or intelligence which God has implanted in the world, to explain to us the meaning, although in an imperfect manner, of the Divine creating Wisdom. For that wisdom which displays itself in the works of God is not the Creator, but a creature. And it is that voice by which "the heavens declare the glory of God, and the firmament showeth His handiwork" (Ps. xix. 1). This wisdom, if men have it within them, they will acknowledge it to be the true Wisdom of God; and they will know that they are made in deed and in truth after the Image of God. Suppose a son of some monarch were to build a city at his father's desire, and that this son should think it desirable to have his own name carved or engraved upon each of the buildings that were now rising, both in order to preserve those buildings from damage and violence, as well as to show the citizens whose authority they lived under, and to put them in continual remembrance of himself and his father. And supposing that when the city was completed anyone were to ask the prince what was the reason of this, and why he had caused this thing to be done, he might be expected to make an answer to this effect, "I took what I considered to be the best means for the security of the buildings; my name is engraved, with my father's approval, on everything; there is a creation of my name in the works." Now, would any sensible person argue from this that this son himself was a part of the buildings in his father's city? or that when he spoke of his name being found on the buildings, he meant that he himself was turned into one of those edifices? If no one would be so foolish as to say this, then our Lord's assertion that "The Lord hath created Him for the works," is very intelligible, and can be easily understood by those who can discern the impress and character of the uncreated Wisdom in the works of the creation. The true Wisdom seems to say, that His impress is in those works, and He has thus accommodated His power in order that He might frame and create all things.

80. This is by no means the only passage of Scripture in which the Son of God speaks of the effects of His power in us, as if it were of Himself. His Church has in it His impress and image, and when Saul was persecuting the Church, He rebuked him, and said to Saul, as if He Himself were being persecuted, "Saul, why persecutest thou Me?" (Acts ix. 4). This expression may satisfy us that the creating Wisdom and Only-begotten Word of God may as truly affirm that God created Him, calling His creatures Himself, because of His love to them, and because of that impress of His Wisdom which they bear in their being, without causing us to conclude that He Himself is a created and dependent being; just as, in the same manner the created wisdom, which represents Him in His works may affirm of itself, "The Lord created Me for His works." Let no one, then, confound together these two wisdoms, lest in so doing they defraud their souls of the truth, and, as it were, mix wine with water. The distinction ought to be as carefully preserved, as in the case of a workman and his work; so let no one think that "He created" is said of the substance of the Wisdom of God. For this Wisdom is the Creator and Framer of all; but its impress is created in the works, as the copy of an image. Moreover, this representative wisdom may be very well said to be "the beginning of God's ways," as it is the first and elementary principle of Divine knowledge. For whosoever sets out, as it were, upon this way first, and keeps it in the fear of God, even as Solomon says, "The fear of the Lord is the beginning of wisdom" (Prov. i. 7, Sept.), and then advances upwards in his thoughts, and perceives the works of creation, will in that wisdom have a full view, and a true knowledge, of the Wisdom of the Father Himself; as our Lord Himself tells us "He that hath seen Me, hath seen the Father" (S. John xiv. 9); and as S. John writes, "He that acknowledges the Son, hath the Father also" (1 S. John ii. 23). And He says, "From the beginning, or ever the earth was, He founded Me," since in its impress the works remain settled and in perpetuity. And yet, on the other hand, to prevent any mis-

takes about this created wisdom, and that it might be clearly distinguished from the uncreated, the Son of God; He tells us, as was necessary He should, that this latter Wisdom was " Begotten from the beginning, or ever the earth was," and that " Before the mountains, before the waters, before the hills was He brought forth " (Prov. viii. 23, 24), that is to say, before God had made any one of His creatures. Can there be a plainer statement, that His nature is absolutely an uncreated one? Certainly it cannot be disputed, that if He was created " for the works," and yet existed before them, it follows that He truly existed before He was created; and, therefore, He was begotten in His nature and substance, before He was created the Beginning of His Father's ways. And wherein creation and generation differ I need not enter again, having shown this in what has gone before.

81. But since our Lord proceeds to say, "when He" (His Father) "prepared the heavens, I was there" (Prov. viii. 27), He must not be misunderstood to mean that His Father prepared the heavens or the clouds above without the presence of His Wisdom. This would not be consistent with what He says elsewhere, that all things were made by God's Wisdom, and that without Him was not anything made that was made. The meaning of the words is as follows :—" All things were made in Me, and by Me, and when it was necessary that there should be a Wisdom created in My works, I, who had My being substantially and from everlasting with My Father, descended, as it were, and accommodated Myself in a special manner in framing the creatures, and impressed upon them something of My own character, and so shaped their nature and qualities, that they might all be in accord and compose a harmonious whole." So, then, all who duly employ that portion of wisdom which has been given them, and proceed to contemplate all created things may well say, " They continue this day according to Thine ordinance" (Ps. cxix. 91); but they who make light of, and despise their talent, must apply to themselves these words, " Professing themselves to be wise they became fools, because that which may be known of God is manifest in them; for God hath showed it unto them. For the invisible things of Him from the creation of the world are clearly seen, being understood by the things that are made, even His eternal Power and Godhead, so that they are without excuse. Because that when they knew God, they glorified Him not as God, but worshipped and served the creature more than the Creator, who is blessed for ever. Amen." And they ought to feel some

shame surely at reading the words, "For, after that in the wisdom of God," which is that representative wisdom we have lately spoken of, "the world by wisdom knew not God, it pleased God by the foolishness of preaching to save them that believe" (1 Cor. i. 21). For no longer, as in times past, has God chosen to be discovered and known by an image and shadow of wisdom, that namely which exists in the creatures ; but He has made the true Wisdom itself to become incarnate, and to be made man, and even to be crucified for us, that henceforth all that believe may obtain salvation. This is that same Wisdom of God, which formed the creatures after His own Image, and from this it may so far be said to be created ; and which has conveyed to us a partial knowledge of Himself and His Father, but has since, as S. John tells us, "been made flesh " (S. John i. 14) ; and after destroying death, and saving our race, has given us a clearer knowledge than ever both of Himself and His Father, according to His own assertion, "This is life eternal, that they may know Thee the only true God, and Jesus Christ whom Thou hast sent " (S. John xvii. 3).

82. And thus is the whole earth filled with the knowledge of the Lord. We behold the Father in the Son and the Son in the Father ; even as the Father rejoices in the Son and the Son reciprocally rejoices in the Father, according to what He tells us Himself, " I was daily His delight, rejoicing always before Him " (Prov. viii. 30). And this again proves unanswerably, that the Son is not foreign, but proper to the Father's substance. He that is a cause of joy to God could not be a creature, made out of nothing, and made only for our sakes, as the heretics assert. It cannot be conceived of God, that He should want some foreign being to complete His joy ; and therefore this passage also declares the true and orthodox belief. Or will our adversaries say that there was a time when the Father did not thus rejoice ? Surely not ; and yet if He always rejoiced, they must confess that He was from everlasting, in whom He rejoiced. And in whom does the Father rejoice, but in His Eternal Word and Son, who exhibits to Him the Brightness of His own Glory and the express Image of His own Person ? And although it is true that after the creation, the Divine nature also "rejoiced in the habitable parts of the earth," and that " His delights were with the sons of men," yet His joy was not a new one, as might seem implied in the verse at first sight ; but it was comprehended in the original joy, as it resulted, not from His creatures as such, but from that resemblance to His Image which had

been imprinted on their natures. It is still His own Image which occasions God's delight here. And what, too, is that which fills the Son with rejoicing, except His contemplation of Himself in His Father? For this must surely be His meaning when He says, "He that hath seen Me hath seen the Father," and "I am in the Father, and the Father in Me" (S. John xiv. 9, 10). I have, therefore, sufficiently proved, from every point of view, the weakness and folly of the impious heresy of these enemies of Christ. In vain do they publish abroad and speak far and wide that passage, "The Lord created Me, the Beginning of His ways;" a text the meaning of which they have altogether misinterpreted, and to which they have attached a sense which Solomon had never known. And not only is it very evident, that they have invented this new explanation of the verse, as appears from what I have already said; but, moreover, that very passage of the Proverbs proves most conclusively that the Son is not a creature either in His nature or His substance; but that He is begotten of the very essence of His Father; and that He is the true Wisdom and Word of the Father, " by whom all things were made, and without whom was not anything made that was made" (S. John i. 3).

THE THIRD ORATION.

1. WHEN once the Arians, so it seems, have determined to set themselves against the truth, their position is exactly that which is described in those words of Scripture which say, "When the ungodly cometh into the depth of the wicked, he becometh a scorner" (Prov. xviii. 3, Sept.). Evidence does not convince them, nor do difficulties stand in their way; but just as there are unclean people who are never ashamed of any indecency, so these wicked ones have entirely abandoned any modest feelings in the propagation of their impious heresy. For when we have clearly proved what is the meaning of those other passages of Scripture, which they alleged to prove their case, namely, "The Lord created Me" (Prov. viii. 22); and, "Being made so much better than the Angels" (Heb. i. 4); and, "The First-born" (Rom. viii. 29; Col. i. 15); and, "Who was faithful to Him that made Him" (Heb. iii. 2); and, when we have shown that they teach the true doctrine concerning our Lord; still they will persist in bearing about with them, as it were, the poison of serpents, "seeing they see and do not perceive, and hearing they hear and do not understand" (S. Mark iv. 12). Now they have laid hold of another passage; they have invented a meaning out of the perverse ingenuity of their evil hearts concerning those words of our Blessed Lord, "I am in the Father, and the Father in Me" (S. John xiv. 10). They wish to know how this can be possible. Can the Son, they say, comprehend or contain the Father? and, at the same time, the Father comprehend and contain the Son? The Father is by the Son's own confession greater then Himself: how can the less contain the greater? And where is there any room for wonder, if the Son is in the Father? since the Scripture affirms even of us, that "in Him we live, and move, and have our being" (Acts xvii. 28). And in this manner are all the powers of their mind blinded by their perverseness, so that they

have got to think that the Divine nature is like a human body, and they cannot understand what are the properties of the Father and the Son, nor what is the meaning of " Invisible and Eternal Light," or of the " Invisible Brightness of that Light and Glory," or of an " Immaterial Representation and Image of that Invisible Substance." For had they known these things, surely they would not have so dishonoured and scorned the Lord of Glory; nor have ascribed the properties of things material to those which are immaterial, nor would they have so perverted the sense of the Holy Scriptures. It ought, indeed, to be quite enough for anyone, when they only hear that any words have been spoken by our Saviour, at once to believe them. It is much more acceptable to God to believe in simple faith, than to search diligently after doubts and objections. However, since our adversaries have endeavoured to make this passage of Scripture also to fit in with their heresy, we must let them see the falseness of their interpretation, and show what is the true sense of it, that, at least, the faithful may be in security. For, first, we must not understand those words, " I am in the Father and the Father in Me," as if the Father and the Son were two distinct natures or essences, blended into one another. It is not, for instance, as if they were like vessels supposed to be capable of being doubly filled at once, as if the Father occupied the same region of space as the Son, and the Son the same as the Father. It is not as if either of them singly were an incomplete and imperfect being. If these things were possible in nature, they could only apply to things material, and therefore to apply them to the nature of things spiritual is most irreligious. The Personality of the Father is infinitely perfect and complete, and the Son is the Fulness of the Father's substance. Again, we are not to conceive the Father to be or dwell in the Son, after the same manner as He is said to dwell in His Saints. The Son is in the very substance and nature of His Father, and He is the Power and the Wisdom of the Father ; and the means whereby the grace of the Holy Spirit is conveyed to us is our communion with the Son. But the Son has not His Sonship communicated to Him by any sort of intervention. It is of His very nature, of His Father's substance, and immediate from the Father, and not in the sense of the passage which says, " In Him we live and move and have our being." The Father is as the Fountain of existence, and the Son is the Life which flows from that Fountain, and by which all creatures have their principle of life, and their preservation in it. For the Life does not continue living in that which gave it its existence, for then it would not be Life, but it is better to say that He gives life to all things.

2. But now let us see what evasions of the truth the sophist Asterius has to bring forth, that champion of this vile heresy. Following the Jews, then, he thus writes :—" There is nothing in the assertion that He is in the Father and the Father in Him, than that His revelations and doctrines were not His own but His Father's ; and that the miracles which He wrought were indeed wrought by His Father ; and that He was only the instrument of His Father's power in working them." Now, had some little child prattled like this, we should have thought nothing of it, on account of his tender years ; but when one who bears the title of sophist, and professes to have received a learned education, says such trash, what punishment is bad enough for him? Nor does this folly prove him in any sense to be a follower of the Apostle S. Paul, who would never have taught him to be puffed up with "enticing words of man's wisdom" (1 Cor. ii. 4), nor to try to deceive others as well as himself, "understanding neither what he says, nor whereof he affirms" (1 Tim. i. 7). The Son of God ascribes certain characteristics to Himself as being such, and He tells us that He is the Word, and Wisdom, and Image of the Father's substance. This sophist attributes the same properties to all God's creatures, and makes them entirely common to the Son and to them. Moreover, this wicked man says that the Power of the Father is a power derived from elsewhere, that he may proceed from this false supposition to assert that the Son was made a Son by another Son, and that one Word communicated its power to another Word. And so he concludes that the Son did not say He was in the Father in a natural sense, as a Son, but metaphorically ; and he considers that the Son is on the same level with all created things, as having done all things entirely by the power of the Father. For if the Son said, " I am in the Father, and the Father in Me," because His words and works were entirely His Father's, and not His own, then, since David says, " I will hear what the Lord God will say by me " (Ps. lxxxv. 8, Sept.) ; and Solomon says, " My words are spoken from God ; " and since Moses' office was to reveal Divine revelations ; and each of the Prophets spoke not their own words, but generally introduced themselves with "Thus saith the Lord ;" and since the works of the Saints, as they admitted, were not their own but God's, who gave the power, Elijah and Elisha, for instance, undertaking to raise the dead, not by any power or virtue in themselves, but because they called upon God to do it,

and Elisha telling Naaman, on cleansing him from his leprosy, "that there was no God in all the earth but in Israel" (2 Kings v. 15); and Samuel, too, prayed to God to send rain in the time of harvest; and the Apostles being careful to say that their miracles were wrought not by their own power but by the grace of God; it is plain that, according to Asterius, such a statement as "I am in My Father, and the Father in Me," must be common to one and all, so that each of them will be able to make those words his own. If this is true, then the consequence must be that these were all of them truly and properly Sons of God; and if so, then our Lord could not be, as we maintain that He undoubtedly is, the Only-begotten Son, and Word, and Wisdom of the Father.

3. If our Lord had meant to affirm what our adversaries would have Him say, He would not have so clearly said, "I am in the Father, and the Father in Me," but rather He would have expressed Himself, "I also am in the Father, and the Father is in Me also." It would not have been right so to express Himself, that anyone would take it for granted that He was in the nature and essence of His Father, his eternal and Only-begotten Son, at the same time that He was the Son of God only in common with others, and that He was only a creature as they were. This is the meaning our adversaries are resolved to uphold. They cannot bear that the Son should be of the substance of His Father, and, therefore, they make Him put a false interpretation on the words, "I am in the Father, and the Father is in Me." These words in their obvious meaning cannot be true of anyone but the Only-begotten Son of God, who is in the nature of His Father, as reason tells us He is, because there must be a complete community of nature between the Son and the Father, in like manner as there is between brightness and light, and between the stream and the fountain. And so it follows that He who sees the Son, sees in Him the Father, and cannot but know that the Son is in the substance of the Father, since His being was communicated to Him out of that substance. And again, the Father is in the Son, as He communicates His substance to the Son, just as the substance of the sun is in its rays, and as the thought is in the word, and the fountain is in the stream. Thus the nature of the Father is contemplated in that of the Son, and thus the Father is confessed to be in the Son. The Father's Divinity and Essence is indeed the Son's, and, therefore, it was a plain truth which the Son uttered in saying that "He was in the Father, and the Father was in Him." And this obvious sense of the words

is beyond all dispute confirmed by what He told the Jews on a former occasion, "I and My Father are one" (S. John x. 30), that is, "We have both one and the same Divinity and Essence."

4. For they are one; not as one thing that is divided into two parts, but which is really but one; nor is it as if the same person may sometimes be called by one name and sometimes by another; may sometimes be called a Father, and sometimes be called a Son; for this was the heresy held by Sabellius, and for which the Church condemned him as a heretic. But there are two Persons, because the Father is the Father, and not the Son; and the Son is the Son, and not the Father, but the nature is one and the same. There cannot be a difference in the nature between the parent and the offspring, for the latter is the image of the former. All things that the Father hath are the Son's, which could not be if the Son were another God, as He must be if His nature were foreign and created. If His were a distinct Divinity, united from without to that of the Father, then there would be more Gods than one. For although the Son, as such, cannot be otherwise than begotten of the Father, and consequently cannot be the Father; yet, as being begotten of the Father, he cannot but be God; and as being God, He cannot but be one in essence with the Father; and, therefore, He and the Father are one, one with regard to their proper and common nature, and one in the unity of the Godhead. Thus brightness also is light, it is not second to the sun, nor a different light, nor does it consist simply in a borrowed nature, but it is an entire and proper offspring. And such an offspring is of necessity one light; and no one would say the sun and its brightness were two separate lights; and yet the sun and that brightness are not one and the same thing. Still, the light from the sun, which enlightens all things by its brightness, is but one. This is an emblem of the Divinity of the Son of God, which is, indeed, essentially one with that of His Father. They are one individual substance; and they are one God, and there are no other Gods but that one. And since they are both one in Essence and Divinity, it follows that whatever can be affirmed of the Father, may as truly and properly be affirmed of the Son, except only the relation of Paternity. Thus the Son is expressly called God, "And the Word was God" (S. John i. 1). He is also called Almighty, "Thus saith the Lord, which is, and which was, and which is to come, the Almighty" (Rev. i. 8). Likewise, He is called the Lord, "One Lord Jesus Christ" (1 Cor. viii. 6). He calls Himself the Light, "I am the Light"

(S. John viii. 12). He tells us that He forgives sins, "But that ye may know that the Son of Man hath power on earth to forgive sins" (S. Luke v. 24). The Scripture abounds with evidences of this kind, so let these suffice, "All things," says the Son, "that the Father hath are Mine" (S. John xvi. 15); and again, "All Mine are Thine" (S. John xvii. 10).

5. He cannot but see the Father in the Son, who hears the attributes of the Father ascribed to the Son. And He cannot but see the Son in the Father, who hears those attributes which are ascribed to the Son, affirmed and confessed to be in the nature of the Father. And how could those attributes be ascribed to the Son, if He were not the Son of His Father's substance? Again, how could the attributes of the Son be ascribed to the Father, if those attributes were in their nature distinct from, and foreign, to the Father's? The Son, therefore, cannot but be properly the Son of His Father's very essence and substance; and being so, He reasonably says, that whatever belongs to the Father belongs to Him. After He had said, very rightly and properly, "I and the Father are one" (S. John x. 38), He adds, "That ye may know that I am in the Father, and the Father in Me" (S. John xiv. 10); and, moreover, He has added this again, "He that hath seen Me hath seen the Father" (S. John xiv. 9). There is a wonderful agreement and harmony in these three passages. For what can be a clearer consequence, than that the Son is in the Father, and the Father in the Son, if He and the Father are one? And if they are one in Divinity and Nature, then it must follow that "He that hath seen the Son hath seen the Father," for the Godhead of the Father is contemplated in the Son. And we may understand this the more easily by the familiar comparison of the Emperor's image on a coin. For there you have in the image the features and form of the Emperor, and in the Emperor himself you have the living picture of that representation. There is such an exact correspondence between the original and the facsimile, that he who has looked upon the latter may, without impropriety, be said to have seen the former; and he who has seen the former recognises at once that he sees the face of him in the latter. And if the coin were sensible how exactly it represents the face of the Emperor, and could speak to those that were going to see him, after they had been looking at the image, it might say, "I and the Emperor are one; for I am in him, and he is in me. What you see in me, you will see in him; and what you have seen in him, that is exactly to be seen in me." Accordingly, he who

worships the image, in it worships the Emperor also, for the image exhibits, and really is, the Emperor's face and form.   As then the Son has declared Himself to be the proper and express Image of His Father, we must necessarily understand, that the Divinity, and all the attributes of the Father, is in the being of the Son.   And this is what is meant in those words of Scripture, "Who being in the form of God" (Philip. ii. 6), and "The Father is in Me" (S. John xiv. 10).

6. Moreover, He is not merely partially in the form of God, but the Son is the Fulness of the Father, and His nature is perfectly adequate of His Father's, and the Son is wholly and entirely God.   Therefore, also, since He is equal to God, He "thought it not robbery to be equal with God" (Philip. ii. 6).   There is a perfect unity and individuality of infinite essence and attributes between Himself and His Father, which is the meaning of those words, "I am in the Father."   Thus "God was in Christ reconciling the world unto Himself" (2 Cor. v. 19), that is to say, the nature of the Father is the same as the Divine nature of the Son, who, having assumed human nature, reconciles it to His Father. Thus the works of the Son are the works of the Father, because that Divinity of the Father which wrought those works is in the nature and essence of the Son.   Thus the Father is seen in the Son, because the Father's Godhead can be contemplated in the Son, and this demonstrates the Father to be in the Son, even in His very nature.   And again, this community of essence convinces us that the Son is in the very nature of His Father, and that it is impossible that He should ever be out of that nature. If, therefore, when we find in Scripture that whatever belongs to the nature of the Father belongs also to the nature of the Son, we do not understand this as if God had only invested a creature with attributes similar to those of His own Divine nature, or as if He were in some way made to partake of these qualities, but in the plain and obvious sense of such assertions, that the whole nature of the Son is of, and in the very substance of, the Father's infinite essence.   Then, as I have said before, we can rightly understand the words, "I am in the Father, and the Father is in Me," and "I and My Father are one."   The Son is such as the Father is, because there is no single attribute which the Father has which the Son has not.   And that the Son is co-eternal with the Father the very nature of the relation proves.   For no one is father of a son until that son exists, whereas when we call God a Maker this does not necessarily imply a co-existence of production; and therefore it does not follow that God could not

be a Creator before the existence of His creatures. But God could not be a Father before He had a Son of His substance, and therefore His Paternity must have been co-eternal with His Godhead. Accordingly, He that believes in the Son believes in the Father, because the object of that belief is co-essential and consubstantial with the Father. And thus we have but one faith in but one God. The Divinity of the Son and Father is so perfectly uncompounded and individual, that whoever worships and honours the Son, worships and honours the Father in the same act. In those addresses which are made to the Son, the Father has an immediate interest, and the Son has the same in those which are directed to the Father. And thus we believe in and worship only one God, for there is but one, and there cannot be another. And therefore most appropriately do we find in Holy Scripture assertions of this Unity of the Godhead, such as, " I am that I am" (Exod. iii. 14); and, " There is no God beside Me" (Deut. xxxii. 39); and, " I am the First and I am the Last" (Isa. xliv. 6). God is but One, and Only and First; but God forbid that this truth should tempt us to deny that these attributes belong also to His Blessed Son. He is in that One and Only and First great Being; He is the One and Only Word and Wisdom and Brightness of His Only and Eternal Father. He is the First from everlasting, as being the Fulness of His Divinity, who is First and from eternity, as being properly and absolutely God. These assertions of the Unity of God are not arguments against the Divinity of the Son, but they are only meant to deny that any other being, besides the Father and His Word, is entitled to Divine honours. And this is so clearly and manifestly the sense of those passages, that anyone can understand them.

7. But since these passages of Scripture, too, must be perverted to the profane purposes of these blasphemers, since they dishonour God and reproach us, and say, " How can God be the One and Only God, and the First and the Last; and yet His Son be truly God too; for if His Son were as truly God as Himself, why did He say, 'There is no God beside Me' (Deut. xxxii. 39), and 'The Lord our God is one Lord'"? (Deut. vi. 4). I shall explain these phrases as well as I have done the rest that it may yet more notoriously appear how maliciously these Arians are set against God. If they had ever heard of any rivalry between the Son and the Father, then such words might be uttered against the Son. If, just as when David had to defend himself against Adonijah and Absalom, so also the Father has

occasion to look upon the Son, then the Father might have asserted His prerogatives in those expressions in order to guard against any rebellion of the Son, which might arise from that Son calling Himself God. He might speak thus to prevent the revolt and apostasy of some of His subjects. But if the contrary is true, if we cannot arrive at a true knowledge of the Father but by our knowledge of the Son, who reveals Him to us; if the contemplation of the Father is only possible in our contemplation of the Son; if the Son, whilst on earth, did not seek His own glory, but that of the Father, saying to one who came to Him, "Why callest thou Me good? None is good save One, that is God" (S. Luke xviii. 19); saying to another that asked Him, "Which is the first commandment of all?" "Hear, O Israel, the Lord our God is One Lord" (S. Mark xii. 28, 29); if He told the people, "I came down from heaven, not to do My own will, but the will of Him that sent Me" (S. John vi. 38); if He said to the disciples, "My Father is greater than I" (S. John xiv. 28); and "He that honoureth Me, honoureth Him that sent Me" (*cf.* S. John v. 23); if this, I say, be the Son's account of Himself, if there is this harmony and agreement between Him and the Father, what difficulty is there, that one must thus pervert those plain words of Holy Writ? On the other hand, if the Father owns the Word to be His Blessed Son, that man must either be mad, or must entertain a strong prejudice against our Lord, who supposes that the Father introduced this doctrine of His Unity, in order to vilify and deny His own Son. Such a thought cannot enter into the mind of any Christian; God forbid that it should. These passages concerning the Divine Unity are not written with any reference to be implied against the Son of God, but simply to deny that those are rightly called gods, which have been falsely styled as such by men. And indeed there was great need for declaration to be made against the worship of these false deities.

8. No one can serve the true God and those false gods at one and the same time; he must choose one or the other. Therefore God, since He is good and full of tender concern for mankind, and because He would recover all wanderers from the error of their ways, says, "I am God alone," and "I am that I am," and "besides Me there is no God," and the like. He makes these assertions that He may condemn those which are so far from being gods that they are nothing, as well as that He may convert and draw all men unto Himself. Suppose that in the daytime, when the sun was shining brightly, that a man, who

wished to show his skill in painting, should daub a piece of wood with various colours, and should try and make people believe, that this painting, which had not the least resemblance towards light, was really the cause of light; and if the sun, resenting this, should say, " I alone am the light of the day, and besides me there is no other light," people would not infer from this that there was no brightness in his rays, but that the object of the words was to rebuke the error into which the painter would lead them concerning his picture, and the evil which would arise from a belief in such a gross absurdity. Why, then, when Almighty God declares that " He is what He is," that He is " the Only God," and that " there is none other besides Him," must we think that He intends any more than this, to make men renounce all false deities, and that they may recognise Him instead as the only true God? And, moreover, when God uttered these declarations, He revealed them through His own Word. For whatever the Father spoke, He delivered by and through His Word, unless these modern Jews will deny this statement also. But this is the fact, no matter what infatuation and malice may possess these followers of the devil. The Word of the Lord came unto the Prophets, and they heard Him speaking unto them. Well, then, if the Father uttered these very assertions by His Word, and if the Father neither speaks nor does anything but by Him, then these enemies of God cannot possibly prove that this Word of God who spoke was one of the beings against whom His assertions were directed, but these declarations all had reference to things foreign to Him, and which were not from Him. For, to resume our late illustration, if the sun had used those expressions, he would have explained away the error, and have made the assertions referred to, not indeed for the sake of implying that his rays were not a part of his nature and substance, but, on the contrary, to plainly declare that they were so. It is, therefore, evident that it was far from God's intention to deny His Son Divine honours, nor, indeed, was it with any reference to Him, that He declared against false deities. And it is remarkable, that God never asserted His Unity in the beginning of the world, nor spoke of it to Adam, although His Word, by whom He made all things, was then certainly with Him. There was not then any occasion for so doing, because there were no such things then as idols. But afterwards, when men rebelled against the truth, and set up gods for themselves as they pleased, then God's protestations against idolatry were very necessary, to put a stop to it. And, I may remark further, that in these assertions of the Divine Unity provision was made against those evil doctrines which God foresaw that wretched heretics would introduce in later days, of worshipping as God a being so far from being the express and true Image of the Eternal God, that they suppose Him to be out of the Divine nature, and foreign, and unallied to it.

9. If, then, the Father be called the only true God, He must not be thought to deny, that His Son, who says, " I am the Truth " (S. John xiv. 6), is also truly God. He only protests against those who by their nature have no pretentions whatever to Godhead, such as His Father and He have. Thus our Lord thought it no presumption to join Himself on terms of equality with the Father, and to say, " And Jesus Christ whom Thou hast sent " (S. John xvii. 3). Had He been a creature, He could not have so spoken, and He would not have ranked Himself with His Creator. For what fellowship is there between the true God and a dependent creature? So that by His joining Himself with the Father He has made a plain declaration that He is of the nature and substance of His Father, very God, truly and properly begotten of very God. And this is the doctrine which S. John has received and which He has delivered to us. He writes in his Epistle, " And we are in Him that is true, even in His Son, Jesus Christ ; this is the true God and eternal Life " (1 S. John v. 20). And this explains what the Prophet says concerning the creation, where he tells us that " God alone spreadeth out the heavens " (Job ix. 8), and when God says that He " stretcheth forth the heavens alone " (Isa. xliv. 24), it is evident that the Word is comprehended in this Unity of the Divine nature, even that Word " by whom all things were made, and without whom was not anything made that was made." And, therefore, if notwithstanding God affirms that He alone made the heavens, and yet it is certain that His Word made them, and therefore must be conceived to exist in and of the infinite substance of, the only Creator; it follows that when God declares Himself to be " One," and " the only God," and " the First and the Last," these expressions must be understood with this necessary restriction, that the Person of God's Eternal Word is in the nature and essence of this " One," " the only God," " the First and the Last," even as brightness exists in the light. And His being thus in and of the nature of the Father can be understood of the Word alone. All other creatures arose out of nothing at His command, and their nature is totally different from His. The Son only is properly and substantially begotten of the nature of His Father.

And, therefore, that assertion, "I am the First and the Last," is so far from countenancing the cause of our adversaries, as they imagine it does, that it utterly defeats and ruins it. For God says, "I am the First and the Last," and "the First" here must signify an antecedency of existence, either from eternity or only in order of time. If they say, that it signifies only the latter, and if He is said to be the first of all creatures, so that they come next to Him, then certainly you will have shown that He is the head of them, as being the first created; and this is the height of atheism and absurdity. But if the meaning of His being First is, that He did not exist from something existing before Him, and that no person or thing was in being before Him, but that He was the Author and Cause of all things, and if He insisted upon this to destroy idolatry and paganism; then these words, "I am the First," and His being called the First-born are parallel to this and declare Him to be, as the Father declares of Himself, that He is not to be ranked with created beings, but that the Son was immediately concerned with the creation and adoption of all things. For as the Father is First, so also is He also First, the First in the First, the full and adequate Image of the First; as truly begotten of His Father's substance, as the creatures were made and adopted by His immediate application.

10. However, they try to explain away the truth by their fictions. They say, that the Church is mistaken, about this unity and likeness between the Son and the Father. They argue, that it consists in the agreement of the will of the Son with that of the Father, and that the Son is one with the Father, because the Son's apprehension and judgment of things agrees perfectly well with the Father's, and because He declares and teaches nothing but what the Father approves of. This is what some of them have had the boldness to say and to write, and there cannot be a more ridiculous and wild imagination. For this is such a unity in which others besides the Son might participate. It would follow, if this were so, that the Angels and the different orders of the celestial beings, Principalities, Powers, Thrones, and Dominions, and even those material things such as the Sun, the Moon, and Stars, might quite as well assume the name of Sons of God as our Lord Himself; and that they might assume and affirm that they, as well as He, are one with the Father, and are Words of God. For what God wills, they will the same; and their wills and judgments are entirely conformable and absolutely subject unto Him. Had this not been the case, they must have forfeited

the state of glory in which they were created, just as he who did not preserve his first estate, but indulged in apostasy, heard the words, "How art thou fallen from heaven, O Lucifer, son of the morning?" (Isa. xiv. 12). But if all this is true, how then can our Lord be the Only-begotten Son, and God's Word and Wisdom? or how can He be the express Image of His Father's Person, if so many are like the Father? For, since the world began, there have been men who have resembled the Father, in some measure, by their goodness and virtue. Such have been the noble army of Martyrs, and before them the Apostles and Prophets, and before them still, the Patriarchs. And even at this day, there are many good and faithful servants of our Blessed Lord, many who try to be "merciful, as their Father also is merciful" (S. Luke vi. 36), and who try to observe the precept, "Be ye therefore followers of God, as dear children, and walk in love, as Christ also has loved us" (Eph. v. 1, 2), that is to say, there are many also who seek to imitate S. Paul, even as he imitated Christ. And yet none of these can be said to be God's Word, or Wisdom, or His Only-begotten Son or Image ; nor has any one of them ventured to say such a thing as "I and the Father are one," or "I am in the Father and the Father is in Me ;" but it is said of them all in general, "Among the gods there is none like unto Thee, O Lord" (Ps. lxxxvi. 8), and "What is he among the gods that shall be likened unto the Lord?" (Ps. lxxxix. 7). But there is only one genuine and adequate and perfect Image of the Father. For although it is true that we ourselves were created after that Image, and although we are called "the image and glory of God" (1 Cor. xi. 7); still, there is not anything in our nature in which this likeness and glory consists, but it is because of the dwelling in us of the genuine Image and Glory of God, even of that Word and Son, who became incarnate for us.

11. This opinion of theirs, then, is, like their other notions, unseemly and ridiculous ; for this likeness and unity must of necessity have reference to the substance of the Son. For if it be understood otherwise, the Son will not have anything beyond ordinary creatures, as we have shown ; nor will He be like the Father, but He will be like the Father's doctrines. And, therefore, it would follow, that the Son would rather be unlike the Father, than like Him ; because the doctrines and teaching of the Father are quite distinct from the substance of the Father. If, then, with regard to the doctrines and teaching, the Son is like the Father, then the Father will be only nominally and metaphorically such, and this will be to take away the propriety

and expressness of that Image and Representation of Him, which the Scripture declares the Son is. For it is impossible that He should be the proper and express Image of the Father's Person, and yet have nothing common with Him in His nature. For example, S. Paul taught doctrines similar to those which our Lord approved, but yet no one would say that he was like our Lord in substance. It appears, then, how miserably our adversaries are mistaken, and that the Father and the Son are one in essence, as has been proved; and that the Son is like the Father Himself, and proceeds from Him, just as children are of the same species as their parents, and are of their substance, and just as the brightness has the same relation towards the sun. And in consequence of this unity of nature, the Father is said to work, or do, whatsoever the Son works, or does. And when the Son comes to His Saints, the Father also come to them in the Son, as He promised when our Lord says, "I and My Father will come, and will make our abode with him" (S. John xiv. 23). For the Father may be always contemplated in the express Image of His Person, just as where there is brightness there cannot but be light. Accordingly we find, as I observed before, that the Son bestows grace and peace as well as the Father, as S. Paul declares in all his Epistles, when he writes, "Grace to you and peace from God our Father, and the Lord Jesus Christ" (Rom. i. 7, &c.). The grace which the Son bestows upon us is really the same as the Father's; just as one light proceeds from the body of the sun and from its rays, and as the sun's illumination is effected through its brightness. S. Paul has plainly expressed and asserted this unity of nature between the Father and the Son, where he prays for the Thessalonians, "Now God Himself and our Father, and our Lord Jesus Christ, direct our way unto you" (1 Thess. iii. 11). In this passage, in the original, the word "direct" is not in the plural, as we should have imagined, as if the direction were to proceed partly from the Father and partly from the Son, and as if it were to be the joint work of two separate individuals. The word is in the singular, to show that the Father bestows the grace through the Son. And this is all so clear, that our adversaries might well blush for shame when they consider it, if they had not lost all sense of modesty.

12. For if there were no unity, if the Word was not the proper Offspring of the Father's substance, as the brightness is of the light, if the Son were of a different nature from the Father, the Son's part in the distribution of mercies and graces would be unaccountable. This is a province which the Father Himself would

not only be sufficient for, but which is peculiar to the Creator, and, in the nature of it, impossible to be communicated to the creature. And, therefore, being ascribed to the Son as well as to the Father, it demonstrates their unity of nature. No one, for instance, would pray to receive from God and the Angels, or from any other creature, nor would anyone say, " May God and His Angels give thee this or that." But whatever we pray for, we pray for from the Father and the Son, because of their essential unity and their unity in bestowing gifts and graces. For all things are given through the Son; and, indeed, whatever the Father acts or does, He does by the Son, and because of Him grace is made secure to him who receives it. But if it be urged against us that the Patriarch Jacob, when blessing his grandchildren, Ephraim and Manasses, said, " God which fed me all my life long unto this day, the Angel which redeemed me from all evil bless the lads " (Gen. xlviii. 15, 16); we must not suppose from these words that he considered created Angels to be equal to God their Creator. Nor did he, putting aside the God who had always sustained and preserved him, ask from an Angel a blessing on his grandchildren. In saying " the Angel which redeemed me from all evil," he showed clearly that he meant no created Angel, but the Word and Son of God, whom he made in his prayer a joint object of worship with the Father, because the Father protects and delivers by the Son. And the Patriarch might as properly style Him his Angel of benediction and deliverance, just as the Prophet called him afterwards by a name which probably Jacob knew, " The Angel of great Counsel " (Isa. ix. 6, Sept.). Nor is it conceivable that Jacob would beseech God for a blessing upon Himself, and that he would ask an Angel to bless his grandchildren. It was, of course, the same Person he addressed now, to whom he had said formerly, " I will not let Thee go, except Thou bless me " (Gen. xxxii. 26); and that the Person to whom the Patriarch then spoke was God, he himself assures us, saying, " I have seen God face to face " (Gen. xxxii. 30). This is He whom he prayed to bless also the sons of Joseph. The Angels are all ministering spirits; they are always ready to obey the commands of God. Thus Angels were deputed to go before and conduct the Israelites, to clear the land of Canaan from the Amorites and other enemies, and to lead and guard God's people in the dangers of their journey. And yet this work is, after all, not properly theirs but God's, who employed and sent them; and who alone is able to defend and deliver whom He will. It was, therefore, the Lord God Himself who chose to show Himself personally to Jacob, when He said to him, " And, behold, I am with thee, and will keep thee in all places whither thou goest" (Gen. xxviii. 15). It was the same Almighty God that came to Laban and prevented his evil purpose against Jacob, and commanded him not to speak roughly to him (Gen. xxxi. 24). And this was that God of whom Jacob implored safety in that prayer, " Deliver me, I pray Thee, from the hand of my brother, from the hand of Esau, for I fear him " (Gen. xxxii. 11) ; and in speaking to his wives he said, " God hath not suffered Laban to hurt me " (Gen. xxxi. 7).

13. And David, too, sought deliverance and rescue from none other but God Himself, as we learn from his words, " When I was in trouble I called upon the Lord, and He heard me ; deliver my soul, O Lord, from lying lips, and from a deceitful tongue " (Ps. cxx. 1, 2). This was the Lord whom the same Prophet celebrated in that Psalm of thanksgiving, in the day in which the Lord delivered him from the hand of all his enemies and from the hand of Saul, saying, " I will love Thee, O Lord my strength ; the Lord is my strong rock, and my defence, and my deliverer" (Ps. xviii. 1, 2). And it was the goodness of this God, which S. Paul, after he had endured many sufferings and persecutions acknowledges and commemorates, saying, " Out of them all the Lord delivered me " (2 Tim. iii. 11), and "in whom we trust that He will yet deliver us " (2 Cor. i. 10). It was not any creature, but God Himself, who blessed His servants Abraham and Isaac ; and Isaac prayed that the blessing of God might descend upon Jacob in these words, " God Almighty bless thee, and make thee fruitful, and multiply thee, that thou mayest be a multitude of people, and give thee the blessing of Abraham my father " (Gen. xxviii. 3, 4). Well then, if blessing and deliverance come from God alone, if Jacob owed his safety and preservation to none other than God, and if he sought and requested it for his grandsons only from Him, it is clear and certain that the Angel, whom he joins with God in his prayer for their safety and happiness, could be no other than God the Word and Son ; and the reason why he called Him an Angel, was because it is He who is the revealer of the Father. This makes this passage of Scripture correspond with that form of Apostolic benediction, " Grace be to you and peace from God our Father, and the Lord Jesus Christ" (Rom. i. 7). As the grace to be conferred was individually one, so was the nature and essence of the two Persons, the Son and the Father, of whom it was sought. And, therefore, both were to be mentioned,

and application was to be made to both. It flows from the Father, but through the Son; and although we receive it immediately from the Son, it is, nevertheless, the Father that communicates it, in and by the Son. And this is fully and distinctly expressed by the Apostle, for he says, writing to the Corinthians, " I thank my God always on your behalf, for the grace of God which is given you by Jesus Christ " (1 Cor. i. 4). And this, indeed, one may see in that illustration of light and brightness. For the light enlightens whatever it shines upon by the action of its rays; and whatever the brightness of the rays illuminates, that brightness comes really from the light itself. Thus the Son is beheld in the Father, as being the Brightness of His infinite Glory, and thus the Father and the Son are essentially one.

14. But this is not so with regard to the relation existing between God and His creatures. No Angel nor created being can properly co-operate with Him. He is, indeed, the singular and only efficient Cause, of which the origin and substance of created things, and all their properties and powers, are produced. God is one and alone; but their natures and abilities are perfectly distinct from, and infinitely inferior to, His. They were made themselves, and cannot make anything. And as they cannot be God's associates or partners in the production of effects, neither can they be so in the donation of blessings. No Angel would dare to say, that he that had seen him had seen the Father, nor would any man say such a thing. For Angels, as it is written, are " ministering spirits sent forth to minister " (Heb. i. 14), and they are ambassadors of those gifts which are given by Him, through the Word and Son of God, to those who are appointed to receive them. And so we find, that the Angels, when they appear to announce a message, say that they have been sent by their Lord. Gabriel declared this in the case of Zacharias, and he also made a similar statement with regard to Mary, the Mother of God. And those holy persons, who beheld visions of Angels, knew very well when they had seen only an Angel, and when they had seen God. Zacharias saw only an Angel; but Isaiah beheld the Lord. Manoah, the father of Samson, saw only an Angel; but Moses beheld God. Gideon saw an Angel; but it was God that appeared to Abraham. They distinguished and knew very clearly, whether it was God or an Angel who conversed with them. The points of difference between God and His creatures were just as evident and plain, as their natures were different and remote from one another.

Nevertheless, it might happen that the vision might be only that of an Angel, but the voice or revelation might proceed immediately from God, as when "the Angel of the Lord appeared unto Moses in a flame of fire out of the midst of a bush, and God called unto Moses out of the midst of the bush, and said, I am the God of thy father, the God of Abraham, the God of Isaac, and the God of Jacob" (*cf.* Exod. iii. 2, 4, 6). The Angel that appeared was not the God of Abraham, and therefore God was speaking on that occasion in or by the Angel. The Angel was seen, but God's voice was heard. That God, who spoke afterwards to Moses in a pillar of a cloud in the tabernacle, made Himself known unto him upon the mount by the vision and voice of an Angel. So also He spoke to Joshua under an Angel's form. Now, it is not to be questioned, but that God speaks by His Word, and not by any other person. And concerning this Word, since He is in the very nature of the Father, and is inseparable from the Father, and equal in perfection to the Father, it follows that the Father's works, efficiencies, and gifts, are truly and properly the Son's. Therefore he who knows that he has seen the Son, or heard the Word, knows that he has not seen an Angel, nor any creature superior in excellence and power to Angels, nor any creature whatsoever, but God Himself, who is the Father. It is just as he who sees the light of the sun shining round about him, does not need to be told that the sun itself diffuses that brightness in its rays.

15. For Holy Scripture applies such illustrations, as this of light or brightness, to the matter under dispute, and most useful and significant they are; for, when we use them, we are able to confound the traitor Jews, and to refute the wicked calumnies of those Gentiles, who groundlessly and maliciously say, on account of the Blessed Trinity, that we worship many gods. It might, indeed, be said, that we declare, with the followers of Marcion and Manichæus, that there are three Fathers or Gods, if we compared the three Persons to three suns in the firmament. But no such objection can be laid to our charge, when we illustrate our meaning by one sun and the unity of its light, rays, and brightness. We maintain that there is one first Cause and Author of all things. We do not imagine the Son to be a different kind of Deity from the Father, or only a colleague with Him in the Godhead. We affirm that His and His Father's Godhead are one, and that His cannot be a distinct and separate one from the Father's, because it is begotten of the very substance of the Father. But the Arians must be regarded, and must own them-

selves, to be both polytheists and atheists; because they acknowledge the Son to be God as well as the Father, although distinct from the Father; and they confess the Holy Spirit likewise to be so, at the same time that they affirm both to be made out of nothing, that is, not to be God. For they are under the unhappy necessity, either of denying the Son to be God, or (if they have not the courage to do this, because the Scripture expressly declares Him to be so, and yet they will not allow Him to be properly God, but affirm that His nature and substance are entirely distinct and separate from His Father's) they must confess, that, according to their view, there are more gods than one. They have but one way in which they can elude this dilemma, and that is, to affirm, that the Son, although God, is only so by way of participation, because of His immediate dependence upon the Divine attributes; and then all creatures, as well as the Son, would be called gods too. But if this is their notion, let such an impious doctrine be immediately banished. It is iniquitous to suppose for one moment, that the Word of God is no more a God than one of His lowest creatures. The Divine Nature cannot but be one. It is one in the Father, and one also in the Word. God is one; the Father is one essence, subsisting in Himself, omnipresent and infinite; and this Divinity both is and manifests itself in the Son, by whom He acts or speaks, in all places, and at all times. The same Divinity is also in the Holy Ghost, operating and influencing by the Word in that Blessed Spirit. And this explains and justifies our doctrine of the Unity in Trinity, which we hold to be far more agreeable to religion, than the godhead of the Arian heretics, with its many kinds and many parts.

16. If the Word was from nothing, and is a creature, either they must own that He is not true God, because He Himself is one of the creatures; or if, from regard for the Scriptures, they will go on to call Him a God, it is impossible for them to deny, that there are two Gods, that is to say, one the God the Creator, and the other a God whom He created. Thus they have got two Lords to serve, one an unmade, the other a made one. Thus they must have two faiths, one in the True God, and the other in one who is made and invented by themselves, and called by them God. And so this absurd delusion proves a great snare to them, for it follows that when they worship the uncreated God, they must renounce the God who is made, and when they worship the created Deity, they turn from the Creator. Both cannot be worshipped in one act, or beheld at one view; because there is no manner of union between their several natures and opera-

tions. And, besides, if our adversaries hold such sentiments as these, they certainly will not stop here, but will go on to more gods, for this is always the way with those who revolt from the one God. Why, then, when the Arians hold these opinions and sentiments, do they not rank themselves with the heathen, and own them as brethren? For what is paganism, but worshipping and serving a creature, instead of the True God the Creator? And this is their religion and practice, although they will not always own it in terms, because some of their followers would be alarmed at such a confession, and would perhaps leave them at once, unless they were thus blinded and deceived. For that subtle statement, which they are continually urging, is in order to deceive the simple. They say, " We deny that there can be two unmade beings." But what follows except this, that they confess and worship two Gods, and these with different natures, the one made, the other unmade. All the difference between them and the heathen is, that the heathen worship one unmade and many made, and the Arians worship one unmade and but one made. But there is no real difference here, after all. For the God whom they call made must be as truly made as all the made ones of the heathen; and all the made gods of the heathen have the same nature as this one of the Arians, for both he and they are creatures. What wretched creatures, then, are these Arians, and the more so because their profession of Christianity has only turned to an opportunity of insulting the Blessed Lord. They are apostate infidels, and are greater traitors than the Jews in denying and renouncing Christ. They are confederates with the heathen, hateful to God, and they worship and serve the creature and many false deities. But there is only one true God, and He has but one Son and Word, and that Word is God, and He alone is the express Image of His Father's substance. And this He Himself has in effect asserted in that expostulation of His with the Jews, where He says, " The Father Himself which hath sent Me, hath borne witness of Me. Ye have neither heard His voice at any time, nor seen His shape. And ye have not His Word abiding in you; for whom He hath sent, Him ye believe not" (S. John v. 37, 38). Here we find the Shape or Image of God, mentioned in conjunction with His Word. Here the Word of God informs the Jews what He is, even the Image, the Representation, or Shape of the Father; and He accuses them for not receiving and believing in that Word, which is the Shape or Image of God, because they did not receive and believe in Him who spoke these words to them. This is He that made Himself visible to the Patriarch Jacob, and gave him His blessing, and changed his name from Jacob to that of Israel, even as Holy Scripture testifies in the words, "And as he passed over Peniel" (the Face of God), "the sun rose upon him" (Gen. xxxii. 31). And this it was who said, "He that hath seen Me, hath seen the Father" (S. John xiv. 9), and "I am in the Father and the Father is in Me" (S. John xiv. 11), and "I and the Father are one" (S. John x. 20). Thus the Godhead is still one, and our faith in the Father and the Son is one faith in one God. We read and know that the Word is God, and being so, He must be of and in the very essence of His Father, His Son consubstantially. And, consequently, although the Word be God, as well as the Father, still "the Lord our God is one Lord" (Deut. vi. 4).

17. But our Arian adversaries have still a shameless answer ready for us. They reply to us in this strain : "It is not, as you say, but as we will ; for although you may have put aside some of our former arguments, still we have others in reserve. Let us see what you will say to this objection. We affirm that the Father and the Son are one, and that the Father is in the Son, and the Son is in the Father, as the Father and we ourselves are one, and as the Father is in us and as we are in the Father, and in no other manner. For this is written in the Gospel according to S. John, and this is what Christ Himself asked for us from the Father. He says, ' Holy Father, keep through Thine own Name those whom Thou hast given Me, that they may be one, as we are.' And a little afterwards, 'Neither pray I for these alone, but for them also which shall believe on Me through their word ; that they all may be one ; as Thou, Father, art in Me, and I in Thee, that they also may be one in us ; that the world may believe that Thou hast sent Me. And the glory which Thou gavest Me I have given them ; that they may be one, even as we are one. I in them, and Thou in Me, that they may be made perfect in one, and that the world may know that Thou hast sent Me' (S. John xvii. 11-23)." Thus, having found a way of evasion, these wretches craftily say, " If the Son and the Father are one, and if the Son is in the Father only in the same sense and manner as we are made or become one with and in the Father ; what evidence can be alleged from the words, "I and the Father are one," and "I am in the Father, and the Father is in Me," of the truth of the doctrine, that the Son is in and of the substance of His Father essentially and really ? For if these last assertions declare Him to be so, those other statements which we argue from, as plainly declare that we are so too. But if it can-

not be inferred from the text we bring forward, that we are so; as little can you support your doctrine from your texts which allege that He is so." And thus they foolishly gossip. But in this obstinacy of theirs, there is nothing to be seen but irrational recklessness and rashness. They seem to be bent on imitating the folly of the devil, saying with him, " We will ascend into heaven, we will be like the Most High " (Isa. xiv. 13, 14). For what is given to man by grace, this they would make equal to the Godhead of the Giver. No sooner do they find themselves honoured by God by the title of sons, than they must fancy themselves equal to the eternal and substantial Son of God. And now, again, hearing from our Blessed Lord, " that they may be one as we are," nothing less will satisfy their presumption and vanity, than that they are to commence as sons and stand in as near and as high a relation to the Father as the very Offspring of His Essence ; that they are to be in the Father as much as He, and the Father in them as much as in the Son, forgetting that this was the arrogance and rebellion which caused the fall and ruin of their father the devil.

18. If, then, it is really the case, as our adversaries will have it, that the Word of God is simply the same as we are, and only differs from us in point of time ; then, as we have had occasion to say before, let Him be like us, and have the same rank in all things as we have. Let Him not be called any more the Only-begotten, nor the only Word and Wisdom of the Father ; but let every one of us have the same names as He has, since we are all like Him. All things of the same species or kind have a common right and title to the name of that species, and seniority makes no difference. Human nature is not in any way altered by lapse of time. S. Paul was as truly a man as Adam, and he that was born to-day is to all intents and purposes a man, and in this matter time is a subject of no consequence at all. If, then, the Word only differs from us with regard to time, this is indeed no difference whatever, and we must be beings such as He is. But we are quite sure that we are not the Word and Wisdom of God, and that He is neither a creature nor a work ; else how is it that we are all sprung from one, and that He is the only Word? The principles of Arianism makes it fitting, I suppose, for them to make such dreadful statements ; but no Christian ought to entertain such considerations for one moment. The passages of Scripture which we have quoted, which our adversaries intended to make so much out of, are to every candid person so manifestly to be reconciled with our doctrine, and carry with them such

proof of its truth and orthodoxy, that it seems almost needless to dilate upon their meaning further. But because a discussion and interpretation of them will strengthen the charge of blasphemy and impiety which we bring against Arianism, we shall proceed to show that these texts are all on the side of that Faith which we profess, and which has been handed down to us from the Fathers of the Church. Now, it is customary in Holy Scripture to use the things of nature by way of images and illustrations for mankind ; and this is done, that these representations may exhibit and describe to us the moral actions of men, and that in this manner these may be shown to be either right or wrong. Thus the Psalmist speaks of those who are vile sinners, " Be ye not like to horse and mule, which have no understanding " (Ps. xxxii. 10). Or, again, when he speaks of those who have become wicked, he says, " Man, being in honour, hath no understanding, but is compared unto the beasts that perish " (Ps. xlix. 20). And, again, Jeremiah says, " They were as fed horses in the morning " (Jer. v. 8). And our Lord has described Herod in these words, "Go ye, and tell that fox " (S. Luke xiii. 32). And when our Lord sends forth his disciples, he says, " Behold, I send you forth as sheep in the midst of wolves, be ye therefore wise as serpents and harmless as doves " (S. Matt. x. 16). No one would be so foolish as to fancy, that there was a command in these words to the Apostles, to change themselves into sheep, or into serpents, or doves. God did not make them so, and they cannot make themselves so. The meaning of these figurative expressions is simply, that we should avoid that fierceness for which some animals are remarkable, and imitate that gentleness which is displayed in others ; we should be on our guard against the wiles of the old serpent, and be meek and patient as the dove.

19. And sometimes our Saviour takes patterns for man from the Divine Persons, for He says, " Be ye merciful, as your Father which is in heaven is merciful " (S. Luke vi. 36) ; and, " Be ye perfect, even as your Father which is in heaven is perfect " (S. Matt. v. 48). And here He certainly does not mean that we should endeavour to become equal to God in the perfections of His nature ; for this is far too high a standard to be attained to by mere creatures. But, as the Psalmist, when he charges us, " Be ye not like to horse," &c., bids us not make ourselves like brute beasts, and thereby tells to beware of degenerating into imitating their lower natures ; so our Lord proposes the goodness and mercy of God, not for a standard of nature, but as a pattern or rule of action. He neither

commands nor expects that we should emulate God in the nature of His attributes ; but only that we should conform our practice as nearly as we can to the Divine goodness; that we should be as serviceable as we can to one another, not so much for men's sake, as for God's sake, so that at length we may be rewarded, not by men, but by God. The Son of God is the Only-begotten One of His nature, and His creatures cannot be such. But, nevertheless, we too are sons of God by adoption and grace, and God is pleased to call us poor mortals by the title of gods. But although this is so, yet no one ought to be so foolish, as to suppose that we can be as the true God, or as His Word. And thus, when God enables us to be merciful, even as He is merciful, this does not alter our nature entirely ; it does not render us infinitely good and benevolent. It does not make us, as God, the source of happiness to the creatures. It is more in this way ; that we are disposed to distribute benefits and to give assistance freely, impartially, and universally, even as God Himself does. For it is only in this manner, that we can in any sense become imitators of God, when we dispense to others, and bestow liberally upon other people, those good gifts which come to us from Him. And we need no more than this, to make the meaning of these passages in the Gospel according to S. John clear and simple, which our adversaries allege against us. Has S. John anywhere told us, that we are in the Father, after the same manner and as properly as the Son is ? Has he said, that we, who are fashioned out of the earth, are as truly within the nature and essence of God as His own Word and Wisdom ? Does he not, on the contrary, expressly assure us that the Word is truly God, even in His very nature and substance ? " We know," he says, "that the Son of God is come, and hath given us an understanding, that we may know Him that is true, and we are in Him that is true, even in His Son Jesus Christ. This is the true God, and eternal life" (1 S. John v. 20). But we are only made God's sons by adoption and grace, and are made so by the communication of the Holy Spirit, as the same Apostle informs us, " As many as received Him, to them gave He power to become the sons of God, even to them that believe on His Name" (S. John i. 12). And, therefore, also our Lord is the Truth, even as He declares of Himself, " I am the Truth" (S. John xiv. 6). The same assertion He repeats in His address to the Father, saying, "Sanctify them through Thy Truth, Thy Word is Truth" (S. John xvii. 17). Whereas our sonship and the best of our perfections are but resemblances and shadows of the great Reality.

20. And, therefore, our Lord did not pray, " that they may be one, even as We are" (*cf.* S. John xvii. 21), in order that we might have a similar nature to His, but that our wills might conform to His ; that we should be enabled to resemble God, as nearly as we can in doing what is right, just as His Son truly equals Him in the infinity of His nature.   He prayed that we should endeavour to preserve an agreement and union of spirit with one another, even as there is a union of essence and attributes between these two Persons of the Trinity ; and that there should be no schism amongst us, as there was amongst the Corinthians, but that we should be like that multitude of believers mentioned in the Acts of the Apostles, who were " of one heart and of one soul " (Acts iv. 32).   We are commanded to act as sons of God, but not to be the Son of God.   We are to be like gods in aiming at goodness, but not to be divinities ourselves.   We are to strive to be " merciful as the Father," but not to partake of the Father's essence and substance.   When God has made us one, as the Father and the Son are one, we shall not be either in the Son or in the Father, as the Father and the Son are in one another. Our union with God has reference to our imitation of His will, and we shall best fulfil the purpose of our Lord's prayer, if, in the duties of brotherly love, we can imitate the unity of the Divine essence, and also, if we can, by acts of kindness and love, imitate the Divine goodness.   For things of the same nature are united together by that very community of nature.   Thus all mankind are one family, from whose nature that of the Word is quite distinct and different ; for it is perfectly equal and like that of the Father, and, therefore, He cannot but be substantially and essentially One with the Father.   As for mankind, they agree in one nature or species, for all were made from one, and so they ought to be as closely united in natural affection as the Father and the Son are in nature and essence, if that were possible.   Thus our Saviour, when He taught us meekness, proposes His own example for us to imitate.   He says, " Learn of Me, for I am meek and lowly in heart " (S. Matt. xi. 29).   It was not that we were to become equal with Him, for that would be an impossibility ; but He meant that we should set Him before ourselves as our example or pattern.   In like manner He recommends the unity of the Divine Persons, as a pattern of that charity which ought to be seen in His disciples.   He says, " that they may be one even as we are one," that is to say, that they may imitate our unity of nature in their unity of affection ; and as we are one individual essence, so they may keep themselves one undivided body.   And

the imitation of things which are in nature is an excellent model and example for us, better, indeed, than the actions and patterns of men. For the latter are very variable, whereas the former do not alter or change. A fixed rule is always to be preferred to an unsteady one, with regard to the regulation of our lives. And so now we may see more clearly what is the proper meaning of the words, " that they also may be one in us," and what they have to do with us.

21. If, for instance, it had been possible for us to be in the nature of the Father as the Son is, and had this been meant or supposed in the text before us, our Saviour ought to have spoken very differently. He should have said, " that they may be one in Thee," as the Son is in the Father. But as it is, He has not said this, but by saying " in Us," He has shown how wide is the difference between the Only Son being in the Only Father, as His Only Word and Wisdom, and between our being in the Son, and through Him in the Father. And by speaking in these terms, His meaning was as follows :—Grant that they may make our unity of nature the pattern, and, as far as they are able, the standard of their unity of affection. Grant that as we are one in nature and in truth, that so they too may be joined together in fraternal unity, after the pattern of our Eternal Union. And that the words " in us" may have this signification, we may learn from S. Paul, who says, " These things I have in a figure transferred to myself and to Apollos, that ye might learn in us not to think of men above that which is is written " (1 Cor. iv. 6). Will our adversaries say that the learning here was to be in the nature or essence of S. Paul and Apollos? Certainly there was no more meant here than the taking their practice for an example. And it is the same thing as if the Apostle had said, that ye may learn " of us," instead of " in us." Why, then, must another meaning be found for the words in the text of S. John? The Son, in the one place, proposes His Unity with the Father as a rule or example for the practice of His disciples ; as the Apostle in the other proposes his example to the Corinthians in the duties of charity and humility. A closer unity there could not be than that between the Father and the Son in the Divine Nature, and, therefore, there could not be a better instance brought forward to express that excellency of brotherly love and charity, which our Lord here enjoined upon His disciples. Or, if we must account in another manner for the text, the words " that they may become one in us," may signify that they may become one in the power of the Father and the Son, and that

they all continue in concord and agreement, " speaking the same things" (1 Cor. i. 10); for without God this is impossible. And we find this mode of expression in other places of Holy Scripture, as, " In God will we do great acts " (Ps. lx. 12); and, " In God I shall leap over the wall " (Ps. xviii. 29); and, " In Thee will we tread down our enemies " (Ps. xliv. 6). Therefore, it is plain, that as our baptism in the Name of the Father and the Son makes us one, so it keeps us firmly one in the bond of charity. For this is what our Saviour has said more emphatically still in those words of His, " And the glory which Thou gavest Me, I have given them ; that they may be one even as We are one " (S. John xvii. 22). Here He has very properly said, not, " that they may be in Thee as I am," but "as We are." And this plainly shows their unity here to be only figurative, as compared with that of the Father and the Son. For had this unity between the disciples and the Deity been the same in kind as His own unity with the Father, He would have worded Himself otherwise.

22. So, then, we see that God the Father and His Word are identically one in nature; whereas we can only be one with them as regards our imitation of that nature. And therefore our Lord adds to the text just quoted, " I in them and Thou in Me, that they may be made perfect in one " (S. John xvii. 23). By saying this our Lord seems to ask for something greater and more perfect for us. And as to our union with the Word, it may truly be said to have begun, and He to be made in us, by His taking upon Him our human nature, and this is the meaning of " I in them." And next He adds, " And Thou Father in Me," that is to say, "for I am Thy Word, and Thy very nature is in Me, as being so ; and as My human nature may be said to be in them, and because of Thee the salvation of men is perfected in Me, therefore I beseech Thee that they also may become one, as members of the same body, and according to their full perfection and happiness. Let them be united to Me, as this My natural body is, let Me, as it were carry them about with Me that all may be actually one mystical body, governed by one Spirit, and let all grow up unto ' a perfect man ' (Ephes. iv. 13)." For, indeed, we all, since we are spiritually partakers of our Lord, become one body, since we have the Lord within us. This is a very plain and reasonable construction of the text, and it shows even more clearly still the falsity of the Arian cause. If our Lord, I repeat, had said simply and absolutely, " that they may be made one in Thee," or "that they and I may be one in

Thee," then these enemies of God might have had something on their side, although even then their argument would have been a shameless one. But our Lord has studiously expressed Himself otherwise, and has said, " As Thou, Father, art in Me, and I in Thee, that they all may be one." Moreover, He would not here have used the word "As " if He wished to let us know that our union with the Father was to be the same in kind and manner with His own ; and therefore that expression plainly shows how distant our union is from His, that is, not in place but in nature ; for in place nothing is far from God, although everything must be infinitely removed from Him in nature. And therefore, as I said before, whenever the particle " As " is used, there is implied only an allegorical likeness or resemblance, but not a natural equality or identity, in the two unions.

23. We have another instance of the same mode of expression in what our Saviour tells us of the Prophet Jonah. He says, " For as Jonas was three days and three nights in the whale's belly, so shall the Son of Man be three days and three nights in the heart of the earth " (S. Matt. xii. 40). For no one would try to prove from this, that Jonah and the Saviour were one and the same person, or that Jonah descended into hell, or that the whale was hell, or that the fish did not only vomit out Jonah at the commandment of the Lord, after he had been swallowed up, but that Jonah also brought up others who had been before swallowed up by the whale. Undoubtedly the comparison here is only of a typical occurrence to the completion of it, and not of the essence or nature of the person that was the type and of the person that was the antitype. And, therefore, it does not at all follow from our being one in the Son, that we are so in Him, as He is in the Father and the Father in Him. It is our duty to be one in communion and in faith, as it is of the nature of the Son to be one in essence with the Father. Our Saviour was to be three days in the grave, as Jonah had been in the whale's belly ; but then, as this Jonah was not our Saviour, so our Saviour was not swallowed up by a fish, but descended into hell ; and so the descents were as absolutely distinct as the persons. In like manner, we are one in communion with Christ, as the Son is one in essence with the Father. But then we neither are, nor can be, either one with, or equal to, the Son in essence ; and therefore the unions here are as evidently distinct as the natures. For on this account is the word " As " applied to us, since things widely different in nature and species have a relative and figurative likeness and resemblance to one another, when they are

viewed in a certain relation. The Son's unity with and in the Father is declared in absolute terms; there is no condition annexed to it, for this attribute belongs to Him by nature. But for us, to whom this union is not natural, there is needed an image and example, that He may say of us, "As Thou art in Me and I in Thee." And when they shall be so perfected, He says, "then the world shall know that Thou hast sent Me," for unless I had come and assumed a mortal body, none of them could have attained to perfection or happiness, but one and all had remained corruptible. Therefore, O Father, do Thou influence them and work upon them, and as by giving Me this body Thou hast made Me one of them, so do Thou communicate to them that Spirit which is united to this Body, that they may be one in that, and perfect in Me. For this perfection will demonstrate that Thy Word has come among them, when they behold this exalted and Divine disposition of their minds. This will convince men that Thy Son has been upon earth, and that Thou hast sent Him. For whence has this perfection been possible for them if I, Thy Son and Word, had not taken that nature into My Divinity, had not I been made man, and performed the work which Thou gavest Me to do? And this work is perfected, because men, redeemed from sin, are no longer in a state of death, but being partakers of the Divine nature in a relative and mystical union with us, that grace is shed into their hearts, which is the bond of their mutual love one towards another.

24. And thus we have given a general account of those passages in the Gospel according to S. John, to which our adversaries have objected. The holy Apostle himself has very clearly explained the meaning of the words much more concisely and exactly in his Epistle. His exposition is such as severely reprimands the Arians and their views, and he declares the true sense of our being in God and God in us, and what is the nature of our unity in Him, and how infinite is the difference between Christ the Son of His substance and us who are His adopted children. This will prevent the Arians any longer from thinking that they shall be hereafter as the Eternal Son Himself, lest they hear these words applied to them, "Thou art a man, and not God" (Ezek. xxviii. 2), and, "Thou that art poor, make not thyself equal to him that is rich" (Prov. xxii. 4). S. John speaks in these words, "Hereby know we that we dwell in Him and He in us, because He hath given us of His Spirit" (1 S. John iv. 13). It is, then, because of the grace of the Spirit that has been given to us, that we are in Him and He in us. That

Spirit is the Spirit of God, and, therefore, they, in whose heart He dwells, may be very justly and truly said to be in God, and thus it is that God is in us. But then it does not therefore follow, that we are not so in the Father, as the Son is. The Father does not unite the Son to Himself by those communications of spiritual grace, by which the Son unites us to Himself. The Holy Ghost is not the principle of unity between the Father and the Word, but rather the Word is so between the Father and the Spirit. And the Son is in the Father, as His essential Word and Brightness. We, on the contrary, if the grace of the Spirit be not in us, are altogether aliens, not only out of His nature, but far from His favour. It is when we are partakers of the Spirit, that we become united to the Godhead itself. But then this union is not from our nature, but from that Spirit which is and continues in us, as long as we keep ourselves worthy of His indwelling, by our constancy in that confession which is mentioned by the same Apostle, when he says, "Whosoever shall confess that Jesus is the Son of God, God dwelleth in him, and he in God" (1 S. John iv. 15). What, then, is our likeness or equality to the Son? Are not the Arians vanquished on this subject, and that on all sides? Does not S. John especially condemn them? Does not he declare, that the Son's being in the Father is quite another thing from our being in Him; and that we must never expect to be such as the Son is, and that the nature of the Word is not as ours? Or will they dare to have recourse to that old opinion of theirs, and say that the Son is only made such by the communication of the Spirit of grace, and that He was admitted into union with the Father, as a reward for His obedience and good services? But this, as we have shown already, is a most shameful blasphemy, a miserable invention, which deserves our utmost abhorrence. For, as has been stated, the Son communicates and gives the Spirit, and whatsoever the Spirit has, He receives from the Word.

25. Our Saviour, then, when He says of us, "As Thou, Father, art in Me, and I in Thee, that they too may be one in us," does not intimate or imply, that our nature will be hereafter identical with His; for this was clearly proved from the instance of Jonah. We learn from the verse, that the passage before us is a prayer of our Saviour to His Father, that He would communicate to those who believe on Him the grace of the Holy Spirit through and in Him, who is the Author and Centre of our union with God, and our unity among ourselves. The Word is in the Father's essence, and the Spirit proceeds from and is given

by the Word. He, therefore, prays that we may be made partakers of this Holy Spirit, that, by the grace of that Spirit, which is the Spirit of that Word, which is the essence of the Father, we might be joined and united and made one in the Word, and through the Word in the Father Himself. And how indissoluble He desired this unity of His Church should be, appears from the nature of that parallel to which He has here likened it, "That they may be one, even as we are one." He beseeches the Father, that He would so establish this unity of grace in His Church, that it should be as lasting and permanent, as even the unity of Persons in the Blessed Trinity. And the Apostle, having this in his thoughts, said, "Who shall separate us from the love of Christ"? (Rom. viii. 35); and afterwards tells us, that "the gifts and calling of God are without repentance" (Rom. xi. 29). We, considered in ourselves, are not in God; for it is not anything of our nature, but only the Spirit inhabiting our persons, which exists in the nature of God. As the Word's indwelling is the means of our adoption and our being made one with God, so the means of our union with and unity in the Father and the Son, is the grace of the Holy Ghost, who is in the essence of the Word, as the Word is in the essence of the Father. And, therefore, when at any time the wickedness of man so grieves the Holy Spirit, that He departs from the sinner; when he repents after his fall, the sinner may be sure that the Holy Spirit will return unto him, and will again make His abode with him. But until he so repents, and the Holy Spirit returns, the sinner is no longer in God; because that Holy Spirit, which is in the essence of God, is no longer in the sinner. This was the miserable state of Saul, when "the Spirit of the Lord departed from him, and an evil spirit troubled him" (1 Sam. xvi. 14). When God's enemies hear this, they ought to be struck with shame, and no longer arrogate to themselves an equality with their Maker. But they neither understand, for, as Solomon says, "the wicked do not understand knowledge" (Prov. xxix. 7), nor will they endure wholesome doctrine or advice, but they find it intolerable to listen to anything of that nature.

26. And see now how active these Arians are, in cultivating their irreligious notions. In this they very much resemble Pharaoh, who wilfully hardened his heart; for, whilst they read and hear of the Saviour's human actions which are recorded in the Gospel, they seem, like Paul of Samosata, to have utterly forgotten the Divinity of the Son of God. And so they pour forth such rash and bold objections as these, "How can the Son

be from the Father by nature, and be like Him in substance, when He says, 'All power is given unto Me' (S. Matt. xxviii. 18); and, 'The Father judgeth no man, but hath committed all judgment unto the Son' (S. John v. 22); and, 'The Father loveth the Son, and hath given all things into His hand; he that believeth on the Son hath everlasting life' (S. John iii. 35, 36); and, 'All things are delivered to Me of My Father; and no man knoweth who the Son is but the Father, and he to whom the Son will reveal Him' (S. Luke x. 22); and again, 'All that the Father giveth Me shall come to Me'? (S. John vi. 37)" And from all this they draw this conclusion, "If the nature of the Son had been what you would have it to be, all these things could not have been given Him, because as being truly God, He must have had them in Himself. Or, once more, how can He be the genuine and natural Power of the Father, who, a little before the time of His Passion speaks in this fashion, 'Now is My soul troubled, and what shall I say? Father, save Me from this hour; but for this cause came I unto this hour. Father, glorify Thy Name. Then came there a voice from heaven saying, I have both glorified it, and will glorify it again' (S. John xii. 27, 28). And He said at another time, 'O My Father, if it be possible, let this cup pass from Me' (S. Matt. xxvi. 39); and, 'When Jesus had thus said, He was troubled in spirit, and testified, and said, Verily, verily, I say unto you, that one of you shall betray Me' (S. John xiii. 21)." From these passages they maliciously argue thus, "If He were really the Father's Power, He would not have felt any trouble or fear, but He would rather have supplied power to others instead." Moreover, they further object, "If He were by nature the true and proper Wisdom of the Father, how is it written, 'And Jesus increased in wisdom and stature, and in favour with God and man'? (S. Luke ii. 52). In like manner we read, 'When Jesus came into the coasts of Cæsarea Philippi, He asked His disciples, saying, Whom do men say that I am?' (S. Matt. xvi. 13.) And when He was at Bethany, He enquired where they had laid Lazarus (S. John xi. 34). Besides, He said to His disciples, 'How many loaves have ye?' (S. Mark vi. 38). How then," say they, "can He be the true Wisdom of God, who increased in wisdom, and was ignorant of what He asked of others?" They next proceed to urge this, "How can He be the Father's essential Word and Son, without whom the Father never was, and through whom He makes all things, as you tell us, who said upon the Cross, 'My God, My God, why hast Thou forsaken Me?' (S. Matt.

xxvii. 46) ; and before that had prayed, 'Glorify Thy Name' (S. John xii. 28) ; and, 'O Father, glorify Thou Me with the glory which I had with Thee before the world was' (S. John xvii. 5). We find Him praying, too, in the deserts, and exhorting His disciples to 'watch and pray, lest they should enter into temptation,' for 'the Spirit indeed is willing, but the flesh is weak' (S. Matt. xxvi. 41). He also says, 'Of that day and hour knoweth no man, no, not the Angels, nor the Son' (S. Mark xiii. 32). Concerning these passages, these miserable men say, "If the Son were, according to your interpretation, the consubstantial Word of God, He could not have been ignorant of the day, but He had knowledge of it. How, too, could He be deserted by His Father, if He existed in His Father's nature from everlasting? Why should He ask His Father to confer glory upon Him, when He always enjoyed an equal state of glory with Him? Or, why should He have any occasion to pray, for He could need nothing if He was of the very substance of His Father? It is proper and necessary for creatures to require things, and to need what they have not, and therefore since the Son thus spoke, and had need for those things which He did not possess, it follows that He must be a creature, and one of things generate."

27. This, then, is what these irreligious men allege in their discourses ; and, if they thus argue, they might consistently speak yet more daringly. They might say, "What need was there, in the first instance, that the Word or Son of God should be made the Son of Man?" And again, "How could the great God be made a creature? How could an Infinite Spirit clothe itself with a human body?" Or they might ask with Caiaphas, after the manner of the Jews, "How is it that Christ, being a man, makes Himself God?" (S. John x. 33.) The Arians now as obstinately refuse to believe what they read, as the Jews did what they saw ; and the voices of the one are not to be distinguished from those of the other, in their invectives and blasphemies. If the arguments of the Jews and the Arians are set over one against the other, we shall see how exactly the infidelity and audacious impiety of one answers to the other, and the Church has to fight against both. The Jews could not conceive how our Lord, being man, could be God. And the Arians ask, "How was it possible for Him to be made man, if He is very God of very God?" The Jews were offended and scandalised at the sufferings of Christ ; they concluded that He could not be the Son of God, because He endured the Cross. And the Arians, arguing in very much the same way, ask us, how we

dare to affirm that a body of such a being as the consubstantial Word or Son of the Father should be thus liable to all these in-dignities and sufferings? Next, the Jews were so incensed at our Lord, because He called God His Father and made Himself equal with God, and because He appealed to the testimony and evidence of His miracles for the truth of His pretensions, that they sought to kill Him. The Arians, likewise, deny that God is properly His Father, and that He is equal with God; and because we hold this to be true, they seek to put us to death. Again, whereas the Jews said, "Is not this Jesus the Son of Joseph, whose father and mother we know? How is it, then, that He saith, Before Abraham was I am, and I came down from heaven"? (S. John vi. 42 ; viii. 58.) The Arians, likewise, tread in their footsteps, and ask similarly, "How can He be the Word of God, who slept, and wept, and asked questions, just like any ordinary man?" Thus they both conspire to deny the Eternity and the Godhead of the Word, in consequence of those human attributes which the Saviour took upon Him by reason of that mortal flesh which He was pleased to assume.

28. Since, then, their heresy thus entirely agrees with the Jewish doctrine, and since it is on a par with the belief of the traitor Judas, either let the Arians candidly confess that they are disciples of Caiaphas and Herod, instead of dressing up Judaism in a garb of Christianity, and let them, as we have before advised them, speak out plainly, and deny that the Saviour has appeared in the flesh, for this doctrine is all one with their heresy. Or, if they are afraid to become Jews openly, and are unwilling to submit to circumcision for fear of displeasing the Emperor, as well as on their account, whom they have deluded and beguiled, then let them cease from asserting these Jewish blasphemies. If they disown the name of Jews, then let them not believe and teach Jewish doctrine. As for us, we are not only called, but we are truly Christians. Let the Arians mark these words, that we are Christians, and, therefore, we try, because it is our privilege and duty, to inform ourselves and others of the reasonable and right meaning of those passages in the Gospels, which relate to the Person of our Blessed Lord. And when we find Him asserting the Divinity and Eternity of His nature, we do not seek to stone Him, with the Jews, nor with you do we raise objections against the truth, when He speaks for our sakes in humility concerning His human nature. If, then, you would return to the Christian Faith, put off from yourselves this Arian madness, and with the words of religion purge your ears, which have been defiled with

blasphemy. If you would but listen to the truth, you would soon be convinced that you were Jews as long as you were Arians, and that you renounced their infidelity at the same instant as you abjured your own heresy. Then, at once, truth would shine upon you out of darkness, and you would no longer reproach us with holding that there are two Eternals. You would no longer find it a difficulty to comprehend that Christ is His Father's co-essential Son, and that, as He is from everlasting, so He has existed co-eternally with the Father. There are, indeed, other things, and those created by Him, which are also said to be eternal. In the Psalm it is written, " Lift up your heads, O ye gates, and be ye lift up, ye everlasting doors " (Ps. xxiv. 7). But, then, it is certain that these eternal things were made by Him ; and if He made what best deserves to be called eternal among the creatures, can anything be plainer than that He must have been in being before whatever is improperly eternal could be so ? Nor would His eternity prove Him to be our Lord, if it were not such an eternity as can only belong to the Son of God. For He must have been always with and in His Father, because, as being truly His Son, He was always of His substance. And, therefore, there could not be a time or period when as yet He was not, or which was before Him. And the nature of His eternity must be the very same with that of His Father's, because, otherwise, He could not be the Image and the Brightness of His Father's Glory. Now, what has been briefly said above must suffice to show, how foolishly our adversaries have misunderstood the passages they then alleged. And they certainly give an unsound interpretation of those other passages which they produce out of the Gospels, and this will soon appear, if we do but give heed to the general tenor of the Christian Faith, and using this rule, apply ourselves, as the Apostle teaches, to the reading of the Holy Scriptures, which were all given by inspiration. If our adversaries had followed this rule of belief, they could not have wandered so widely from the way of truth ; they had not then indulged in fancies in which they should not have revelled ; nor would they then have fallen on that stone of offence which has dashed their faith to pieces.

29. Now, the whole design and tendency of Holy Scripture, as we have often said, is this, to inform and satisfy mankind with regard to our Saviour upon these two fundamental points, namely, that He is God from eternity, the very Son of His Father's substance, as being His Word, His essential Brightness and Wisdom ; and that He was afterwards made man, of the substance of the

Virgin Mary, Mother of God. Our Lord Himself informs us, that these two things run through the whole of the inspired Scriptures. He says, " Search the Scriptures, for they are they which testify of Me" (S. John v. 39). But lest I should transcribe too many passages, by bringing together all that is written on the subject, let the few following suffice for a specimen. " In the beginning was the Word, and the Word was with God, and the Word was God. The same was in the beginning with God. All things were made by Him, and without Him was not anything made that was made." Again, " And the Word was made flesh, and dwelt among us, and we beheld His glory, the glory as of the Only-begotten of the Father" (S. John i. 1-3, 14). Thus also S. Paul writes, " Who, being in the form of God, thought it not robbery to be equal with God, but made Himself of no reputation, and took upon Him the form of a servant, and was made in the likeness of men, and being found in fashion as a man, he humbled himself, and became obedient unto death, even the death of the Cross" (Philip. ii. 6-8). And he that will take pains to examine and trace the sacred Oracles with the same purpose and view, will easily have a right conception of the manner in which the Father uttered His creating will and pleasure at the beginning, and said, " Let there be light," " Let there be a firmament," and " Let us make man" (Gen. i. 3, 6, 26). He will rightly understand, how, in the fulness of time, " God sent not His Son into the world to condemn the world, but that the world through Him might be saved" (S. John iii. 17) ; and how it is written, " Behold, a Virgin shall be with child, and shall bring forth a Son, and they shall call His Name Emmanuel, which, being interpreted, is God with us " (S. Mat. i. 23).

30. These, and similar passages, are the testimonies and authorities which the books of the Old Testament afford us in this matter, as whoever has read them knows very well. And then, on the other hand, he will find in the Gospels the account of the mystery of our Lord's becoming man. S. John tells us that "the Word became flesh and dwelt among us " (S. John i. 14). And we must particularly observe, that the Apostle does not say, that He only descended and entered into a human body, but that He became and was made man ; and our adversaries ought to pay special attention to this, lest they should fall into a certain foolish notion, and beguile others into the same conceit. For a curious opinion was prevalent with some, in former times, that the Word descended into a man's form only in such a manner as He descends into the persons of His Saints, and that

He discovered and revealed Himself in that person, just as He does in them. There needs no more to confute such an extraordinary notion as this, than the surprise and wonder which the spectators showed at our Saviour's presence, and His declarations concerning the nature of His Person. They asked, " Whence He was?" (S. John xix. 9), and the Jews said, " Why dost Thou, being a man, make Thyself God ? " (S. John x. 33). They were quite familiar with the language of the Prophets, "And the Word of the Lord came unto me," &c. But that the Word of God, by whom all things were made, should condescend to become the Son of Man, that He should humble Himself and assume the form of a servant, and die upon a Cross, this was " unto the Jews a stumbling-block," but to us Christ is " the Power of God and the Wisdom of God " (1 Cor. i. 23, 24). " The Word was made flesh," S. John tells us, that is, in the language of Holy Scripture, " was made man," for "flesh " in those writings often signifies "man," or " men." Thus Joel the Prophet says, " I will pour out My Spirit upon all flesh " (Joel ii. 28). And Daniel said to King Astyages, " I may not worship idols made with hands, but the Living God who hath created the heaven and the earth, and hath sovereignty over all flesh " (Bel. and Dr. 5). Here, and in Joel, it is plain the word " flesh " stands for " mankind."

31. The Word of the Lord had visited His Saints individually from the beginning, and had sanctified those who rightly received Him ; and yet when they were born or suffered, it is not said that He was made man, or that He suffered and died. Afterwards, " when the fulness of the time was come," that it pleased the Father to send His Son, " made of a woman," the Blessed Virgin Mary, " made under the Law" (Gal. iv. 4), to destroy and abolish the dominion of sin ; then it is said that He took flesh and was made man, and in that flesh He suffered for us, as S. Peter says, " Forasmuch, then, as Christ hath suffered for us in the flesh " (1 S. Peter iv. 1). And here our adversaries are taught very briefly, but plainly, to believe, that the Person who was God from everlasting, the Sanctifier of those to whom He came, and the great Agent of all His Father's counsels, was made man for our sakes ; and that, as the Apostle says, in this man dwells " all the fulness of the Godhead bodily " (Col. ii. 9), that is to say, that He, although He was God, had His proper human body, formed and organised exactly as ours, and made for our sakes and salvation. And on account of this, the properties of human nature are said to be His, because He existed in that nature, and He hungered, thirsted, suffered, laboured, and was

perfectly sensible of those infirmities, of which our flesh is capable. On the other hand, those powers and operations, which were peculiar to Him as Divine, such as raising the dead to life, restoring sight to the blind, and giving health to the sick, are ascribed to Him, because He did them by the instrumentality of His own Body. The Word truly bore the infirmities of our human nature, since He was truly and properly man. Again, His human nature was subservient to the powers and works of His Divine nature, for it was personally joined to it. His body, indeed, was the body of God, and, therefore, the Prophet Isaiah has rightly used the word "carried" (Isa. liii. 4). He does not say, "He hath healed," lest as being external to the body, it should only denote that this was done by some outward method of application, such as He had made use of by Himself or His Prophets before ; and this would by no means have freed us from the penalty of death. When, therefore, we are told that "He carried our infirmities," and that "He Himself bare our sins," to make it quite certain that He was made man for our sakes, and that body which bore our sins was properly and personally His ; we must remember that His Divine nature sustained no detriment by His "bearing our sins in His own body on the tree," as S. Peter says (1 S. Peter ii. 24). But this to us men was great gain, for we were redeemed from our own evil ways, and our nature was filled with the grace and righteousness of the Word of God.

32. It was on this account, that when our Lord's flesh or human nature suffered, it was not separated from the Divine nature, and, therefore, the Word of God is rightly said to have suffered. Neither was it separate when He wrought with Omnipotent Power the works of His Father, but He wrought them in His body, and by its ministry. Hence, after He was made man, He said, "If I do not the works of the Father, believe Me not ; but if I do, though ye believe not Me, believe the works, that ye may know and believe that the Father is in Me and I in Him" (S. John x. 37, 38). And thus when there was need to restore to health Peter's wife's mother who was sick of a fever, our Lord's hand touched her, but His Godhead cured her (S. Matt. viii. 14). It was not the spittle and the clay, but Christ's Almighty Power that gave sight to the man that had been blind from his birth (S. John ix. 11). The voice of man called Lazarus out of the grave, but it was the Word of God which raised him from the dead (S. John xi. 43). And our Lord, by acting in this manner, gave evidence of His manhood, and prevented any suspicion of His

being only an apparition or phantom. The very fact of our Lord's taking upon Him our nature required, that He should not assume it in an imperfect manner, or divested of those properties which belong to that nature; in order that as His body was a true and proper human body, so it should truly have in it all those dispositions and properties which a human body ought to have; that they should be in His body, although they would not affect or act upon His Divine nature. Had His body been another's, then those human actions and affections could not be ascribed to Him but to some other person; but if the flesh is the Word's, and S. John says definitely "The Word became flesh," then it follows of necessity that the affections also of the flesh are ascribed to Him, whose the flesh is. And thus the same person, who performed such mighty works, and effected our redemption and sanctification, is said to be judged and condemned, to be scourged, to thirst, to be nailed to a Cross, to die, in short, to labour under as many bodily pains and infirmities, as if He was another man. For this cause then, consistently and fittingly, are such affections and dispositions attributed to our Lord, and not to anyone else; that the grace also may be from Him, and that we may not become worshippers of any other, but truly devout and thankful towards God. And this is so because we do not pray to a mere man or a creature, but to the genuine Son of God, of the very substance of His Father, who is not at all the less our Lord and God and Saviour, by becoming our fellow-creature and brother in the flesh.

33. Now, who is there who will not admire this? or who is there who will not give it as his candid opinion that such an appointment is an evidence of God's Infinite Wisdom? For had not our nature been so closely united to the Son's Divinity, man could not have been made a sharer of Divine perfection. And again, had not the Son of God admitted the imperfections of our nature to a place in His person, it had been impossible for our nature to be entirely delivered from them. For if they had ceased for some little time, yet, as I have said before, they had still revived again. Sin and death might have been laid to rest for a short time, but man had still been under their dominion, as we find our forefathers were. And that this is so is sure and certain; for former ages have produced many holy and good men, persons of innocence and integrity. The Prophet Jeremiah was "sanctified from the womb" (Jer. i. 5), and at the voice of Mary, Mother of God, S. John the Baptist "leaped in the womb for joy" (S. Luke i. 44). "Nevertheless, death reigned from Adam to Moses, even over them that had not sinned after the similitude of Adam's

transgression" (Rom. v. 14); and thus man remained mortal and corruptible as before, liable to the corruptions to which our nature is liable. But now these hostilities have ceased, since God has made Himself man, and has impersonated our nature, with all its infirmities and defects. God now dwells, in and rules over, our nature in His own person; and our evil desires and passions yield submission to Him. Henceforth men no longer remain sinners, and dead, according to their sinful passions and inclinations; but, having risen, according to the Almighty Power of the Word they ever abide both immortal and incorruptible. Accordingly, the Son of God is said to be born, when His human nature was conceived of Mary, Mother of God; even He, whose Infinite Power gives birth and being to all mankind. And He truly was born; and by being born He made our nature and whatever naturally appertained to it His own; and by that union He has exalted us, who before were only dust, and sentenced to return to dust, into a participation of His own incorruptibility and immortality; and, as it were, carried us up along with Him, at His Ascension, into Heaven. Hence it appears what necessity there was, that, with our bodies He should take into Himself, those infirmities and affections which naturally belong to them. This was in order that we, no longer as being merely men, but as being intimately connected with the person of Christ, may have a share with Him in everlasting happiness and glory. The nature which descended to us from Adam was frail and under sentence of death; but since God the Word has assumed it and united it to Himself, and with it all its natural imperfections and infirmities, we are able to rise out of the grave, the curse from sin being removed, because of Him who is in us, and who has become a curse for us. And there is great reason for this; for as in the nature and person of Adam we are all from the earth and under a necessity of dissolution, so, in the person of Christ, we recover a state of immortality, a new life and frame, both of mind and body, by the means and application of the baptismal Water and the Holy Spirit. We may say of our bodies, that now they are no longer simply earthly, but the very body, the members of that God, who made Himself man, in order that He might work out our redemption and sanctification.

34. And that we may attain to a more exact knowledge of this point, that Christ's Divinity could not suffer, and that those passages which speak of His infirmities are to be understood of Him only as man, let us attend to what S. Peter tells us of Him, for certainly he will be a trustworthy witness concerning the

Saviour. He writes then in his Epistle the following words, "Forasmuch then as Christ hath suffered for us in the flesh" (1 S. Peter iv. 1). Do we read, then, that He hungered and thirsted, and laboured, and suffered, that He was ignorant of certain things, that He slept, wept, prayed, withdrew Himself, or made His escape, that He was born of a woman, that He besought His Father that the cup might pass from Him; in a word, that He was not insensible of the passions of human nature, and the common calamities of life? All this, no doubt, is very true, and perfectly consistent with His being truly God. He hungered and thirsted, as the Apostle says, "for us in the flesh." He stooped to defectiveness of knowledge, was buffeted and scourged, and underwent sad scenes of sufferings and sorrow "for us in the flesh." He was exalted too, and was born, and increased in stature "in the flesh." His fears and His flights only concerned "the flesh." He said, "If it be possible, let this cup pass from Me" (S. Matt. xxvi. 39), and He was beaten and received violence "for us in the flesh." In short, whatever else is ascribed to Him, implying any infirmity or pain, must be understood with the same limitation; it was "for us in the flesh." For on this account the Apostle himself has accurately said, "Christ then having suffered," not in His Godhead, but "for us in the flesh." And, therefore, what we find affirmed of our Saviour as man, should not give the least ground or occasion for any cavil or scruple. All that can be inferred from it is, that the person who, although He was God as well as man, could not be passive or capable of any infirmity in His Divine nature, yet, as man, had a proper human body, and in it all those passive properties and affections which belong to human bodies as such. Wherefore, as nothing of imperfection can touch the nature of the Word of God, so He abides for ever the same infinite immutable being. And so little do the frailties of the manhood molest or discompose Him, that they are obliterated before His Power, and they disappear at His presence. Our weaknesses and infirmities, which He admitted into His own person, were so vanquished and extinguished, that we were delivered from those evils which had encompassed our nature ever since the fall, according to what S. John says, "And ye know that He was manifested to take away our sins, and in Him is no sin" (1 S. John iii. 5). And so there is no room left for heretics to raise such objections as these, "Are human bodies naturally mortal? If so, how is it possible that they shall rise again? Or, if they must rise again, how is it that they do not rise mortal, and are as sensible as before of want and pain? If they came from the earth, how can their natural condition pass away from them?" To these and such like heretical questions, the flesh itself is now able to make reply and say, " I am from the earth, it is true, and my original condition was mortal. But the Eternal Word of God, who cannot have anything in Him defective or weak, united Me to Himself. He has made Me one person with Him, so that I am His flesh and His body; and so by this union, I am set out of the reach of death and above the power of sin, and because of the Lord's goodness I am no longer in subjection to those two evils. For if you make any objection to the fact, that I have been thus delivered from my natural depravity, corruption, and mortality, how will you be able to entertain this other fact, that the Word and Son of God assumed the form of a servant, and became such as we are? For by this means I obtained this glorious change. God Himself took a human body into His nature, and by that impersonation made us sharers with Him of the Divine nature, and made us co-heirs with Himself of Life and Glory everlasting."

35. It was necessary, then, first of all, to examine these points, that, whenever we find our Lord either doing or saying anything by the action of His body, which at the same time proves His Divine power, we should ascribe all such actions and words to to Him as God; and that, when the manner of His acting or speaking is represented as human, and when any infirmity seems to encompass Him, we should understand that He bore our flesh and became man, and that, as such, He did and said and suffered these things. We cannot fail to have a right notion and belief concerning the person of Christ, if we distinguish, as we should, between the two natures; and if, at the same time, that we attribute to each nature its proper faculties and functions, we look upon both as the powers and acts of one person. He whose contemplation of Christ's Divine powers and miraculous acts induces him to deny the propriety of His manhood, and he who suffers himself to be misled by the consideration of any weakness or defect in Christ's human nature, so as to deny the personal union of His Divine with it, and to form unworthy conceptions and propagate dishonourable doctrines of this Divine Person; both the one and the other is equally in the unhappy condition of the Jew, who "mixed his wine with water" (*cf.* Isa. i. 22), and who makes the Cross a "stumbling-block," or he is like the Gentile who accounts the Gospel of Christ "foolishness" (*cf.* 1 Cor. i. 23). This, then, is what happens to God's enemies the Arians; for looking at what is human in the

Saviour, they have judged Him to be no more than a creature. Therefore, they ought, looking at the Divine works which the Word of God performed, to adopt the views of the Manichees, and to deny that He was truly conceived and born as a man. May grace be given them, before it be too late, to believe God when He tells them, that "the Word was made flesh." And may God help us to retain and uphold the Faith, and to preserve and promote a right understanding of those passages of Scripture, which these men so grievously misinterpret.   For it is absurd to infer imperfection and dependency from such passages as these, "The Father loveth the Son, and hath given all things into His hand" (S. John iii. 35); and, "All things are delivered unto Me of My Father" (S. Matt. xi. 27); and, "I can of Mine own self do nothing, as I hear I judge" (S. John v. 30).   For it is impossible that He, who is the Only-begotten Word and Wisdom of His Father, should ever have wanted in any degree any one of these perfections which are essential to the Father.   And this is what He tells us expressly Himself, "All things that the Father hath are Mine" (S. John xvi. 15); and, "All Mine, O Father, are Thine" (S. John xvii. 10).   We see that the Son is not destitute of any attribute or perfection whatsoever that belongs to the nature of the Father, and we know that the Father's perfections are from everlasting, and so it cannot but follow that they are in the nature and person of the Son from everlasting too.   Well, then, all that is suggested in these and similar passages is this, that the Son's Divine perfections and person result or flow from the Father's, which is far from proving that there was not always a fulness of perfection in the nature of the Son.

36. It was, no doubt, on purpose to prevent that other extreme view, which was the error of Sabellius, that our Saviour made use of those expressions, such as, "All power is given unto Me" (S. Matt. xxviii. 18), "This commandment have I received" (S. John x. 18), and "All things are delivered unto Me" (S. Matt. xi. 27).   Had not the distinction of the persons been thus asserted, the declaration of Scripture concerning the likeness and equality of the Divine attributes and perfections, which is between the two persons, might leave us exposed to the danger of confounding the two persons, and believing but in one.   This mistake is admirably provided against by those very expressions we are now considering.   They declare very plainly, that the Son is not the Father, but the Eternal Word and Son of the Father; that, as being so, He has all the Divine perfections

communicated from His Father by an Eternal Generation ; and that He could never have been without any of them, because they are essentially the same infinite perfections as His Father's. Moreover, the expressions, " is given," and " are delivered," and the like, do not disparage the Godhead of the Son, but they rather confirm and establish it, if we will but duly consider the force of the passages. Thus, when our Lord informs us that " all things are delivered unto Him," He lets us understand that He Himself is not in the number of the things received ; and that, being the Heir of all things, He must be the only Son of His Father, and the proper Son of His substance. The whole universe could not be His heritage, if He Himself were a part of that heritage. He could not have been, in that case, the sole " Heir of all things," but only a co-heir with His fellow-creatures. And, therefore, as certainly He is a single and universal inheritor, He and His inheritance are distinct and separate things, and the Father's essence and attributes are in Him and do not extend to them. There is another declaration of our Lord's which makes it yet more plain, that the expressions " given " and " delivered " do not show that there was once a time when He did not possess them, and this teaches us how to understand such expressions, wherever we find them applied to the person of our Blessed Saviour. The text is this, " As the Father hath life in Himself, so hath He given to the Son to have life in Himself " (S. John v. 26). Now, the words " hath given " show us that the Son is a distinct person from the Father ; but in using the word " so," this is a clear proof of His being the natural Son, and equal to and co-essential with the Father. And, therefore, if a time can be imagined when the Father was a less perfect being than afterwards, then I suppose the same may be imagined of the Son, but not otherwise ; for, as the Father hath, so hath the Son from the Father, self-existence. But if this is an iniquitous opinion to hold, and if it is a funda-mental doctrine of all religion, that the Father is alike perfect and infinite from everlasting ; then is it not extravagant to main-tain that the Son has not all things which the Father has, and that the Son's attributes differ in kind and extent from the Father's, although the Son Himself expressly assures us of the contrary ? Let us rather believe, that everything that the Word of God tells us is true and faithful, and when He tells us that all things that the Father hath are His, and consequently that the Son has them from the Father, let us be satisfied that the Son had them in His nature everlastingly. The Father has these perfections uncommunicated; but the Son has them from, and holds them of, the Father. For as in the instance of the sun's brightness, if the brightness itself were to speak and say, "The light has appointed me to enlighten all places, and I do not enlighten from myself, but as the light wills," yet, in saying this, it does not imply that the brightness, at some time or other, was destitute of the nature of the sun. On the contrary, the meaning would be this, "The sun and its brightness are of one nature, and the same properties and powers are common to us both." Much less can we doubt, whether the Son of God is indeed of His Father's nature and substance, when He tells us, that all things that the Father hath are His, and that He receives them all from the Father. The Father communicates His whole nature to Him, and the Father has in Him the whole that He communicates. And so, again, all things and the very same things that the Son hath, are the Father's, for the Son's Godhead is the Father's Godhead, and thus the Father conducts all His dispensations, and orders everything, by and in His Son.

37. And while such is the sense of these passages of Scripture, those too which concern our Lord as man, are equally capable of a religious meaning also. For with this in view, we have examined them beforehand, that if objections should be raised, because our Lord enquired where Lazarus was laid (S. John xi. 34), or because He asked when He came into the region of Cæsarea, "Whom do men say that I am?" (S. Matt. xvi. 13), or, "How many loaves have ye?" (S. Mark vi. 38), or, "What will ye that I should do unto you?" (S. Matt. xx. 32), we may know from what has been already said, what is the true meaning and sense of the passages, and keep clear of all such perverse constructions which the Arians make them bear, so as to make them agree with their errors. First, then, let these impious ones tell us the reason why they consider our Lord to be ignorant? Because anyone asks certain questions, this is no infallible proof that the questioner is unacquainted with the things he asks about. There may be sometimes occasion for a man to speak, as if he doubted or wanted instruction about a matter with which he is well acquainted. Thus, in the instance of the question, "How many loaves have ye?" S. John tells us that he was aware that our Saviour was not ignorant, for he adds, "And this He said to prove him, for He Himself knew what He would do" (S. John vi. 6). And if He knew what He would do, undoubtedly He knew the number of the loaves, with which He

was to work the miracle. S. John's explanation of this instance sets all the parallel ones in a clear light. He knew as well before as after He had asked where Lazarus was buried, and what notion the people entertained of Him. He was perfectly well informed of the thing which He was asking, and He was very well aware of what He was about to do. And thus with the greatest ease are their foolish quibbles confounded. But if they will still persist in saying, that our Lord must be only a man because of His asking questions, then I must tell them that it is simply impossible that there should be any degree of ignorance in our Lord's Divine nature, and that He could only be capable of it in His human nature. And the truth of this will at once commend itself to anyone who recollects that our Lord, at a considerable distance from Bethany, knew Himself, as if He had been upon the spot, that Lazarus was dead, and in what place he died; although when afterwards He arrived there, He was pleased to enquire where the place was. What a grievous misrepresentation then it is for our adversaries to consider Him as an ignorant creature, who knew, even beforehand, the secret and inmost conceptions and thoughts of all men. He "needed not that any should testify of man, for He knew what was in man" (S. John ii. 25), and that perfectly. And even more than this is true of Him, for He alone knows the Father, and says, "I am in the Father, and the Father is in Me" (S. John xiv. 11).

38. Wherefore, it is plain that our Lord's knowledge was not universal only as He was man; but that as the Word and Son of God there is nothing hid from Him, and there is nothing unknown to Him, even from eternity. His Incarnation did not lessen His Divinity; and His Divinity did not hinder His Incarnation, or unqualify Him for the assumption of human nature and all its properties. Let us not cherish any such wicked fancies. The great Eternal God made Himself man, and imparted a sort of Divinity to our very nature, by assuming it into His person. Did He not raise the dead in that very nature in which He asked questions, and in which He seemed to be ignorant of certain matters? And can it be supposed, that He, who was able to call back a departed soul, and raise a dead body to life, could be shut out of any mysteries or secrets whatever? He had seen Lazarus laid in his grave, although He enquired after the place; for the most holy Word of God, who endured all things for our sakes, did this, that so, bearing all our imperfections and infirmities, He might vouchsafe to us the knowledge that the Father is properly and essentially His Father; and that He was sent by that Father to

redeem and sanctify us all, which was an office which manifested the perfection of infinite goodness and mercy. When, then, the Saviour uses the expressions, to which our adversaries make objection, namely, "All power is given unto Me," and "Glorify Thy Son," and "Power is given unto Him," we must understand all these passages in the same sense, and that, as we have shown, they are only applicable to our Lord's human nature. For although He had no need whatever of anything, still He received in His manhood an ample supply of grace and glory, which were conveyed to our nature by a grant as firm and irreversible, as the union of our nature with our Lord's Divine nature is close and indissoluble. For while a mere man receives, he is liable to lose again, as was shown in the case of Adam, who received and then lost. And therefore to prevent another such forfeiture, and to provide sinners with the means of making their peace with God and obtaining His favour, therefore He Himself appropriates the gift, and He speaks of the great advantages which we receive in His person, as if only He Himself received them. As God His glory was always complete, but as man He declares that it was entirely derived, and that He has received power. And when He, who is the author of all our glory and happiness, says to His Father, "Glorify Me," what He would have us infer from this is plain, that He is truly man, and that as such He has need of many things. He assumed our nature into Himself, and that nature, thus impersonated, received this glory; and so God the Son may very truly and properly say of Himself, that He received it.

39. If then, as we have said many times, the Word was not made man, then it must have been the Word whose glory was defective and imperfect, and whose knowledge was so limited, that He was obliged to ask questions; and then you Arians will be in the right. But if the Word was made flesh, as we are assured, and if ignorance and want only belong to human nature, then we must be careful to avoid mistaking the nature which gives, for the nature which receives. We must not think that He who supplies everything to all the world is Himself in need of anything. We must not represent the Son of God as being feeble and poor, and consequently separate from His Father's nature; for this would be to deprive mankind of all grace and blessing. For if it were true, that the Word as such, and in His own nature, received all that grace and glory which Christ is said to have received; if it had been His Divinity, which was sanctified and raised out of the grave, what had we been the better for all this? We should have just remained in our former state, helpless and

miserable and mortal, having no interest whatever in those things which were given to the Son of God. Why, too, did the Word come among us at all, and become Incarnate? Was it that He might receive these advantages which He says that He has received? If so, then He was without them before, and so will be thankful to this human nature of ours which He assumed, because it was the means of making Him so much richer than He was before, and so much more an object of God's goodness and bounty. In short, if what the Arians say is true, our nature advanced the condition of the Word, and not the Word the condition of our nature, and this is what the Jews would believe. But if, on the contrary, the Word came down and was Incarnate, as we hold, to be our Redeemer, Sanctifier, and to make us sharers of the Divine nature; then there is no doubt, but that whatever change of condition He was pleased to submit to, by assuming our nature, He did not consult His own, but our interest and advantage, in embracing it. The advantages which He Himself bestows from the Father upon the creatures, He made over and appropriated to His human nature; and it was in this nature that He revealed and declared this communication. Further, if it is possible in any way to move our adversaries to a right conviction, let us next observe the nature of the things about which He asked questions, and see too what were the things which He said He had received. The same person, then, that asked for glory, yet had said, "All things are delivered unto Me" (S. Luke x. 22). And after the Resurrection He says that He has received all power; but even before that He had said, "All things are delivered unto Me," He was Lord of all; for "all things were made by Him" (S. John i. 3), and "there is one Lord, by whom are all things" (1 Cor. viii. 6). And when He asked for glory, He was, as He is, the Lord of glory, as S. Paul says, "If they had known it, they would not have crucified the Lord of glory" (1 Cor. ii. 8); for He had that glory which He asked for when He said, "The glory which I had with Thee before the world was" (S. John xvii. 5).

40. Again, it is evident concerning the power which our Lord said He received after the Resurrection, that He had this before He received it, and before the Resurrection. For He of Himself rebuked Satan, saying, "Get thee behind Me, Satan" (S. Luke iv. 8), and He invested His disciples with power against him too, when, on their return from their journey, He said, "I beheld Satan, like lightning, fall from heaven" (S. Luke x. 18, 19). He cast out devils, and He loosed what Satan had bound, as in the

instance of that daughter of Abraham, who had a spirit of infirmity eighteen years (S. Luke xiii. 16). He forgave sins, saying to the paralytic, and to the woman who washed His feet, " Thy sins be forgiven thee" (S. Matt. ix. 2 ; S. Luke vii. 48). He restored the dead to life, and gave the power of seeing to the man who had been born without it. And He did all this, not waiting till He should receive power, but being possessed of power already. He had, it is clear from all this, before His Incarnation and Resurrection, what He says He afterwards received, and what He received He transferred into our nature. He made us as gods, and our being made so had this effect, that the powers of hell were no longer too strong, nor the glories of heaven too pure and sublime for us. The Word was God, and it was as impossible that God should want any excellency, as that the man should not receive whatever excellency He wanted. And thus our nature being endowed and glorified in His person, our persons may be secure of the stability and perpetuity of this endowment and glorification. And this explains the meaning of S. Peter, where he tells us that " He received from the Father honour and glory" (2 S. Pet. i. 17), and that " Angels are made subject unto Him " (1 S. Pet. iii. 22). As in the case of Lazarus, it was the Man that enquired where He was buried, and God the Word that raised him to life ; so here His receiving proves Him to be a Man, and the subjection of the Angels declares Him to be God.

41. Cease, then, ye objects of the Divine displeasure, from thus seeking to degrade the Word of God. Do not detract from His Godhead, which is the same as the Father's, as though He lacked anything, or was ignorant of anything ; lest, by so doing, you are casting your arguments against the Christ, just as the Jews formerly sought to cast stones at Him. There could be nothing defective in the Word of God, I repeat again ; whatever imperfection we read of was entirely in the man. His miracles were Divine, although they were wrought by the instrumentality of a human body ; as when He spat on the ground and made it clay, and when He stretched out His hand, and when He raised His voice to call Lazarus out of the grave. But when our Lord's actions and passions are represented and described as properly human, then we may be sure that these are only his actions and passions as a Man. Those weaknesses and imperfections, which are implied very plainly, are attributable to His humanity. The qualities and affections of that man which the Word was made were circumscribed within the human nature,

and could have no place in the Divine. Again, the Divine kept its own powers entire and incommunicable, at the same time that it comprehended our nature in a personal union. His body was the instrument by which He wrought the works of the Father. But notwithstanding the manhood was assumed into the Deity, yet none of its properties and affections were lost there. It was the man that existed in the nature of God that asked questions, that raised Lazarus, that reproved His Mother, saying, " Mine hour is not yet come " (S. John ii. 4), and then at once he turned the water into wine. For our Lord was very God in the flesh, and He was true flesh in the Word. The first He demonstrated by His miraculous works, and the last by His human actions and affections.

42. Let us now pass on to the consideration of that assertion which our adversaries, being weak and blind in heart, insist upon as an unanswerable evidence of their doctrine, namely, "But of that day and hour knoweth no man, no, not the Angels which are in heaven, neither the Son " (S. Mark xiii. 32). When these heretics bring forward this passage, and base their arguments upon it, it is just like the giants of old who sought to fight against God. They call in question the knowledge of Him who created heaven and earth, and all things, about a day and hour. They despise that Word, from whom nothing can be concealed, as if He knew no more than they themselves, at what time He should come to judge His creatures. And they look upon the time of that day, as a secret withheld from that Son of God, who has told them that He knows the Father, and that no one knows Him besides Himself. Now, I ask, what can be spoken more contrary to sense than this, or what madness is there to excel it ? Through the Word all things were made, times and seasons, and day and night, and the whole creation. Is, then, the Framer of all things to be declared to be ignorant of His work ? And the very context of the passage shows that the Son of God knows that hour and day, although the Arians fall headlong into error in their ignorance and folly. For after saying that He knows not the day and hour, He relates to His disciples the various occurrences which were to precede that day, saying, " These different things shall come to pass, and then cometh the end." But He who speaks of the antecedents of the day, knows certainly the day also, which shall be manifested subsequently to the things foretold. Had he been utterly in the dark about it, He could no more have told that it was to be after, than that it was to be before, the completion of such events. It is just as if anyone who, in

order to inform some stranger of the locality of some house or city, should give an account of those things that preceded the one or the other, and having described all particulars, should tell him, " Then immediately comes the city or the house." The stranger would know then very well where the house or the city was, for if his informant had been ignorant of the facts, he would not have ventured to describe what went before, lest from ignorance he should mislead anyone out of their way, or in speaking of what he was unacquainted with, he should unawares lead anyone astray. In like manner, when our Blessed Lord tells us plainly what shall precede the day and the hour of the end, He knows exactly, and He is not ignorant of, the time when the day and hour shall arrive.

43. If we should be asked why our Saviour did not tell His disciples plainly when the time was, if He knew it Himself, I answer that no one may curiously seek to know those things which He has concealed; for, "Who hath known the mind of the Lord, or who hath been His counsellor?" (Rom. xi. 34). But if it be demanded why He told them that the Son did not know this thing at the same time that He certainly did know it, of this I think none of the faithful are ignorant; because He only declared that He knew it not as man, by the faculties of His human nature. For human nature cannot have a deep and thorough knowledge of matters; whereas Omniscience is a special characteristic of the Word of God. And this, again, will be clearly seen by carefully examining into the occasion, when and to whom the Saviour spoke this. Our adversaries might with reason have argued from this, if our Lord had declared Himself ignorant when He made the heavens, and when He was by His Father disposing all things, or at any time before He was made man. But this is not the case. It was God Incarnate who spoke these words; and so, whatever expressions that savour of imperfection He applied to Himself after His Incarnation, ought, with fairness, only to be understood of His human nature. The Word Himself, since He created and formed all creatures, knew exactly the constitution and duration of every one of them; when each had its beginning, and when it was to have an end. He was the Author of all things, and so He knows how many things He has made, and the length of their existence. And since He is acquainted with the beginning and end of each, it consequently follows that He cannot be ignorant of the general and common end of all. Certainly when our Lord says in the Gospel concerning Himself as man, " Father, the hour is come, glorify Thy

Son " (S. John xvii. 1), yet He clearly shows us that He knew, as God, when the hour of the end of all things should come. And this alone proves what we contend for, that, as the Word, he was not ignorant of the time of the consummation of all things, although His human nature, as such, knew it not. For the sphere of human knowledge is very narrow, and things of this nature especially lie far beyond it. And yet so great was the affection and love of our Saviour, that, since He had assumed our flesh He is not ashamed because of His union with our frail nature to say, " I know not ; " although there is nothing, nor can there be anything, of which He has not a complete and perfect knowledge of as God. And it must be remarked that He does not say that the " Son of God " does not know, lest any should think that the Godhead was ignorant ; but He simply says, " not the Son," which implies that the " Son of man " did not know, and that the ignorance only concerned His humanity.

44. And if this were not the meaning of the word " Son " in this place, after He had confessed Himself jointly ignorant with the Angels, no doubt He would have likewise added the Holy Ghost. From His not doing this, two conclusions naturally arise, first, that the Holy Spirit knew this day and hour, and consequently that the Word, as such, from whom the Holy Spirit proceeds, could not but know it. And, secondly, it follows, that the Son here was the Son of Man and not the Son of God ; for if it had been the latter, the Holy Ghost had been certainly mentioned too. And a proof of it is this, that He who confesses the ignorance of His human nature in this particular, asserts the perfection and universality of His knowledge as God. He asserts that He has a perfect knowledge of the nature, acts, and purposes of His Father, although the time when He was to come to judge the world was a secret of which He was ignorant. This very Son tells us that " no man knoweth the Father, save the Son " (S. Matt. xi. 27). And all men but the Arians would join in confessing, that He who knows the Father, much more knows the whole history of creation, and, among the other schemes of Providence, the time of the world's dissolution. And if already the day and the hour are determined by the Father, it is plain that they are determined through the Son, and He knows Himself His own determination. For this neither is nor can be disputed, that the Father made all His creatures and established all His counsels by the Son. And it is inconceivable, that He, who was the Framer of all things with the Father, should not know all the nature and properties of the things He had made, their number,

and the term of their duration ; which, if He knew, it is impossible He should be ignorant of the time of their dissolution.   And again, our Lord has told us, that all things that the Father has are His.   If, therefore, the Father has in Himself the knowledge of this day and hour, the Son cannot but have it too, and that on account of His union of nature with the Father.   Again, the Father knows that day and hour, and the Father is in the Son, and the Son is in the Father, and knows whatever is in the Father ; therefore the Son knows that day and hour.   Again, the Father knows that day and hour, and the Son is the express Image of His Father's person ; therefore the Son knows them too.   For otherwise, there would be one part or instance of knowledge in which the Son is not the express Image of His Father, and in which He does not exactly represent and resemble Him.   And although it is no great matter for astonishment, that He, who made all things, and by whom all things consist, should have a thorough knowledge of the nature and framing of them, and of the period of duration assigned to each and all of them ; yet in truth it is a matter which may well call forth surprise, that this perverse mania of these Arians, suitable as it is to their mad doctrines, should require us to enter into such a copious and lengthy vindication of the truth against them.   Let our adversaries consider how, by ranking the Son of God, the Eternal Word, among created things, they approach within reasonable distance of that awful blasphemy, of believing that the Father Himself is inferior to His creatures.   If that day and hour is unknown to that person who only knows the Father, I do not see how they can pretend to deny, that the knowledge of the nature and motions of God's creatures, or even of perhaps a very small part of them, is something above the knowledge of the Divine nature itself.

45. Our Lord has told us that those wicked ones who dare to utter blasphemies against the Holy Spirit cannot ever expect forgiveness for their great impiety.   But let us who love Christ, and in whom He dwells, know better things.   When we hear the Son of God saying, " I know not," considering that this cannot possibly refer to His Divine Omniscience, let us turn our thoughts to His human nature, and there we shall find what it was in Him that knew not all things.   Let us observe that our Lord, having told His disciples that the Son did not know that day and hour, and having compared the condition of those who should be surprised at the end of the world with that of mankind in the time of Noah, applies this warning, " Watch, therefore,

for ye know not what hour your Lord doth come," and again, " In such an hour as ye think not, the Son of Man cometh " (S. Matt. xxiv. 42, 44). He means here, that He, the Son, who has taken upon Himself their nature, in that nature is as ignorant as any of them of the day and hour. Had His meaning been that the Word of God Himself knew it not, His warning would have run as follows, " Watch ye therefore, because I know not, and in such an hour as I think not of." But in fact He has not said this, but by saying, " Ye know not," and " When ye think not," He has signified that it belongs to man to be ignorant; for whose sake He, too, having a body like theirs and having become man, confessed, that, speaking only of His human nature, He knew no more of that matter than another man. And, again, the example from the men of Noah's time discovers to us yet further the blindness of these insolent enemies of Christ. He does not say, " I knew not," but " They knew not until the flood came " (S. Matt. xxiv. 39). Mankind did not expect it, until they were overwhelmed with it, but our Blessed Lord, who brought it upon the earth, knew very well the day and hour when He determined to " open the windows of heaven, and to break up all the fountains of the great deep " (Gen. vii. 11). He said to Noah, " Come thou and all thy house into the ark," and He told him precisely on what day the flood was to begin, saying, " Yet seven days, and I will bring a flood upon the earth " (Gen. vii. 1, 4). But if in describing the day, He makes use of the parallel of Noah's time, and He did know the time of the flood, therefore it follows of necessity that He knows also the day of His coming to judgment.

46. And, moreover, the application which our Saviour makes of the parable of the Virgins shows us still more clearly who they are who are ignorant of the day and the hour, for He says, " Watch, therefore, for ye know neither the day nor the hour " (S. Matt. xxv. 13). Here He does not say, " I know not," but " Ye know not," which is a plain suggestion that the Son who, He had told them before, knew it not, was only the Son of Man and in the nature of one of them. And that by the Son He meant only His human nature, which only could be limited in its knowledge, is evident to anyone who has not forgotten that this Son of Man is also the Word and Son of God, and that He is the Judge and the Bridegroom who is to come at that day. For it is simply inconceivable that He should not know the time when He was to come, and when He was to say, " Awake, thou that sleepest, and arise from the dead, and Christ shall give thee

light" (Ephes. v. 14). For as on becoming man, our Lord hungers and thirsts and suffers like other men, and had no more than other men have, a universal knowledge of things; but as He was the Father's Word and Wisdom, and in the Father's very essence, as such He was Omniscience itself. He that desired to know where Lazarus was buried, was the very person that came to the grave and raised him out of it. He knew, it seems, where the departed soul of Lazarus resided, for He called it back from thence into the body. And surely He who knows where a departed soul is, knows also, without asking anyone, where the body lies which it has left. But it seemed good to His Wisdom that the question should prove Him man, as the miracle proved Him God. And when He enquired of His disciples, when He came into the region of Cæsarea, what the world thought and said of Him, He knew what answer He should have from S. Peter, even before He made the enquiry. For if the Father revealed to S. Peter the answer to the Lord's question, we know that He had revealed it by and through the Son, for "No man knoweth who the Son is but the Father, and who the Father is but the Son, and he to whom the Son will reveal Him" (S. Luke x. 22). It is by the Son alone that any man receives whatever knowledge He obtains either of the Father or of the Son. And, therefore, the Son was as much the author of S. Peter's answer as of His own question. He revealed to Him from the Father what the Apostle told Him again, and He made His asking the question, as we said before, an occasion of asserting and proving the propriety of both His natures. He who knew all things, He who had a full and entire knowledge of the nature and person of the Father, must have known all about these things, and such other things as these; for the knowledge of the Divine nature comprehends the knowledge of all things.

47. What has now been said is really quite sufficient to confute entirely the Arian heretics. But, in order that we may let all men see yet more plainly, how keenly these enemies of Christ are opposed both to the truth and to our Blessed Lord, it will be necessary to question them concerning a passage in S. Paul's Second Epistle to the Corinthians. The Apostle writes, "I knew a man in Christ above fourteen years ago, whether in the body I cannot tell, or whether out of the body I cannot tell, God knoweth" (2 Cor. xii. 2). What have you to say about this text? Did the Apostle truly know what happened to him in this vision, although he says, "I know not," or did he really not know? If you reply that he did not know, you will fall into another heresy,

and you are quite familiar enough with error ; for this is the profane notion of the Phrygians, who say that the Prophets and all the other ministers of the Word were absolutely insensible and unconscious of their own extraordinary acting and speaking. But if you think that the Apostle knew when he said, " I know not," for he had Christ within him revealing to him all things, then how defiled is the mind and conscience, and how corrupt and self-condemned 'are the hearts and inclinations of these fighters against God ! For they confess that the Apostle knew what he says he did not know, and yet they affirm that our Lord was ignorant of the day of judgment, merely because He uses the words, " I know not." It is absurd to imagine that S. Paul should, by Christ's immediate presence and communications, understand and know what he tells the Corinthians he did not know ; and yet that our Lord Himself should be utterly unacquainted with His Father's decrees, simply because He words Himself as S. Paul does. The Apostle, then, because the Lord revealed it to him, knew what happened ; for on this account he says, " I knew a man in Christ ; " and therefore it is reasonable to believe that he knew in what manner this man was carried up into heaven. Elisha saw the manner of Elijah's translation, and yet when the sons of the Prophets thought that " the Spirit of the Lord had taken him up, and cast him upon some mountain," as fully as Elisha was convinced of the reality of what he had seen, and notwithstanding he had assured them that Elijah was carried up into heaven ; when " they urged him to let men be sent to seek their master even till he was ashamed," he no longer insisted upon the truth of what he had said, but suffered them to do as they wished (2 Kings ii. 16, 17). Will any one say, because he allowed them to send, that he did not know that the messengers would search in vain ? Certainly not, but it only means that he was willing that they should satisfy themselves of the truth of Elijah's assumption, of which they seemed to be not sufficiently satisfied upon his testimony. And can we suppose that S. Paul, who was the person himself caught up, and not, like Elijah, only an eye witness of another's translation, knew nothing of the manner and circumstances of his own translation ? If Elijah was asked to give an account of his translation, no doubt he could have described the manner of it. And yet S. Paul says, " I know not," and there seem to be two reasons why the Apostle did not expressly tell his readers the particulars of his own translation. And first, because, as he tells us, lest, on account of the abundance of the revelations, any one should be induced to think him a person of much more importance than he really was; and, secondly, because our Saviour having said, " I know not," it became him also to express himself in a similar fashion, lest the servant should appear above his Lord, and the disciple above his Master.

48. He, from whom S. Paul had the knowledge of his own condition under those peculiar circumstances, undoubtedly knew the things which concerned Himself. Since He spoke of the antecedents of the day, He could not but know, as I observed before, when that day and hour were to come, although He says that the Son did not know. And if we should be asked to give the reason, why our Lord declared the Son of Man to be ignorant of what the Son of God knew? we may safely and prudently answer, that we have good reason to believe that it was altogether with regard to our interest and benefit, that He expressed Himself as He did. And we seriously hope that we are not mistaken in this opinion of His purpose. The good of mankind was the motive which directed Him, for He has made known what comes before the end, that, as He said Himself, we might not be startled or terrified when these remarkable occurrences take place, but when they happen, we may have due warning that we may shortly expect the end to arrive. And so He found it more expedient for our advantage to say nothing of His knowledge of the day and hour, as He was God; but He rather chose to mention His ignorance in that particular, as man. For, had He told His disciples that He knew it, probably they would have been eager in their desire to know it, and if He had not gratified them, the refusal would have pained them; and, on the other hand, if He had told them, it might have been prejudicial to them and to us all too. It was purely for our sakes that the Word was made flesh, and whatever our Lord does or says is to promote our welfare. It was for our good, then, that our Lord made the assertion, " Neither the Son knoweth." And there was nothing untrue in the statement, for He said humanly, as man, "I know not;" nor did He allow His disciples to press their enquiries about it, for by making this declaration he kept them from doing so. And so in the Acts of the Apostles it is written, when He was borne up by the Angels, ascending as man, and carrying up to heaven the flesh which He had assumed, that the disciples, who were the witnesses of His Ascension, thought it a good opportunity to renew their enquiries as to when the end should be, and when He would come to judgment. He then said to them more clearly, " It is not for you to know the times

or the seasons which the Father hath put in His own power" (Acts i. 7). And He did not then say that the Son did not know, as He had said before when speaking as a man, but He said, " It is not for you to know." Our Lord's human nature had now risen from the dead, and had put off its mortality and had been deified. He was now going into the heavens, and therefore it did not become Him now to answer after the flesh; but henceforth He would only use language appropriate and suitable to His Divine nature. Therefore He said, " It is not for you to know the times or the seasons which the Father hath put in His own power." And then He adds, " But ye shall receive power," that is, " Ye shall receive Me," for Christ is the "Power of God, and the Wisdom of God" (1 Cor. i. 24).

49. The Son, then, did know, as being the Word; for He implied this in what He said, " I know, since I am God, what you cannot possibly have knowledge of as men. I told you when I was sitting and talking with you on the mount, that that day and hour were unknown even to the Son of man as such, and I told you this for your advantage as well as that of all men." For it is profitable for you to hear so much both of the Angels and of the Son, because of the pretenders and impostors that shall come. Although the devils should transform themselves into Angels of light, and pretend to tell you the time of the world's dissolution, you are assured beforehand that not even the Angels in heaven are aware of the time when it shall take place. And when Antichrist shall arise, and shall show great signs and wonders, saying, " I am Christ," and when He shall attempt to persuade you that He knows and can tell you the time, the remembrance of what I now say to you, that the Son does not know the day, will prevent you from believing Him. It would not be in any way expedient for mankind, to know certainly and exactly the day when the world is to end, and when the judgment is to begin. This would make men, if they knew it, negligent of the intermediate time, and they would wait to prepare themselves for the days near the end, for they would think that then only was it necessary to amend their lives. And it is for the prevention of this evil, that God leaves man in uncertainty of the time of his death, lest our foreknowledge of it should encourage us to make a bad use of the greatest part of it. The Son of God has thought fit to keep concealed from us both the end of all things and the limit of each, for in the end of all is the end of each, and in the end of each the end of all is comprehended; that, living in a continual expectation, and under

daily apprehensions about both, we might be the more diligent in our application of the time present, "reaching forth unto those things which are before, and forgetting those things which are behind" (Philip. iii. 13). Where is the man who would not give way to the temptations of the present, if he knew for certain that he had plenty of time before he could possibly come to the end of his life? But if he was ignorant of it, then he would strive each day to be prepared for the end. It was on this account that our Saviour added the words, "Watch, therefore, for ye know not what hour your Lord doth come" (S. Matt. xxiv. 42) ; and, "The Son of man cometh at an hour when ye think not" (S. Luke xii. 40). He said that He was ignorant of the time, then, that we should reap the advantage which comes of our ignorance of this matter; for in saying it, He wishes that we should always be prepared; "for you," He says, "know not, but I, the Lord, know when I come, although the Arians will not wait for Me, who am in deed and in truth the Word of the Eternal Father."

50. And thus our Blessed Lord, who understands our true interests much better than we do ourselves, admonished his disciples; and they, having received this instruction, were able afterwards to set right the Thessalonians when they were liable to fall into error on this very point (*cf.* 2 Thess. ii. 12.) However, since these enemies of Christ do not yield even to these considerations, I should like to ask them some more questions about these matters, although I fear that the heart of Pharaoh was not so hard as theirs. We read that God called unto Adam in Paradise, and said unto him, "Where art thou?" (Gen. iii. 9); and that the Lord said unto Cain, "Where is Abel thy brother?" (Gen. iv. 9). What, then, do the Arians say to these things? Did God make these enquiries because He really wanted to be informed about the matter of them? If you think so, then you must really belong to the party of the Manichees, for this is their daring conception. But if, rather than attach yourselves to them, you find yourselves under the necessity of confessing that God perfectly knew what He asked about before He asked; then why should you be so surprised and amazed at finding the Son declaring His ignorance of something in His human nature, or of His asking questions? The same God the Father which had interrogated Adam and Cain by His Word and Son, before that Son's Incarnation, puts forth enquiries by the same Word and Son now after it. Or, perhaps, you have indeed now become Manichees, and you wish to blame the

question that was then put to Adam, and all because you wish to have full scope for your hateful and perverse doctrines. And now, having so far successfully prosecuted the controversy, since you raise objections from certain words of S. Luke, which have a good and right meaning, but which you have impiously misunderstood, we must proceed to refer to this passage, that here also we may clearly lay bare your corrupt opinions.

51. Now, S. Luke says, "And Jesus increased in wisdom and stature, and in favour with God and man" (S. Luke ii. 52). This is the passage the Arians allude to, and since they make of it a difficulty and stumbling-block, we must ask them, as the Pharisees and Sadducees might be asked, of the person concerning whom S. Luke speaks. And the case stands thus. Is Jesus Christ merely a man just like other men? or is He God who assumed our nature? That He was only the former was the opinion of Paul of Samosata, and it is yours in the meaning of your assertions, although you are unwilling to rank yourselves along with him, because you shun unpopularity. And yet it is the only thing that can make you appear consistent with yourselves. For it is very easy to understand how He should increase and improve as other men do, if He is only a mere mortal man, as they are. But if He is God Incarnate, as we know He is, for "the Word was made flesh," and if, being God, He descended upon earth, then how such a Divine person should be capable of growth and improvement, how He that is equal with God should increase beyond that equality, how He that is in the Father from eternity should advance to some state beyond, is inconceivable. Can there possibly be any perfection out or beyond the Father? And next it will be fitting to repeat here what was said about the Son's receiving, and His being glorified. If the Son increased and improved after He was made man, it follows that before He was made man He was but an imperfect being; and then it cannot be denied but that our nature perfected and exalted His, not His ours. And again, what greater or more perfect being can the Word of God be than what He is Himself? Can God's Wisdom, and Son, and Power, have any superior? And the Word of God is all these. If a single ray, as it were, of these perfections, could be communicated to any one of us men, such a man would become exalted into a kind of perfect being, and equal to Angels. For Angels, and Archangels, and Dominions, and all the Powers, and Thrones, as partakers of the glory of the Son of God, always behold the Face of His Father. Will any one be so foolish as to say that the person, who supplies per-

fections to others, advances in perfection Himself later than those to whom He supplies these gifts? For Angels even ministered to our Lord's human birth, and the event recorded in the passage of S. Luke occurred several years after our Lord's Nativity. It is amazing that such an absurd imagination should ever have entered into the mind of anyone. How could Wisdom advance in wisdom? How did He who gives grace to all others advance in grace? S. Paul knew very well that Christ is the author of all grace, as he says in every Epistle, "The grace of our Lord Jesus Christ be with you all." Either, then, let our adversaries say that S. Paul is to be charged with falsehood, or let them shamelessly deny that Christ is the Wisdom of God. Or else, if our Lord is Wisdom, as Solomon has said, and if, as S. Paul has written, "Christ is the Power of God and the Wisdom of God" (1 Cor. i. 24); let them tell us how it was possible that the Wisdom of God should be more perfect and extensive at one time than at another.

52. For men, since they are only creatures, are capable of, and are qualified for, progress and advance in virtue. Enoch, for example, arrived at such a state of perfection that he was translated into heaven. Moses increased and attained to considerable perfection. Isaac "waxed great, and went forward, and grew until he became very great" (Gen. xxvi. 13). The Apostle declares of himself that he "reached forth unto those things which are before" (Philipp. iii. 13). There was a scale and gradation of improvement and proficiency marked out for all these. They were to rise and advance from being small and weak to being great and strong. But what was that excellency or perfection towards which God's essential and Only-begotten Son can be supposed to reach forth and press forward? All creatures advance by looking towards Him, and since He is the only Son of His Father's nature, it is impossible that either His desires or occasions should dispose Him to look beyond that nature, because He has in that all that can be desired. It is common to man's nature to advance; but because the Son of God, who was already perfect in the Father, could not advance to any more glorious state than He possessed, He condescended to humble Himself for our sakes, that in His humbling, we, on the other hand, might be able to increase. And this is properly our increase: to renounce and give up all earthly things, and to partake of the Son of God's perfection and glory, in order that we may grow up to be like Him in that nature wherein He made Himself like us. It was not, then, the Word, considered as the

Word of God, who advanced, because the Son of God is as infinitely perfect from everlasting as the Father. He is the Giver of all good things, and there can be no good thing that is not to be found in Him. The growth and improvement here has only relation to our Lord as man; and to prevent all possibility of mistake, S. Luke has specified his stature, as one of the things in which He increased. Now, measurement of stature belongs to bodies, and is proper to bodies; but this kind of measurement cannot possibly be applied to the Word and Son of God. As man, then, His human body increased; still, in the course of its growth, He gave, time after time, clear manifestations of His being truly God. And as the Godhead was more and more revealed, by so much more did His grace as man increase before all men. For as a little child He was carried by His Mother to the Temple; and when He became a youth He betook Himself there again, and He questioned the priests concerning the Law. And as by degrees He arrived at man's estate, so His Divinity continued to manifest itself through His mortal nature, that He was confessed, first of all by S. Peter, and afterwards by all the other Apostles, to be the true Son of the Living God. However, as the ancient Jews in former times could not, so these modern Jews in the present day cannot be prevailed upon to acknowledge this great truth. They wilfully close their eyes, for fear they should perceive this fact, that Divine Wisdom cannot acquire increase or improvement, and consequently that our Lord is said to have increased in His human wisdom or knowledge only. For S. Luke says, " Jesus advanced in wisdom and favour," which is just the same as if he had said that He advanced in Himself. For " Wisdom had builded Herself an House " (Prov. ix. 1), and She caused this house to be filled with wisdom and knowledge.

53. This advancement that is spoken of, consisted, as I observed before, in that grace and Divine nature which the Wisdom of God communicated to mankind. For this cancelled our guilt and abolished the power of sin, since God's Son immortalized our species by taking upon Himself our human nature. For thus, as the body of our Lord increased in stature, there advanced in and with it the manifestation of the Godhead also, and all men were shown that the body was the temple of God, and that God was in the body. And if our adversaries tell us, that the Word said to be made flesh is that man whose name was Jesus, and that this advancement and improvement must be understood of Him, they must be told that this objection does

not diminish the Brightness of the Father's Glory. The only consequence that follows is that very true one, that the Word was made flesh, and that He was properly and truly a man. The same person grew and improved as a man, that hungered and laboured, and underwent pain and death as a man, and yet not as a man divided from God. As our human nature was in God, so it grew up and improved in Him. And thus we are assured that we advance and improve in Him, by virtue of that union which exists between Christ's humanity and ours. And this, in short, is the state or account of this incomprehensible mystery, that the Word of God did not grow or improve, and that the Wisdom of God was not flesh or man, but such a body as ours became the body of God's Infinite Wisdom, and was taken into it by a personal union. God's Wisdom did not advance, but that which made progress was the human wisdom received into the Divine. And it was this reception or admission that raised it far above itself, that caused it to reflect the Infinite Wisdom, and rendered it fit for the Godhead to make use of, and which particularly caused it to manifest its union with our human nature. And that the growth or improvement belongs only to that, in such a sense and manner as we have shown above, we need no other argument to prove than this, that S. Luke tells us, that Jesus, which was the Name of our Blessed Lord after He became man, and not that the Word of God, increased in wisdom, stature, and favour.

54. Our Lord's weeping, His being troubled, and, in a word, the whole narrative of His pains and sufferings, require the same interpretation. For these particulars and circumstances our indefatigable adversaries are very ready to lay hold of, as so many testimonies and confirmations of their heresy. How frequently do they bring forward such weighty objections as these. " Behold," they say, " He wept " (S. John xi. 35), and said " Now is My soul troubled " (S. John xii. 27), and He besought that the cup might pass away from Him (S. Matt. xxvi. 39); how then, if He spoke in such a manner, can He be God, and the Essential Word of the Father? It is very true, O ye enemies of God, that our Lord wept, that He said His soul was troubled, that He cried with a loud voice on the Cross, " Eloi, Eloi, lama sabachthani," that is, " My God, My God, why hast Thou forsaken Me? " (S. Matt. xxvii. 46), and He besought that the cup might pass away. Thus certainly it is written ; but again I would ask you, for the same rejoinder must of necessity be made to each of your objections, was He of whom these things are related merely an

ordinary man? If He was, then He would naturally weep and fear death, as being man. But if He was the Word of God Incarnate, and I must not mind repeating the same truths, whom had He to fear, being Himself God? Why should He fear death, who was Himself Life, and who was rescuing others from death? How, when He had said, " Be not afraid of them that kill the body " (S. Luke xii. 4), should He Himself be afraid? And how should He who had said to Abraham, " Fear not, for I am with thee " (Gen. xxvi. 24), and who encouraged Moses against Pharaoh, and who said to Joshua, " Be strong and of a good courage " (Joshua i. 6); how should He, I say, feel any alarm before Herod and Pilate? And, further, did He who strengthened and succoured others against fear, for David says, " The Lord is on my side, I will not fear what man doeth unto me " (Ps. cxviii. 6); did He fear judges who were but poor mortal men? Did He, who Himself had come to rob death of its sting, feel any terror of death? Is it not both ridiculous and impious to say, that He should be in the least frightened at death or hell, at whose presence the keepers of the gates of hell are filled with consternation and confusion? But if, as you would have us believe, the Word was in terror of death, why, when He foreknew that He was to be betrayed and delivered up into the hands of His enemies, did He not flee away? Why did He say to those who were sent to apprehend Him, " I am He "? (S. John xviii. 5). It was entirely in His own hands whether He would suffer or not, for these are the very words He makes use of, " I have power to lay down My life, and I have power to take it again," and " No man taketh it from Me " (S. John x. 18).

55. By this time we have made it quite plain, that the Son of God, as such, is absolutely devoid of any of these affections alluded to, and that He is said to be sensible of them only because His humanity was liable to them. Would that Christ's enemies, the Arians and unthankful Jews, would take these words to heart! And it is to be noted, that these affections and passions are never ascribed to the Son of God before His Incarnation. They were then born with Him; and, therefore, are attributed only to His human nature. It is certainly of Him that these things are written, that He raised Lazarus from the dead, that He made the water wine, that He vouchsafed sight to the man born blind, and that He said, " I and My Father are one " (S. John x. 30). If, then, our adversaries make our Lord's human attributes a ground of imagining Him to possess a mean and inferior nature, a plea for considering Him to be of merely human origin, and not to have

descended from heaven at all; why, then, should His miracles, which were such as never man did, be thought a less fair and just proof of His Divinity and equality with the Father? This should surely oblige them, from this time forth, to confess and renounce the perverse error of their ways. They cannot deny that it was one and the same person, who wrought these miracles, and underwent these inconveniences and sufferings. And, indeed, it was necessary that we should be quite sure and certain of the reality of these properties and affections of that human nature, which He held in common with us, such as weeping, hunger, and the like. For if men had not actually seen it, we should have found it difficult to believe, that an impassible and perfect being had really and positively assumed our passive, imperfect, and feeble nature. Again, His miracles were necessary to convince us, that the man we saw, beset with sorrows and infirmities like our own, was also God. And therefore for the proof of this, our Lord appeals to His miracles, saying, "If I do the works of My Father, though ye believe not Me," who to your sight and apprehension am no more than a man, "believe the works, that ye may know, and believe that the Father is in Me, and I in Him" (S. John x. 37, 38). And Christ's enemies seem to me to take a pride in showing forth their depravity and blasphemy, for when they read, "I and My Father are one," they do utter violence to the sense of the passage, and seek to separate the unity of the Father and the Son. On the other hand, when they read of His weeping, or sweating, or suffering, then they make no reference to His human body. Then it is that they say, that the whole person is signified, and not one of the natures in that person; and so, that person, by whom all things were created, must be brought down into an equality of nature and condition with the works of His own hands. What difference then, I ask our adversaries, is there between them and the Jews? The Jews blasphemously ascribed the miracles of our Saviour to the power of Beelzebub. And so, these wretched unbelievers, who strive to place the Lord who made all things on the same level with His own creatures, the works of His hands, will undergo the same condemnation as the Jews, and they can expect no mercy.

56. Had our adversaries reasoned rightly, they would have recognised the true meaning of the words, "I and My Father are one." They would have readily seen in our Lord the unity of the Godhead, and the propriety of the Father's substance. And when they read that this Divine person wept and the like, they would have owned that He was certainly also a man, and

that these passions and affections belong to Him as such. The nature of the thing and the necessity of reconciling such seeming contradictions, make us have recourse to this interpretation. It could not be said of an immaterial person, that he has in him any of those qualities or properties which are peculiar to the body, unless such a mortal and corruptible body as ours was personally united to a spiritual and immortal nature. And such a mortal body did our Lord possess, for it was derived from the substance of a mortal woman, Holy Mary. And no wonder that, having this body, He should have the properties of it too, and that He should endure the common portion of human nature, and should suffer, and weep, and toil. If, then, He wept and was troubled, it was not the Word, considered as the Word of God, who endured these things, but they were proper to the flesh He had assumed. And if, too, our Saviour besought that the cup might pass away from Him, it was not the Godhead that was in terror, but this only appertained to His human nature. And this is what we have observed before of the exclamation, "Why hast Thou forsaken Me?" The Word of God is absolutely impassive, and infinitely happy. But our Lord might be very properly said by the Evangelists to suffer, and say, and do, what strictly his human nature only suffered, and said, and did. For that nature was in or of His very person, and He made all the affections and natural infirmities of it so too; for this purpose, that its union with the Divinity might entirely refine it, and purge it from all such imperfections. And, therefore, our Lord could never be forsaken by the Father, for He was from everlasting in the bosom of the Eternal Father, both before He spoke and when He uttered these words. Let no man be so bold and wicked as to say, that our Lord could know what it was to be frightened at any horrible scene, at whose approach the keepers of the gates of hell quaked with fear, and before whom the graves were opened, and many bodies of the saints arose, and appeared to their kindred and friends. Therefore, let every heretic close his lips, and never more dare to insinuate that that Blessed One ever knew what terror was; at whose advent death flees like a serpent, before whom devils shudder, and the sea is in alarm; at whose look the heavens roll asunder, and all the powers are shaken. For so it seemed good to the Father, that when the Son cried out, "Why hast Thou forsaken Me?" at that instant heaven and earth bore witness to Him that He then was, as He had been from everlasting, in the very essence of the Father; for the earth, knowing that it was the Lord of all who spoke, straightway trembled, and the vail of the temple was rent, and the sun was hidden, and the rocks were torn in pieces, and the sepulchres, as I have said, unlocked themselves, and the dead in them arose. And one thing happened which is, perhaps, the greatest miracle of all, that those who were present on this occasion, and who had hitherto denied Him, when they saw those things that were done, openly confessed that "truly this was the Son of God" (S. Matt. xxvii. 54).

57. And it is certain, that although our Lord said, "If it be possible, let this cup pass from Me" (S. Matt. xxvi. 39), yet we must observe how He rebuked S. Peter, saying, "Thou savourest not the things that be of God, but those that be of men" (S. Matt. xvi. 23). He expressed His willingness to endure that suffering, for which He had come into the world. He was, therefore, not only not averse to it, but forward and eager to embrace it; but the terror which encompassed Him belonged only to His human nature. It was only as man that He uttered this exclamation, and yet both the sayings we have just referred to were spoken by our Lord to show that He was God, willing to perform all things for our sakes, and yet that when He had become man, His human nature was capable of feeling terror. It was for the sake of man, that He suffered human infirmity to take possession of His human will or inclination, that He might perfectly reform it and regulate it in Himself, and so destroy everything in it that was base, as to raise it above the fear of death and to render man undaunted at the thought of dissolution. What a wonderful thing, then, is this Divine plan! We see Him, to whom Christ's enemies impute words of terror, by that very terror rendering men undaunted and fearless. The blessed Apostles knew this very well. They were witnesses of their Master's firmness, and from His words and actions they learned to have such a contempt of death that they were not afraid of their judges, but warned them of the uselessness of their proceedings, saying to them, "We ought to obey God rather than men" (Acts v. 29). And all the other holy Martyrs were so brave, that they thought they were rather passing to life than undergoing the pains of death. It is absurd, then, to admire the wonderful courage of the servants and disciples of the Son of God, and at the same time to represent Him of a timorous spirit, who actually influenced them to despise death and all other evils. But from the fixity of purpose and bravery of the holy Martyrs, we have abundant proof that the Word of God was so far from being capable of anything like fear or alarm, that nothing less than

His power and grace divested our human nature of the very principle of fear; for as He abolished death by death, and cleared our nature of all its infirmities and imperfections by taking them into His person, and thereby abolishing them, so He extinguished the passion of fear in men, and caused men never more to be afraid of death. His words and His actions must be placed side by side. For the words were, indeed, those of human nature, which cried, " Let the cup pass," and " Why hast Thou forsaken Me?" but the actions were Divine, whereby the same person caused the sun to be eclipsed and the dead to arise. He that declared in His human nature, " Now is My soul troubled" (S. John xii. 27), also said in His Divine nature, " I have power to lay down My life, and power to take it again " (S. John x. 18). For to be troubled is natural to the flesh, but to have the power of laying down His life and taking it again when it pleased Him, is altogether foreign to man, and cannot be ascribed to any person or being inferior to the Son of God. It is not at the discretion of any mortal to live as long as he likes, or to die when he likes, and to revive when he likes. But the Lord, being Himself immortal, but having assumed a mortal nature, had power, as God, to become separate from the body, and to take it again at His pleasure. And it is concerning this that David thus speaks in the Psalm when he says, " Thou shalt not leave My soul in hell, neither shalt Thou suffer Thy Holy One to see corruption " (Ps. xvi. 10) ; for it was not fitting that the flesh, since it was unsuitable to the dignity of the Godhead on account of its corruptible character, should remain in its old frail and perishing state ; but because it was personally united to the Word of God, it was endowed with incorruption. God made Himself one of us, a mortal man, by assuming our nature, and He caused us to partake of His own immortality, by communicating to us its principle in the person of His Son.

58. All to no purpose, then, do these Arians raise up stumbling-blocks, and form base and degraded opinions of the Word of God, because it is written that, " He was troubled," and " He wept." For they seem not to have ordinary human feeling, and to be utter strangers to the general properties and affections of their own nature. For it is certainly a most remarkable thing, that the Word of God should have consented to have put on our flesh with all its infirmities ; that He should have suspended His power in the way He did ; for He neither hindered those who were conspiring against Him from carrying out their designs, nor did He execute vengeance upon those who were putting Him to

death. And all this was the more extraordinary, since He was able, as He showed us by His miracles, to hinder people from dying, and He could also raise those who were dead to life. And He permitted His own body to endure pain and suffering, for that was the end and occasion of His coming into this world, as I said before, that He might suffer in the flesh, and so from this time forward the flesh might be made impassible and immortal, and that injuries and indignities might lose their sting in their encounter with His person, and so might have no evil effect on mankind, being utterly abolished by Him. In short, all this took place, that henceforth men might for ever abide incorruptible, as living temples of the Word. Had these enemies of Christ thus dwelt on these thoughts, and recognised the Holy Scriptures and sound tradition as an anchor of their faith, they would not have made shipwreck of that faith, as they have done. They would not have been so shameless as to resist those who have endeavoured to raise them up after their deplorable fall, and they would not treat those as their bitter foes who have sought to bring them to the acknowledgement of the truth. But, alas! the whole creation cannot show a more vile being than a heretic. Such a one is utterly depraved, and his heart has become completely corrupt. Even when these men are overwhelmed with confutations of their objections and arguments, and their foolishness and stupidity is clearly demonstrated on all sides, they will not confess that they are in the wrong. They very much resemble the hydra which pagan mythology speaks of, a monster that when its former serpents were destroyed, produced a number of fresh ones; and so it contended against the slayer of the old heads by the production of new ones. And, in like manner, these hostile wretches, who are hateful to God, resemble the hydra, and shoot out new short-lived heads, or, I should rather say, old Jewish ones, of objection and difficulty, as fast as they lose their old ones. They will not come to any terms with truth and piety, which the Lord offers them, and as soon as they are vanquished in one place, they make preparations for war in another.

59. Even the devil himself, who is their father, I venture to think, would have been abashed at last, and would have yielded to the invincible arguments which have been employed in this conflict. But it is not so with the Arians. From their subtle hearts they only mutter and whisper evil insinuations in the ears of some, and in other company they hum and buzz like gnats. They say, " Let it be so, interpret these passages as you please,

and gain the victory in reasonings and proofs. Still, when all is said and done, you will not pretend to deny that the Son has been begotten by His Father, at His will and pleasure." Many people has been imposed upon by this misapplication of the terms, the will and pleasure of God. Now, if any orthodox believers were to make use of expressions of this kind, in the simplicity of their hearts, we should not think anything of it. We should hardly think it to be dangerous, or, at the most, we should say that the expressions were incorrect and inexpedient. But we must deal otherwise with the hardened heretics. Let a phrase seem quite harmless and plausible in itself, still when it comes from them, we may be sure there is something suspicious about it. It is written, "The counsels of the wicked are deceit," and "The words of the wicked are deceitful" (*cf.* Prov. xii. 5, 6). There is nothing but insincerity with them, and a very small thing may show us what opinion we are to have of them, and how to understand them. Accordingly, let us examine this phrase also; since, although we have convicted them on all sides, still, as hydras, they have invented fresh difficulties, and by their clever language and specious evasions, they once more seek to convey their irreligion in different and various directions. For he who affirms that the Son's existence is wholly the effect of His Father's will and choice, affirms, in other words, that there was a time when the Son was not, that He arose out of nothing, and that He is a creature. Being driven from the openness and ingenuity of these assertions, they bring the very same doctrine forward again, disguised in another sort of language. Their object is really to put forth the word "will," and to cover and secure themselves and their heresy under this word, and also by this to deceive the simple ones, just as the cuttle-fish surrounds itself in the water with its blackness. But let the Arians tell us, from what source, or from what passage of Scripture they obtain the expression "by will and pleasure." Let them give us this information we require, for we are suspicious of their words, and of their designs and meanings. For the Almighty Father, who revealed from heaven His own Word, declared, "This is My beloved Son" (S. Matt. iii. 17). By the mouth of David He said, "My heart has given forth a good Word" (Ps. xlv. 1). He bade S. John say, "In the beginning was the Word" (S. John i. 1). David says in the Psalm, "With Thee is the well of Life, and in Thy Light shall we see Light" (Ps. xxxvi. 9); and the Apostle writes, "Who being the Brightness of His Father's Glory" Heb. i. 3), and "Who, being in the form of God" (Philip. ii. 6), and "Who is the Image of the invisible God" (Col. i. 15)

60. All the sacred writers tell us of the being of the Word, but none of them speak of His being "by will," or as a mere creature. Where, I ask, did the Arians find it stated, that God willed and resolved upon the existence of the Word before He was? These ideas are entirely foreign to the truths of Holy Scripture, so, doubtless, our adversaries have borrowed them from Valentinus, and are imitating his perverseness. It was the doctrine of Ptolemy, the Valentinian, that there were two attributes in the uncreated power, Thought and Will. God, says this heretic, first of all thought, and then He willed. He could not reduce His own ideas into act, before He exerted the force of His will. It is plain that the Arians have adopted this strange fancy, and imagine that the mere arbitrary will and pleasure of the Father preceded the being of the Word. And let them and Valentinus enjoy themselves in the harmony of their philosophy. But we have our rule of faith, even the Holy Scripture, which we must not depart from; and that tells us that the Son of God was in the beginning and was from eternity; that He is in the Father, His Only Son; and that He is the express Image of His person; and that in the case of generate things only, must we recognise a precedent will or pleasure, since even the very nature of these things demonstrates that they once were not, but afterwards came into existence. And so David says, " As for our God, He is in heaven, He hath done whatsoever pleased Him " (Ps. cxv. 3). And again, "The works of the Lord are great, sought out unto all His good pleasure " (Ps. cxi. 2, Sept.), and " Whatsoever the Lord pleased, that did He in heaven, and in earth, and in the sea, and in all deep places " (Ps. cxxxv. 6). If the Son is only a creature, a created being, and one amongst others, then let it be granted, that He received His being by a mere act of His Father's will, even as Scripture shows us that all other things are brought into being. And Asterius, one of the leaders of the heresy, seems to agree with us on this point. He writes thus, " If we ought not to conceive of God as a voluntary agent, then let us not suppose Him creating anything whatsoever by an act of volition, properly so called, lest His honour and dignity should suffer some diminution by such a mistake. But if we may truly and safely attribute a proper volition to God, then it must be confessed, that the First-begotten owes His origin entirely to a special and eminent act of the Divine will. For there cannot be a plainer contradiction, than that it should be very suitable to His nature to give being to everything else by a proper effort of volition; and yet that we cannot conceive Him

producing one particular creature out of nothing by a proper volition, without dishonour and injustice offered to the perfection of His attributes." Here is, indeed, abundant blasphemy crowded into a few words, in the assumption of the argument which makes " made " and " begotten " convertible terms, and supposes the Son to be " made " because He is " begotten." But it is not to be denied, that the conclusion of the sophist follows rightly from what he laid down at first, namely, that whatever God made, He made without any one exception by the force of His will and pleasure.

61. If, therefore, as we have shown above, the Son is so far from being one of the creatures, that He is the Maker and Creator of them all, let us never entertain such an absurd idea as that the Son exists only in dependence upon an act of His Father's will. For what can be more contrary to common sense than to fancy, that He, who produced all things out of nothing by a simple act of will, should first have been produced out of nothing Himself? and this, too, by an act of will, the very same with His own. S. Paul was not an Apostle until he was called to be so " through the will of God " (1 Cor. i. 1). Our calling, which was not actually eternal, but which took place in the course of time, was the result of the previous counsel of God. It came to pass, as S. Paul expresses it, " according to the good pleasure of His will " (Ephes. i. 5). And Moses, in the history of the creation, says, " Let there be light," and " Let the earth appear," and " Let us make man " (Gen. i.) These instances are, as we observed before, all significant of the will of the Creator. The Creator chooses and determines when anything is to be made out of nothing, and whether He will give it a being. But, in the generation of the Word, there is no prior act, analogous to what we call deliberation or choice. And whatever the Father does or creates with regard to other things, He does or creates by His Word or Son. This is the doctrine of S. James, " Of His own will begat He us with the Word of Truth " (S. James i. 18). The operation, therefore, of the Divine will concerning all things, whether as regards creation or regeneration, is in the Word ; in and by whom the Father makes and regenerates whatever He pleases. And the truth of this appears further from those words of S. Paul, which he writes to the Thessalonians, " For this is the will of God in Christ Jesus concerning you " (1 Thess. v. 18). The will of God is in that person by whom He creates all things ; the Father's will is in Christ His Son ; how, then, can that Son Himself, as others, come into being simply by will and pleasure ?

If, as you say, He was only a voluntary production, there must have been some other Word of God, by the act of whose will He was to be created. For it has been shown that God's will is not in the things which He brings into being, but that this power can only be in Him by whom and in whom the Father creates all things. And since asserting that any person in the mere production of God's will, is, in substance, the same as to say, that there was a time when this person was not in being, they had better make up their minds to say, "Once He was not," that perceiving with shame that times are signified by the latter, they may understand that if Divine appointment preceded the production of the Son, so it did that of the other creatures, and He no more existed before the execution of that decree than they did. But if the Word existed before the whole creation; if He made all things out of nothing, and was co-eternal with the Father; how can it possibly be that the being of an Eternal Person should be a subsequent production of only an arbitrary act of the Divine will? Whatever was created, God created by His Son, and nothing but what was created could be the effect of such an act. How, then, could the Son be so, from whom all created beings received the beginning of their existence? Well, then, if nothing will satisfy our adversaries but a created Word, the mere product of a prudential act, even as we are begotten according to the will of God by the Word of Truth; it follows that they will find themselves, as has been said, under the necessity of discovering another Word who created this one, and everything else which it pleased the Divine Wisdom to bring into being.

62. And if there is really another Word of God, then we must allow that the Son has been made by him. But if there are not two, as we know there are not, for "without Him was not anything made which was made," then this again manifests to us the extraordinary versatility of the craft and subtlety of the Arians. They pretend to be unwilling to say openly that God's Son was made, or that He is only a creature, or that He was not before His generation; and yet, in another way, they plainly assert that He is a creature, bringing the Divine will into the question, and saying, "Unless the Son's existence be not the effect of the Father's voluntary act, then God had a Son by necessity, and against His good pleasure." And so these most wicked atheists, dragging in all the blasphemies they can think of, if they will only serve their cause, make out that the Almighty and Omnipotent God is liable to compulsion. They see and

understand whatever they imagine to be contrary to will, but what is greater and altogether surpasses it, of that they seem to have no knowledge or perception. For, just as inclination and aversion are in conflict one with the other, so whatever is immediately according to our nature, this precedes in act and excels in nature, whatever is only formed or produced by our mechanical faculties. A man, for instance, builds a house by exercising counsel and deliberation, but he begets a son by nature. Whatever is built comes to pass gradually, and there is no identity of substance between the materials and the person of the builder. But the son is the proper offspring of the father's substance, and is not external to him; wherefore, neither does he exercise counsel about him, lest he should appear to counsel and deliberate about his own being. Wherefore, as a natural product is much more excellent than a mere voluntary one, so the nature and the generation of the Son is far superior to the nature and formation of the creature. These obvious considerations, which could not escape our adversaries, ought to have prevented them from the wickedness of confounding God's physical from His arbitrary acts. But, forgetting that they are talking about the Son of God, they boldly venture to apply contradictory human arguments with regard to Him. They apply the phrases " of necessity" and " beside purpose" when discussing points connected with the Godhead, and all that they may be able to deny the sure and certain fact, that there is a true Son of Almighty God. Now, let them give us an answer to the following questions :—" Is God's goodness and mercy in His very essence or substance, or is it only in His will? Had He not been good, but simply by His choice? And did it, or does it, depend entirely upon His own discretion, whether He would or will be a good and gracious being, and how long?" For that power of a rational soul or mind, which we call freewill and choice, implies, in the exercise of it, reviews and comparisons of motive and circumstances, and an irresolution between opposite counsels and measures. It must and will be granted, therefore, that there cannot be a greater absurdity than to say, that God's essential goodness and mercy are not in Him, as a physical principle, but merely as a voluntary or arbitrary habit. And if this be so great an absurdity, then what must be our adversaries' consequence? If God is not voluntarily good and merciful, He is forced to be so, that is, He is good and merciful against His will. Now, who is it who puts this force upon Him? But if it be extravagant to speak of necessity in the case of God, and therefore it is by nature that He is good and merciful, much more is He, and more truly, the Father of the Son by nature and not by will.

63. And now, in the next place, I wish to put forth another question against their recklessness. It is a most important and fundamental one, but I ask it with a righteous intention, and so may the Lord look favourably and graciously upon me. I would ask, whether the Father Himself took His own existence into consideration, and decreed His being before He had it? or whether He existed first, and consulted with Himself about existing afterwards? Since our adversaries are so bold with regard to the person of the Son, we must let them see, that in dishonouring Him, they equally affront and attack the majesty of the Father Himself. If the notion of the Son's being only a production of the Father's will is what, upon mature deliberation, they are resolved to adhere to, and if, consequently, they are ready to confess, as they must be then, if they will reason consistently, that the Father's existence is also the result of will; then we must ask them, what being was there, or what being was He, before there had been an act of that deliberative counsel? or what did He gain, do they think, by His counsel and deliberation? But if such a question be extravagant, unnecessary, and shocking even to ask—for it is quite enough for us only to hear God's Name for us to know and understand that He is the self-existent One—will it not also be against reason to indulge in similar wicked notions concerning the Word of God, and to pretend that He is only the effect of God's will and pleasure? In like manner, it is quite enough for us only to hear the Name of the Word, to know and understand that He who is God not by will, has not by will but by nature His proper Word. What madness, then, can be compared to theirs, who can represent Almighty God to themselves and to others, as deliberating and counselling with Himself, whether He shall furnish Himself with His own Wisdom and Intelligence, and as proposing and persuading Himself to provide them? He that counsels about producing a property or part of his own being, disputes with himself whether he exists, and enquires with himself whether he shall be or not. And the blasphemy of that Arian fallacy of which we are now speaking, when it is thus exposed, establishes the truth and certainty of our doctrine. Whatever was created, we hold was created by the Divine Counsel, and Will, and Power; but the Son of God is no such mere voluntary effect of God's power, but He is by nature the proper Offspring of God's substance. In declaring Himself the Son and Word of the Father He does

not allow us to think, that the Father deliberated upon and decreed His existence before He began to be. He could not properly and truly be what He assures us, if He were not Himself the vital and personal Will of the Father, the Omnipotent Power, and the Author of all His Father's creatures. This is what He says of Himself in the Book of Proverbs, " Counsel is Mine, and sound Wisdom, I am Understanding, I have Strength " (Prov. viii. 14). For since, although He is Himself the " Understanding," by which He established the heavens, and although He is Himself " Strength and Power," for Christ is the " Power of God and the Wisdom of God " (1 Cor. i. 24), yet He has here altered the terms and said, " I am Understanding, and I have Strength." And so by asserting that counsel or will is His, He confirms the meaning of that title which is given Him by the Prophet, " The Angel of great Counsel" (*cf.* Isa. ix. 6), and this proves to us that He is the essential and substantial Will of His Father. In this manner, then, we must refute our adversaries by the use of human illustrations concerning God.

64. Is it true, then, that God's creatures only subsist by His will and favour? Was it God's good pleasure that called the whole universe into being? Was S. Paul called to be an Apostle "by the will of God"? (2 Tim. i. 1.) Was our calling brought about " according to the good pleasure of His will"? (Ephes. i. 5.) And have all creatures that exist been brought into being by the Word? What, then, can be a clearer truth than that the Word Himself is not one of the effects of His own agency or power, but rather is Himself the Living Counsel of the Father, by which all things were made, and which is the subject of David's thanksgiving in the Psalm, where it is written, " Thou hast holden me by my right hand ; Thou shall guide me with Thy Counsel" (Ps. lxxiii. 23, 24)? How, then, can that Word, who is the Counsel and Good Pleasure of the Father, come into being Himself " by good pleasure and will " as everything else, unless, as I said before, in their madness they will repeat that He was brought into being by Himself or by some other? Who, then, can there be that should give Him being? Will our adversaries create out of their imaginations another Word? Will they say that there is another Christ according to the scheme advanced by Valentinus, but concerning which Holy Scripture is altogether silent? And although they fashion another, yet assuredly he, too, comes into being through some one ; and so while we are thus counting up and investigating the succession of them, the many-headed heresy of

these impious wretches is found to issue in polytheism and in perfect lunacy.   First of all they exclaim, that the Son of God is a creature and made out of nothing, and then they go on to imply the same thing in other words by pretending that the terms "will and pleasure" are capable of being referred to the Word, when they rightly only belong to things generate and to creatures. It is most irreligious to impute the properties and affections of His own creatures to the Creator and Maker of all.   It is also blasphemous to affirm that the Will of the Father was in His Person before the Word was in it.   For if His Will was there first and His Word afterwards, then what our Lord tells us of Himself cannot be true in the proper sense of the words, that He is in the Father and in His nature.   Or, if He could be supposed to be in that nature eventually, yet, in that case, He could only be an inferior power, and in the second place, and it was not right that He should say, "I am in the Father," since that Will, by the act of which all creatures were brought into being, and He among the rest, was in the Divine nature before Him.   And then, although He might be said to excel in glory, still as regards His origin and production, in which is the thing we are concerned for, that will be all the same with one of His own creatures, which have come into being by the exercise of Will.   And if this be so, as we have observed before, how does it come to pass that He is declared to be our Lord, and that all creatures everywhere are His servants?   It is undoubtedly because He is Lord of all things jointly with His Father, since He is of His Father's essence; and all creatures are His subjects and servants, since they are external and foreign to that Divine essence, and because they wholly derive and hold their existence by a mere voluntary act of its power.

65. "Counsel" and "understanding" I consider to be only two words for the same thing.   For what a man counsels, concerning that he certainly has understanding; and what he has in his understanding, about that he also counsels.   Our Saviour, we see, thought them so closely allied and connected with one another, that He has joined them together in that saying which we before referred to, "Counsel is Mine, and sound Wisdom; I am Understanding, I have Strength" (Prov. viii. 14).   "Strength" and "Security" (*i.e.*, sound wisdom, firmness of purpose) are the same, or they are both equivalent to "Power."   And so we may say, that "Understanding" and "Counsel," which our Lord here appropriates to Himself, are terms which are equivalent and convertible.   But these impious men are unwilling that the Son

should be considered to be God's Word and Living Counsel; but they resolve all these appellations of God's Understanding, His Will, and His Wisdom, into such mere acts, habits, or operations, as those which we acquire and experience in our mortal nature, and which are attended with intermissions and repetitions. They leave nothing undone, and they put forward the "Thought" and "Will" of Valentinus; and all this to establish what they have most at heart, the doctrine and belief of the Son's being out of the essence of the Father, and only a created, not the Eternal Word of God. That curse which S. Peter addressed in the case of Simon Magus is applicable to the Arians, "The blasphemy of Valentinus perish with you." Let us, on the contrary, take our instructions and learn our faith from Solomon, who says, "The Lord by Wisdom hath founded the earth, by Understanding hath He established the heavens" (Prov. iii. 19). And the words of the Psalmist are to the same effect, "By the Word of the Lord were the heavens made" (Ps. xxxiii. 6). And as the heavens were made by the Word, even so "He hath done whatsoever pleased Him" (Ps. cxxxv. 6, Sept.); and as the Apostle writes to the Thessalonians, "The Will of God is in Jesus Christ" (1 Thess. v. 18). Here is full proof, then, that the Son of God is the "Word" and "the Wisdom," the "Understanding" and "Living Counsel" of God, that in Him is the "Good pleasure of the Father," and that He is the "Truth," and the "Light," and the "Power" of the Father. Wherefore, if the Son is the Wisdom of God, and the Wisdom and Counsel of God is His Will, it follows that he who affirms that the beginning of the Son's existence was only an effect of the Father's Will, must maintain such doctrines as these: that God's Wisdom is a creature of God's Wisdom, that the Son of God made the Son of God, and that one Word produced another Word out of nothing. And these notions cannot possibly be reconciled with God's character or attributes, and, moreover, they are directly opposed to the Holy Scriptures. The Apostle informs us that our Lord is "the Brightness of His Father's Glory and the express Image of His Person" (Heb. i. 3); and none of the inspired writers anywhere describe Him as the arbitrary result of His Father's Counsel or Will. And so I must repeat what I said before, that as certainly as the Father's own essence and substance is not voluntary, neither can His be so, who is co-essential with the Father, and the Son of His substance. Just such as the nature of the Father is, such the nature of His Son and Offspring, properly so-called, cannot but be. And accordingly, the Father

I

did not say, " This is the Son who is the production of My
Will," or " This the Son whom I have by the exercise of My
favour," but His words are simply, " This is My beloved
Son, in whom I am well pleased " (S. Matt. iii. 17). And the
meaning of the words is this, " This is My Son by nature,
in whom is placed My will concerning those things which
please Me."

66. Since, then, the Son is by nature, and not by will, does
He exist without the Father's good pleasure, and without the
Father's will? God forbid that we should entertain such a
thought. The Father not only exists with the Father's will and
good pleasure, but as He says Himself, " The Father loveth the
Son, and showeth Him all things " (S. John iii. 35, v. 20). As
it is not from His own will that His Son became good, and as it
is no less certain that the Father is not good against His own
will and inclination; for what He is, that also is His good
pleasure to be; so the Son did not receive His existence from
only an effort of the Father's will, much less in opposition or
with violence to it. The Father's essence and attributes are
altogether such as He would wish them to be, if His being were
His choice; and so are those of His Only-begotten and consubstantial Son. And thus we see how the Son is the subject of the
Father's pleasure and love, and how the necessity of the Son's
existence and the freedom of the Father's will are reconciled.
It is perfectly consistent with sound religion and true piety to
believe and confess, that God is perfectly pleased with that, both
in Himself and in His Son, which is essentially and therefore
necessarily in Him, by the glorious perfection of His nature.
This pleasure and happiness is mutual and reciprocal between
the Father and the Son. For with the same delight and affection that the Father wills, approves, and honours, the existence
and person of His Son, the Son also wills, approves, and honours
the existence and person of the Father. For the will and affection of the Divine nature in the Father and the Son is one,
which enables us to understand how we may contemplate the
Son in the Father, and the Father in the Son. For as in the
case of the sun and its brightness, one might say that the brightness does not counsel and deliberate with itself about shining
before it shines; for the brightness is the mere natural act and
property of the sun. There is no will and deliberation implied
here, although the brightness exists at the pleasure of the sun.
So also in the same manner one would be right in saying, that
the Father has love and good pleasure towards the Son, and the

Son has love and good pleasure towards the Father, although neither exerts an act of will in order to produce the other.

67. Therefore let us not call the Son a work of good pleasure, and let us never bring the erroneous doctrine of Valentinus into the Church. Let the Son of God be ever, and everywhere, confessed to be what He is, the Living Counsel, the genuine and co-essential Offspring of the Father, just as the Brightness is of the Light. For thus has the Father Himself spoken, " My heart has given forth a good Word" (Ps. xlv. 1), and the Son says the same thing in other words when He tells us, " I am in the Father, and the Father is in Me" (S. John xiv. 10). Now, if the Word was in the heart of the Father, what place or room is there for the exercise of any mere arbitrary will? If the Son, indeed, is in the Father, where is there any opportunity for the Father's good pleasure? If the Son is the Father's essential Will and Counsel, how can He owe His existence entirely to the act of that essential Will? Or are these two Wills in the Divine essence? Is there one Word, Son, and Wisdom dependent upon another Word, Son, and Wisdom? Let no one, then, presume to embrace that detestable opinion of Valentinus, and introduce a precedent Will, nor let anyone, by this pretence of " Counsel," intrude anything whatsoever between the only Infinite Father and His Only begotten Son. It is simply an extravagant and insane idea to place " Will " and " Counsel" between them. It is one thing to say that the Son is the production of His Father's will, and quite another to say that the Father is full of love and good pleasure towards His Son who is proper to Him by nature. To assert that the Son is only an effect of the Father's will implies, first, that He had a beginning of existence; and, secondly, that the Father need not have begotten Him, as has been said, so that one might suppose that it was open to the Father either to give Him His being or not. But to say of the Son that He might never have been, then that which is of the essence and substance of the Father might never have been; which is the very height of atheism and blasphemy. For if that which is essential to the Father might possibly not have been, then it was possible that God might not have been a good Being. But He is eternally good, and eternally a Father, because He is equally both, by His nature and in His substance. Wherefore, when we say, " The Father's good pleasure is the Son," and " The Word's good pleasure is the Father," we must not be supposed to imply by these expressions that there is here a precedent will, but genuineness of nature and propriety and likeness of substance.

For, as we have said more than once before, this is an impious and ridiculous absurdity. There is no perfection in the essence of the Father which is not in the essence of the Son; neither was there ever anything in the Father before the being of the Son; but the Will of the Father dwells in the Word, as its proper subject; and whatever work or creature God wills or decrees to have its being, He performs that work and accomplishes that will, by the agency of His Word. And this is all evident from the Holy Scriptures. And I could wish that these impious Arians, having shown such an utter lack of reason, as to invent this absurd notion of the Son's being only a production of the Father's will, would now suspend their method of questioning women and enquiring of the mothers, whether they had children before they conceived them? and that they would instead ask fathers whether they became fathers by counsel, or by the natural law of their will, or whether their children resemble their nature and substance? If they will ask these questions of the fathers, they will soon be put to shame and be confounded by them, from whom they assumed this proposition about generation, and from whom they hoped to gain additional arguments to uphold their hateful opinions. Surely the fathers will turn to them and reply to them in some such way as follows, "What we beget is like ourselves, but not according to our will and pleasure. We do not become parents by previous counsel and deliberation, but by a natural act. Our children are born of us, just as we were born of our fathers. Either, then, let our adversaries allow that they have been entirely and altogether in the wrong, and let them cease from asking women questions about the generation of the Son of God; or else let them learn from them that the Son is begotten not by any arbitrary will, but in nature and truth. If these wilful men will discourse and argue in this manner about the Divine nature, just as if they conceived it to be finite and defective, and as if it differed little or nothing from human nature; it is but reasonable that they should allow us to bring forward against them those arguments which we gather from human instances. Why, then, do these enemies of Christ still rage so madly? For these opinions of theirs, as well as their others, we have shown and proved to be but fables and foolish fancies. On this account they ought, although it is late, to reflect in all seriousness, and contemplate from what a height they have fallen, and into what an awful abyss of folly and wickedness they have plunged themselves. Would that our warnings and calls may arouse them to struggle to arise out of their wretched state, and to free themselves from the snares of the devil! For God's truth is full of love and mercy, and is never weary of exclaiming to men, "If, because of my bodily appearance you do not believe Me, yet believe the works" (S. John x. 38), that ye may know that "I am in the Father, and the Father is in Me" (S. John xiv. 10), and that "I and the Father are one" (S. John x. 30), and that "He that hath seen Me hath seen the Father" (S. John xiv. 9). But the Lord is loving to every man, according to His unfailing mercy, and He "helps them that are fallen" (Ps. cxlvi. 8), as David says. But these impious men, who will not hear the Lord's voice, and who cannot bear to see the Word acknowledged by all men as God and the Son of God, fly about in all quarters just like beetles, under the leadership of their father the devil, and seek everywhere fresh pretexts for their irreligion, abandoned wretches that they are. Where they will next betake themselves I cannot imagine, unless it is to the Jews and Caiaphas. They will be able to borrow blasphemies from these, and then they will perhaps go to the heathen to find atheism. As for the Holy Scriptures, these sacred books are closed against them; for in every part of them, these impious men, who are indeed bitter enemies of our Blessed Lord and Saviour, are convicted of folly, and reproved for their wickedness.

THE FOURTH ORATION.

1. THE Word is God of God, for "The Word was God" (S. John i. 1), and again, S. Paul says, "Whose are the Fathers, and of whom as concerning the flesh Christ came, who is over all, God blessed for ever, Amen" (Rom. ix. 5). Moreover, since Christ is God of God, and the Word, and the Wisdom, and the Son, and the Power of God, therefore it is plain that there is but One God revealed to us in the Holy Scriptures. For the Word, since He is the Son of this One God, must be so in a proper unity of essence. And thus the distinct personalities are consistent with the individuality and indivisibility of the One Divine nature. And so there are not two distinct self-existing Principles. The Father did not reign from everlasting by Himself, and the Son by Himself, but both in One make only One Creator and Monarch of the universe. The Word is the proper Son, existing in the very substance of this eternal Principle. He does not subsist apart from Him, by His own especial capacity of self-subsistence, nor is He born or begotten of the substance of any other than the one self-existent Principle. For, then, there would be two, or three, or more infinite Principles, subsisting independently of one another from eternity; and this is absurd. Therefore we say that the Son is substantially and essentially the Wisdom, the Word, and the Offspring of that infinite and self-existing Principle, which cannot be but One. This is that Eternal Principle, in which S. John tells us that "the Word was." And this Principle was that God, in union of essence with whom the same Apostle in the next words affirms "the Word was" (S. John i. 1). For God is here styled "the Principle," and in this Principle, that is, in that self-existing nature, which is the author of existence to all created beings, was the Word; and as being in and of this Principle, the Word was also truly and properly God. And as there can be but One Eternal Principle and One Infinite Nature, so that God, which

is this Principle, declares this of Himself, in these proper terms,
"I am that I am;" "I am Existence in the abstract, and
consequently but One Essence. For if there were another besides Me, there would be two separate, infinite, self-existent
Principles, which is impossible." And of, and in, this one
essence or substance is the Son of God, by a proper, although
inconceivable generation, even His Word, His Wisdom, His
Omnipotence. And it is not possible that the Son should leave
His Father's substance, and exist out of it, or separately. And
as the Divine substance or nature can be but One, because
there cannot be two infinite Principles; so the Word which is
from that one Divine nature cannot be like one of our ideas or
words, a mere transient act or articulate sound, but is undoubtedly God's substantial Word and substantial Wisdom, that
is to say, His true and proper Son. If the Word of God signified, according to the common meaning of the "Word" among
men, simply His speech, we should have to imagine the Deity
as having a body like ours, and uttering his will or mind in an
audible manner. But such a notion of the Deity would be derogatory to Him, and also to His Word or Son, and would seem
to place Him merely on a level with men. For as the One
Self-existent Principle is One Substance, even so that Word and
Wisdom, which is essential to that Principle, and substantial in
it, can only be One. Thus as He is God of God, and of, and in,
the Infinite Wisdom, and the Divine Word in that Infinite
Mind or Spirit, and also the true Son of the Father; so He is
God's substantial Word, as being of the Divine substances and
God's essential Word, as being of the Divine essence, and He
is Self-existent, as being from the Self-existent One.

2. Did those appellations, God's Wisdom, His Word, and His
Son, signify nothing substantial or personal, and if the last is
only a figurative expression, and the two former are only transient things, then it would follow that this Wisdom and Word
are two component parts of the Father's nature. Now we have
already intimated the absurdities that would follow if this were
true. For if this were all the meaning of Father and Son, then
the Father would be His own Father, and the Son His own Son,
and the same person would beget, and be begotten of Himself.
Or is there nothing in these appellations of the Word, the
Wisdom, and the Son, but a mere arbitrary variety or diversity
of denomination or title applied to one and the same person?
Has He, who is said to be all these, no real and proper subsistence, but is He a mere name, and only the meaning of an in-

scription? If so, they must be very unnecessary and superfluous thus applied, unless it be said that the Wisdom and the Word are in the nature of God Himself. But if the Father and the Son are only two titles of the same person, then indeed the same person would be Father to Himself, and Son to Himself. As being Wise, He would be the Father, and as being Wisdom, He would be the Son. But, then, the Wisdom of God thus conceived would be no other than a mere accident or quality, such as might be in any of His creatures; and this would be such a representation of God, which would be totally unworthy of the Almighty. Far be it from us to entertain such an idea! For what is this but resolving the Divine nature into a composition like our own, of substance and quality? For whereas all quality is in substance, it will clearly follow that the Divine One, since that is indivisible, must be compounded, since it would thus be divided into substance and accident. We must, therefore, again call upon these rash and foolhardy men to explain themselves. The Holy Scripture declares the Son of God to be His Wisdom and Word. How, then, is He such? Is it as a quality? Then we have shown already what an absurdity this would be. Or, is that Wisdom nothing else but only another Name for God Himself? Then, this is the heresy of Sabellius, and nothing but folly can result from such a doctrine. What remains, therefore, but that we acknowledge the Son to be truly and properly the Offspring of the Father's substance? even according to the illustration of light. For as there is light from fire, so from God there comes the Word, and Wisdom from the Wise, and from the Father the Son. For in this way the Unity of the Divine nature is preserved entire and indivisible; and yet the Father's Eternal Son loses nothing of His substantiality or personality; He is not one merely subsisting, but He is, in a substantial sense, the Word and Son of the Father. For unless it were so, all that is said would be only said metaphorically, and without any literal meaning. But if we must avoid that ridiculous idea, then is a true Word substantial. For as there is a Father truly, so there is a Wisdom truly. And thus the Father and the Son are not one in person, as Sabellius would have them be, but they are truly and properly two Persons. The Father is the Father, a Person by Himself, and the Son is the Son, a Person by Himself. And yet these two Persons cannot but be one in unity of essence, because the Son as such is of His Father's own substance, and the Word or Wisdom of God cannot be of or in any other substance but God's. And this is the meaning of the assertion of our Lord, "I and My Father are One" (S. John x. 30). The Word never existed apart from the Father, and God was never destitute of His own Word. The Word, therefore, is God, and was always in the nature of the Father; and on this account He says, "I am in the Father, and the Father is in Me" (S. John xiv. 11).

3. That Christ is the Word of God is certain. Did He, then, give Himself being, and after subsisting was He joined to the Father? Or, did the Father create Him, and then call Him His Word? If the first is true, that is, if He gave Himself being and is God, then He is a Deity by Himself; not properly the Son of the Father, but the Son of Himself; and then there will be two self-existing Principles. Again, if His substance is foreign to the Father's, and made of nothing, He must be a creature. And it is impossible to avoid these two absurdities, except by confessing Him to be the Son of the Divine substance; and this confession forces us to distinguish between the Son which is of or from that substance, and that substance which He is of or from. And this is the distinction of the Divine Personalities. If you deny that there is more than one Person in the Godhead, and if those personal characters and affections which are attributed to the Son, do truly belong to the Person of the Father, then the same Person is His own cause and effect; He that is begotten is the same as He who begets. And this is the blasphemous doctrine of Sabellius. For if you will say that He gave Himself being, and yet He who gave the being is the Person to whom the giver gave it, then the same Person must be the origin or cause of this being, and yet not so. He must be so, because He gives it Himself, and He must not be so, because He is the very same Person with Himself. And if the Father and the Son are so, that is, One Person, considered only under two different characters, then the union between them is not substantial or essential, but merely speculative and ideal. But if this be unseemly and unfitting to say, then the Father and the Son are truly and distinctly two Persons, and, moreover, these two Persons are united in One essence, because the Son is not from without, but He is begotten of God. But if anyone shrinks from that expression "Offspring," and would rather have it said that the Word exists with God, let such who take exception to this and similar phrases remember, that these terms are constantly used in the Scriptures, and let them fear lest they fall into any heretical doctrine, and make God a being of double nature. For if this co-existence implies an essential Unity of the persons

co-existing, then it is exactly the same thing as consubstantiality. But if the meaning of it is only this, that both exist together from everlasting, but not in one essence or nature, then it supposes the two co-existing persons to have two distinct and separate essences, and neither of them the Father or Son of the other. And exactly the same thing will hold good with regard to the term " Power." And we may see this more clearly, if we consider it with reference to the Father. For as the Father can be but one Person, so He can have but one essence or nature, and consequently the Son must be of that one essence or nature. And, therefore, as there are not two Fathers, but one Father; so there are not two Eternal Principles, but one; and the Son is of and in that. Now, then, the Arians must be questioned from an opposite point of view. To insist upon that propriety of person which is implied in the name and relation of a Son is the way to confute the Sabellians; but the effectual method of dealing with the Arians is to explain what is the true and proper meaning of the word Father.

4. Let us then proceed. Either it is true that God is wise, and has His Word in His nature, or it is false. If you say it is false, you deny, in other words, that God is God. But if it is true, we are then to enquire what is the proper meaning of God's having His Wisdom and His Word in His nature? Does He possess the Word and the Wisdom from without, or from Himself. If from without, there must be some one who first gave it to Him, and before He obtained it His nature lacked His Wisdom and His Word. But if His Word was from Himself, then it must be false that His Word arose out of nothing, and that there was a time when He was not. For we must remember that this Word is the Son of God, the express Image of His Father's Person, which He could not be, if He had not existed eternally with the Father, because otherwise He could not have represented or expressed the Father in His attribute of being Eternal. But if they should reply that the Deity is indeed Wise and not without His Word, and this always was so, that is to say, that He has and ever had His essential Wisdom and Word in Himself; but still that this Wisdom and Word is not Christ, but that by which God created Christ; then our adversaries must allow, that the Word by which Christ was created is He who brought all things into being, that is to say, that He is that Word, as S. John declares, "by whom all things were made" (S. John i. 3), and to whom the Psalmist refers in the words, "In Wisdom hast Thou made them all" (Ps. civ. 24). And then Christ Himself will be

found guilty of untruth, when He says, "I am in the Father" (S. John xiv. 10), if there is another Word who is in the Father. And that assertion of S. John, "The Word was made flesh" (S. John i. 14), will, according to this belief, be false as well. For if that Word which was Incarnate was that Word in the Essence of the Father which made all things, and Christ is not that Essential Word; then Christ was not made flesh, and is but a nominal, not a real Word of God. And, if so, then these results are inevitable, first, that Christ is not properly and truly what He has expressly declared Himself to be; and secondly, that He is so far from being the Person that made all things, that all things were made by another Word, and Himself among the rest. But if they say that Wisdom is in the Father as a quality, or that the Father is His own Word or Wisdom, what ridiculous absurdities will follow, as we have already observed. If the first were true, the Father's essence must be a compounded one; and if the latter were true, then the Father would be Father to Himself, and the Son Son to Himself. Moreover, we must confute them and put them to silence on this ground, that the Word which is essential to God cannot have been created, and cannot have had a beginning of existence. That such a Word Christ is, His own words, "I am in the Father and the Father is in Me," abundantly testify. And that there is no other Word but Himself in God appears from His being the Only-begotten of the Father. The Son of God, the Word, the Wisdom, and the Power, are all one Person under different names; and this Son is the one and only Son of God. He is the proper Offspring of God, and these names are not so many parts or elements of which God is compounded. Of His own nature God begets the Word, and by the agency of that Word He creates and disposes and governs all things. This was that Word and Wisdom from whom all creatures derive their being, and "according to whose ordinance they continue to this day" (*cf.* Ps. cxviii. 91). And as this Word is that Son "without whom was not anything made that was made," so is it certain that if God did not beget this Son, He neither makes nor ever did make anything. And so it is plain that our reckless adversaries must allow that we have overwhelmed them with convincing proofs to their objections, or else they must be utterly confounded with the frightful consequences of their error.

5. In Deuteronomy we find these words, "But ye that did cleave unto the Lord your God are alive every one of you this day" (Deut. iv. 4). This passage compared with our Lord's

assertions, " I and the Father are One," and " I am in the Father, and the Father is in Me," shows us the difference there is between the Son of God and His creatures, and proves His existence from eternity. The Word is in the Father, but the creatures only cleave unto the Lord ; they subsist and increase by cleaving to Him, that is, depending entirely upon His Power. Their nature and His are widely separated, and entirely dissimilar. They may, indeed, be united to God in the conformity of their wills to His ; but the Word is united to Him in essence. He, who is the very Son of His Father's nature, derives His very nature and substance from His Father, whereas adopted children come from another stock, and are not born or begotten, but are simply attached to the family. And so the Prophet says, " What nation is there so great, who hath God so nigh unto them ? " (Deut. iv. 7). And elsewhere we read this question, " Am I a God at hand ? " (Jer. xxiii. 23). His creatures are in their nature very remote from and inferior to His ; and, therefore, to them He only descends or approaches. But He does not come to His Son, nor His Son to Him, for the Son co-exists with the Father. And, therefore, Moses says afterwards in the same Book of Deuteronomy, " Ye shall obey His voice, and cleave unto Him " (Deut. xiii. 4). Now that which cleaves to a thing is without the substance of that which it cleaves to.

6. And in answer to that impious conclusion which the Arians pretend to draw from those expressions in Scripture where we read of our Saviour having " all power given unto Him " (S. Matt. xxviii. 18), of His being " highly exalted " (Philip. ii. 9), and of His " sitting at the right hand of God " (Col. iii. 1) ; for they infer from these passages that our Lord is just such another dependent and needy creature as we are ourselves ; we shall here confute them from a consideration of the nature, extent, and end of His office as Mediator. The Divine assumed our human nature in order that our Lord, being both the Word and Son of God, might interpose between God and man for the glory of the former and the benefit of the latter ; that from God, He might dispense to us His blessings, and that from man, He might represent our needs and recommend our interests to God. When, therefore, He is said to be hungry, and to weep, and to feel weariness, and when He cries out that God has forsaken Him, these are all our human affections. He receives these from us and offers them to the Father, and He intercedes for us that our human woes and weaknesses may be remedied and redressed. And when it is said, " All power is given unto Me,"

and that He "received," and that "God hath highly exalted Him," these are our privileges and gifts which are given to us from God through His intercession. For as the Word never did nor could want anything, so man always did and could not but want ; and man was not able, by his own strength, to procure those things which he needed. The things which are necessary for us are conferred upon us in and by the Person of the Son. They are said to be given to Him, because He takes or receives them to give them to us. For this was the very end and purpose of His Incarnation, that our human nature might in His Person obtain and receive whatever it could not otherwise have obtained, and that we might be partakers both of the same nature and of the same blessings with Him. A mere man could never have merited, and God, not made man, could never have wanted any of these graces and gifts. It was necessary, therefore, that God and man should be personally united, in order that human nature might be invested with power and exalted to glory. The Divine exalted the human nature, which it had taken into itself; and the human nature, being assumed into the Divine, received from that its glory and power. Our nature neither had, nor could have, any other title to these blessings, but by virtue and in consequence of its personal union with God. And as "the Word was made flesh" (S. John i. 14), so also man received the gifts which came through the Word. For all that man has received, the Word is said to have received ; that we might thereby understand, that man himself being unworthy to receive, as far as his own nature is concerned, yet has received because of the Word thus uniting Himself to man. Wherefore, whenever we find the Scripture speaking of our Lord as receiving, needing, or the like, we must consider that it is not given to the Word in His own nature, or because He needs anything, but it is given to our human nature through Him. When one person intercedes for another, only the person interceded for is supposed to want a favour bestowed upon him, and no reference is implied to the intercessor himself.

7. As He, who had no infirmities of His own, transferred ours to Himself ; and as He, who was incapable of hunger, yet felt the pangs of hunger, that He might make our case and condition His, and might offer up our sufferings to the Father that they might be done away ; so He receives of the Father those advantages and blessings which His intercession procures for us, instead of our weaknesses and infirmities, in order that man, being united to Him, may be able to partake of them. And this is the

meaning of our Lord's words, " All things whatsoever Thou hast given Me I have given them," and again, " I pray for them " (S. John xvii. 7-9). For He prayed for us, having taken on Him our nature and condition, and then He gave to us those things which He received in answer to His prayers. It was entirely for the sake of the Word that the Father was so merciful and gracious to our human nature, as to exalt and glorify it when it was assumed by the Word, as to invest it with all power, and the like. And, therefore, those privileges are said to be given to the Word, because, indeed, the Father does immediately bestow them upon Him, and from Him they descend to us. He humbled Himself for our sakes, and we are exalted for His sake. And He may very fairly and properly be said to be exalted for our sakes, by the means of whose humiliation our nature is exalted and glorified in Him. And when we read that God " gave to Him," we must understand that God gave to us for His sake ; and when we are told that God " highly exalted Him," we are to understand that God exalted our nature and ourselves in Him. And so the Word Himself, when we are exalted, and receive, and are succoured, just if He Himself were exalted, and received, and were succoured, gives thanks unto the Father, and He refers what is ours to Himself, and says, " All things whatsoever Thou hast given Me, I have given them " (S. John xvii. 7, 8).

8. Those of the Arians who are specially called Eusebians deny that the Son had a beginning of kingly power, although they affirm that His nature and existence had a beginning. But this is ridiculous, for it is self-evident that He could not reign from everlasting, if He did not exist from everlasting. This is confessing and denying the same thing at the same time, and shows the men to be both foolish and blind. Again, those amongst the Arians, in whose opinion the Son of God has nothing of essence or substance, but is only a name or appellation, pretend to be angry with others of their party for asserting the doctrine that there was a time when the Son of God was not. And this is ridiculous also ; for they who deny that the Son of God has or ever had any being at all, are angry with those who at least grant that He had a beginning in time. Thus, in quarrelling with their brethren, they confute and contradict themselves. Again, the Eusebians are divided amongst themselves into those who admit of the name or title of the Son, but deny the Son to be the Word of God, or anything but a title arbitrarily attached to Him by the Father. And then there are others who grant Him the name and title of the Word of God, but deny

Him to be the Son, or anything but a mere title assigned by the Father to the Son. And both thus equally find themselves striving to no purpose in darkness and obscurity.

9. Our Blessed Lord says, "I and My Father are One" (S. John x. 30). That two are one, you will say, means either that one has two names, or that one is divided into two. Now, if one is divided into two, that which is divided must undoubtedly be a body, and neither of the two perfect, for each is a part and not a whole. But if one thing has two names to it, this is the expedient of Sabellius, which has been long since condemned. He would have it that the Father and the Son are one Person. And this made it impossible that either of them should be a person at all, unless the Father could be His own Son, and the Son His own Father. But if one thing in one respect, one may be two in another; then the nature and essence of the Deity may be one, and yet the Persons in that nature more, the Son a Person consubstantial with the Father, and the Word begotten of and in the Father. Thus God is One, the Father is One, the Son or Word is One, and yet the Father and the Son are two in that One. Had they been two, He would not have said, "I and the Father *are* One," but "*I am* the Father," or "I and the Father *am ;*" whereas the Persons here are distinguished by the known and common significations of the terms. The word "I" declares the Person of the Son, and the word "Father," as evidently expresses Him who begat the Son, and the word "One" the one Godhead and His consubstantiality. And it must be observed that the heathen entirely mistake us, when they charge us with the absurdity of making two things one and the same thing, of making God and His Son or Wisdom, the Father and the Word, one and the same Person. Nothing, indeed, can be more repugnant to reason and nature than that the same person should be His own Father and His own Son. But this is a doctrine which the Christian religion has nothing to do with. We acknowledge a distinction of persons, the Father and the Son, the Wise and His Wisdom, God and His Word, and we are most careful to explain that the nature of God in all things is indivisible and inseparable and indissoluble.

10. But sometimes when people hear that we maintain that the Father and the Son are two distinct Persons, they misrepresent us by saying that we assert that there are two Gods. This is what we have often been reproached with, and so we have been held up to scorn as defenders of polytheism. But to all those who raise this objection, we make this reply, If to confess

that there are two Persons, the Father and the Son, is to assert in other words that there are two Gods, and therefore the Son must no longer be considered to be a Divine Person, then Sabellius was in the right when he asserted the doctrine of one Person. For if to speak of two Persons is heathenish ; on the other hand, to say that there is but one is Sabellianism. But this is no part of our belief, and God forbid that it should be ! We assert the Unity of the Godhead, as expressly as the diversity of the Persons. We believe the Father and the Son to be two, perfectly distinct from one another in their relative and personal characters ; but still we believe these two to be but One God, One Infinite Essence or Nature, and that the Son or Word begotten of the Father is indissoluble and indivisible and inseparable from Him. And that illustration which we have made use of before explains this very well in the way of example, for fire and the brightness which comes from it are truly distinct ; they are two in being and in appearance, and yet they are both one as to substance and general properties ; and brightness cannot exist without fire.

11. The men that cast these objections against us ought to know that they are falling into the same folly as the Arians. There is only the difference of a word between them, which is that of " Emission," instead of their original word " Creation." They both suppose that the Son had a beginning of existence, and that God gave it to Him in order that we might be created, and consequently at some convenient time before it. The Arians, then, attribute a much higher excellence to us, God's creatures, than to His Only-begotten Son. Both must own that if God produced Him that He might produce us, then He was made for us, and not we for Him. And this second party, who are even more irreligious than the Arians themselves, seem to think that God is more imperfect and more feeble than we are. For very often we are able by thought and meditation, even when we are silent, to execute our purposes and projects, and to shape and frame our productions and compositions. But these men represent the Deity as incapable of acting in any other manner, except by the emission of His Word and Voice. When He is silent, they say, nothing is done or made ; it is only when He speaks that He begins to create. Moreover, we will proceed to ask them whether they think the Word of God was something so real and perfect in God, before His emission, as to be able to make or create ? If He was not so before, and our creation was the end of His emission, then are we the cause of His per-

fection, for had it not been for God's purpose of creating us, He had not been qualified to create at all. But if He was perfect in God, so as to be able to make, then His generation is altogether superfluous; since He, even when He was in the Father, could frame the world. The consequence of which reasoning will be, either that He was not begotten at all, or that He was not begotten on our account, and that He might make us; but that He was everlastingly begotten of the nature and substance of the Father. For His generation proves, not that we were created, but that He is from God; for He was in God before that, even from everlasting.

12. And all this offers as great indignity to the Father as to the Son. For if, when silent, He was incapable of creating, then it follows that by begetting His Son, He has acquired a new power He did not possess before, that is, by emitting His Word or Speech. Now, how did He acquire this capability? For what purpose did He receive it? If, when He had the Word within Him, He could create; then the generation of the Word was wholly unnecessary, because He might have created the world as well without it. Again, if the Word was in God before He was begotten, then He was not properly begotten of God, but subsisted out of Him and separate from His nature. But how does this agree with His assertion, "I am in the Father and the Father is in Me"? (S. John xiv. 10). If He is now in the Father, certainly He was always so. He is not one thing at one time, and another thing at another; and so it is absurd to say that He was begotten on purpose for creating us, and then that He reverts into the Person of the Father afterwards, that He may be as He was before. He never was what He is not now, and what He is now, He always was. The properties of His essence, and the manner of His existence were always the same; or else His Nature must be strangely defective and variable. If at first He was one thing, and then another, and then again the thing which He was at first, then He is not now what once He was, and what again He will be. Let me explain this further. If He formerly was, and will hereafter be again, in God, it plainly follows that the Word is not now in God. And how shall we account for that positive and express declaration of our Lord, "I am in the Father, and the Father is in Me"? If this be true, then He is now the same that He always was; and if He is now the same that He always was, it cannot be true that once He was unbegotten, and that afterwards He was begotten; nor that the Deity was first in a state of silence and inactivity, and afterwards uttered

or sent forth His Voice or Word. On the contrary, the Father and the Son and Word always co-existed, the latter in Unity of nature and substance with the former, not a mere Word in name alone, or a Son by appointment or decree, and not begotten simply on purpose to create us, for we were created for His honour and glory. For, if He were begotten for us, and in His begetting we were created, and in His generation all creatures were brought into being, and then He returned into the same state in which He was before, it cannot be denied but that He would have been first begotten, and then again unbegotten. He would be begotten by His emission, and unbegotten by His recession; and after that God's state of silence would re-commence, and consequently that former state of inactivity, and then there would have been an end of the world. For if the emission of the Word was the cause of the being of all creatures, His retreat and silence must put a stop to their existence. For what purpose, then, were they created, if they were to be thus soon annihilated? Why did God send forth His Word, if He were to recall it so soon? Why did He speak once, and then utter His Voice no more? Why did He beget a Son, who was to continue with Him so short a time? Again, we do not know, nor can we imagine, what the future will bring forth. Either God will ever be silent, or He will again beget and create another universe, for it is not to be supposed that He will revive the old one, else that which was already made would have remained. And then in due course He will bring that also to a close, and will create another world, and so on without end.

13. It is very likely that this wild theory is borrowed from the Stoics. It is one of their peculiar fancies that there is an eternal inactivity in the essence of God, and that His creating consists in the expansion of His nature, and then He enjoys a continuous rest. The substance expanded and the substance contracted is the same; only the Deity, according to this notion, is in a different state at one time from what it is at another, and undergoes various modifications and alterations. If, therefore, the Unity of the Divine nature thus expanded makes the Trinity; if the Person of the Father is the Unity, and the Trinity is the Father, Son, and Holy Ghost in the expansion of that Unity; first, it is certain that the Divine essence sustains a change of condition, and is shaped or changed into another form; for it was expanded, whereas before it was contracted. Next, if the Unity is thus expanded into a Trinity, and the Trinity consists of the Father, Son, and Holy Ghost, the consequence will be that the Father

becomes the Son and the Holy Spirit, as Sabellius taught. Unless, indeed, he supposed that the Unity which he speaks of is something besides the Father; and then he ought not to speak of expansion, since the Unity would produce three Persons out of itself, and would turn itself into what it was not before, even into a Trinity of Persons. Its expansion of itself neither takes from, nor adds to, its substance or essence; it must itself be that which was originally expanded. A Trinity, when it is expanded, is no longer a Unity, and when there is a Unity, there is not yet a Trinity. While the Father was not expanded, He was not the Son and the Holy Ghost; and after He was expanded and turned into these, He was no longer the Father. Now these are such hateful conceptions of God, that no one can entertain who has any worthy notions whatever of His glorious character. For what is this but circumscribing that Blessed Being within narrow and confined limits, and making no more of Him than passive matter? Expansion implies an impression or force upon the thing expanded, and that which is distended keeps its substance and only changes the situation of its parts. It may be larger at one time than at another, and change its outward appearance and form, but the matter or substance of it neither increases nor decreases.

14. And this S. Paul knew very well, for he thus writes to the Corinthians, "Ye are not straitened in us, be ye also enlarged" (2 Cor. vi. 12, 13). S. Paul exhorts his readers to change from straitness to enlargement and expansion. Now, in either of these states, the Corinthians were, or would have been, the same men. And so if the Trinity only consisted of the expansion of the Father, then the Trinity would be only the Father. And the Apostle says the same thing in the verse before, "Our heart is enlarged" (2 Cor. vi. 11); and Noah says, "God shall enlarge Japheth" (Gen. ix. 27). Now, the Apostle's heart, and no other person's, in the former verse is to be enlarged, and Japheth, and no other person, in the latter verse is to enlarged likewise. Either, therefore, the object of the expansion of the Unity was not itself, but some thing or things out of itself; or if the Unity expanded itself, then it was the same before its expansion as after it; that is to say, it was the Son and Holy Ghost before, as well as after, the Father's expansion. And I should like to be informed, when speaking about these matters, what authority is there for supposing that this principle of expansion exists in the Deity, and what is the motive or cause of it all? For certainly we cannot suppose that God would effect such a change in the

Divine nature for no end or purpose at all. If, then, it was in order that the Word and Spirit should be with Him, it is unnecessary to speak first of the Unity, and then to say it was expanded ; for the Word and Spirit did not come into being afterwards, but they always existed, or else, as the Arians says, God was at some time without His Word. For so it was, if this doctrine of the expansion be true, until such time as the Unity expanded itself. Or, was the purpose of this expansion the assumption of our human nature? Did the Incarnation bring forth the Trinity? If so, then there was no Trinity before the Incarnation. Besides, this view would make the Father to be Incarnate ; for the Father was that Unity, which expanded itself for the assumption of our nature; and then the Son will be out of the Trinity, and the Trinity will consist of the Father, the flesh, and the Holy Ghost. And thus, again, the Trinity will be only three names or titles. Or, was this expansion necessary for the creation of the world? But this is a most absurd thing to imagine. For the Unity in its original state was able very easily to create and make all things, and it is gross blasphemy to fancy that the Deity could not work or create without this expansion. And another extravagance also would result here. If this expansion was necessary for the sake of the creation ; and if, while there was only a Unity, there was not a single creature in existence ; and, if this expansion was to be followed, after the creatures were once made, by a return to the state of Unity, then when that state began to be, the creation, too, will come to nought. For if this expansion was necessary, in order that creation should take place, then it follows, that when the expansion ceased, the creation will cease also.

15. These and such like are the absurdities which attend this doctrine of the expansion. And there is another great error which those who hold this doctrine fall into as well as this, namely, that the Word and the Son are two distinct beings, that the Word was first in existence, and the Son afterwards. And this is such a wicked invention that we ought not to let it pass unnoticed. Now, the asserters of this doctrine are divided among themselves in the explanation of it. Some of them say that the Son was the human nature, which our Saviour assumed ; and others say that the Word and the human nature were made the Son upon their being united. Others, again, hold that the Word Himself then became the Son when He was made man ; for from being the Word, they say, He became the Son, and that He was not the Son before this, but merely the Word. Now,

for both these doctrines our adversaries are indebted to the Stoics, both for the doctrine of the Son's distinction from the Word, as well as for that of the expansion. To confess the being of the Word, and to distinguish Him as a Person by that very title, and yet to deny that the Word is the Son is very ridiculous indeed. For if the Word were not from God, then they might reasonably deny Him to be the Son; but if He is from God, then certainly it is but right to confess Him to be the Son of the Divine Nature. For what is a son, but a substance or person, resulting out of the nature and substance of his father? Now, since God is properly and truly a Father, whom can we suppose to be the Son of this Father, but the Word, that is confessedly of the Divine substance? A father is said and known to be a father with regard to that person who bears the name of his son; and a son is said and known to be a son with regard to that person who is called his father. If, therefore, God is not the Father of Christ, then the Word is not the Son of God; but if He is His Father, then there can be no doubt but that the Word is His Son. There is, however, another Arian doctrine which comes in here. Some of these wicked men say that the Father was God first, and that He only became the Father afterwards. But then this makes the Divine nature corporeal, and it is, besides, a terrible sin to say that God is liable to change and alteration. But if they reply to this, " How is it, then, that God could be first God, and afterwards a Creator?" Then I would answer them thus, " Creation implies no change at all in the nature of the Creator, and any change that took place had only regard to the things which were afterwards made."

16. If, therefore, the Son were a creature, then, indeed, His Father would be only such in a temporary or improper sense. But if the Son is not a creature, then the Father is the Father, and the Son is the Son, from everlasting. And if the Son is from everlasting, then certainly He must be the Word. And if anyone has the presumption to deny this, then he will be obliged to affirm, either that the Son is the Father Himself, or that the Son is a more excellent being than the Word. Now, we read that the Son is "in the bosom of the Father" (S. John i. 18). Either, therefore, the Father is not before the Son, for nothing can be before Him who is in the Father, or if the Word is distinct from the Son, then who can He be but the Father Himself, in whose bosom the Son is? Or, if the Word is not the Father, but the Word in contradistinction to the Father, then the Word must be external to the Father, since it is the Son "who is in the

bosom of the Father." For we nowhere find that both the Word and the Son are in the bosom of the Father, and therefore they must be one and the same Person, even the Only-begotten Son of God. Again, if the Word is not the Son, we are sure, from another reason, that the Son is a more excellent being than the Word. For He tells us Himself that "no man knoweth the Father save the Son" (S. Matt. xi. 27), and consequently the Word does not know the Father, unless He is the Son. Either, then, the Word does not know the Father, or if He knows Him, then our Lord's words are not true that no one knows Him but the Son. And the same arguments are equally applicable to the texts, "He that hath seen Me hath seen the Father" (S. John xiv. 9), and "I and My Father are One" (S. John x. 30). The Person here speaking of Himself was not the Word as opposed to the Son, but the Son. And though our adversaries deny this, the context very plainly proves it. For, according to S. John, when the Lord said, "I and My Father are one," "Then the Jews took up stones again to stone Him." "Jesus answered them, Many good works have I shown you from my Father, for which of those works do ye stone Me? The Jews answered Him, saying, For a good work we stone Thee not, but for blasphemy, and because that Thou, being a man, makest Thyself God. Jesus answered them, Is it not written in your law, I said, Ye are gods? If He called them gods unto whom the Word of God came, and the Scripture cannot be broken, say ye of Him, whom the Father hath sanctified and sent into the world, Thou blasphemest, because I said, I am the Son of God? If I do not the works of My Father, believe Me not. But if I do, though ye believe not Me, believe the works, that ye may know and believe that the Father is in Me, and I in Him" (S. John x. 30-38). Our Saviour's words, which so enraged the Jews, were, "I and My Father are One," although He did not actually say either "I am God," or "I am the Son of God."

17. The Jews, then, when they heard the word "One," thought, as Sabellius did afterwards, that He said He was the Father Himself. But our Saviour shows them what a mistake they had made by this argument, "Although I said God, you should have remembered what is written in the Old Testament, I said, ye are gods." And then to explain the words, "I and the Father are One," He shows them what is the unity that exists between the Son and the Father in those words in which He gives them to understand that He is the Son of God. For although He does not expressly declare this to them, yet by comparing His

statements it is very clear that this is their sense and meaning. For as He said at first that He was one with the Father, so a little after we find how He was thus one with Him, even as being His Son. For nothing can be co-essential with the Father, which is not of the same substance with the Father, and who is that who partakes by generation of the substance of the Father, but His Only-begotten Son? And it is on this account that He adds, " That ye may know that I am in the Father, and the Father is in Me." He does not say, in explaining the Divine Unity, that He is in that Person which is numerically in Himself; but that He is in that nature, which is common to the Father and the Son, and in which they are substantially, eternally, and inseparably united. And thus He confutes and condemns the opinion of Sabellius, who imagines that Christ was the Father, by saying, " I am the Son of God." And He also convicts Arius when He says, " I and the Father are One." If, then, the Son and Word are distinct and separate Persons, then the Son, and not the Word, is One with the Father; and " He that hath seen the Son hath seen the Father," but not He that hath seen the Word. And from this it follows, either that the Son is greater than the Word, or that the Word is co-equal with the Son. For what can express greater excellency or a higher state of perfection than those assertions, " I and the Father are One;" " I am in the Father, and the Father is in Me;" and " He that hath seen Me hath seen the Father"? Now all these assertions and declarations are uttered by the Son. And in the same way we can understand the following passages of Scripture, " He that seeth Me seeth Him that sent Me " (S. John xii. 45); " He that receiveth Me receiveth Him that sent Me " (S. Matt. x. 40); " I am come a Light into the world, that whosoever believeth on Me should not abide in darkness. And if any man hear My words and believe not, I judge him not; for I came not to judge the world, but to save the world. He that rejecteth Me and receiveth not My words hath one that judgeth him; the word that I have spoken, the same shall judge him in the last day " (S. John xii. 46-48), " because I go unto My Father" (S. John xiv. 12). The word that I have spoken, our Lord says, shall judge him who has not observed My commandments; " For if," He says, " I had not come and spoken unto them they had not had sin, but now have they no cloke for their sin " (S. John xv. 22). He here tells us that those who have heard His words and make a right use of them, shall not fail, by that observance, to obtain eternal salvation.

18. Perhaps these impious men will have so little shame as to say that it is the Word, and not the Son, who uttered these sayings. But from what preceded these passages it plainly appears that the speaker is the Son. For He who here says, "I came not to judge the world, but to save the world," is shown to be none other but the Only-begotten Son of God, because the same S. John says of Him before, "For God so loved the world that He gave His Only-begotten Son, that whosoever believeth in Him should not perish, but have everlasting life. For God sent not His Son into the world to condemn the world, but that the world through Him might be saved. He that believeth on Him is not condemned, but he that believeth not is condemned already, because he hath not believed in the Name of the Only-begotten Son of God. And this is the condemnation, that light is come into the world, and men loved darkness better than light, because their deeds were evil" (S. John iii. 16-19). If He who says, "I came not to judge the world, but to save the world," is the same who says, "He that seeth Me seeth Him that sent Me" (S. John xii. 45); and if He who came to save the world, and not to judge it, is expressly declared to be the Only-begotten Son of God, it is plain that it is the same Son who says, "He that seeth Me, seeth Him that sent Me." For He who said, "He that believeth on Me," and "If anyone hear my words, I judge him not," is the Son Himself, of whom Scripture says, "He that believeth on Him is not condemned already, because He hath not believed in the Name of the Only-begotten Son of God" (S. John iii. 18, 19). And again we read, "And this is the condemnation, that Light is come into the world" (S. John iii. 19); and men did not believe this Light, that is, in the Son of God; for He is "the true Light which lighteth every man that cometh into the world" (S. John i. 9). As long as our Lord was upon earth in that human nature which He had assumed He was a Light in the world. And so He said to all men, "While ye have Light, believe in the Light, that ye may be the children of Light" (S. John xii. 36). And He says in another place, "I am come a Light into the world" (S. John xii. 46).

19. All this, then, abundantly proves that the Son and the Word are one and the same Person. But if the Son is the Light which has come into the world, it cannot be disputed that this world was made by the Son. For in the beginning of the Gospel, the Evangelist, speaking of S. John the Baptist says, "He was not that Light, but was sent to bear witness of that Light" (S. John i. 8). For, as we observed before, Christ Himself

was "the true Light, which lighteth every man that cometh into the world." For if " He was in the world, and the world was made by Him " (S. John i. 10), then of necessity He must be the Word of God, concerning whom also the Evangelist testifies that "all things were made by Him " (S. John i. 3). For either our adversaries will be obliged to speak of two worlds, one created by the Son, and the other by the Word, or, if the world was all of it created by one person called sometimes the Word and sometimes the Son, then the Son and the Word are certainly one and the same Person. Therefore, if the Word is that Son which created the universe, it will not be contradictory, but just the same for the Evangelist to say, for instance, " In the beginning was the Word," or " In the beginning was the Son." And if these two phrases are the same, then the one does not exclude the propriety and truth of the other, as our adversaries would tell us they do. And if they will perversely deny that what is here affirmed of the Word is to be understood of the Son, because the Word, and not the Son, was the subject of that first assertion, " In the beginning was the Word ; " then by analogy of reason they must affirm that what is declared of the Son cannot have reference to the Word, and ought not to be ascribed to Him. But, as we have already demonstrated, those words, " I and the Father are One," refer to the Son, and also the words, " Which is in the bosom of the Father," and " He that seeth Me seeth Him that sent Me," are spoken of the Son ; and the creation of all things is ascribed as expressly to the Son as to the Word ; all this incontestably proves that the Son was in being before the world, for of necessity the Creator must exist before the things He brings into being. And, again, what is said to S. Philip must have reference to the Son, and not to the Word, as our adversaries would tell us. For, as the Evangelist narrates, "Jesus saith unto him, have I been so long time with you, and yet hast thou not known Me, Philip? He that hath seen Me hath seen the Father ; and how sayest thou, then, show us the Father? Believest thou not that I am in the Father, and the Father in Me? The words that I speak unto you I speak not of Myself ; but the Father that dwelleth in Me, He doeth the works. Believe Me that I am in the Father, and the Father in Me, or else believe Me for the very work's sake. Verily, verily, I say unto you, he that believeth on Me, the works that I do shall he do also, and greater works than these shall he do, because I go unto My Father. And whatsoever ye shall ask the Father in My Name, that will I do, that the Father may be glorified in the Son" (S. John xiv. 9-13). Therefore, if the Father be glorified in the Son, the Son must be He who said, "I am in the Father, and the Father is in Me," and He who said, "He that hath seen Me, hath seen the Father;" for the Person who spoke to S. Philip declares Himself to be the Son in those very words, "That the Father may be glorified in the Son."

20. But if our adversaries bring forward that other opinion that the human nature of Christ, and not the Word, is the Only-begotten Son of God, then He that is in the Father, and in whom the Father is, would be only a mere man. He that declares Himself to be One with the Father, who lives in the bosom of the Father, and who is the True Light, even this Person, according to this theory would be simply a man. And these wicked men will be compelled to say that it was a man, like one of themselves, who created the world, and that it was but a man, who came not to judge the world but to save it; and that this man, too, was in being before Abraham was born. But how ridiculous it is to suppose that this could be true of a descendant of Abraham, born two-and-forty generations after him? How could the creation be the work of a man that was not in being, until He was conceived of the Virgin Mary? The same Evangelist had said before that "He was in the world," that is to say, that He existed before His Incarnation, for that is the meaning of these words. Again, how could the Son, if He were not the Word, but only a man, redeem or save the world, Himself being a part of it? And if this does not put these men to shame, let them tell us where the Word is, whether it is not He, but the Man, that is in the Father? How can the Word be one with the Father, if not the Father and the Word, but the Father and the Man are one? If the Man is the Only-begotten, then what becomes of the Word? They must either say that He is second and inferior; or if He is above the Only-begotten, that He is the Father Himself. For as the Father is One, so the Only-begotten of the Father is One. Again, if the Word is not the Son, what has the Word more than the Man? The Scripture informs us that the Son and the Word made the world. Creation is equally ascribed to Him under both names. But, then, as to seeing the Father and saving the world, these two things are attributed in Scripture, not to the Word, but to the Only-begotten Son. For our Saviour Himself says, "Have I been so long time with you, and yet hast thou not known Me, Philip? He that hath seen Me, hath seen the Father" (S. John xiv. 9). It is not said that the Word, but that the "Only-begotten Son who is in the bosom of the Father," knows and sees the Father.

21. If the Son is one Person and the Word another, as these men would have us believe, let me ask what does the Word do more for our salvation than the Son? We are commanded to believe in the Son, and not in the Word, for S. John says, " He that believeth on the Son hath everlasting life, and He that believeth not the Son shall not see life " (S. John iii. 36). And Holy Baptism, in which is the very foundation of our Christianity, is not administered in the Name of the Word, but in the Name of the Father, the Son, and the Holy Ghost. If, therefore, the Word is not the Son, but a Person distinct from the Son, then the Word has no connection whatever with Baptism. And if, as they hold, the Word is with the Father, how is it that He is not joined with Him in the administration of Baptism? But perhaps they will tell us that the Word is comprehended under the Name of the Father? Then why should not the Holy Ghost be so too? Or does the Holy Ghost exist out of, and separate from, the Father? Moreover, if the Word is not the Son, but the Man-hood, then the Man should be named after the Father, and the Spirit after the Man; and thus the Unity will no longer be ex-panded into Three Persons, but into Four—the Father, the Word, the Son, and the Holy Ghost. But being vanquished on this point, they have recourse to another argument, and they say now that the Man alone is no longer the Son, but the Word and Man united make up the Son; for both joined together are named Son, they tell us. Which, then, was the cause of the other? Did the Word make the Man the Son? Or, did the Man make the Word the Son? To speak more clearly, Did the Word become the Son in consequence of the Man being united to Him? Or, did the Man become the Son in consequence of the Word being united to Him? Or, did neither of them give the other this new character, but does it wholly consist in the abstract in their union? If they answer, that the Word became the Son in consequence of the Man being united to Him, then they must return to their old assertion that the Man is really the Son, and then all those ridiculous absurdities follow which we have seen must happen from saying such a thing as this. Or, if they say the Man became the Son in consequence of the Word being united to Him, then they must confess that the Word was the Son before the Incarnation. For, how could He, who is Himself not a Son, make others the Sons of God, and especially when the Father was existing at the same time? If He makes Sons for Himself, then He must Himself be a Father; but if He makes Sons for the Father, then He Himself must be the Son of the

Father, or rather that particular Son, for whose sake the rest are made Sons.

22. For if our Lord is not the proper Son of God, and if we are truly sons, it follows that God is our Father, and not His. Why, then, does He assert His Sonship in such plain and emphatic terms, saying, "My Father" (S. John v. 17), and "I came forth from the Father" (S. John xvi. 28). If God is the common Father of us all, He is not His Father only, nor did He only come forth from the Father. He tells us, it is true, that God is sometimes called our Father, because He has Himself become a partaker of our human nature. For on this account the Word was Incarnate, that, since the Word is God's Son, therefore, because of the Son dwelling in our nature, we might become God's adopted sons. And so the Apostle says, "God hath sent forth the Spirit of His Son into your hearts, crying, Abba, Father" (Gal. iv. 6). Therefore the Son, who is in our nature, gives us the privilege of calling His Father our Father as well; and whosoever has not the Son in his heart cannot call upon God as His Father. Now, it is plain that long before our Lord's Incarnation, there were those that were called the sons of God. And this alone proves the Word was the Son before that time; for Scripture says, "I have nourished and brought up children" (Isa. i. 2); and in Noah's time we read, "The sons of God saw the daughters of men" (Gen. vi. 2); and in Moses' song we find the words, "Is not He thy Father?" (Deut. xxxii. 6). There must, therefore, have been at that time that proper and true Son of God, for whose sake these persons were also called God's sons. But if these men will insist upon it, that neither the Word nor the Man is the Son, but the conjunction and union of both, then the cause of Sonship must lie in something else that united and joined them; and this cause must be prior to the union; and consequently the Sonship must be so. When this argument is put to silence, then these men take refuge in another pretext, saying that neither the Man is the Son, nor the conjunction of the Man and the Word, but that the Word, which in the beginning was only such, came to be called the Son when it had assumed our human nature. Until then, they say, this was not the Son, but only the Word; and therefore as the Word was in time made flesh, which it was not before, so it was also in time made the Son, which it had not been before. Such are the foolish notions in which our adversaries indulge, but they can be refuted without much trouble.

23. If it was the Incarnation that caused the Word to become

the Son, then His Sonship is the result of His connection with our nature ; and, therefore, if the Man or the Union of the Word with the Man be said to be the cause of the Word's Sonship then the same absurdities we have noticed before will take place. And, moreover, if the Word existed first and the Son afterwards, then it will appear that He knew the Father afterwards, not before, for He does not know Him as being the Word, but as being the Son ; for "no one knoweth the Father, save the Son" (S. Matt. xi. 27). And this too will follow, that He was afterwards "in the bosom of the Father" (S. John i. 18), and afterwards He and the Father became one, and it is to some time afterwards that those words have reference, "He that hath seen Me hath seen the Father" (S. John xiv. 9). For all these things are said of the Son. The consequence of all this will be, as they cannot but confess, that the Word was nothing but a name. For it is not the Word but the Son that is said to be in us with the Father ; and it is not the Word, but the Son in whom the Father was and is to be seen. Nor, if this were so, could the Father, who makes Himself known through the Son, be known to anyone until the Incarnation, for so it is written, "And he, to whomsoever the Son will reveal Him" (S. Matt. xi. 27), for the Word, since He was not yet the Son, did not yet know the Father. How then does it come to pass that He was seen by Moses and the Fathers? for He tells us that He was so seen in the following words, "Did I plainly appear unto the house of thy father?" (1 Sam. ii. 27). But if God was thus revealed, then there must have been a Son to reveal Him ; even as our Lord plainly tells us that God appears, or reveals Himself to no one but by the Son. It is then very wicked and foolish thus to divide the Word from the Son, and the Son from the Word. What pretext can our adversaries have for putting forth such a shocking opinion ? They answer, Because they find that no mention is made in the Old Testament of the Son, but only the Word ; and so they conclude that the Son came later than the Word, because He is only spoken of in the New Testament, and not in the Old. This is what they have the wickedness to say, but what is this separating between the Testaments, and saying that one does not agree with the other, but the device of Manichees and Jews, the former of whom oppose the Old Testament, and the latter the New ? Moreover, if, as they say, what is contained in the Old Testament is of more ancient date, and what in the New of later, and times depend upon the date of the writing, then it follows that the phrases, "I and the Father are one," and

" Only-begotten," and " He that hath seen Me hath seen the Father," are of later date, because these testimonies are not to be met with in the Old Testament but in the New.

24. But as a matter of fact the statement itself is not true, for the Son is frequently mentioned in the Books of the Old Testament. For instance, in the second Psalm we read, " Thou art My Son, this day have I begotten Thee" (Ps. ii. 7); and in the ninth Psalm the title, " Unto the end, concerning the hidden things of the Son, a Psalm of David" (Sept.); and in the forty-fourth Psalm the title, " Unto the end, concerning those that shall be changed, to the Sons of Core, for understanding a song about the Well-beloved." And in like manner the Prophet Isaiah says, "Now will I sing to My Well-beloved a song of My Beloved touching His vineyard. My Well-beloved hath a vineyard " (Isa. v. 1). Who is this Well-beloved but the Only-begotten Son; even He of whom God declares that begat Him " from the womb of the morning," and " before the morning star " (Ps. cx. 3, Sept.), of which we shall have occasion to speak afterwards. And so, again, we read in the Proverbs, " Before the hills was I brought forth" (Prov. viii. 25); and in the Book of Daniel, " And the form of the Fourth is like the Son of God " (Dan. iii. 25); besides many other places. If, then, the antiquity of the Old Testament implies the antiquity and age of the person mentioned in it, then our adversaries must confess that the Son of God must be a much more ancient Person than they suppose Him to be; for we frequently read clear descriptions of Him in many passages of the Old Testament. To meet this objection, they tell us that these passages in the Old Testament concerning the Son are only prophetical. And we answer again, that we may as reasonably say, that all the texts in the Old Testament, where mention is made of the Word, are only prophetical too. The expressions relating to the one must be considered in exactly the same way as those relating to the other. For if the words " Thou art My Son " are a prophecy, then the following words must be one too, " By the Word of the Lord were the heavens established " (Ps. xxxiii. 6, Sept.); for the word here is " established," and He does not say that the heavens were " created by the Word." And that the word " established " may have reference to the future appears from other passages, such as " The Lord reigneth; He hath so established the earth that it can never be moved " (Ps. xciii. 1). And if the title of the forty-fourth Psalm, which we lately quoted, is a prediction of the future, so the words that follow them are also predictions, " My heart

has given forth a good Word" (Ps. xlv. 1). And if it may be argued that the Son is only a mere man from the words "from the womb" in the Psalm before referred to, then the same thing may be inferred of the Word from these words concerning the heart. He only implies a body as much as the other. But if the Word who proceeds from the heart is eternal, then it must be granted that He is born of the womb is eternal too. And if it is not denied that the "Only-begotten" is in the bosom of the Father, neither can it be denied that the "Well-beloved" is in that bosom too. For that the "Only-begotten" and the "Well-beloved" are one and the same Person, those words of the Father Himself declare to us, "This is My Well-beloved Son" (S. Matt. iii. 17). In calling Him His "Well-beloved Son," He did only wish to tell us what there could not be any doubt of, that God loved His Son, or to make it be believed that He hated everything besides His Son; but it was simply that He might thereby proclaim Him to be the Only-begotten Son, and that He might show us that He alone was from Him. And thus when the Divine Word commanded Abraham to offer up his only-begotten son, He bade him take his "only son Isaac whom he loved" (Gen. xxii. 2); and it is plain to anyone that Isaac was the only son that Abraham had by Sarah. The conclusion, then, at which we arrive from all this is, that the Word is truly the Son; that He is neither a novel nor a nominal Son, but that He is the proper Son of God from eternity. For if He is not truly and properly God's Son, then neither is He His Word; as, on the other hand, if He is not God's Word, neither can He be His Son. For he is a son that is of the substance of his father; and undoubtedly He is of the substance of the Father, who is the Word that went forth from the heart, and was born from the womb. For we are sure that the Father Himself is not the Word, nor the Word the Father; but the Father is one Person, and the Son another; the Father begets, the Son is begotten.

25. Here, then, we see the insanity of Arius on the one hand, and of Sabellius on the other. We see the folly of Arius, who says that the Word is from nothing, and that there was a time when He was not. We see also the madness of Sabellius, who says that the Father is the Son, and that the Son is the Father, Two in name, but personally One. Sabellius, to support his ridiculous notion, brings forward S. Paul's account of the grace of the Holy Ghost as an example of his meaning, "Now there are diversities of gifts, but the same Spirit" (1 Cor. xii. 4). He says that so also the Father is the same, but is expanded into Son

and Spirit. But this is utterly absurd; for if the parallel holds good, then the Father must be in One Person Himself the Word and the Holy Ghost; and not always all these together, but at one time the Father, and at another time the Son, and at another time the Holy Ghost; that is, in plainer words, He will be in Nature and Person only the Father, and but in name the Son and Holy Ghost; and upon commencing to be the Son in name He must lose His title of Father, at least for a time. And then it will follow that it was not a Person, but only a name and title that was made man; and that the Son did not come down from heaven, but that only a title descended upon earth; and that the Son spoke what was untrue in saying, " I and My Father," being, indeed, according to this doctrine, not another Person, but the Father Himself. It is, in fact, impossible to enumerate all the impossible absurdities which are involved in the heresy of Sabellius. According to him, even the very names of the Son and the Holy Ghost must necessarily cease, when there is no occasion or need for the use of them; and all the things which have been transacted, according to the accounts in the Scriptures, will seem to have been but visionary and imaginary. And when the Name of the Son ceases to be, as they hold, then the grace of Baptism will cease too, for it is administered in the Name of the Son. And, further, what must follow but the annihilation of creation? For if the Word came forth that we might be created, and when He came forth all things were given their being; it is plain that when He goes back into the Father, as they say, we shall no longer exist. He will be then in the state He was in before; and we shall be so too, that is to say, in nothing. And thus there could be no world, until He was pleased to come forth and exert Himself a second time.

26. But these, indeed, are most fanciful and most ridiculous absurdities. Could S. John affirm in plainer words that the Son had no beginning of existence, but that He abode with and in the Father before His assumption of our nature, and indeed from everlasting, than in those with which he begins his first Epistle? He writes thus, " That which was from the beginning, which we have heard, which we have seen with our eyes, which we have looked upon, and our hands have handled, of the Word of Life; for the Life was manifested, and we have seen it, and bear witness, and show unto you that Eternal Life, which was with the Father, and was manifested unto us " (1 S. John i. 1, 2). And then in the conclusion of his Epistle, he tells us that the Son is that Life, which here, in the beginning of it, he says was

not made, but was Eternal and with the Father. He writes, " And we are in Him that is True, even in His Son, Jesus Christ ; this is the True God and Eternal Life " (1 S. John v. 20). But if the Son is the Life, and the Life was with the Father, and if the Son was with the Father, and the same Evangelist says, "And the Word was with God" (S. John i. 1), then it is plain that the Son must be that Word which was everlastingly with and in the Father. And as this Son is the Word, so God must be the Father. Moreover, the Son, according to S. John, is not merely "God," but "Very God." And, therefore, the Word, which he tells us elsewhere was God, is doubtless properly so too. And the Son Himself declares Himself to be that Life, which the Apostle tells us is eternally with the Father. Thus, then, we see that the Son, the Word, and the Life, are all declared to be with and in the Father. And, again, another evidence and proof of the Son's being from eternity, the same Apostle exhibits where he styles Him "the Only-begotten Son, which is in the bosom of the Father" (S. John i. 18). This Son is the Person whom the Psalmist calls the " Hand of God," saying, " Why pluckest Thou not Thy Right Hand out of Thy bosom " (Ps. lxxiv. 12)? Here the Hand is in the bosom, as the Son was said to be before, and therefore we infer that the Son is this Hand, and this Hand the Son, by whom the Father made all things. For, says the Lord, " All those things hath Mine Hand made" (Isa. lxvi. 2) ; and " The Lord hath brought you out with a mighty Hand," that is, by His Son (Deut. vii. 8). Compare those words of the Psalmist, "This is the change of the Right Hand of the Most Highest" (Ps. lxxvii. 11, Sept.), with the title of the forty-fourth Psalm, " Unto the end, concerning the things that shall be changed, a song for My Well-beloved." Now, the " Well-beloved " in the latter text is plainly the " Hand that has been changed " in the former, concerning whom the Divine Voice also says, " This is My beloved Son " (S. Mat. iii. 17). And this clearly shows that the " Son " and the " Hand " are equivalent terms.

27. The text we lately produced and argued from, " I begat Thee from the womb before the morning " (Ps. cx. 3, Sept.), is by no means conclusive and satisfactory to many ignorant and inconsiderate men. They say that this cannot possibly refer to the Divine essence ; that the womb must be interpreted of the Blessed Virgin, affirming that Christ was conceived of her before the morning star arose in its ordinary course. Let me explain their error in a few words. If they think the expression used in the text is unworthy of the Deity, they ought also to find fault

K

with the mention of the heart, for this part also belongs to the human body.   And therefore, since both are human, we must either deny both, or seek to give an explanation of both.   Now, as a word issues from the heart, so an offspring proceeds from the womb.   The Scriptural metaphor of the Heart of God the Father does not mislead us into a notion of His being a body, or having one; why, then, should we take the words " from the womb" in any other but a metaphorical sense?   In treating of Divine and supernatural persons and things, Holy Scripture explains itself by descriptions and ideas borrowed from various parts of the natural world, particularly from the frame and constitution of human nature.   Thus, speaking of the creation, it says, " Thy hands have made me, and fashioned me " (Ps. cxix. 73); and " All those things hath Mine Hand made " (Isa. lxvi. 2); and, "He commanded and they were created" (Ps. cxlviii. 5). These are familiar images, which serve as illustrations to express the work or act of creation, just as those others signify the propriety of the Divine Sonship.   For some things God makes and creates, but He begets the Son from Himself, as His Word and Wisdom.   That the Son is of the Father's genuine and proper substance is plainly manifest from His issuing out of the heart, and being born from the womb; for thus it is with our nature, from which these allusions are taken.   What we beget is the issue of our nature, but what we make is the work of our hands.

28. But, these objectors reply, what does that part of the text mean which speaks of His being begotten "before the morning star?"   I answer that this very thing should be enough to convince them that this passage is not to be considered of our Lord's birth from the Virgin Mary.   For many others besides our Lord have been born before the rising of that star.   There is no extraordinary or singular circumstance involved here, for this is common to very many.   We must observe further that " begetting " is one thing and " production " another, and that the former is antecedent to the latter; and therefore this passage cannot relate to Christ's human nature, which was not conceived at that time when the Angels appeared to the shepherds in the night, and brought to them the glad tidings of His birth, but before this, at the time of the Annunciation, which we do not find took place in the night, as the Scripture tells us His birth did.   Thus His being begotten before the morning star is plainly distinguished in Scripture from His conception and birth, the latter of which the Psalmist expresses by the figure of His

proceeding from the womb, as when He says, "Thou art He that took Me out of My mother's womb" (Ps. xxii. 9). Besides the words are not "Before the rising of the morning star," but, "Before the morning star," that is, before its existence. And if the being, and not the motion or course of the star, is meant in these words, then it is plain that the passage has no relation to the Saviour's being born of the Virgin. For if it had, then the body born of the Virgin must have had a being before Adam; for all the stars were in being before him. But let us look out elsewhere for a passage of Scripture to explain the sense of this. Let us turn to the Book of the Revelation of S. John, where we read this, "I am Alpha and Omega, the Beginning and the End, the First and the Last. Blessed are they that do His commandments, that they may have right to the tree of life, and may enter in through the gates into the city. For without are dogs and sorcerers, and whoremongers, and murderers, and idolaters, and whosoever loveth and maketh a lie. I, Jesus, have sent Mine Angel to testify these things in the Churches. I am the Root and Offspring of David, and the Bright and Morning Star. And the Spirit and the Bride say, Come. And let him that heareth say, Come. And let him that is athirst come. And whosoever will, let him take the water of life freely" (Rev. xxii. 13-17). If, then, the Offspring of David is the Bright or Morning Star, then it is plain that our Saviour here styles Himself the Morning Star as man, or as He was of the seed of David, and not as the Son of God, of the substance of the Father, which He had from all eternity. And thus the sense of the passage in the Psalm will be this, "I have begotten Thee from Myself before Thy appearance in the flesh;" and so "Before the Morning Star" will signify "before the Incarnation of the Word."

29. We have seen that the Old Testament makes very explicit statements concerning the Son. But we need not lay any very great stress upon this after all, for we have another very troublesome argument which will puzzle the most perverse and obstinate of our adversaries to deal with. Let me proceed to ask, then, if what is not stated in the Old Testament is of later date, where in the Old Testament is any mention made of the Holy Spirit, the Paraclete, or Comforter? Mention is made, no doubt, of the Holy Spirit, but there is not the least intimation anywhere of the existence of the Paraclete. Now, will our adversaries also make two Persons of the Holy Spirit and the Paraclete? and will they venture to affirm that the Paraclete is the later because He is not mentioned in the Old Testament? But God

forbid that anyone should say such a thing as this, either that the Comforter began to exist but lately, or that the Holy Ghost is one Person, and the Comforter another. For undoubtedly He is that one and the same Blessed Spirit, who then did, and still does, both sanctify and comfort those that are worthy and qualified to receive Him. And so is the Word and the Son that one and the same Blessed Person, by whom as many as were, or are now, worthy, were then, and are still, adopted. For it appears that God had His sons in the times of the Old Covenant, and these were made such only by the operation of His Son. For unless there was a Son who was of God, even before the Son was born of the Virgin Mary, how can He be said to be before all, when there were sons before Him? And how, again, can He be said to be the First-born, if He comes second after many? But neither is the Paraclete second, for He was before all, nor is the Son later; as it is written, "In the beginning was the Word" (S. John i. 1). And as the Holy Spirit and the Paraclete are the same, so are the Son and the Word the same. Our Saviour expressly declares the Holy Ghost and the Comforter to be one and the same Person, for He says, "The Comforter" (or the Paraclete) "which is the Holy Ghost, whom the Father will send in My Name" (S. John xiv. 26). And S. John as fully asserts the same of the Son and the Word, when he says, "And the Word was made flesh and dwelt among us, and we beheld His glory, the glory as of the Only-begotten of the Father" (S. John i. 14). Here He does not distinguish between the Word as one Person, and the Only-begotten of the Father as another; for this is a direct and clear affirmation that they are both One Person. It is therefore evident that as the Paraclete is not one person and the Holy Ghost another, but both are one and the same; so neither is the Word one Person and the Son another, but both are the Only-begotten Son. For the glory of the Only-begotten in this passage is not the glory of the flesh or man, but it is the glory of the Word. If, therefore, these men are not afraid of dividing the Paraclete from the Holy Ghost, then indeed there will be no wonder in their presuming to divide the Son from the Word. But if the Paraclete and the Holy Ghost must not be separated, neither must the Word be parted from the Son, who is also the Wisdom and the Power of God. Moreover, even those heathens who are versed in grammatical knowledge and classical writings know very well that "Well-beloved" is a very proper equivalent for "Only-begotten." And this is that epithet, which Homer in the second book of the Odyssey gives Telemachus, who was the only-begotten son of Ulysses :

> " O'er the wide earth, dear youth, why seek to run,
> An only child, a well-beloved son ?
> He whom you mourn, divine Ulysses, fell,
> Far from his country, where the strangers dwell."

Here, then, we see an instance of one who was the only son of his father, being called well-beloved.

30. But there are those who belong to the heresy of Paul of Samosata, who also divide the Word from the Son, affirming that the Son is the Person called Christ, and that the Word is quite another Person. And for this view they appeal to those words of S. Peter in the Acts of the Apostles, which are in themselves most edifying, but which are lamentably misapplied by these men. The words are these, "The Word which God sent unto the children of Israel, preaching peace by Jesus Christ : He is Lord of all" (Acts x. 36). For, they say, that since the Word spoke through Christ, as the Prophets tell us He formerly did by them, in their usual form, "Thus saith the Lord," the Prophet was one person, and the Lord who made use of him, was another. Now, to refute this notion it will be well to turn to those words of S. Paul's, which we find recorded in the first Epistle to the Corinthians, namely, "Waiting for the coming of our Lord Jesus Christ, who shall also confirm you unto the end, that ye may be blameless in the day of our Lord Jesus Christ" (1 Cor. i. 7, 8). One Christ does not confirm or establish the day of another Christ, but the One and Only Christ confirms those that wait for Him, at His own day. Thus likewise the Father sent the Word made flesh, that being made man He might preach Himself to the children of Israel. He that is here declared Lord of all is Jesus Christ. Jesus Christ, therefore, is the Word, for the Word is Lord of all.

31. "And Moses said unto Aaron, Go unto the altar, and offer thy sin-offering and thy burnt-offering, and make an atonement for thyself and for the people ; and offer the offering of the people, and make an atonement for them ; as the Lord commanded Moses" (Levit. ix. 7). Here Moses is named twice, but certainly it is the same man ; yet Moses is called so by Moses, as if he were another. So in that passage of the Acts, S. Peter says that "the Word is sent to the children of Israel by Jesus Christ, although it is no more a distinct person from Christ, than Moses is from Moses, but He is one and the same Person, Divine as well as human, because of His

gracious and merciful assumption of our nature into His Person. And although our Lord's natures may and ought to be distinguished, yet this ought not to be done so as to divide the Word ; for no division of the Word can be reconciled with the statement of S. John, "And the Word was made flesh and dwelt among us" (S. John i. 14). What, then, is said in a proper and right manner by S. Peter, the disciples of Paul of Samosata put such a perverse and misleading construction upon, that it is altogether wide of the truth. For in Holy Scripture Christ is spoken of under two titles, as when we read that Christ is "the Power of God, and the Wisdom of God" (1 Cor. i. 24). If, then, S. Peter says that the Word was sent through Jesus Christ unto the children of Israel, let him be understood to mean that the Word Incarnate has manifested and revealed Himself to His people ; for this will then correspond to S. John's words, "And the Word was made flesh." Now, if these men confess the Divinity of the Word, and then separate the human nature from it, affirming that the Divine Person of the Word sent the human Person of Jesus Christ, then they are, without knowing it, contradicting themselves. For those who in this place separate the Divine Word from the Divine Incarnation, have, it seems, a base and low notion of the doctrine of the Incarnation, imagining that this was simply a change or alteration of the Word. And this is an opinion in which the very heathens will agree with them.

32. But this is not so. God forbid it should be. For as S. John here asserts that mysterious union, "the mortal being swallowed up of life" (2 Cor. v. 4), and that this takes place by Him who is the Principle of life and being, even as He Himself said to Martha, "I am the Life" (S. John xi. 25); so when S. Peter says that the Word was sent though Jesus Christ, he implies the Divine Unity also. It is a wicked thing to say, and we have proved it so, for anyone to infer from the words, "The Word was made flesh," that our Lord ceased to be the Word on assuming our flesh. And in like manner when anyone hears of the Word which has been united to the flesh, let him understand that this Divine mystery is one and simple. But the answer of the Archangel to the Mother of God supersedes all our disputing and reasoning upon this point, and shows us plainly the unity of the Divine Word and Man. For He says, "The Holy Ghost shall come upon thee, and the Power of the Highest shall overshadow thee: therefore also that Holy Thing which shall be born of thee shall be called the Son of God " (S. Luke i. 35). Very foolishly

then, do these Samosatenes seek to separate the Word, who is here clearly declared to be united to that human nature which was conceived of the Virgin Mary. And, therefore, the Word was not sent by Christ, but He did indeed send others in and by Christ; for He commissioned and commanded the Apostles to "go and teach all nations" (S. Matt. xxviii. 19.)

33. Moreover, it is customary for Holy Scripture to express itself in plain and simple terms. So, for example, in the Book of Numbers we read as follows, "And Moses said to Hobab, the son of Raguel the Midianite, Moses' father-in-law" (Num. x. 29). The Moses who spoke, and the Moses whose father-in-law was Raguel, were but one Moses. The Word of God has many names; He is called God's Wisdom, His Power, His Right Hand, His Arm, and the like, and all these very justly and properly, without being supposed to be so many different Words. Why, then, after He has taken our nature into His own, and has made Himself the first-fruits of our immortality by uniting Himself with us, must the two natures be thus divided into two persons? The nature of man which was assumed was the work of the God who assumed it. It was one of those things which were made by that Word, who was in the beginning with God, and who was God Himself, and without whom was not anything made that was made. And if it pleased the Word of God to take our human nature upon Himself, even when it was corrupted, and to rescue it from destruction, and to renew it in Himself, in order that it might eternally enjoy His attributes and glory; and for this purpose He made it indeed Himself, a part of His own person, that within Him it might obtain this blessed state; how shall we possibly persuade ourselves to imagine that this human nature, which was born of the Virgin Mary, sent or commissioned the Word? Shall the Lord and Master, who sent the Apostles and Prophets, be at last enrolled amongst those who were sent by Him? And again, is it not simply impossible that a mere man should be called Christ? But when even a man is united to the Word, then there is no wonder that He should be called Christ and the Son of God. And this exactly corresponds with that prophecy which so clearly asserts His consubstantiality with the Father, which says, "I will send My Son Christ" (*cf.* Isa. xix. 20. Also, *cf* Acts iii. 20), and with that testimony of the Father at the river Jordan, "This is My beloved Son" (S. Matt. iii. 17). For when the promises and predictions which concerned Him were fulfilled; then He shewed, as was fitting,

that the words spoken referred to Him of whom it was said that He was sent.

34. Thus we see that our Blessed Lord has two natures in One Person, the Divine Word, and the human nature which is united to it, even that which was born of the Blessed Virgin Mary. For in the Virgin's womb the Word formed Himself His house, as it were; just as at the beginning He formed Adam from the dust of the earth. I had better say, however, that our Lord did this in a more glorious manner altogether, which is well described by Solomon, who rightly understood that the Word was also called Wisdom, for he says, "Wisdom hath builded Her house" (Prov. ix. 1), the meaning of which the Apostle explains when he says, "whose house are we" (Heb. iii. 6). Elsewhere S. Paul calls us "the temple of God" (1 Cor. iii. 16), as much as to say, that we are a habitation not unworthy of God, the material type of which Solomon was commanded to build of stone. This was the resemblance or type, which was to disappear when the reality was manifested. The wicked men of that time were so blind and obstinate that they mistook the shadow for the substance, the type for the person typified. They sought to destroy that true and living Temple which He was, that Habitation which was made by His union with ourselves. And we must notice, that instead of warning the Jews of the evil consequences of their mistake, since He knew they were but bringing calamities upon themselves, He says to them, "Destroy this Temple, and in three days I will raise it up" (S. John ii. 19). And our Saviour also intimated in these words that all those things in which men interest themselves must very soon perish and come to nought, according to those words of the Psalmist, "Except the Lord build the house, their labour is but lost that build it. Except the Lord keep the city, the watchman waketh but in vain" (Ps. cxxvii. 1). And so the works of the Jews are now lost and gone, because they were only a shadow and a type of things to come. But the Church stands firm and immovable, for it is "founded on a rock," and "the gates of hell shall not prevail against it" (S. Matt. xvi. 18). The Jews found fault with our Lord, and asked Him "Why dost Thou, being a man, make Thyself God" (S. John x. 33)? Paul of Samosata is their willing disciple, and he is continually teaching his heresy to those who are foolish enough to be taught by him. But "we have not so learned Christ, if so be that we have heard Him, an' have been taught by Him; that we put off the old man, which is corrup. according to the deceitful lusts; and that we put on the new man, which after God is

created in righteousness and true holiness" (Ephes. iv. 20-24). We conclude then, that we ought to believe in Christ as both God the Divine Word, and man personally united to that Word.

35. Moreover, Holy Scripture often calls only the human nature by the name of Christ. S. Peter tells Cornelius "How God anointed Jesus of Nazareth with the Holy Ghost" (Acts x. 38); and again, he says to the Jews, "Jesus of Nazareth, a Man approved of God among you" (Acts ii. 22); and again, S. Paul tells the Athenians that God will judge the world "by that Man, whom He hath ordained, whereof He hath given assurance unto all men, in that He hath raised Him from the dead" (Acts xvii. 31). Our Saviour's mission and manifestation of Himself are often expressed by His unction; and any one may at once see from this that there is no disagreement among the sacred writers. There is no dissension among them as to the thing itself, that is, the personal union of God the Word with the Man born of the Virgin Mary; only they use various terms about it, sometimes calling it an unction, sometimes a mission, and sometimes a manifestation. And so it follows that what S. Peter says agrees very well with all this, and so far from separating the person of God the Word from the human nature, which God forbid anyone should try to do, it is a plain declaration and testimony of the propriety of our Lord's Divinity as the Only-begotten Son of God. How could He say otherwise, who had so frequently had the words brought before Him, "I and My Father are one" (S. John x. 30), and "He that hath seen Me hath seen the Father" (S. John xiv. 9)? After our Lord's Resurrection His body entered the room, where His Apostles were assembled, although the doors were shut, and to satisfy them that it was really His body, which otherwise they might have found it hard to believe, He removes all their doubts by saying, "Handle Me and see, for a spirit hath not flesh and bones, as ye see Me have" (S. Luke xxiv. 39). And we must observe here that He does not say "Handle this body or this human nature, which I have assumed," but "handle Me." And so it is nothing but perverseness and obstinacy on the part of Paul of Samosata and his followers, that notwithstanding they find themselves overpowered by so many arguments to the contrary, yet they will not confess the proper union of the two natures. They will not be convinced by God the Word Himself, who so clearly expressed and asserted Himself to all His Apostles after His Resurrection, assuring them of the reality of His union with our human nature by eating before their eyes, and by allowing them to handle His body,

which they did. There is no question but that at least He touched their hands with His, and they touched His with theirs, when He supplied them with food; for the words of Scripture are, "And they gave Him a piece of a broiled fish and of an honeycomb. And when He had eaten before them, He took what remained and gave unto them" (S. Luke xxiv. 42, 43). This satisfied them of the truth and reality of His Resurrection, since He was actually touched by them, and we may now pass on to see how S. Thomas was convinced, although it was not quite in the same manner. But if nothing less than examining our Lord's sacred wounds will give faith to these men, let them learn the truth from S. Thomas. God the Word said to him, "Reach hither thy finger and behold My Hands, and reach hither thy hand and thrust it into My Side" (S. John xx. 27). He calls that Side and those Hands a part of His Person, and thus He declares Himself to be a Person consisting of the Divine and human nature. Another evidence and proof of which was His entering the room when the doors were shut, and presenting His body before His disciples, and demonstrating its reality to their senses. These reasonings and arguments may very well suffice for establishing the faithful in sound doctrine, and for convincing and reclaiming the unbelieving.

36. And so let Paul of Samosata renounce his error, and listen to the Divine voice of our Saviour, who said, "This is My Body" (S. Matt. xxvi. 26); and not, "This is Christ, a Person distinct from Me, who am the Word," but "This is My Body, one in Person with Me, and I one with that." For I the Word am the anointing oil, and the Man that belongs to Me is anointed by Me; and, therefore, the Christ is not to be imagined as separated from Me, but belongs to My Person, and I am in Him. Therefore, the mention of the mission of the Word signifies its union with Jesus born of Mary, which is interpreted Saviour, because He was personally united with God the Word, but not because of anything else. This is that mission mentioned in those passages of S. John, "The Father that sent Me" (S. John viii. 10), and "I came not of Myself, but the Father sent Me" (S. John viii. 42). For He has given the name of "mission" to His assumption of our body, by whose visible nature He made known to us His invisible nature. Not that God changes His place, as we finite beings do, who are in various places at different times; for nothing of this kind must be inferred from the small dimensions of our poor mortal bodies, in one of which He was pleased to appear during His sojourn in

our human nature. How could He, who fills heaven and earth, be thus contracted? The word "mission," therefore, is only metaphorical for the word "Incarnation."

Therefore, Christ is God the Word, and is both God and Man, born of the Virgin Mary. He is not some other Christ, but the Word and the Man are one and the same Person. He was begotten of His Father before all worlds, and born of the Blessed Virgin in these last days. He was before invisible in heaven even to the celestial powers themselves, but now by the union of His invisible nature with His visible, made visible to all. He is visible, I say, not in His invisible Godhead, but by those manifestations of the Divinity, which are exhibited in the acts and operations of His human nature; and this human nature He has entirely renewed by receiving it into a personal union with Himself. All honour and adoration be therefore ascribed to Him, who was in the beginning, and is now, and ever shall be, world without end. Amen.

Turnbull & Spears, Printers, Edinburgh.

2 M.—D. 11/93.

ern human nature. "How could He, who fills heaven and earth
be thus concealed?" The word "mission," "baptism," is only
metaphorical to the word "incarnation."

"Hermann Cramer, How far Word, and is both God and Man,
born of the Virgin Mary? He is not some other Christ, but the
Word and this Man the one and the same Person. He was
begotten of His Father, above all worlds, and born of the Blessed
Virgin in these last days. He was, before, invisible to heaven,
even to the Celestial powers themselves; but now by the union of
the invisible nature with His visible form, visible to all. He is
without Place, not in His material existence, but by those means
expressions of the Divine nature, and His human nature. He has
represented by expressing in His personal nature, with His
visual rays in the beginning, and is not, and ever shall be, world
without end. Amen."